Developing
Web Sites with
Macromedia® Flash™ MX

Rickard Müller

THOMSON
™
COURSE TECHNOLOGY

Australia • Canada • Mexico • Singapore • Spain • United Kingdom • United States

THOMSON
★
COURSE TECHNOLOGY

Developing Web Sites with Macromedia® Flash™ MX

by Rickard Müller

Product Manager:
Alyssa Pratt

Managing Editor:
Jennifer Locke

Acquisitions Editor:
Bill Larkin

Development Editor:
Lisa Ruffolo

Associate Product Manager:
Janet Aras

Editorial Assistant:
Christy Urban

Associate Marketing Manager:
Angela Laughlin

Production Editor:
Melissa Panagos

Cover Designer:
Joseph Lee, Black Fish Design

Compositor:
GEX Publishing Services

Manufacturing Coordinator:
Laura Burns

BRIEF
Contents

TABLE OF
Contents

Preface

Developing Web Sites with Macromedia Flash MX introduces you to Flash MX, a Macromedia product used to develop enticing, low-bandwidth animations as well as complex Web sites. Using Flash MX, you can design appealing Web pages that can also function as interactive software tools or games. Instead of creating Web sites where visitors scroll through static images and read pages of text, you can use Flash MX to create an interactive Web site that lets users view animated logos, for example, watch movies, click graphic buttons to make choices and respond to questions, and design personalized versions of products or services. Flash is a complete Web development tool that allows programmers to create truly interactive sites that respond to the visitor's request in fully animated ways. Because both Web designers and developers use Flash to create Web sites and interactive presentations, this book begins by examining Flash design features and then focuses on development tools and techniques.

The Intended Audience

Developing Web Sites with Macromedia Flash MX is intended for anyone who wants to learn how to use the Flash design and development tools to create appealing, interactive, customized Web sites, presentations, and online learning resources. Readers should already be familiar with HTML; knowledge of JavaScript is also helpful. Additionally, you should be comfortable working with computers and know your way around your operating system, whether it be Microsoft Windows or the Mac OS.

The Approach

As you progress through the book, you learn fundamental and advanced concepts, review guidelines and principles for creating effective Flash documents, and then apply what you have learned as you work with sample files to create a full range of Flash movies that you can play on Web sites or as stand-alone presentations. Each chapter concludes with a summary, review questions, and project ideas that highlight and reinforce the major concepts of each chapter.

Overview of This Book

The examples and exercises in this book will help you achieve the following objectives:

- Understand the role of Flash MX on the Web
- Learn to use the Flash MX design tools
- Create and control Flash animations
- Enhance Flash documents with other media resources
- Learn advanced animation techniques
- Learn ActionScript techniques and uses
- Design applications with Flash MX components
- Explore Flash MX design techniques with XML, CGI, and JavaScript
- Optimize and publish Flash movies
- Use Macromedia and third-party tools, technologies, and resources

Chapter 1 introduces Flash MX and discusses how it is useful as a Web design and development tool. You examine the capabilities of Flash MX, its new and improved features, and how to apply them. You also review how to develop a typical Flash project. **Chapter 2** provides the basic information you need to create a Flash document. You review the Flash MX tools to create and edit objects and work with animations, focusing on learning to use the drawing tools to create images that you can manipulate. You also learn the basic elements of working with animations. In **Chapter 3** you learn to take advantage of reusable objects such as symbols, and how to create different types of animations in Flash. This chapter also provides a brief introduction to the common ActionScript commands you can use to make your animations interactive. In **Chapter 4**, you import bitmap and vector images, add sound to button events, synchronize music with the Timeline, and integrate QuickTime movies with your Flash documents. In **Chapter 5**, you learn advanced design techniques to make your movies more sophisticated and interactive. **Chapter 6** explores advanced design techniques with ActionScript, the Flash scripting tool. In **Chapter 7**, you learn to add user interface components to your Flash movies. (Components are movie elements you use to save time and solve common problems.) In **Chapter 8**, you integrate Flash MX with other popular and powerful technologies, including Extensible Markup Language (XML), the Common Gateway Interface (CGI), and JavaScript. In **Chapter 9**, you learn how to optimize your Flash movies, which involves generating your final output with the highest possible quality and the lowest possible file size for your Flash movie file. Finally, in **Chapter 10**, you explore a variety of tools and technologies available for enhancing your Flash movies and building upon your designer toolkit.

Features

Developing Web Sites with Macromedia Flash MX contains many teaching aids to assist the student's learning.

- **Chapter Objectives** Each chapter in this book begins with a list of the important concepts to be mastered within the chapter. This list provides you with a quick reference to the contents of the chapter as well as a useful study aid.

- **Illustrations and Tables** Illustrations help you visualize common components and relationships. Tables list conceptual items and examples in a visual and readable format.

- **Tips** Chapters contain Tips designed to provide you with practical advice and proven strategies related to the concept being discussed.

- **Chapter Summaries** Each chapter's text is followed by a summary of chapter concepts. These summaries provide a helpful way to recap and revisit the ideas covered in each chapter.

- **Review Questions** End-of-chapter assessment begins with a set of approximately 15 to 20 Review Questions that reinforce the main ideas introduced in each chapter. These questions ensure you mastered the concepts and understood the information you learned.

Hands-on Projects Although it is important to understand the concepts behind Flash design and development, no amount of theory can improve on real-world experience. To this end, along with conceptual explanations, each chapter provides Hands-on Projects related to each major topic and aimed at providing you with practical experience. Most of these projects involve using Flash to create or enhance a movie or presentation. Because the Hands-on Projects ask you to go beyond the boundaries of the text itself, they provide you with practice implementing Flash design and development skills in real-world situations.

Case Projects The case projects at the end of each chapter are designed to help you apply what you have learned to business situations much like those you can expect to encounter as a Web designer or developer. They give you the opportunity to independently synthesize and evaluate information, examine potential solutions, and make recommendations, much as you would in an actual design or development situation.

Teaching Tools

The following supplemental materials are available when this book is used in a classroom setting. All of the teaching tools available with this book are provided to the instructor on a single CD-ROM.

Electronic Instructor's Manual. The Instructor's Manual that accompanies this textbook includes:

- Additional instructional material to assist in class preparation, including suggestions for lecture topics. It is critical for the instructor to be able to help the students understand how to use the help resources and how to identify problems. The Instructor's Manual will help you identify areas that are more difficult to teach, and provide you with ideas of how to present the material in an easier fashion.

- Solutions to all end-of-chapter materials, including the Review Questions, and when applicable, Hands-on Projects and Case Projects.

ExamView®. This textbook is accompanied by ExamView, a powerful testing software package that allows instructors to create and administer printed, computer (LAN-based), and Internet exams. ExamView includes hundreds of questions that correspond to the topics covered in this text, enabling students to generate detailed study guides that include page references for further review. The computer-based and Internet testing components allow students to take exams at their computers, and also save the instructor time by grading each exam automatically.

PowerPoint Presentations. This book comes with Microsoft PowerPoint slides for each chapter. These are included as a teaching aid for classroom presentation, to make available to students on the network for chapter review, or to be printed for classroom distribution. Instructors can add their own slides for additional topics they introduce to the class.

Data Files. Files that contain all of the data necessary for the Hands-on Projects and Case Projects are provided through the Course Technology Web site at *www.course.com*, and are also available on the Teaching Tools CD-ROM.

Solution Files. Solutions to end-of-chapter Review Questions, Hands-on Projects, and Case Projects are provided on the Teaching Tools CD-ROM and may also be found on the Course Technology Web site at *www.course.com*. The solutions are password protected.

Distance Learning. Course Technology is proud to present online test banks in WebCT and Blackboard, as well as MyCourse 2.0, Course Technology's own course enhancement tool, to provide the most complete and dynamic learning experience possible. Instructors are encouraged to make the most of your course, both online and offline. For more information on how to access your online test bank, contact your local Course Technology sales representative.

Read This Before You Begin

The following information will help you as you prepare to use this textbook.

TO THE USER OF THE DATA FILES

To complete the steps and projects in this book, you will need data files that have been created specifically for this book. Your instructor will provide the data files to you. You also can obtain the files electronically from the Course Technology Web site by connecting to *www.course.com* and then searching for this book title. Note that you can use a computer in your school lab or your own computer to complete the steps, Hands-on Projects, and Case Projects in this book.

Using Your Own Computer

You can use a computer in your school lab or your own computer to complete the chapters, Hands-on Projects, and Case Projects in this book. To use your own computer, you will need the following:

- Macromedia Flash MX
- Web browser, such as Microsoft Internet Explorer 5.0 or later or Netscape Navigator version 6.0 or later.

TO THE INSTRUCTOR

To complete all the exercises and chapters in this book, your users must work with a set of user files, called a Data Disk, and download software from Web sites. The data files are included on the Teaching Tools CD-ROM. They may also be obtained electronically through the Course Technology Web site at *www.course.com*. Follow the instructions in the Help file to copy the user files to your server or standalone computer. You can view the Help file using a text editor, such as WordPad or Notepad.

After the files are copied, you can make Data Disks for the users yourself, or tell them where to find the files so they can make their own Data Disks. Make sure the files are set up correctly by having students follow the instructions in the "To the User of the Data Files" section.

Course Technology Data Files

You are granted a license to copy the data files to any computer or computer network used by individuals who have purchased this book.

Visit Our World Wide Web Site

Additional materials designed especially for this book might be available for your course. Periodically search *www.course.com* for more information and materials to accompany this text.

ACKNOWLEDGMENTS

I'd like to take this opportunity to thank the team for their efforts with this project. This is a true testimony that a team effort carries its weight in gold and that authoring is not a single person's mission. Thanks to Bill Larkin, Acquisitions Editor, Alyssa Pratt, Product Manager, Melissa Panagos, Production Editor, and Margarita Leonard, Product Manager, for all of your efforts and patience. A special thanks to Lisa Ruffolo, our Development Editor, who served with enormous diligence and kept the focus on the reader. Also, a special acknowledgement for my aunt Dar, who has inspired me to pursue creativity as life's calling.

Thanks to the reviewers who provided plenty of comments and positive direction during the development of this book:

- Sherrie Geitgey, Wright State University
- Gene Klawikowski, Nicolet College
- Brian Morgan, Marshall University
- Marty Hanlin, Hocking College
- Nickie Little, Florida State University

This book is dedicated to my wife and daughter, who continue to be my *North Star*. Thank you for your continuous support, encouragement, and love.

It's the North Star...

It's the only star in the sky that never moves...

It's constant...unwavering...a guide...

Rickard Müller

INTRODUCTION TO MACROMEDIA FLASH MX

Understanding the Role of Macromedia Flash MX on the World Wide Web

In this chapter, you will:

♦ Learn a brief history of multimedia on the Web
♦ Understand the role of Macromedia Flash MX as a multimedia tool
♦ Explore what's new in Macromedia Flash MX
♦ Learn how to launch a typical Macromedia Flash project

As a Web designer or developer, you can use Macromedia Flash MX to design appealing Web pages that can also function as interactive software tools or games. Instead of creating Web sites where visitors scroll through static images and read pages of text, you can use Flash MX to create interactive Web sites that let users view animated logos; watch movies; click graphic buttons to make choices and respond to questions; and design personalized versions of products or services. This chapter introduces Flash MX and discusses how it is useful as a Web design and development tool.

If you are familiar with previous versions of Flash, you'll find that Flash MX includes improvements that make it easier for novice users and provides a new toolset for experienced designers. Flash MX streamlines the tasks of developing artwork, managing projects, and creating interactivity with ActionScript, the programming language that Flash uses to extend its features.

After completing this chapter, you will understand the capabilities of Flash MX, and you will learn how to apply its new and improved features. You will also review how to develop a typical Flash project. You will see why more people are using Flash now than ever before.

A Brief History of Multimedia on the Web

The Internet is the world's largest communications network. It supports the World Wide Web, which is a collection of Hypertext Markup Language (HTML) pages, protocols, and Hypertext Transfer Protocol (HTTP) servers. The Web is used every day by millions of people around the world for selling, buying, advertising, entertaining, communicating, and researching. As the popularity of the Web has increased over the last few years, so, too, has competition among Web sites for traffic. With millions of Web sites competing for viewers' attention, Web developers and designers are constantly looking for new ways to enhance the presentation of their information, to attract more users, and to encourage more sales of their goods and services. The most popular and effective way to attract users is to develop Web sites that use **multimedia**, a combination of imagery, animation, sound, and video.

Until the mid-1990s, Web developers could present information only through pictures and text. HTML, the coding language used to create Web pages, was limited in its options for designing pages and providing interactivity. Using HTML, designers could create only static Web pages using page formats that did not change much from one site to another. When developers introduced animated graphics and scripting tools such as JavaScript, designers could create Web pages with features such as buttons that changed color and form, online quizzes that recorded users' answers, and simple animations using images in the Graphics Interchange Format (GIF), called **animated GIFs**. These innovations made Web pages more interactive, engaging, and visually interesting. However, because the GIF animations were short and repetitive, they lost their appeal after one or two viewings.

In 1995, Sun Microsystems introduced **Java applets**, small programs that can be transported over the Internet and run in a user's browser. Web developers can use applets to provide animation that is longer and more sophisticated than GIF animations. Web pages can also use applets to allow for interactivity by responding to user actions. The drawback to applets, however, is that they require heavy programming. In addition to using applets, Web developers can also make sites respond to user actions by using a technique called **back-end scripting**, where scripts allow a Web page to interact with a Web server to update a database, for example; however, you cannot use this technique to produce effective animations.

In the past, the limitations to adding animation and interactivity to Web sites were imposed by the browser and server capabilities, and by the slow modems and processors on most user systems. In recent years, as the performance and power of browsers, servers, and user systems have improved, so, too, has the demand for increased interactivity on Web sites. A struggle for dominance in the browser market left only two major players: Netscape Navigator and Microsoft Internet Explorer. Both companies responded to user demand and improved the capabilities of their browsers by supporting browser add-ons called plug-ins. **Plug-ins** are software applications that work with your browser to provide added functionality. Plug-ins let browsers use newer technologies such as the Flash Player to play movies or Adobe Acrobat Reader to provide formatted text documents.

1

UNDERSTANDING THE ROLE OF MACROMEDIA FLASH MX AS A MULTIMEDIA TOOL

When you work with Flash MX to create graphics and animation for Web sites, you create Flash documents, which have a .fla filename extension. Flash documents contain all the information that you need to develop, design, and test interactive content. After you create a Flash document, you save it as a Flash movie, which has a .swf filename extension, and then you publish it on a Web site. A visitor to the Web site views a Flash movie by using a browser, such as Internet Explorer or Netscape Navigator. The browser uses a plug-in to download the SWF file and play the Flash movie, such as the one shown in Figure 1-1, which was shown on the CBS Web site (*www.cbs.com*).

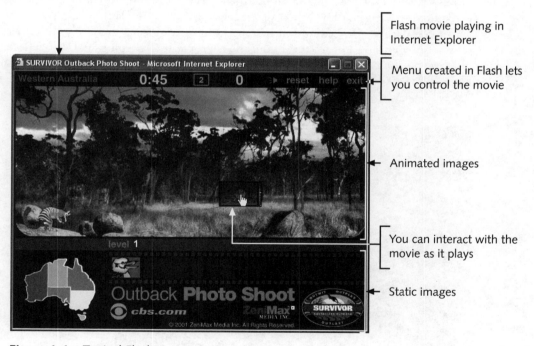

Flash movie playing in Internet Explorer

Menu created in Flash lets you control the movie

Animated images

You can interact with the movie as it plays

Static images

Figure 1-1 Typical Flash movie

 You can visit the Macromedia Web site at *www.macromedia.com/showcase* to see samples of movies Flash users have created. You can view the current Macromedia Web site of the day and browse a showcase of Web sites designed with Flash.

In addition to playing animations, you can use Flash on a Web page to provide visual and audible feedback to your users. When you include visual and audio clues to let users know where they are on your Web site, where they have been, and where they are going, you increase their confidence and help them navigate more easily and efficiently. This feedback is part of the look and feel of the Web site design. Flash can integrate many media elements and formats into the SWF file because of its powerful compression capabilities. When Flash produces a SWF file, it takes all the Flash content, including static graphics, animated images, and sound, and publishes it in a browser-friendly format. Other standard Web technologies do not compress data as efficiently, causing slower load times. Flash can integrate all of the standard Web image formats—GIF, JPG, PNG, and Adobe Photoshop and Illustrator—and can also import audio and video into the SWF file. Using these multimedia tools means that you can use Flash to create a full, dynamic experience for the users of your Web site. You can also design Flash to respond to mouse events and user input, allowing you to create effects that change, either on their own or through user actions.

Although Flash was originally created as a Web animation tool to be used with your browser, Flash also creates stand-alone movies. A stand-alone movie means that no plug-in is required to view the file. When you create a stand-alone Flash movie, you create a Flash Player file with a SWF extension that you can distribute to users who might not have a browser or are using a browser without the appropriate Flash plug-in. Users who have Flash installed on their computer can then double-click the SWF file to view the movie in the Flash Player window instead of in a browser. Figure 1-2 shows an example of a movie in the Flash Player, version 6.

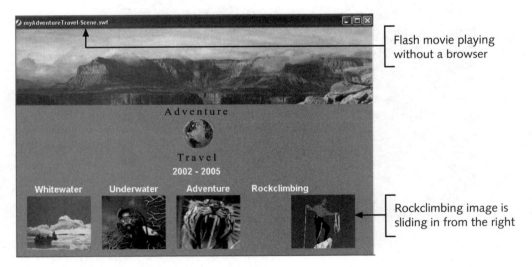

Figure 1-2   Flash Player window

Exploring Macromedia Flash MX Animation Features

Animation capabilities are what first attract most developers to Flash. Flash creates complex and sophisticated animations with unprecedented ease of manipulation. For example, you can add two effects to a simple graphic to animate a sphere flying across the screen while it changes shape and transparency levels. The Flash environment, tools, and sample files help you get started with an animated movie, and a suite of panels helps you manipulate scenes, objects, and symbols. (See "Exploring What's New in Macromedia Flash MX" later in the chapter for more information on panels.)

Recall that in the past, computer animators relied on scripting languages such as JavaScript to create animations. However, because Web browsers interpret scripting languages, the differences between browsers such as Internet Explorer and Netscape Navigator made it difficult to create scripts that worked on all browsers. In addition, developers had to rely on the script-interpretation features offered by the browsers, which limited the types of animations they could create.

Most recent versions of the popular browsers now include the plug-in for playing Flash movies. Macromedia provides the plug-in free for downloading if your browser does not already include it. This means Flash movies are compatible with most browsers and platforms, overcoming the drawbacks of using a scripting language to create animations.

Besides showing images that change over time, animations can also include streaming sound. With a **streaming sound** file, your browser can begin to play music before it downloads the entire file. Originally, computer sound was limited to brief Waveform (WAV) or Musical Instrument Digital Interface (MIDI) files. These are digital sound file formats that are often used for short pieces of music or sound, such as error beeps or chords, because their file size increases as the length of the music or sound increases. In Flash, you can also use Moving Picture Experts Group (MP3) audio files, which use an advanced compression method to keep file size low but sound quality high. MP3 files also stream the sound so that the animation and the sound are always in sync, even if the user has a slow Internet connection or computer processor. With sound streaming, Flash skips frames as necessary to keep the animation and the sound at the same speed.

Developing Interactive Animations with ActionScript

ActionScript is the language a developer uses to programmatically manipulate objects, perform calculations, and communicate with the users of a Flash movie. With ActionScript, Flash becomes more than a simple animation program; it lets you develop a more creative design by responding to user actions (called user events), controlling objects, and integrating a movie with Extensible Markup Language (XML). **XML** is a markup language that segregates the data from the design. In an XML document, structured information contains content (data), such as text and images, and formatting information that indicates the role of that content. For example, content in a section heading has a different meaning from content in a body area, which, in turn, means something different from content in a figure caption or a database table. By expanding into XML, Flash lets you change content without changing its design. As a developer or designer, this means you can create common information formats and share both the format and the data on the Web.

ActionScript syntax is based on the European Computer Manufacturers Association's standard ECMA-262, which is the protocol for the JavaScript programming language. JavaScript has been a core programming language for the Web since its inception, and is widely used by developers. With ActionScript, you can use Flash to develop instructional tools such as online tutorials or computer-based training courses that display text along with animated demonstrations. For example, you can use ActionScript to create a Flash movie that integrates instructional videos and uses event-driven programming to allow users to control their paths through the movie. These movies can also keep track of and apply math to variables, allowing you to build online quizzes that automatically grade the user. Figure 1-3 shows an online geography quiz from *www.k-international.com*.

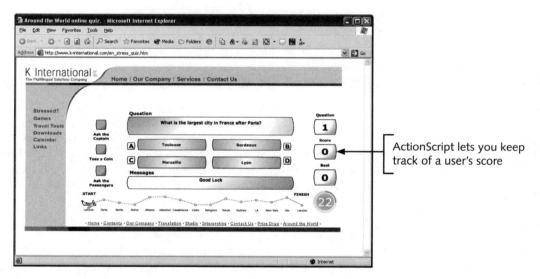

Figure 1-3   Online quiz

You can use the advanced features of ActionScript to create games, with Flash keeping track of objects on the screen. For example, in a game where the user hits a ball, the ball can move in a different direction each time it is hit. Flash keeps track of whether the user has hit the ball, and updates the score at the same time. Figure 1-4 shows an example of a game.

Because ActionScript can also communicate with back-end database technologies, you can create e-commerce sites in Flash. On the Web, a **back-end technology** is one that operates behind the scenes and doesn't require user interaction. For example, a back-end application interacts with a Web server to provide online weather forecasts that change every hour or so. With this back-end connectivity, Flash can integrate with online databases, shopping carts, and product catalogs, for example, enhancing the users' experience and connecting consumers and merchants. A Web site can function as a virtual store, with an animated interface that keeps track of what a user has selected. At checkout, Flash sends all information to the back-end server for verification and approval, informing users immediately whether their transaction is valid.

1

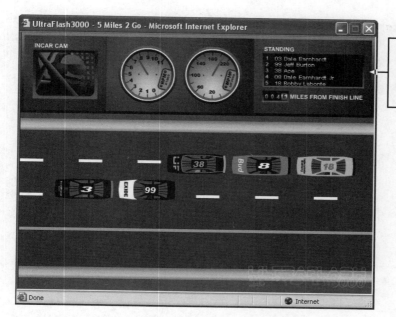

When you control the vehicle, Flash ActionScript starts playing and updates the game's statistics

Figure 1-4 Game created using advanced ActionScript

Increasing Audience Acceptance

As previously mentioned, low bandwidth has always been an obstacle for Internet users. Slow Internet connections and processors and outdated browsers have prevented potential Flash users from obtaining the necessary plug-in, causing some Web sites to opt out of using Flash. To meet the demands of users and Web site sponsors, Flash now allows for smaller file size and shorter download times.

One reason Flash files are smaller than other animation files is that Flash is a vector animation program. A **vector** is a mathematical equation interpreted by Flash as a line or series of lines and fills. Flash performs these equations to create vector images, which contain line strokes and filled areas. In other words, what the viewer sees as a square is actually a combination of numbers that specifies its color, shape, size, and location. Because a vector image is simply a combination of lines and fills, its file size is much smaller than a bitmap image, such as one in JPG format, a popular format for photograph-quality Web graphics. The bitmapped image formats have larger file sizes because they use every pixel to store information, meaning they take longer to download into the user's browser. Bitmapped images can also become distorted when they are scaled (or resized), leading to undesirable results. On the other hand, vector graphics look the same and use the same amount of data no matter how large or small you resize the image.

Another feature that minimizes the file size for Flash movies is object reuse. After you create an object, you can use the object as many times as needed without adding to the file size of the animation. Once Flash loads the object into memory, it does not have to load it again, making playback more efficient.

While Flash is increasing its audience with features that reduce file size and download times, faster modems and Internet connections are becoming available at affordable prices. Most browser users can now view Flash movies on their computers without a problem. In fact, Macromedia states that over 98.3% of all Web users now have a version of the Macromedia Flash Player.

EXPLORING WHAT'S NEW IN MACROMEDIA FLASH MX

Flash MX is a significant improvement over earlier versions of Flash, especially those prior to Flash 5. If you have used earlier versions of Flash, read through this section to learn about the new and enhanced features of Flash MX. In addition to those features discussed in detail in the following section, Flash MX also introduces the following tools and features:

- Enhanced video support that enables you to import any standard video file supported by QuickTime or Windows Media Player, including MPEG, Digital Video (DV), QuickTime (MOV), and AVI

- Dynamic loading of images and sound so that the Flash Player loads external JPEG and MP3 media files during runtime, resulting in smaller file sizes

- Components and templates that let you provide user interface elements such as scroll bars or form controls

- Timeline enhancements, including folders for organizing layers and the ability to manipulate multiple keyframes

- New graphic design tools such as the Free Transform tool and Pixel–Level Snapping Control tool for more creative freedom and control over graphic content

- Color Mixer panel enhancements that make creating, editing, and using colors and gradients easier and more consistent to industry standards such as the RGB, CYMK, or Pantone color models

- Accessibility support such as assistive technologies, screen readers, support of Microsoft Active Accessibility, and integration of tools for creating accessible content

- More multilingual support for Unicode for designing multilingual content and applications

- More options for publishing content to any browser or platform that supports the Flash Player, such as Microsoft Windows, Apple Macintosh, Linux, Solaris, MicrosoftTV, Symbian EPOC, Pocket PC PDAs and WebTV

- A customizable ActionScript Editor for changing text display properties such as font, size, color, syntax coloring, and toolbox content

The Pen Tool

Flash MX, like Flash 5, includes the Pen tool, which you use to draw complex lines and edit images directly in Flash. If you are familiar with Adobe Illustrator or Macromedia Freehand, you probably know that only the Pen tool can provide complete accuracy when drawing complex images. In previous versions of Flash, the Pencil or Brush tools were designed for drawing simple shapes. However, these tools are less accurate than the Pen. Figure 1-5 shows the difference between the Pen and the Pencil tool.

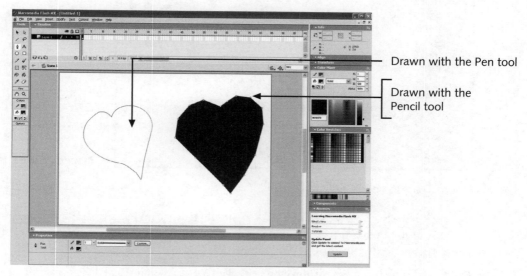

Drawn with the Pen tool

Drawn with the Pencil tool

Figure 1-5   Comparing the Pen tool to the Pencil tool

User Interface Features

Flash MX features a familiar yet enhanced interface, providing the new Property inspector and Answers panels for managing your movies. When you select an object in Flash, the Property inspector shows options you can set for that object. The Answers panel displays information it downloads from the Web to provide useful advice for Flash designers and developers. Other new features include selection highlights that help you identify selected lines, fills, and groups as well as the color of selected objects. These selection highlights make it easier to edit, move, and copy images and parts of images. You can also drag guides to arrange objects in your movie.

To perform most tasks in Flash MX, as in Flash 5, you use panels instead of dialog boxes and keyboard shortcuts. Panels, shown in Figure 1-6, are small windows docked on the screen that allow quick access to Flash tools. You can collapse a panel to show only its title bar, or expand it to work with its options. If you have worked with Flash 5, Adobe Photoshop, or Macromedia Dreamweaver, you are already familiar with using panels to select commands and modify settings.

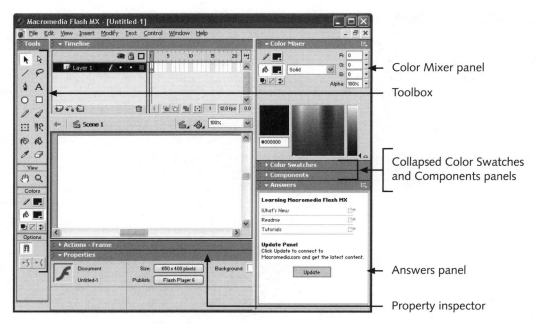

Figure 1-6   Panels in Flash MX

You use panels to view, change, and manage Flash movies and their images, including objects, colors, text, frames, scenes, and entire movies. For example, you use the Align panel to select alignment options for images and text.

Panels offer a significant improvement over earlier versions of Flash, which used dialog boxes that are harder to access than panels. For example, in Flash 4 or earlier, to check or change the color of a graphic, apply an action to a button, or name a movie, you open the appropriate dialog box, find a property, change the property, and then close the dialog box. In Flash MX, you can access these properties on a panel so you can select and then apply the changes all at once, seeing the effect immediately.

You use the Actions panel in Flash MX to create and edit **actions**—ActionScript instructions that run when a specific event occurs, such as a user clicking a button. The Actions panel is fully resizable, color-coded, and provides two modes, one for beginners and another for more experienced users. In Normal mode, the Actions panel helps you create an action by providing lists of appropriate options. You can also use Expert mode to create actions without using menus. Figure 1-7 shows the Actions panel in both Normal and Expert modes.

Normal mode

Expert mode

Enter ActionScript code directly into the Actions panel

Use text boxes to guide you when creating ActionScript

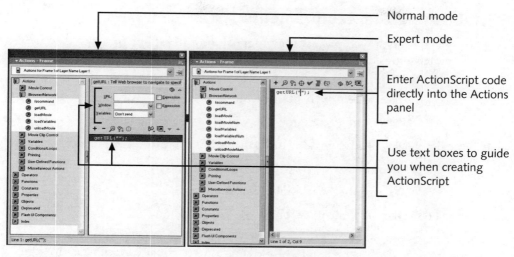

Figure 1-7   Actions panel in Normal and Expert modes

ActionScript Syntax

Flash 5 and MX provide a redesigned syntax for ActionScript. Instead of using a confusing script code involving combinations of dots and slashes, the updated ActionScript syntax uses dot notation to separate objects, methods, and properties. The syntax is based on JavaScript, so users who already know JavaScript should quickly adapt to ActionScript. Even those not familiar with JavaScript usually find dot notation easier to use than earlier versions of ActionScript, which uses a longer syntax to call and perform even simple tasks.

Flash MX also includes new built-in functions and objects that track down the mouse, perform date and other mathematical calculations, and interact with XML.

LAUNCHING A TYPICAL MACROMEDIA FLASH PROJECT

This section explains how you can use Flash MX to create a multimedia or Web project. Recall that Flash MX movies are graphics, text, animation, and applications that you publish on Web sites. To create an effective Web site, you first establish the requirements—what you want the site to accomplish. Next, you design the site, including its organization and appearance. These first two steps involve work you do outside of Flash. Devoting time to prepare for a multimedia project will save you time and effort when you are working in Flash. After you identify the requirements and design the site, you build the site, which involves creating the separate multimedia components in Flash.

Establishing the Requirements

Implementing a Web project is a progression of steps. The first step is to determine your audience and the purpose of the Web site. Before you start working in Flash, ask the following questions:

1. What kind of Web site do you want?

2. What are the demographics of the target audience?

3. What bandwidth can the target audience most likely handle?

4. How much content will the site contain?

5. What are the main topics and subtopics?

6. What are your main objectives for the site?

Ask these and other questions to determine whether Flash is the most appropriate tool for the job. Flash is best suited to giving users a visual experience, providing visual and audible feedback, integrating other media elements, and providing a rich interactive interface. Before you choose Flash as your Web design tool, make sure that your Web site will take advantage of these characteristics. For example, a Flash Web site would not be appropriate for a company with an inventory of thousands of items, catering to people with low-end computers and 28.8 kbps modems. If Flash were used on a Web site of this sort, sales and productivity might decline due to slow connectivity.

On the other hand, if you want to design a cutting-edge Web site featuring a hot new product that will hit the market soon, Flash would be the tool of choice, especially if it were likely that the target audience had high-speed Internet connections and recent browsers.

Designing the Site

Once you have determined the main requirements for the Web site, you can begin the design process. This process involves creating a storyboard and prototype to show the site structure and overall design. When you create a storyboard, you create the elements of the design—the images, text, and animations—and sketch the relationship of one page to another. You can draft a Web page model with software tools such as Adobe PageMaker, InDesign, Microsoft Publisher, or Word. Some traditional designers still prefer the paper and pencil. Figure 1-8 shows a Web page storyboard for a community recreation Web site.

You can also create a Web site map to help you determine on which particular pages graphics, video, and other multimedia files will appear. Your site structure or site map is a hierarchy of all Web pages in your project. Your site map starts with home, showing the relationship among all other pages on the site. You can use visual diagramming software, such as Microsoft Visio 2002, to automate the mapping process. Figure 1-9 shows a sample Web site map.

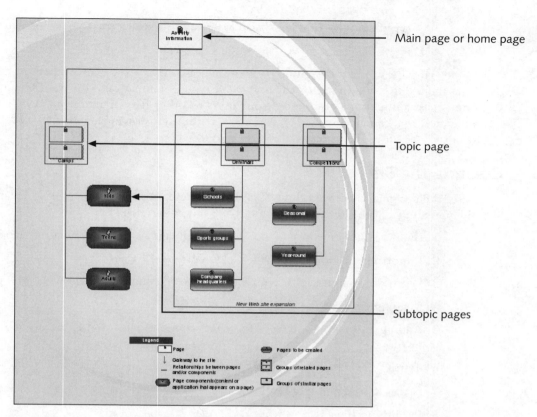

Main page or home page

Topic page

Subtopic pages

Figure 1-8 Sample Web page storyboard

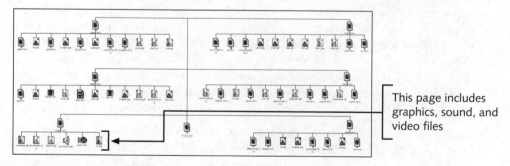

This page includes graphics, sound, and video files

Figure 1-9 Web site map

As you design the site, update the site map. Also ask the following questions:

1. Does the design allow you to comfortably display all of the necessary content?

2. Does the design leave enough room for animations and transitions to occur without overlapping or otherwise covering the content?

3. Is the design so complex that it will slow the processor and performance?

4. Does your design meet the overall objectives?

When you are finished designing, you should also have a rough flowchart of the content, including the number of pages and the type of animations you want to include. If your Flash animation can connect your users to other files or media, identify the ways in which this interaction will occur, such as through downloadable files and links to databases or other Web sites.

Creating the Site

After the design and content flowchart are complete, you can begin actually creating the site. Creating a Web site usually includes the following tasks:

1. Building the site components, including images, symbols, animations, and audio

2. Importing any sounds or video elements

3. Setting the sequence in which the media elements appear

4. Keeping track of the size of the movie file

5. Adding animation and links to other scenes, movies, and external Web pages or files

6. Testing the movie in multiple platforms and browsers

7. Saving the movie in a SWF format

8. Publishing the Flash movie on the Web site

Start by producing the individual elements you want to use in your animation sequences. These elements include text, graphics, symbols, sound, and music that you plan to include in the Flash movie. You can create these elements using the Flash drawing tools and panels, use common elements from the libraries and then edit them, or import media elements from other sources. You can create graphic elements directly on the **Stage**, the main workspace in Flash, or you can use the Stage to arrange imported elements. To improve your view of the Stage, you can leave the Flash panels docked to the sides of the window, as they are by default, or drag them so they become floating panels. See Figure 1-10.

After you create, import, and modify your media elements, you construct the sequence, links, and ActionScript commands, connecting all of the pieces as one product. To integrate the elements into a movie, you work with the **Timeline**, a Flash tool you use to organize and control a movie's content over time. If you want to organize the movie thematically, you can use scenes. For example, you could use one scene for the introduction, another for the main content, and another for the conclusion.

As you work in the Timeline, you can provide interactivity by adding actions to your movie. For example, you can create a navigation action that shows a particular part of the movie when the user clicks a button. (You can also work with actions outside of the Timeline.)

Drawing tools in the
toolbox

Layers

Scene indicator

Stage

Timeline

Floating Transform panel

Docked panels

Floating Property inspector

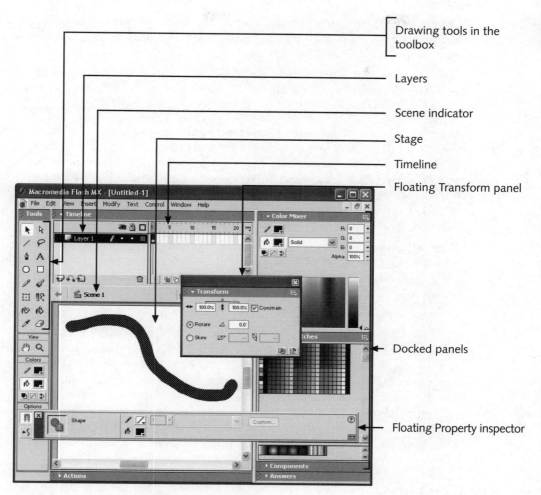

Figure 1-10   Working with the Flash tools

After you create the Web site, test it for bugs and for downloading time. As you will learn in later chapters, Flash MX comes equipped with tools that help you with both tasks. Finally, you use the Publish command to create a Web-compatible version of your movie with the SWF extension. Flash prepares the SWF file and an HTML document that includes the tags necessary to display the SWF on a Web page.

CHAPTER SUMMARY

- At one time, Web content could be displayed with only static images and text. Now Web pages can include multimedia, a combination of imagery, animation, sound, and video.

❏ One reason the Web has changed so quickly is that people continue to demand information, services, and products on the Web. Another reason is that processor and bandwidth quality have increased dramatically in recent years.

❏ Flash plays an important role on the Web because it creates a rich multimedia experience for computer users, provides cross-platform consistency, and can stream sound.

❏ You can use Flash to create Web sites, quizzes, tutorials, games, and e-commerce sites.

❏ When you work with Flash MX to create graphics and animation for Web sites, you create Flash documents, which have a .fla filename extension. After you create a Flash document, you save it as a Flash movie, which has a .swf filename extension, and then publish it on a Web site. You need a copy of the Flash Player or a Flash plug-in for your browser to play Flash movies. Because Flash plug-ins are now included on most browsers, most Internet users can open and play Flash movies on their computers.

❏ Flash MX has many new features, including new drawing tools, an enhanced Timeline and layers, a new interface, and new ActionScript syntax. ActionScript is the programming language that makes Flash interactive, and is based on the same technology as JavaScript.

❏ Creating a Flash project involves three major steps: establishing the requirements, completing the design, and creating the project components.

❏ To create a Flash movie, you assemble text, graphics, symbols, sound, and music on the Stage, the main workspace in Flash. You can create these elements using the Flash drawing tools and panels, use common elements from the libraries and then edit them, or import media elements from other sources. Then you construct the sequence, links, and ActionScript commands, connecting all of the pieces as one product. To integrate the elements into a movie, you work with the Timeline, a Flash tool you use to organize and control a movie's content over time.

REVIEW QUESTIONS

1. Considering that Web sites compete for viewers' attention, what can Web designers do to attract visitors to their sites?

2. The introduction of animated _____ meant that developers could add limited animation to their Web pages.

3. Web designers could use _____ to achieve a higher level of animation and interactivity than animated GIFs, but this would require heavy programming.

4. Early limitations on the Web were caused in part by:
   a. low bandwidth
   b. slow processors
   c. browser limitations
   d. all of the above
   e. none of the above

5. Flash can be used only to display information online. True or false?

6. Flash movies are interpreted by the browser. True or false?

7. A(n) _____ is a small application that can be downloaded to view a Flash movie in a browser.

8. With Flash, animations can now have _____ sound.

   a. loud

   b. streaming

   c. soft

   d. ultra

9. Flash can set a movie to skip animation frames to keep up with the sound. True or false?

10. Which of the following is the language a developer uses to manipulate objects within the Flash authoring environment?

   a. VBScript

   b. ActionScript

   c. JavaScript

   d. FlashScript

11. JavaScript is based on ActionScript. True or false?

12. _____ files are a series of lines and fills.

13. The computer reads lines and fills in Flash documents as mathematical equations. True or false?

14. How is a bitmap image different from a vector image?

   a. Bitmap images become distorted when you resize them, whereas vector images do not.

   b. Bitmap images are a combination of lines and 3-D images.

   c. Vector images can have only one color, whereas bitmap images can have an unlimited number of colors.

   d. Bitmap image files have a .jpg extension, and vector images have a .vtr extension.

15. The Pencil tool is as accurate as the Pen tool. True or false?

16. In Flash MX, you must close a panel after you use it. True or false?

17. ActionScript in Flash MX uses which of the following types of syntax?

   a. dot

   b. slash

   c. comma

   d. quote

18. New features in Flash let it communicate with XML. True or false?

19. The first step when creating a Web project is to _____.

20. Multiple image formats integrate seamlessly with Flash MX. True or false?

HANDS-ON PROJECTS

To complete the following projects, use a word processor such as Microsoft Word or WordPad to prepare and then print your responses or evaluations.

Project 1-1

Visit the Macromedia Web site at *www.macromedia.com* and look for the Flash Player. What information does Macromedia provide about the browser plug-in? If you do not have the plug-in on your computer, download and install it, and follow the instructions that Macromedia provides to verify that the plug-in works with your browser. Find and print information about the Flash Player.

Project 1-2

Visit the Macromedia Web site at *www.macromedia.com/showcase* and browse the showcase of sample Flash movies. View two or three samples in your browser. Select one and evaluate its use of text, static graphics, animation, interactivity, and sound, if appropriate. Also identify other features or elements that make the sample an effective Flash movie, such as consistent design, color scheme, pace, and timeliness.

Capture a screen image of the sample movie by displaying a page from the movie and then pressing the PrtScrn key to copy the image to the Clipboard. Open your Windows word processor, such as Microsoft Word, and then press Ctrl+V to paste the image in a document. (On the Macintosh, press Cmd + Shift + 3 to copy a screen image.) Write a two- to three-page evaluation and include at least one screen image that illustrates and supports your critique.

Project 1-3

Access the Internet and look through popular Web sites, such as *yahoo.com*, *www.travelocity.com*, *www.cnn.com*, and *www.espn.com*. Use the technique described in Project 1-2 to capture the home page of three Web sites that you would not create in Flash. Paste these images in a text document. Provide the address for each Web site, and then explain why Flash is not the best tool for creating the Web site. Review three other Web sites that use Flash or features that Flash provides. Capture the home pages of these three Web sites and paste them in a text document. Explain how the Flash features affect your experience of the Web site.

1

Project 1-4

Access the Internet and look for Flash Web sites that play music. Identify at least one Web site and evaluate its use of music. What effect does the audio have? Does it make the site more appealing or is it distracting to the audience? Is the music appropriate for the theme of the site? Does the site provide any form of sound control? Write your answers in a word processing document.

Project 1-5

For what do your acquaintances use the Internet? Conduct a small informal survey among your family and friends to determine their primary uses for the Internet. List the results. Based on the results of your survey, what kind of Web site would most interest your friends and family? Complete the following tasks, writing your responses in a word processing document:

1. List two to three topics for Flash Web sites that would appeal to your target audience.
2. Select one of these topics and list the types of information, products, and/or services the Web site would offer.
3. Indicate where and how you would use Flash elements such as static graphics, animations, sound, and video.

Project 1-6

Return to the topic and Web site you described in Project 1-5. Sketch a simple site map for this Web site. Set the sequence in which the media elements should appear. Determine where and how you could add links to external elements, such as other Flash movies, external Web pages, or other files.

Project 1-7

Write down all the changes that you have seen on the Internet since you started using it. What is your opinion about these changes? Do you think that the Internet is going to continue to change? What changes do you expect to see a year from now? Two years? Five years?

CASE PROJECTS

Case Project 1-1

You work in a Web development studio as a Web site designer. Your client owns a shoe company and wants you to create a Web site that will showcase the shoes. Your client is not ready to sell them online, but does want to connect to a Web page that provides current shoe news. Based on these requirements, do you think that Flash would be an appropriate tool for this project? Explain why or why not. Then sketch a simple Web site map for this client, indicating where and how you would use Flash, if possible. Refer to Figure 1-9 for a sample Web site map.

Case Project 1-2

As you work through the Case Projects in this book, you will create a Web site using Flash MX. You will plan and design the site, create Flash objects and movies, import media files, create animations, and add interactivity. You can develop a Web site showcasing yourself and your interests, or one for a fictional business that you would like to start or run.

For Case Project 1-2, determine the type of Web site you want to create—a personal or business site. Then create a planning document that answers the questions listed in the "Establishing the Requirements" section of this chapter. Review Web sites similar to the one you want to create, and then complete the tasks described in the "Designing the Site" section of this chapter. Add this information to your planning document.

CHAPTER

2

CREATING THE GROUNDWORK

Learning to Use the Macromedia Flash MX Tools

In this chapter, you will:

- ♦ Use the Macromedia Flash drawing tools to create objects
- ♦ Use the View tools
- ♦ Use the Color tools
- ♦ Use the Timeline to work with animations
- ♦ Edit images

In Chapter 1, you learned how Macromedia Flash evolved as a powerful animation tool as the Web evolved. You also evaluated the types of Web sites for which Flash is the most useful, and learned about the multimedia development process. You can now put that knowledge into practice by creating your own Flash MX documents.

This chapter provides the basic information you need to create a Flash document. In this chapter, you will review the Flash MX tools to create and edit objects and work with animations, including the drawing tools, panels, and Timeline. The focus is on learning to use the drawing tools to create images that you can manipulate. You also learn the basic elements of working with animations. Guidelines for designing animations are provided in Chapter 3, "Animation Fundamentals."

USING THE MACROMEDIA FLASH DRAWING TOOLS TO CREATE OBJECTS

Flash movies are a combination of graphics and animation for Web sites, and include animated games, product demonstrations, or entire Web sites. Working in Flash, you can create a document by drawing or importing artwork and other objects, arranging them on the Stage, and animating them with the Timeline. The main features of the Flash work environment include the Stage, the Timeline, and panels that display the tools you use to select and modify image and document settings. See Figure 2-1.

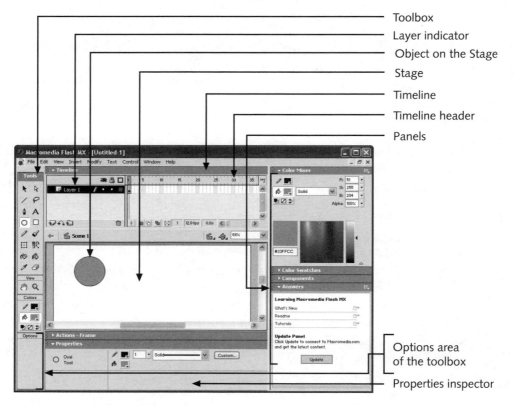

Toolbox
Layer indicator
Object on the Stage
Stage
Timeline
Timeline header
Panels
Options area of the toolbox
Properties inspector

Figure 2-1   Flash work environment

These features are described in Table 2-1.

You add images to a Flash document by creating or importing them, using the Flash drawing tools to create or modify those images. Even if you import graphics, you will probably change them by resizing the graphic, for example, or by adding images or text. Recall from Chapter 1 that Flash is a vector-drawing program; this means that everything you draw in Flash is either a stroke (a line) or a fill (an area of color). Figure 2-2 shows examples of strokes and fills.

Table 2-1   Main features of the Flash work environment

Flash feature	Description
Toolbox	Displays tools for drawing and editing images
Options area of the toolbox	Lists options available for the selected drawing tool
Timeline	Contains frames, layers, and animations; and lets you organize and control a movie's content over time
Stage	Provides the work space where you perform most of the drawing and editing tasks; whatever is displayed on Stage is part of the final document
Panels	Help you view, organize, and change the characteristics of selected elements
Property inspector	Shows the attributes of an object on the Stage, and lets you change them
Layer indicator	Shows the layers in a document

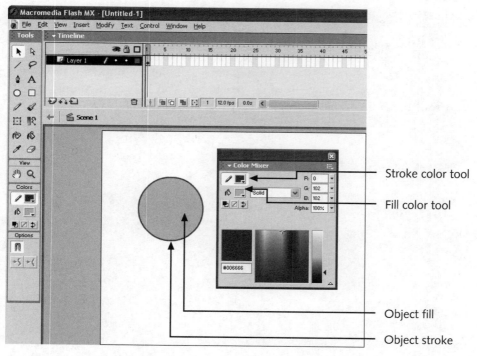

Figure 2-2   Strokes and fills

Vectors are different from bitmaps or raster images. **Bitmaps** are groups of pixels, with each pixel displaying a color. **Vector** images are actually mathematical equations that Flash uses to display strokes and fills, which you see as drawings. The advantage of using vectors is that the graphic designer can enlarge or shrink any vector image, to any degree, without deteriorating the image quality or increasing the file size. The drawbacks are that vector images can look cartoon-like, while bitmap images lose their definition, as shown in Figure 2-3.

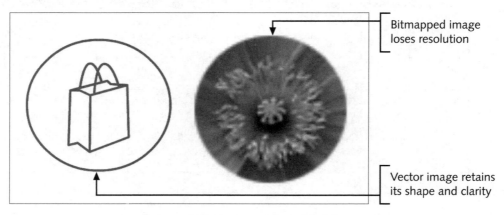

Figure 2-3   Vector and bitmapped images enlarged by 600 percent

You use the Flash drawing tools to create vector objects and to modify imported vector and bitmap images. The drawing tools are included on the **Tools panel**, also called the **toolbox**, which is displayed by default on the left of the Flash window. Figure 2-4 shows the toolbox. You can move the toolbox, if you like, by dragging its title bar. Point to a tool to see its name and keyboard shortcut in a ScreenTip.

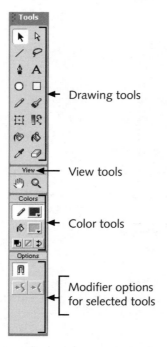

Figure 2-4   Toolbox

The toolbox includes four categories of tools: Drawing, View, Color, and Modifier Options. If you click a drawing tool in the toolbox to select that tool, the pointer changes to reflect the current tool. For example, when you select the Pen tool, the mouse pointer changes to a fountain pen; it changes to a hand when you select the Hand tool for panning or moving the Stage.

The toolbox contains the drawing, painting, and selection tools described in Table 2-2. Use these tools to select and draw freeform or precise lines, shapes, and paths, and to select and paint filled objects. For example, you use the Arrow, Subselection, and Lasso tools to select images or parts of them. The Line, Pen, Pencil, and Brush tools are for drawing or coloring an image.

Table 2-2   Tools in the Toolbox

Drawing tool	Tool icon	Use this tool to:
Arrow tool		Select objects by clicking or dragging the Arrow tool to enclose the object within a marquee.
Subselection tool		Adjust a straight or curved line segment drawn with the Pen tool.
Line tool		Create a straight line.
Lasso tool		Select objects by drawing a freehand or straight-edge selection area.
Pen tool		Draw precise lines or curves.
Text tool	A	Place single lines of text or wrapped text blocks on the Stage.
Oval tool		Create ovals and circles.
Rectangle tool		Create rectangles and squares.
Pencil tool		Draw lines and freeform shapes.
Brush tool		Create brush strokes and fills.
Free Transform tool		Transform objects, groups, instances, or text blocks, such as by moving, rotating, scaling, skewing, and distorting.
Fill Transform tool		Change the color, line width, and style of lines or shape outlines according to the options set in the Property inspector.
Ink Bottle tool		Change the color, line width, and style of lines or shape outlines.
Paint Bucket tool		Fill enclosed areas with the current fill color.
Eyedropper tool		Copy fill and stroke attributes from one object to another.
Eraser tool		Remove stroke and fill areas of an object.
Hand tool		Move or pan the Stage to change its view, not the magnification.
Zoom tool	Q	Zoom in or out on a certain area of the Stage to change the magnification.

Table 2-2   Tools in the Toolbox (continued)

Drawing tool	Tool icon	Use this tool to:
Stroke Color modifier		Set the line color of new objects and change the line color of existing objects.
Fill Color modifier		Set the fill color of new objects and change the fill color of existing objects.

Arrow Tool

Use the Arrow tool to select an object on the Stage. You select an object to move or change it, for example, to reposition an object on the Stage or to change its color. To select an object, click it with the Arrow tool, or use the Arrow tool to click outside the object and then drag to draw a selection box around it, as shown in Figure 2-5. Flash displays the selected object with a blue outline.

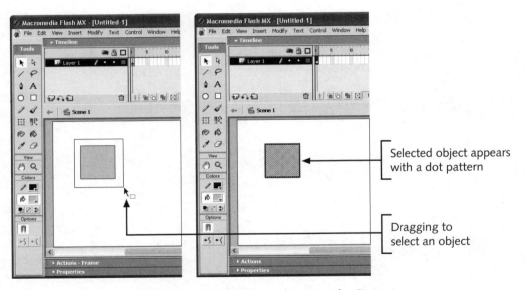

Selected object appears with a dot pattern

Dragging to select an object

Figure 2-5   Using the Arrow tool to select an object on the Stage

Some tools come with options called modifiers. **Modifiers** let you change the way a tool works. For example, you can set modifier options that determine how the Pencil tool smoothes or straightens lines or that set the size of the brush for the Brush tool. The Options area of the toolbox shows the modifiers for the selected tool. The Options area of the toolbox illustrated in Figure 2-6 includes modifiers that you can use with the Arrow tool.

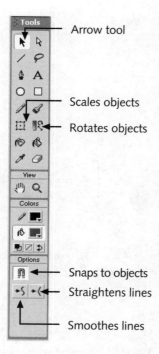

— Arrow tool

— Scales objects

— Rotates objects

— Snaps to objects

— Straightens lines

— Smoothes lines

Figure 2-6   Arrow tool options

Note that a selected option in the Options area of the toolbox has a white background. The options you can set for the Arrow tool are described in the following paragraphs.

Snap to Objects. When you select a stroke or fill with the Arrow tool, you can drag the object to move it and change its shape. The Snap to Objects option helps you align one object with another. When you move or reshape an object, the position of the Arrow tool on the object provides the reference point for alignment. For example, if you move a rectangle by dragging from its center, Flash aligns the center of the rectangle with the center of other nearby objects. When the Snap to Objects option for the Arrow tool is selected, a small black ring appears under the pointer as you drag an object. This small ring changes to a larger ring when the object is within snapping distance of a grid line, as shown in Figure 2-7.

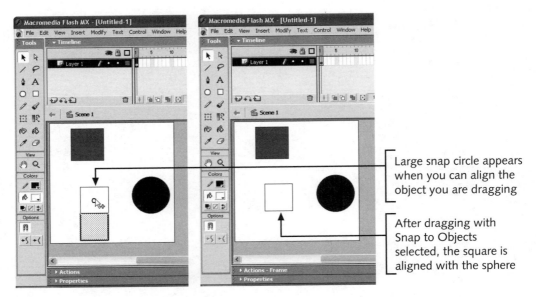

Large snap circle appears when you can align the object you are dragging

After dragging with Snap to Objects selected, the square is aligned with the sphere

Figure 2-7   Moving an object with Snap to Objects selected

Smooth. Select a curved line with the Pencil tool, and then click the Smooth option to smooth the curve, as shown in Figure 2–8. Use the Smooth option when you want to soften the curvature of a line.

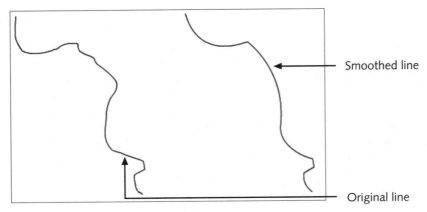

Smoothed line

Original line

Figure 2-8   Smoothing lines

Straighten. Select a line or curve, and then click the Straighten option to straighten the line or curve, as shown in Figure 2-9.

2

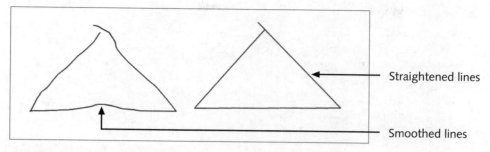

Figure 2-9   Straightening lines

Rotate. Select an object to rotate or turn it around an axis or registration point. The registration point is at the center of any object. Then click the Rotate option to highlight the object. Eight circles also appear around the object. Drag a corner circle to rotate the object. Drag an inside circle to skew the object. **Skewing** an object transforms it by slanting it along one or both axes. Figure 2-10 shows the effect of rotating and skewing objects.

Scale. Select the Scale option on the toolbox, and then click an object to resize it. Eight square selection handles appear around the object. Click and drag a corner selection handle to shrink or enlarge the image proportionately, as shown in Figure 2-11, or click an inside selection handle to change only the width or the height.

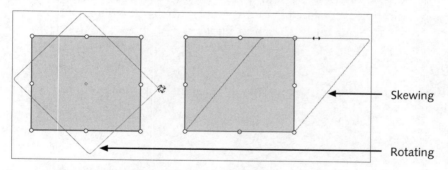

Figure 2-10   Rotating and skewing objects

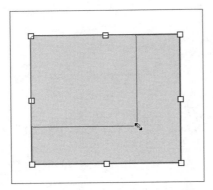

Figure 2-11   Scaling objects proportionately

Subselection Tool

Use the Subselection tool to adjust straight and curved line segments, or a section of line between two points or tangent handles, which are movable points on a curve. Use the Pen to draw a straight or curved line with control points on each line endpoint or tangent handle. Then click the Subselection tool and drag points on the path to change their position. Doing so adjusts the length or angle of straight segments or the slope of curved segments. To add points, click the Pen tool and then click a line segment, also called a **path**; the pointer changes to a fountain pen with cross hairs when you point to a line segment, indicating you can add control points. Click a line segment to set a new control point on that segment, as shown in Figure 2-12.

Line Tool

Use the Line tool to draw straight lines by dragging from one point to another, as shown in Figure 2-13.

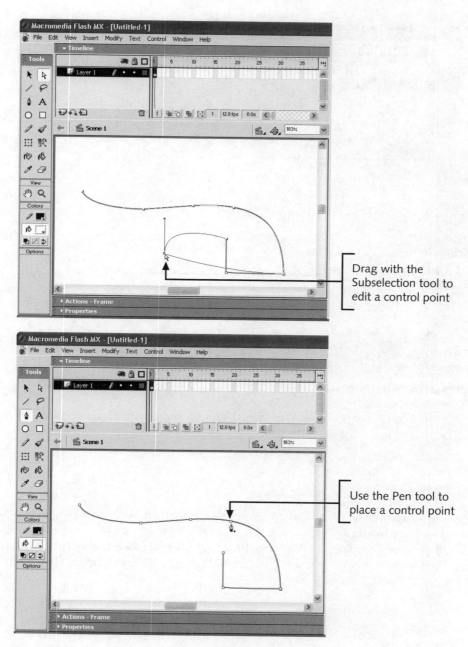

Figure 2-12 Using the Subselection and Pen tools

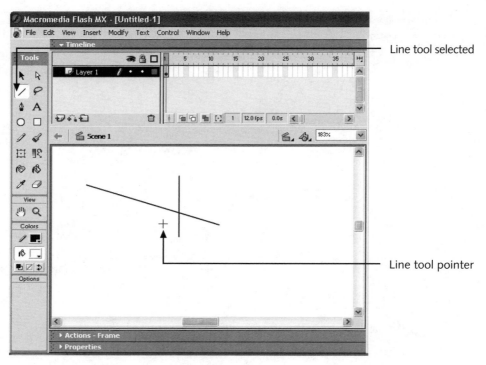

Figure 2-13   Drawing with the Line tool

 To draw perfect vertical, horizontal, and 45-degree lines, press and hold the Shift key while using the Line tool.

Lasso Tool

Use the Lasso tool to select objects by drawing a freehand or straight-edge selection area around objects on the Stage. Create a freehand selection area to select complex or odd-shaped areas of an object, as shown in Figure 2-14. The Lasso is particularly useful when selecting imported bitmaps. See Chapter 4, "Designing with Other Media File Types," for more information on importing bitmaps.

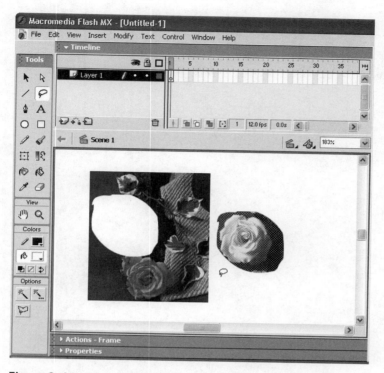

Figure 2-14   Using the Lasso tool to select odd-shaped areas

When the Lasso tool is selected, the Options area of the toolbox includes the tools shown in Figure 2-15 to help you select a shape area.

Use the Lasso tool options to determine what the Lasso selects and the shape of the selection area. Click the Lasso tool, and then click a Lasso option according to the following descriptions:

- *Magic Wand*—Use this option for freehand selections of images.

- *Magic Wand Properties*—Use this option to specify the color threshold and the smoothing of the Magic Wand. The **color threshold** defines how closely the color of adjacent pixels must match to be included in the selection. A higher number includes a broader range of colors. The **smoothing** setting defines how much the edges of the bitmap are smoothed, with options for varying degrees of roughness or smoothness.

- *Polygon Mode*—Select this option to create a straight-edged selection area with the Lasso tool. In Polygon mode, to create a straight-edged selection area around objects, click the Lasso pointer at the starting point of your selection and every other point where the angle of the selection area changes. The Lasso tool then creates a straight line between each point.

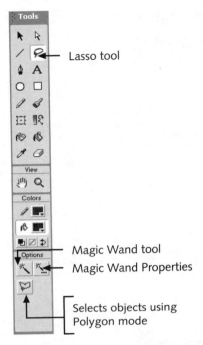

Figure 2-15   Lasso tool options

 To use the Magic Wand on an imported bitmap, break it apart first by clicking Modify on the menu bar, and then clicking Break Apart. See Chapter 4, "Designing with Other Media File Types," for more information on working with imported bitmaps.

Pen Tool

This tool is the most accurate drawing tool in Flash. Use the Pen tool to draw precise straight lines and smooth curves.

To use the Pen tool:

1. In Windows XP, click the **Start** button, point to **All Programs**, point to **Macromedia**, and then click **Macromedia Flash MX** to start Flash. A new document opens in Flash, named Untitled-1 by default.

   On the Macintosh, click the **hard drive** icon, navigate to the Macromedia Flash MX folder, and then double-click the **Flash MX** icon. A new document opens in Flash, named Untitled-1 by default.

2. In the toolbox, click the **Pen** tool. (If the toolbox does not appear in your Flash window, click **Window** on the toolbar, and then click **Tools**.)

3. Click the Stage; a point appears.

4. Click elsewhere on the Stage. Another point appears, and the Pen draws a straight line between the two points.

5. Click to add other control points and lines to the drawing, as shown in Figure 2-16.

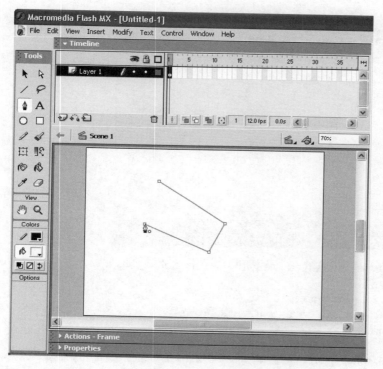

Figure 2-16   Drawing straight lines with the Pen tool

6. Double-click a blank area of the Stage to add the last line segment and to indicate you are finished drawing.

7. Use the **Arrow** tool to select each line, and then press **Delete** to delete the lines.

Now that you have a feel for using the Pen tool to draw straight lines, try drawing curves with the Pen tool.

To draw a curved line with the Pen tool:

1. With Untitled-1 still open in Flash, click the **Pen** tool, if necessary, to select it.

2. Click the Stage. A point appears.

3. Click elsewhere on the Stage and, holding down the mouse button, drag from right to left to make the line curve, as shown in Figure 2-17.

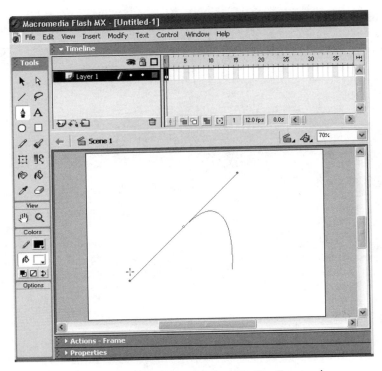

Figure 2-17 Drawing a curved line with the Pen tool

4. Click **File** on the menu bar and then click **Close**. When Flash asks if you want to save the document, click **No** in Windows XP or **Don't Save** on the Macintosh.

 When drawing with the Pen tool, you can leave lines open or you can close them. If they are closed, Flash fills the shape with the current fill color, which is shown in the Colors area of the toolbox.

 You can use the Subselection tool to move points after you initially place them. Change lines by clicking the points with the Pen tool again to straighten lines or delete points as necessary.

Text Tool

Use the Text tool to create text blocks. Click or drag on the Stage with the Text tool, and a text box appears. As you type text, the text box widens to accommodate the characters. You can also click the Text tool, drag on the Stage to create a text block with a fixed width, and then type. The text is enclosed in a white box with a black outline. A small symbol appears in the upper-right corner, either a circle or a square, as shown in

Figure 2-18. The circle indicates that you can type text on a single line; in this case, the text box expands to accommodate the type. Use this type of text box for short text items that do not wrap. A square indicates that the text wraps within the text box. Use a text box to insert longer text.

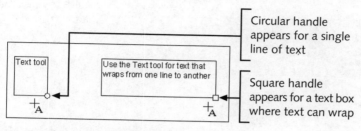

Figure 2-18   Using the Text tool

To add more than one line of text:

1. Click **File** on the Flash menu bar, and then click **Open**. In the Open dialog box, navigate to the Chapter2 folder of your FlashSamples folder, and then double-click **Text.fla**. A cartoon character with a text bubble appears. Use the vertical and horizontal scroll bars to scroll the Stage, if necessary, to see the complete image.

2. Click the **Fill Color** icon in the toolbox, and then click a black square or type the hexadecimal value (**#000000**) to change the stroke to black, if necessary.

3. Click the **Text** tool as shown in Figure 2-19.

4. Click in the text bubble on the Stage, and then drag to create a text box with a square text block handle.

5. If you need to change the width of the text block, drag the text block handle.

6. Type **You can use a text box to insert more than one line of text** in the text box. The text wraps to the next line when it reaches the right border of the text box. If the text box is outside the clown's speech bubble, drag the text box into the bubble by clicking the outer edge of the text box and dragging with a four-headed arrow pointer.

7. Click the **Arrow** tool, and then click outside the text box to deselect it.

 By default, the color of the text is the fill color. Change the fill color before selecting the Text tool, if necessary.

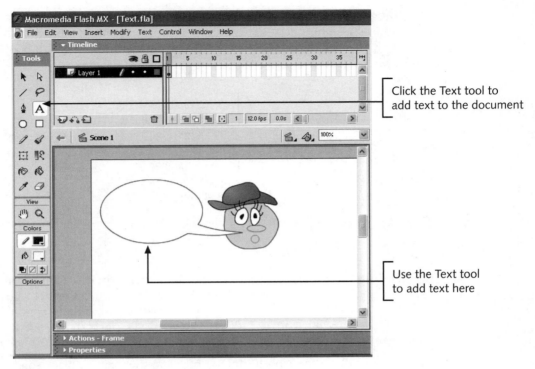

Figure 2-19   Adding text to a Flash document

Now that you've added a block of text that wraps to fit in the text box, you can add a single line of text. In the following steps, you add a label to identify the cartoon character.

To add a single line of text:

1. Using the Text tool, click the Stage just below the cartoon character. A text box appears with a circular text block handle.

2. Type **Jim the Clown** in the text box.

3. Click the **Arrow** tool, and then click outside the text box. See Figure 2-20.

4. To save the document, click **File** on the menu bar, and then click **Save As**. Navigate to your Chapter2 folder in the FlashSamples folder, if necessary, and then save the document as **myText.fla**. Close the document by clicking **File** on the menu bar, and then clicking **Close**. Leave Flash open for the next set of steps.

If you add a text block with more than one line of text, and you want to convert it to a single line of text, click the text box and then double-click the square text block handle.

Figure 2-20   Using an expanding text box

You can set and change text properties such as font, point size, and alignment by using the Property inspector. You'll learn more about the Property inspector later in this chapter, and have a chance to work with it in the Hands-on Projects.

Oval Tool

Use the Oval tool to draw round shapes. Click the Oval tool, and then drag on the Stage. By default, a circular outline appears while you drag, giving you a preview of the oval size. Release the mouse button when you create the shape you want.

To draw a perfect circle, press and hold the Shift key while dragging.

Rectangle Tool

Use the Rectangle tool to draw rectangular shapes. Click the Rectangle tool, and then drag on the Stage. By default, a rectangular outline appears while you drag, giving you a preview of the rectangle size. Release the mouse button when you draw the shape you want.

To draw a perfect square, press and hold the Shift key while dragging.

Pencil Tool

Use the Pencil tool to draw strokes freehand. To use the Pencil tool, click to select it on the toolbox, and then drag to draw the desired shape. You can also use the Pencil tool to sketch text. Select a Pencil tool option to set the following stroke options:

- *Straighten*–Straightens lines that you draw
- *Smooth*–Smoothes the curves in your drawing
- *Ink*–Lets you draw freehand lines with no modification

Figure 2-21 compares the effects of using the Pencil tool with various options.

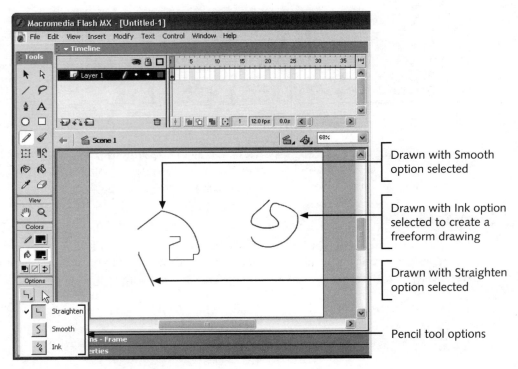

Figure 2-21   Using the Pencil tool options to create shapes

2

Brush Tool

Use the Brush tool for freehand drawing of fills, creating the effect of painted brush strokes. Click the Brush tool in the toolbox, and then select a fill color in the Colors area. You can also select a painting mode and brush size and shape in the Options area. Drag on the Stage with the Brush pointer to create a filled line. When you select the Brush tool, you can set its options in the Options area of the toolbox, as shown in Figure 2-22.

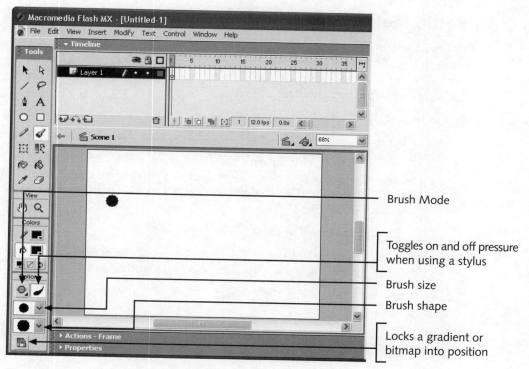

Figure 2-22   Options for the Brush tool

Click a tool in the Options area to set the following options for the Brush tool:

- *Brush Mode*—Click to select an option that determines what you paint when you use the Brush, including Normal (painting over lines and fills), Fills (painting fills only, not lines), Behind (painting blank areas), Selection (applying the fill color to the selected area), and Inside (painting inside existing lines).

- *Use Pressure*—If you are using a pressure-sensitive tablet attached to your computer, click this button to vary the width of the brush stroke as you vary pressure on a stylus and paint on the tablet.

- *Brush Size*—Click the list arrow to select a brush size.

- *Brush Shape*—Click the list arrow to select a brush shape.

- *Lock Fill*—When the fill color for the brush is a gradient or a bitmap, click this button to lock the gradient or bitmap into position to make it appear that you are applying a single gradient or bitmap fill to separate objects on the Stage. A gradient is a smooth transition from one color to another. For example, if you use a gradient that ranges from light blue to navy blue, and apply it to a row of circles on the Stage, the first circle is light blue, the middle a medium blue, and the last a navy blue.

Ink Bottle Tool

Use the Ink Bottle tool to outline an existing fill with a stroke and to change the stroke color, line width, and style of lines or shape outlines. You might use the Ink Bottle tool to change the style and color of line segments. For example, you can change any stand-alone line or a line surrounding an object.

To use the Ink Bottle tool:

1. Click **File** on the Flash menu bar, and then click **New** to start a new document.
2. Create a filled black line with the Brush tool. (Click the **Brush** tool, click the **Stroke Color** icon in the Colors area of the toolbox, click a black square, if necessary, click the **Fill Color** icon, click a black square, if necessary, and then drag on the Stage.)
3. Click the **Ink Bottle** tool.
4. In the Colors area of the toolbox, click the **Stroke Color** box, and then click **bright green** (the second-to-last color box in the first row, #66FF00).
5. Click anywhere inside the fill. The outline of the filled line is now bright green, as shown in Figure 2-23.
6. Save the document as **Shapes.fla** in the Chapter2 folder of the FlashSamples folder, and leave the document open in Flash.

Paint Bucket Tool

Use the Paint Bucket tool to fill enclosed areas with a color or pattern, such as a solid color, gradient fill, or bitmap fill. You select a solid color in the Colors area of the tool-box, or from the Swatches or Mixer panels. A **gradient fill** gradually changes from one color to another, and is useful when you create objects that look multi-dimensional, such as a sphere or a 3-D navigation button. Bitmap fills are sections you copy from existing bitmaps on your Stage; you can use these bitmaps to fill other objects. For example, you can use a textured background as a bitmap fill and apply it to the fill of text.

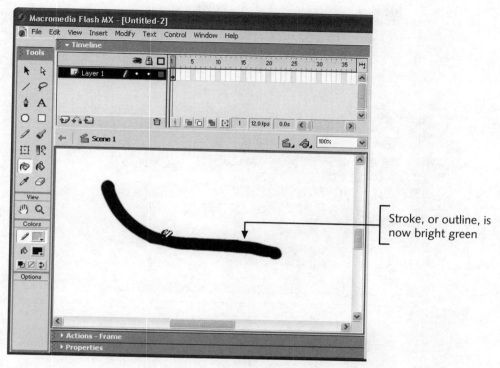

Figure 2-23   Using the Ink Bottle tool to color lines or shape outlines

To use the Paint Bucket:

1. With Shapes.fla still open in Flash, use the Rectangle tool to create a filled black square on the Stage. (Click the **Rectangle** tool, click the **Stroke Color** icon in the Colors area of the toolbox, click a black square, click the **Fill Color** icon, click a black square, if necessary, and then drag on the Stage.)

2. Click the **Paint Bucket** tool.

3. In the Colors area of the toolbox, click the **Fill Color** box, and then click **bright green** (the second-to-last color box in the first row, #66FF00).

4. Click anywhere inside the rectangle to fill it.

5. Click **File** on the menu bar, and then click **Save** to save Shapes.fla. Leave it open in Flash.

Select a Paint Bucket tool option according to the following descriptions:

- *Gap Size*—Choose this option to open the menu shown in Figure 2-24. Choose an option to specify the tolerance of the gap size between the starting and ending points of the stroke. For example, suppose you draw an oval then erase an edge of it and its stroke outline, thus leaving a gap. You refill the oval, depending on the gap size, by selecting an option from the Gap Size modifier: Don't Close Gaps, Close Small Gaps, Close Medium Gaps, or Close Large Gaps.

- *Lock Fill*–When the fill color for the brush is a gradient or a bitmap, choose this option to maintain the gradient or bitmap locked into position so that overlapping lines are consistent.

- *Transform Fill*–Choose this option to modify the appearance of a gradient. This tool is discussed in more detail later in this chapter.

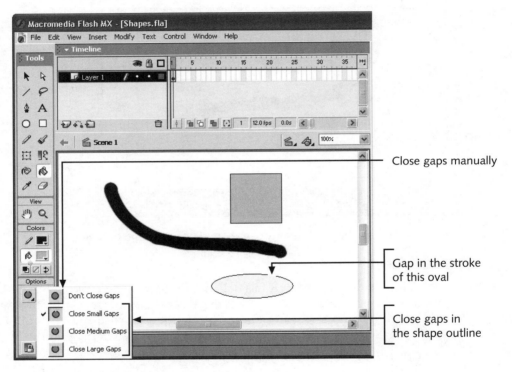

Figure 2-24   Gap Size menu

Eyedropper Tool

Use the Eyedropper tool to select any color on the Stage and then immediately apply it to another object. Click the Eyedropper tool, click a colored area in an object, and then click another object where you want to apply the color.

 When the pointer changes to an eyedropper with a paintbrush, you can use the Eyedropper tool to select a color. When the pointer changes to a paint bucket, you can use the Eyedropper tool to apply the selected color to another object.

Eraser Tool

Use the Eraser tool to delete content on the Stage. To erase strokes or filled areas, click the Eraser tool and then drag over the area you want to delete. To delete everything on the Stage, double-click the Eraser tool. Click an Eraser tool option according to the following descriptions:

- *Eraser Mode*–Choose this option to select the parts of the image you want to erase. For example, erase only strokes and fills, erase only fills, or erase only strokes. See Figure 2-25 for the Eraser Mode options.

- *Faucet*–Choose this option to delete color from the entire selected area.

- *Eraser Shape*–Click this list arrow to set the shape and size of the eraser.

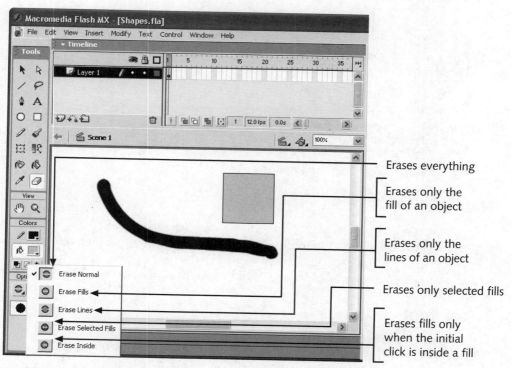

Figure 2-25   Specifying what the Eraser tool deletes from the Stage

USING THE VIEW TOOLS

The View tools on the toolbox help you change your view of images, especially large ones. For example, use the Hand tool to pan, or move, the entire Stage and put certain areas in view. Use the Zoom tool to enlarge or reduce the magnification levels. Use the Zoom options to set the zoom mode, as shown in Figure 2-26.

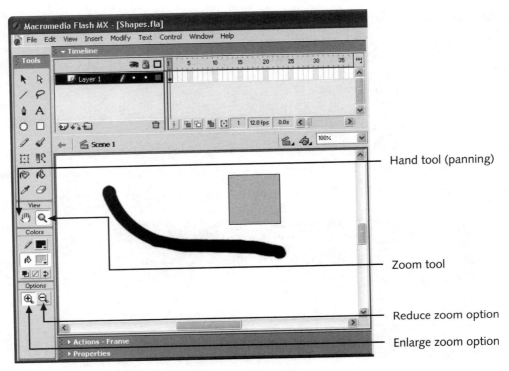

Figure 2-26   View tools and options

Hand Tool

When the image is larger than the Stage, use the Hand tool to change the view of the Stage. This is especially helpful when the Stage is magnified. (See the following "Zoom Tool" section.) Use the Hand tool to pan the Stage without using scroll bars or changing the magnification. To use the Hand tool, click anywhere on the Stage and drag.

Zoom Tool

Use the Zoom tool to change the magnification of the Stage. The Zoom tool does not enlarge or shrink an image; it merely changes your view of the Stage. To magnify a certain part of an image, click the Zoom tool and then drag over the portion of the Stage you want to magnify.

To return to 100 percent magnification, double-click the Zoom tool. To switch from enlarging or reducing the view, hold down the Alt key (Windows) or Option key (Macintosh) while double-clicking.

USING THE COLOR TOOLS

Use the Color tools in the toolbox to specify stroke and fill colors. For example, when you select the Brush tool, you can also select the fill color by clicking the Fill Color box and then clicking a color. Figure 2-27 shows the Color tools.

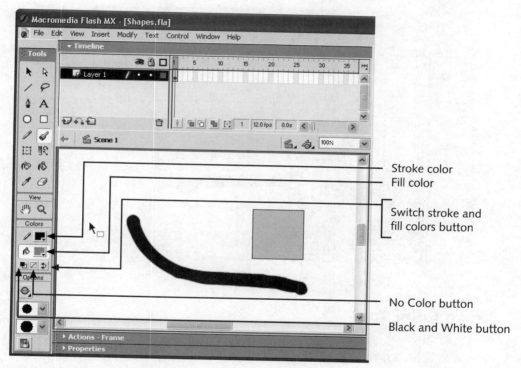

Figure 2-27   Color tools

To select a color for drawing:

1. With Shapes.fla still open in Flash, click the **Oval** tool.
2. Click the **Fill Color** box. A color palette opens. Point to the **red gradient** box at the bottom of the color palette. See Figure 2-28.
3. Click the **red gradient** box to select it as the fill color.
4. Drag on the Stage to draw an oval filled with a red gradient.
5. Click **File** on the menu bar, and then click **Save** to save Shapes.fla. Leave it open in Flash.

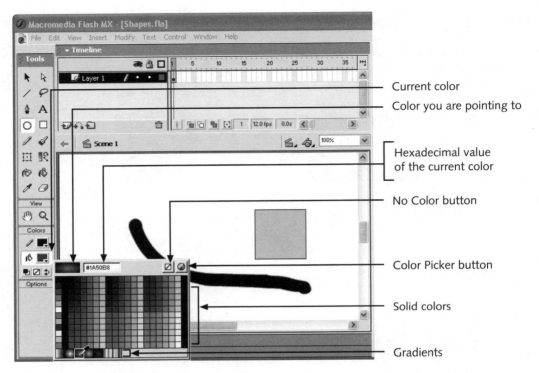

Figure 2-28   Color palette

Stroke Color Tool

Use the Stroke Color tool in the Colors area of the toolbox to change the color of an outline stroke. To change the outline of an existing object, select the object with the Arrow tool, and then choose a color from the Stroke color palette on the toolbox. To set the stroke color of an object you are about to draw with any drawing tool, choose a stroke color just before you draw with that tool. Alternatively, you can select the colors from the Color Swatches or Color Mixer panel.

Fill Color Tool

Use the Fill Color tool in the Colors area of the toolbox to change an object's fill color. To change the fill of a drawn object, select the object with the Arrow tool, and then choose a color from the Fill Color palette. To set the fill color of an object you are about to draw, choose a fill color just before you draw with that tool. As with the stroke color, you can also select fill colors from the Color Swatches or Color Mixer panel.

The Colors area includes three buttons that let you manage the color options quickly by applying colors to any drawn object on the Stage using a black stroke and white fill, using no color at all, or switching the fill with the stroke color. Table 2-3 describes these color selection options.

Table 2-3   Color selection options

Option	Description
Black and White	Uses black strokes and white fills
No Color	Prevents either the stroke or the fill from being drawn
Swap Color	Changes the fill color to the stroke color and vice versa

2

USING THE TIMELINE TO WORK WITH ANIMATIONS

When you are working with static images, you do most of your work on the Stage. When you are working with animations, you also work on the Timeline. Located by default at the top of the Flash window, the Timeline helps keep track of where an image appears in a movie. Figure 2-29 shows the Timeline and identifies its parts.

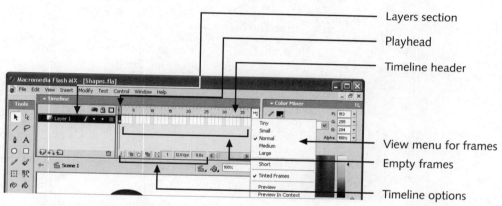

Figure 2-29   Parts of the Timeline

Layer Options

The Layer section and its options are located on the left side of the Timeline. A **layer** is like a clear sheet of plastic. You can draw on a layer, and the parts of the layer not covered by the drawing remain transparent. A Flash movie can have many layers stacked on top of one another, with a different image on each layer. Having separate layers lets you manipulate each image on its own, without affecting the other images. For example, if your movie shows a beach umbrella, sand, and a seagull, you could include each image on a separate layer, and then change the color of the umbrella, for example, without affecting the sand and seagull.

In Flash, a layer has its own band in the Timeline and is separate from the other layers. You work with layers to organize the objects in your movie. You can also organize and manage layers by creating layer folders and placing layers in them. You can expand or collapse layers in the Timeline without affecting what you see on the Stage. It's a good idea to use separate layers or folders for sound files, actions, frame labels, and frame comments. This helps you find these items quickly when you need to edit them. Following are tasks you can perform when working with layers:

- Rename a layer or layer folder by double-clicking the layer name and typing the new name.

- View the layer or layer folder properties by double-clicking the icon to the left of the layer name.

- Add a layer by clicking the Insert Layer icon in the lower-left of the Layers section.

- Add a layer folder by clicking the Insert Layer Folder icon in the lower-left of the Layers section.

- Add a motion layer by clicking the Add Motion Guide icon at the bottom of the Layers section. See Chapter 3, "Animation Fundamentals," for more information on motion layers.

- In editing mode, hide or show a layer or layer folder by clicking the dot under the eye. You can also hide or show all the layers by clicking the eye (called the Show/Hide All Layers icon).

- Prevent or allow editing to a particular layer by clicking the dot under the lock. You can also lock or unlock all layers by clicking the lock (called the Lock/Unlock All Layers icon).

- View a layer as an outline or full shapes by clicking under the square next to the lock. You can also view all layers as outlines or full shapes by clicking the box (called the Show All Layers as Outlines icon).

- Delete a layer by selecting it and clicking the trash can (called the Delete Layer icon), located in the lower-right of the Layers section.

Timeline Header

The Timeline header is at the top of the Timeline, to the right of the Layers section. (Refer back to Figure 2-29.) Each number on the Timeline header represents a frame. A **frame** is a period of time within your animation. You use frames to organize the objects in your movie, such as drawings, imported artwork, or audio clips, placing them in a sequence to create the illusion of motion when Flash plays the frames one after the other. To show a particular frame on the Stage, click the frame number in the Timeline header, or drag the playhead to the desired position.

When you play an animation, Flash shows the frames in order according to their position and other settings in the Timeline. In addition, every layer that is stacked under each number plays at the same time. If a movie has 20 layers, each with a different image, and if all the layers are on frame 15, all of those images appear when Flash plays frame 15.

2

Playhead

The playhead is the red rectangle on the Timeline header (refer back to Figure 2-29). The playhead moves through the Timeline to indicate which frame is currently displayed on the Stage. To display a frame on the Stage, move the playhead to the frame in the Timeline. You can navigate all the frames in the movie by dragging the playhead across the Timeline header.

Frames and Keyframes

Recall that a frame is a discrete period of time within your animation. A **keyframe** is a frame where a significant action takes place. You use keyframes to define where an action begins and where that action ends. Figure 2-30 shows how frames and keyframes are represented by a series of rectangles and circles under the Timeline header.

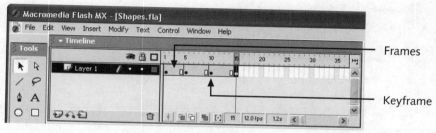

Figure 2-30 Frames and keyframes

 In some movies you create, you might want to reuse certain objects or animations. To reuse a movie element, you select the frame or frames containing the objects or animation you want to reuse, and then copy the frames to another location on the Timeline. To cut, copy, or paste part of a Timeline onto another section, select the area on the Timeline; right-click the selected area, and then click Cut Frames, Copy Frames, or Paste Frames on the shortcut menu. To remove unwanted frames or keyframes, select the appropriate area on the Timeline, click Insert on the menu bar, and then click Remove Frames.

 To change the appearance of the Timeline, click the Frame View menu icon, which looks like miniature ticks of a ruler and is located on the right side of the Timeline header. You can change the appearance of the Timeline to reflect your viewing needs by changing the size of the frames from tiny to small, normal, medium, or large; selecting to toggle on or off the shaded tint on every fifth frame; or choosing to show tiny images of your Stage on the frame.

Timeline Options

At the bottom of the Timeline are eight controls, shown in Figure 2-31, that provide information about the current document and allow you to control the Timeline. For example, you can center the playhead on the Timeline to easily move it to the current frame you are working on; this is useful when working with many frames that don't fit on the Timeline. You can also view all the objects in an animation and multiple frames at one time by displaying the Timeline with the Onion Skin option. This is ideal when you need to see several frames of an animation at one time. You can see where the playhead is by displaying the current frame number. You can also view and edit the frame rate, or view the elapsed time of your movie.

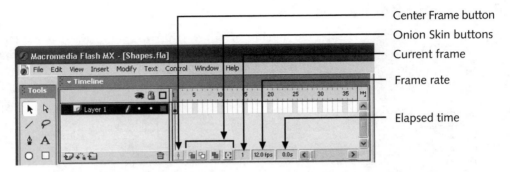

Figure 2-31 Timeline options

Each Timeline option is described in the following list:

- *Center Frame*—Select a frame, and then click the Center Frame button to center the playhead on the selected frame in the Timeline. This option is especially helpful when you are working with a long Timeline because it brings the playhead into view.

- *Onion Skin*—Click the Onion Skin button to display sequential semitransparent frames, like the skin of an onion, as shown in Figure 2-32. This is useful for observing or editing an object's position and for editing animations frame by frame.

- *Onion Skin Outlines*—Click the Onion Skin Outlines button to display the outlines of semitransparent frames in sequence.

- *Edit Multiple Frames*—Click the Edit Multiple Frames button to show sequential frames at one time; this option allows you to modify more than one frame at a time.

- *Modify Onion Markers*—Click this button to open a menu containing options for modifying an onion marker. The onion marker is displayed on the Timeline header when an onion skin feature is selected.

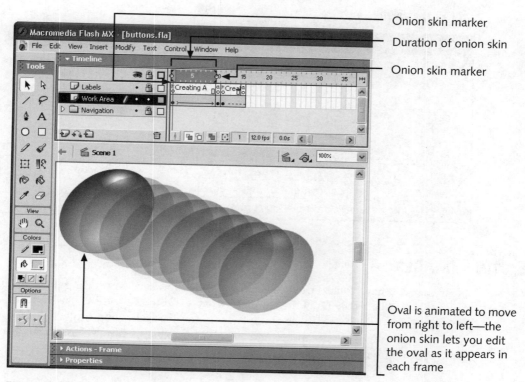

Figure 2-32   Onion skin frames

- *Current Frame*—Click this button to display the number of the frame at the position of the playhead.

- *Elapsed Time*—Click this button to display how much time has passed from the first frame to the selected frame.

- *Frame Rate*—Refer to this indicator to determine the Frames Per Second setting of the current movie. Double-click the Frame Rate indicator to open the Document Properties dialog box, and then specify settings for the current document, as described in Table 2-4.

Table 2-4   Setting Document Properties

Property	Description
Dimensions	Enter the height and width of the Stage for the document.
Match	Click Printer to match the dimensions of the document to the printed page dimensions specified in the Page Setup dialog box. Click Contents to change the dimensions of the document so that the Stage provides equal space around the content on all sides. Click Default to match the default dimensions (550 px by 400 px).
Background Color	Specify the color of the background.
Frame Rate	Specify the number of frames the playhead shows in one second.
Ruler Units	Choose a unit of measurement, such as pixels or inches.
Make Default	Click to save the current settings as defaults to use in other documents.

EDITING IMAGES

Now that you have toured the tools and Timeline, you can start editing images. The "Using the Macromedia Flash Drawing Tools to Create Objects" section earlier in this chapter explained how to create strokes and fills using the Flash drawing tools. The following section explains how to edit strokes and fills. It also explains how to use other Flash panels that support the drawing tools.

Editing Images with the Arrow Tool

Besides selecting objects, you can use the Arrow tool to alter an image. As shown in Figure 2-33, you can drag one edge of an image to distort its appearance.

To resize, or scale, an object, you first select the object. Then you can drag with the Arrow tool to resize the object. (Note that you can also use the Free Transform tool to resize objects.)

You can also use the Arrow tool to select strokes, fills, or both. Flash highlights selected fills and strokes with a dot pattern. To select a stroke, click the outline of an image. To select a fill, click the inside of the image. To select both, Shift+click (press and hold the Shift key and then click) the image, or double-click the fill.

To resize an image using the Arrow tool:

1. With Shapes.fla still open in Flash, click the **Oval** tool, press and hold the **Shift** key, and then draw a circle on the Stage with the current stroke and fill colors.

2. Right-click the **circle** (press Ctrl+click on the Macintosh), and then click **Scale** on the shortcut menu. A bounding box with eight square handles appears around the circle. You can drag any handle to stretch or shrink the circle. Hold down the Shift key and drag a corner handle to resize proportionally.

3. Use the **Arrow** tool to drag a corner handle to the right to enlarge the circle. Click the handle again and drag to the left to shrink the circle.

4. Click **File** on the menu bar, and then click **Save** to save Shapes.fla. Leave it open in Flash.

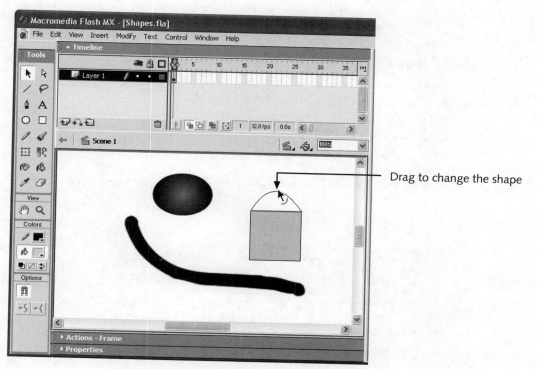

Drag to change the shape

Figure 2-33 Changing an object by dragging with the Arrow tool

Grouping Images

Normally, when you place one image on top of another, Flash deletes the image on the bottom. To prevent this from happening, either place each image on a separate layer, or group the images. To group the images, select one image, click another image as you hold down the Shift key, click Modify on the menu bar, and then click Group. The images stay together as one group. Additionally, grouping images changes their behavior to act as one element. When you move, size, or rotate a group, the changes apply to all objects in the group.

When grouping more than one image on the same layer, the newest grouped image is at the front of the layer. You can organize your document by using multiple groups and arranging the stacking order, or z-order. The stacking order represents groups as they overlay one another. To change the stacking order of grouped images, click Modify on the menu bar, point to Arrange, and then select a stacking order for the grouped image. For example, you can click Bring to Front to move the selected group to the front of the layer.

Editing Strokes

Use the Property inspector to change the type, color, and thickness of a stroke. By default, the Property inspector appears collapsed at the bottom of the Flash window. To expand the Property inspector, click its name in the title bar. If the Property inspector is not open, click Window on the menu bar, and then click Properties. See Figure 2-34.

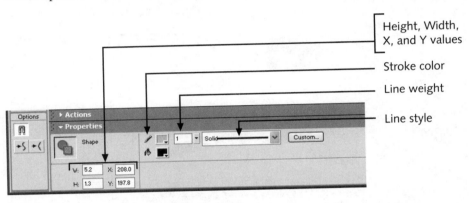

Figure 2-34   Property inspector

To modify a stroke:

1. With Shapes.fla open in Flash, create a shape with the Rectangle tool.

2. Use the **Arrow** tool to drag a selection box around the rectangle.

3. If the Property inspector is not open, click **Window** on the menu bar, and then click **Properties**. If the Property inspector is open but collapsed, click its name in the panel title bar to expand it.

4. Click the **Stroke Style** list arrow in the Stroke panel and then click a dashed line. The rectangle now appears with a dashed border.

5. Click the **Stroke Weight** list arrow and then drag the **slider** up to **3.5** to increase the thickness of the line. See Figure 2-35.

6. Click a blank area of the Stage to deselect the rectangle. Save Shapes.fla, and then close the document by clicking **File** on the menu bar and then clicking **Close**.

The other panels in Flash work in a similar way, so once you are familiar with one panel, you should also be able to easily work with other panels.

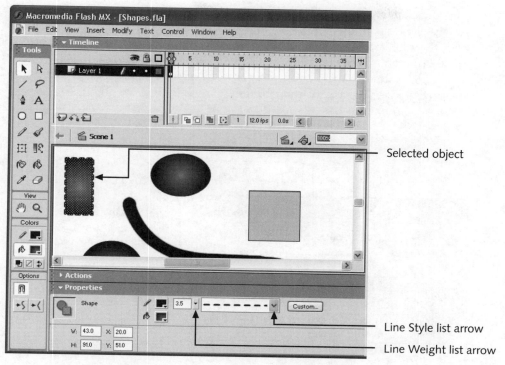

Figure 2-35   Editing strokes

Using the Color Swatches Panel to Review Colors

The Color Swatches panel shows all the color combinations in use for the current project. The Color Swatches panel includes gradients that may have been created in addition to the default colors and gradients. By default, the Color Swatches panel appears in the lower-right corner of the Flash window. To expand the Color Swatches panel, click its name in the panel title bar. To open the Color Swatches panel, click Window on the menu bar, and then click Color Swatches.

Choosing Colors with the Color Mixer Panel

You use the Color Mixer panel to create and edit solid colors and gradient fills, and to apply color options to a selected object. You can select existing colors, create new colors, choose colors in RGB or hexadecimal mode (where you specify colors based on their hexidecimal values, which is ideal if you are creating images for the Web), and specify an alpha value to set the degree of transparency for a color.

By default, the Color Mixer panel appears on the right of the Flash window. To expand the Color Mixer panel, click its name in the panel title bar. To open the Color Mixer panel, click Window on the menu bar, and then click Color Mixer. In the Color Mixer panel, select a stroke color, fill color, and related options, just as you do when working with the Color tools in the toolbox. You can use the R, G, and B text boxes to specify the RGB (red, green, and blue) color combinations. Doing so means you can specify these color values to match your desired color precisely. Click the Alpha list arrow to set levels of alpha—degrees of transparency—by dragging the slider. You can also select a color from the color bar, as shown in Figure 2-36.

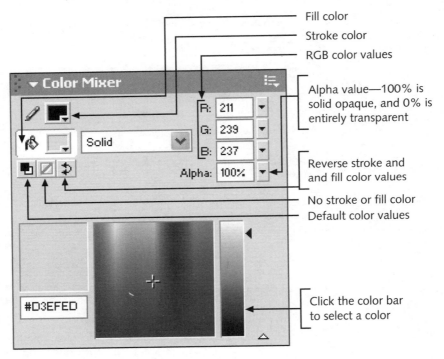

Figure 2-36   Color Mixer panel

If you are creating images for the Web, use the Web-safe color palette in Flash. This palette contains the 216 colors that are most likely to display correctly on most monitors, fixed screen resolutions, and browsers. To open the Web safe color palette, click the triangle in the upper-right corner of the Color Swatches panel to open the Color Swatches menu. Then click the Web 216 command. Using this color palette, you can feel confident using any standard solid color on the Color Swatches panel.

Editing Fills

You also use the Color Mixer panel to modify the appearance of a fill. To modify a fill, first select it with the Arrow tool. On the Color Mixer panel, click the Fill list arrow and choose an option according to the following descriptions:

- *None*–Deletes the current fill

- *Solid*–Lets you specify a particular solid color

- *Linear*–Combines more than one color into one fill. The colors appear parallel to one other.

- *Radial*–Combines more than one color into one fill. The colors appear as concentric circles.

- *Bitmap*–Lets you use part of a bitmap used as a fill

CHAPTER SUMMARY

- ❑ Flash movies are a combination of graphics and animation for Web sites. Working in Flash, you can create a document by drawing or importing artwork, arranging it on the Stage, and animating it with the Timeline. The Flash work environment consists of several panels that display the tools you use to select and modify image and document settings. The main features of the work environment are the toolbox, panels, Timeline, and Stage.

- ❑ Flash provides many drawing tools, including the drawing, painting, and selection tools; the View tools; the Color tools; and the Timeline. When a tool is selected, the Options area of the toolbox shows the options you can use with that tool.

- ❑ You use the drawing tools to work with shapes you draw in Flash and with images you import. In Flash, you create and edit vector images, although you can also import bitmap and vector images. Vector images are comprised of lines and fills that are calculated by mathematical equations. Because of this, resizing a vector image does not affect its quality.

- ❑ The View tools on the toolbox help you change your view of images, especially large ones. For example, use the Hand tool to pan, or move, the entire Stage and put certain areas in view.

- ❑ When you are working with static images, you do most of your work on the Stage. When you are working with animations, you also work on the Timeline. Located by default at the top of the Flash window, the Timeline helps keep track of where an image appears in a movie.

REVIEW QUESTIONS

1. Use the Arrow tool to _____ objects on the Stage.

2. Use the Pen tool with the _____ tool to place or modify points in a stroke.

3. To draw perfect horizontal and vertical lines, hold down the _____ key while dragging with the Line tool.

4. You can use the Magic Wand with:

    a. vector images

    b. bitmaps

    c. none of the above

    d. all of the above

5. Use the Pen tool to create straight lines and curved lines. True or false?

6. The Text tool automatically takes the current color of the stroke. True or false?

7. You can enlarge a(n) _____ image without compromising the quality of the image.

8. In Flash, a line is called a:

    a. bar

    b. stroke

    c. line

    d. none of the above

9. The _____ tool draws freehand strokes and the _____ tool draws freehand fills.

    a. Pencil / Pen

    b. Pen / Brush

    c. Pencil / Brush

    d. Brush / Pencil

10. The Eraser can erase fills and not strokes on an image. True or false?

11. Use the Hand tool only when the image on the Stage is larger than the space available. True or false?

12. You cannot rename layers. True or false?

13. The _____ allows you to navigate through the Timeline header.

14. Which of the following indicates a populated frame that causes a change on the Timeline?

    a. keyframe

    b. blank frame

    c. frame

    d. full frame

15. You can view the content of your layers as outlines. True or false?

16. You cannot prevent a layer from being edited. True or false?

17. The Arrow tool can:

    a. select an area of the Stage

    b. separate a stroke from a fill

    c. modify the shape of an image

    d. all of the above

18. A gradient is the combination of two or more colors that flow smoothly into each other. True or false?

19. The feature that reveals more than one frame at a time is called _____.

20. The Color Mixer panel specifies the _____ of a color.

HANDS-ON PROJECTS

Project 2-1

In this project, you work with the Flash drawing tools to begin creating a Flash resume and portfolio on a Web page. You add text and a photograph in this project, and continue to work on the resume and portfolio in Projects 2-2 and 2-3.

1. Open a new Flash file, and save it as **MyResume.fla** in the Chapter2\Projects folder of your FlashSamples folder.

2. In the Colors area of the toolbox, click the Fill Color box to select any dark blue shade as the fill color.

3. Use the Text tool to add the following line of text in the upper-left corner of the Stage:

Home | Contact Me | Experience | Education | Portfolio
See Figure 2-37.

This text will serve as a navigation bar on the Web page.

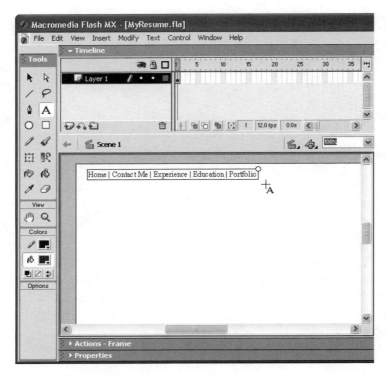

Figure 2-37

4. Use the Text tool to create a text box about as wide as the navigation bar.

5. Open or expand the Property inspector. Make sure Times New Roman appears in the Font list box; if it doesn't, click the Font list arrow and then click Times New Roman. Click the Font Size list arrow and then drag the slider to 18 to increase the point size of the text. Then click the Bold button.

6. Type Cover Letter: and press Enter five times.

7. Repeat Steps 4 to 6 to add **Objective:** in one text box and **Summary:** in another text box. Close the Timeline panel, if necessary, to see more of the Stage. See Figure 2-38.

8. Around each text box, draw a rectangle with a solid black stroke and no fill to add a border to the text boxes. To do so, click the Rectangle tool, click the Stroke Color tool and then click a black square, click the Stroke Style tool, and then click Solid, click the Fill Color tool, and then click the No Stroke button (a white button with a red diagonal line).

2

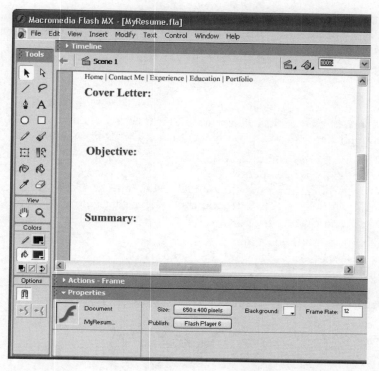

Figure 2-38

9. On the upper-right corner of the Stage, place a text box containing your name, address, phone numbers, and e-mail address in Times New Roman 12-point italic text.

10. Import an image of your photograph. If you do not have an electronic copy of your photo, you can import **Photo Female.gif** or **Photo Male.gif** from the Chapter2\ Projects folder in the FlashSamples folder. To import an image in Windows XP, click File on the menu bar and then click Import. In the Import dialog box, navigate to the folder containing the image you want to import (such as the Chapter2\Projects folder of your FlashSamples folder), and then double-click the image file. (*Hint*: If you can't find your image, click the Files of type list arrow in the Import dialog box, and then click All Image Formats to show all image files.)

On the Macintosh, click File on the menu bar and then click Import. In the Import dialog box, navigate to the folder containing the images you want to import (such as the Chapter2\Projects folder of your FlashSamples folder), click the appropriate GIF file, and then click Open.

11. Use the Arrow tool, if necessary, to move your photo just under your name and address. If you need to resize the photo you imported, right-click the photo (press Ctrl+click on the Macintosh) and then click Scale on the shortcut menu. The photo should be about as wide as the text box containing your name and address.

12. Click the Property inspector title bar to collapse the panel. Then save the MyResume.fla file in the Chapter2\Projects folder of your FlashSamples folder. Leave this file open in Flash for the next project.

Project 2-2

In this project, you work with the Flash color tools to continue creating a Web page for your resume and portfolio. You change the background and text colors and then add colored shadows to the photograph and text boxes. You will complete the Web page in Project 2-3.

1. In the MyResume.fla file you created in Project 2-1, change the background color of the Stage. To do so, open the Document Properties dialog box by clicking Modify on the menu bar, and then clicking Document. Click the Background Color box to open the color palette, and then select pale gold (10th row, 13th column, hexadecimal #CCCC99). Click OK to close the dialog box.

2. To the right of the photo you imported, draw a rectangle with a fill color of dark blue and no stroke. To do so, click the Rectangle tool, make sure the Fill Color tool shows dark blue (#000099), click the Stroke Color tool in the Colors area of the toolbox, and then click the No Stroke button (a white button with a red diagonal line). Make the rectangle about the same size as the photo. See Figure 2-39.

Figure 2-39

3. If you need to resize the rectangle, right-click the rectangle (or Ctrl+click on the Macintosh), and then click Scale on the shortcut menu. Drag the sizing handles to scale the rectangle to the size of your imported photo.

4. Use the Arrow tool to drag the rectangle over your photo, leaving some of the bottom and right side showing, as in Figure 2-40. It should appear behind the photo by default. If it does not, select the rectangle, if necessary, click Modify on the menu bar, point to Arrange, and then click Send to Back.

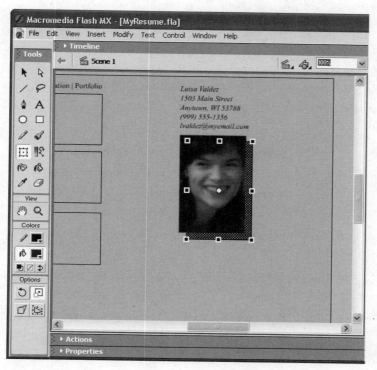

Figure 2-40

5. Save the document as **MyResume02.fla** in the Chapter2\Projects folder of your FlashSamples folder. Leave this document open in Flash for the next project.

Project 2-3

In this project, you work with layers and the Timeline, and continue working on your resume and portfolio. You add layers to the file to help you organize its contents, and then you increase the size of the frames in the Timeline to make them easier to manipulate.

1. In the MyResume.fla file you created in Project 2-1 and revised in Project 2-2, you have been working with Layer 1, which is the background layer by default. With MyResume02.fla open in Flash, rename this layer to Background. Expand

the Timeline panel, if necessary, double-click Layer 1 on the Timeline, type Background, and then press Enter.

2. To add a second layer, right-click the Background layer on the Timeline (or Ctrl+click on the Macintosh), and then click Insert Layer. Repeat Step 1 to change the name of Layer 2 to Navigation. You use this layer to store the navigation bar at the top of the page.

3. You can lock the layer to prevent accidental moving, deleting, or editing images on the Background layer. To do so, click the Background layer in the Lock/Unlock All Layers column (a lock icon appears at the top of this column). A lock icon appears on the Background layer in the Timeline.

4. You can hide the Navigation layer until you need to work with it to focus on the Background layer. To do so, right-click the Background layer in the Timeline (or Ctrl+click on the Macintosh), and then click Hide Others.

5. In the upper-right corner of the Timeline, click the button that shows a tick mark image to open the Frame View menu. Click Medium to adjust the size of the Timeline frames.

6. Save the file as **MyResume03.fla** in the Chapter2\Projects folder of your FlashSamples folder, and then close the document, leaving Flash open.

Project 2-4

In this project, you work with the Flash drawing tools to create a watercolor painting. Open a new Flash file and save it as **Watercolor.fla** in the Chapter2\Projects folder of your FlashSamples folder. To find a painting you can use as a model, visit *www.photodisk.com* or *www.gettyimages.com*, search for "watercolor" or keywords such as "flowers," and then view or download the image file, if possible.

The goal of this project is to let you experiment with the Flash drawing tools. Use some or all of the following techniques as you create your painting:

❐ Work with the Pencil tool and related options to draw rough sketches and outlines.

❐ Use the Paintbrush tool and change the brush size and shape options to paint with different types of strokes. Select a variety of fill colors by using the Fill Color tool or the Color Mixer and Color Swatches panels. Create and modify paint smear gradients with the Fill panel.

❐ Use the Ink Bottle tool and Stroke panel to set the stroke color, style, and height to paint brush strokes and other fills.

❐ Use the Eyedropper tool to select various ranges or colors to apply to a fill.

❐ You can immediately use the Paint Bucket tool after the Eyedropper tool to paint enclosed or partially enclosed fills.

❐ Use the Eraser tool to remove lines and fills. The Eraser tools has many options that let you delete content accurately. You can erase entire stroke or fill segments with one click by selecting the Faucet option for the Eraser tool. Use the Brush Size and Mode options to change the thickness of the Eraser and the specific area being erased: all, selected or all fills, and lines.

Project 2-5

In this project, you work with the Flash drawing tools to design a Web site interface. Examine an existing design and then recreate the design elements in Flash, enhancing them to add visual appeal. Browse the Web, and find a topic of interest. Choose an existing Web site that you can improve. Open a new Flash file and save it as **Web Site.fla** in the Chapter2\Projects folder of your FlashSamples folder. Use the Flash drawing tools to create new versions of the graphic elements on the Web site, such as navigation bars, buttons, logo, and icons.

CASE PROJECTS

Case Project 2-1

A record store hires you to design a dynamic Web site to attract more customers. Using the Flash drawing tools, sketch the designs for the home page and the intermediate pages of this site. Include objects for each of the following:

❑ All pages should let users search for music products. The search features should include ways to find music by media (CD, tape, etc.), genre, artist, and decade.

❑ Featured artist and CD area

❑ A form users can fill out to provide demographic information and to indicate their interests

❑ A favorite artists list

❑ A page that lets users sign up for an e-mail newsletter

Case Project 2-2

A pharmaceutical company has asked you to design a presentation in Flash that allows the public to search for information about prescription drugs and related information. Use the Flash drawing tools to design the first page in the presentation. Use text and graphics that could serve as links to other areas of the presentation, such as general health topics, drug information, drug interactions, and news and updates. To include graphics, you can create images yourself, use clip art, or import other graphics created elsewhere. (If you use graphics from a Web site, be sure they are in the public domain or otherwise free of copyright.)

Case Project 2-3

A gaming company has hired you to design a graphic background for a role-playing adventure computer game. The game will be set in a medieval time somewhere in Europe. Use the Flash drawing tools to sketch an appropriate scene, which may eventually include a rocky mountain range, a forest area, a wasteland area, and hazy colorful objects, such as clouds.

Case Project 2-4

For your personal Web site or fictional business, refer to the plan you created in Chapter 1. Then sketch the design of the home page for your Web site. If necessary, find images of yourself or generic images representing the products you want to sell. For example, if your fictional business is an online gardening service, look for drawings of rakes and hoes rather than brand-name tools. (Make sure the images are free from copyright before you use them.) Add the images to a Flash document, and then use the Flash drawing tools to edit the images to fit your design.

3

ANIMATION FUNDAMENTALS

Creating and Controlling Macromedia Flash Animations

> **In this chapter, you will:**
> ◆ Understand Macromedia Flash animation basics
> ◆ Work with frames
> ◆ Use symbols in animations
> ◆ Create animations with tweening
> ◆ Assemble frame-by-frame animations
> ◆ Control animations with basic frame actions

In the previous chapters, you created and manipulated static images in Macromedia Flash MX. Now you are ready to enliven these images by animating them. **Animation** is the movement or change of an image over time and includes effects such as flashing, spinning, and changing colors. When you animate an image, you make it appear to change its position, shape, size, color, opacity, rotation, or other properties. You achieve the effect of animation by displaying the same image with gradual changes over a period of time. Each time the image changes, you show it in a new frame. When the animation is complete, you play all the frames in sequence, and the image appears to move or change. In the past, even the simplest of animations, such as a box changing color, involved graphic artists drawing every step or frame of the animation, resulting in hundreds of frames and many hours of work.

You will also learn to take advantage of reusable objects such as symbols and their libraries. A significant advantage to a Flash designer, **symbols** store instructions you need to quickly reuse and recreate an object. For example, the Drawing.fla sample file that comes with Flash uses six buttons, and each button has identical features, such as size, color, and shape. It is therefore more efficient to create one symbol of a button, and then use and modify multiple copies of it, than to recreate each button. Symbols improve a Flash file's effectiveness because they lower the file size of a Flash document, increasing the speed the document downloads to the user's browser.

In addition to working with symbols, you will learn how to create different types of animations in Flash. The chapter begins by examining the different types of Flash frames: keyframes, blank keyframes, and unused frames. You will learn how to create three different types of animation with frames: frame-by-frame, motion tweening, and shape tweening.

This chapter also provides a brief introduction to common ActionScript commands. ActionScript commands, also called **actions**, are predefined behaviors you can assign to objects and events. You will learn how to use ActionScript to make your animations interactive by allowing the user to control the movie elements you design. (See Chapter 6 for a detailed discussion of ActionScript.)

UNDERSTANDING MACROMEDIA FLASH MX ANIMATION BASICS

Cartoonists use frame animation to make images move. In Flash, any time you apply a change to an object, such as when you change its shape, color, or position, the change occurs in a frame. When you work with frames, you work in the Timeline, shown in Figure 3-1.

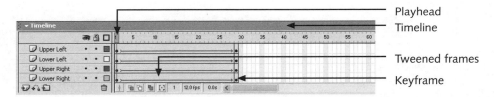

Figure 3-1 Frames in the Timeline

You can create three different types of animation with frames: frame-by-frame, motion tweening, and shape tweening. Each animation method is defined in the following list:

- *Frame-by-frame*—Inserting the same image (not a symbol) with a slight variation in subsequent frames

- *Motion tweening*—Inserting a symbol in the first frame and another object with different properties in the last frame, letting Flash do the rest of the work

- *Shape tweening*—Inserting an image (not a symbol) in the first frame and another image in the last frame, letting Flash do the rest of the work

In the simplest type of animation, frame-by-frame, you create the image for every frame, much like creating a flip book, where each page shows an image that is slightly different from the next and previous images. For example, to use the frame-by-frame method to create an animation of a bouncing ball, you draw one ball on the initial frame, another on the second frame, and so on, until the final frame. You draw the balls in different positions on the frame to simulate bouncing. When you test and play the movie, you see the ball bounce, as shown in Figure 3-2.

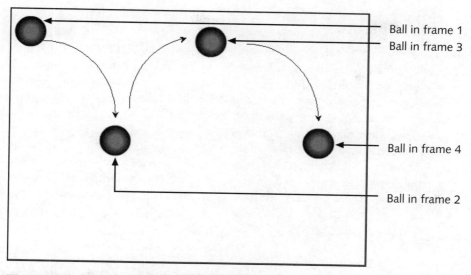

Figure 3-2   Frame-by-frame animation

In motion tweening and shape tweening, you create keyframes at significant positions on the Timeline and let Flash create the frames in between. A **keyframe** is where you specify changes in the animation. Flash varies the object's properties evenly between keyframes to create the appearance of gradual movement. In Figure 3-3, notice the motion tween's appearance; the black dot signifies a keyframe in the final frame.

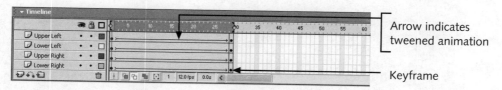

Figure 3-3   Black dot signifying a keyframe

An arrow appears on every frame between the keyframes, indicating that Flash has created the images that show the ball changing from the first frame to the last. To test the animation, you can click Control on the menu bar and then click Test Movie to see your animation of a bouncing ball. Flash automatically creates a SWF file when you test a FLA file, and saves the SWF files with the same filename and in the same location.

Use the frame-by-frame animation method when a complex set of objects changes in every frame, where every frame is a keyframe. For example, you would use the frame-by-frame method to control an image of blades of grass blowing in the wind. Use motion-tweening animation when you want to show one object changing position, color, and shape over time. Use shape-tweening animation to create morphing effects, such as transforming one object into another object over time, or changing the location, size, or color of the shape itself.

WORKING WITH FRAMES

You use frames to create action within a Flash document. Recall that a frame is a single instance in time within an animation. A frame can be compared to a single cel in a traditional animation. By default, Flash provides a single empty frame—frame 1—when you start a new document. Frames are contained in layers on the document Timeline. You navigate or select frames by dragging the playhead or clicking directly on the frame. Frames are the basis of animation, and for animation to move, you must work with a series of frames. The point where a movement or action takes place is called a **keyframe**. In traditional animation, a master animator would create the main storyboard frames—keyframes—and the in-between or interpolated frames, also called **tweens**, are drawn by apprentice or intermediate artists. When you create the keyframes, Flash produces the in-between frames for you.

Flash uses different kinds of frames and keyframes when creating animations. Table 3-1 identifies and describes the purpose of each frame type.

Table 3-1   Flash Frame Types

Frame type	Appearance on the Timeline	Frame usage
Isolated blank keyframe	Blank unfilled keyframe, usually frame 1	A blank keyframe becomes a keyframe when an object is placed on it.
Keyframe	A single keyframe is indicated by a black dot. Light gray frames after a single keyframe contain the same content with no changes and have a black line with a hollow rectangle at the last frame of the span.	A keyframe is a frame in which an object changes.
Motion-tweened keyframe	Motion-tweened keyframes are indicated by a black dot, while intermediate tweened frames have a black arrow with a light blue background.	Flash uses motion-tweened keyframes for changes in a motion-tweened animation.
Shape-tweened keyframe	Shape-tweened keyframes are indicated by a black dot, while intermediate frames have a black arrow with a light green background.	Flash uses shape-tweened keyframes for changes in a shape-tweened animation.
Tweened frames missing the last keyframe	A dashed line indicates that the final keyframe is missing.	With a tweened animation, an ending keyframe is required. Without it, the tweened frames appear with a dashed line as an indicator.
ActionScript frame	A small "a" indicates that the frame has been assigned a frame action with the Actions panel.	You can apply actions to a frame to control its objects or other Timelines.
Labeled frame	A red flag indicates that the frame contains a label or comment.	When creating complex animations, it is a good practice to use a descriptive label for each frame to indicate its role in the animation.

To summarize, a keyframe is where you define changes in the animation. When you create frame-by-frame animation, every frame is a keyframe because you insert a different object in each frame. See Figure 3-4.

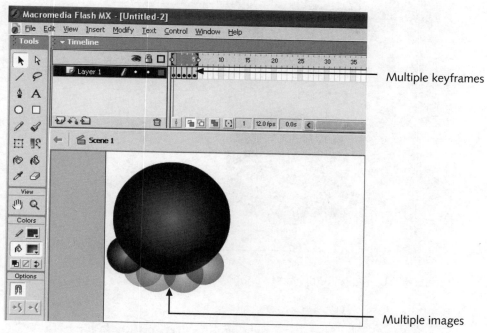

Figure 3-4 Frame-by-frame animation

In tweened animation, you define keyframes at important points in the animation and let Flash create the content of frames in between. See Figure 3-5.

When you play any type of animation, Flash attempts to play it at the speed determined by the **frame rate**, the number of frames it displays per second. You specify only one frame rate for the entire Flash document, so it is a good idea to set this rate before you begin creating animation in a document.

When you create a document, Flash uses the settings in the Document Properties dialog box to determine the Stage size, frame rate, background color, and other properties of the new document. The frame rate is set at 12 frames per second (fps) by default, but you can change this if you like. The standard speed for the Web is 12 fps, which is the setting that QuickTime and AVI movies use, and the standard for motion picture movies is 24 fps. For now, you can use a slower frame rate so you can closely examine the frames in your animations.

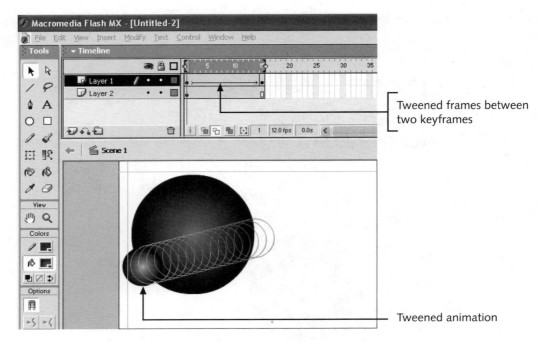

Tweened frames between two keyframes

Tweened animation

Figure 3-5   Using keyframes in tweened animation

To modify your document's frame rate:

1. Start Flash, if necessary, and open the **FrameRate.fla** file from the Chapter3 folder in the FlashSamples folder. Save the file as **myFrameRate.fla** in the same location. If necessary, click the **Properties title bar** to expand the Property inspector. See Figure 3-6 and note the frame rate shown in the Property inspector and on the Timeline.

2. Click **Modify** on the menu bar, and then click **Document**. The Document Properties dialog box opens, as shown in Figure 3-7.

3. In the Frame Rate text box, type **3**.

4. Click **OK** to accept your changes. The frame rate changes in the Property inspector and on the Timeline.

5. Save and close **myFrameRate.fla**, but leave Flash open.

You can also open the Document Properties dialog box by pressing the Ctrl+J keys (Command+J on the Macintosh) or by double-clicking the frame rate on the Timeline.

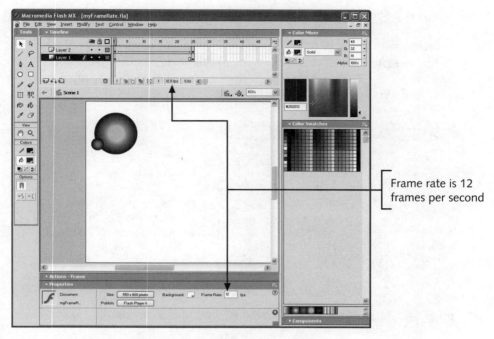

Frame rate is 12
frames per second

Figure 3-6   myFrameRate.fla with default frame rate

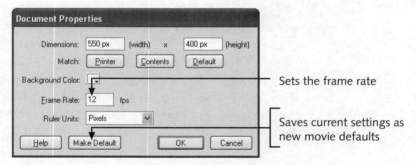

Sets the frame rate

Saves current settings as
new movie defaults

Figure 3-7   The Document Properties dialog box

You can use the Document Properties dialog box to adjust the Stage dimensions. The Stage dimensions determine the size of the resulting SWF document that users will view in a Web browser. You adjust the size by entering the dimensions in the Width and Height text boxes, or by clicking the Printer or Contents buttons. Click the Contents button to allow equal space on all sides of the Stage. Click the Printer button to set the Stage size to the maximum available printer area.

You can use the Document Properties dialog box to change the background color by clicking the Background Color box and selecting a color. Hexadecimal values appear when you point to a color, as shown in Figure 3-8. For any Web document that uses color, knowing the hexadecimal value helps you keep your color schemes precise. Finally, you can use the Document Properties dialog box to reset the way the Stage is measured by choosing the unit of measure from the Ruler Units list box. This option also affects the rulers on the Flash window surrounding the Stage and the Info Panel's units used to display and edit an object's XY values and size dimensions.

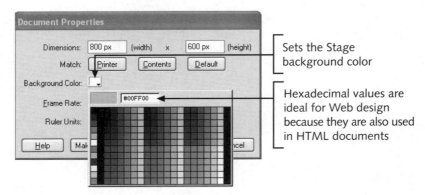

Figure 3-8   Hexadecimal values in the background color palette

USING SYMBOLS IN ANIMATIONS

Symbols are reusable elements for your documents. Symbols can be graphics, buttons, movie clips, sound files, or text. Symbols reduce file size because no matter how many times you use a symbol in an animation, Flash stores the symbol in the file only once.

You create symbols by converting an object into a symbol, or by creating a new symbol and adding shapes and other artwork. Flash stores symbols in the symbol library for that particular document. Every symbol in the document is a reusable copy, or **instance**, of that symbol. While a symbol is a reusable object (including images, buttons, and animations), an instance is an occurrence of the symbol on the Stage; in this way, an instance references a symbol. For example, if you are working on a document that shows a happy face graphic more than once, convert the happy face graphic to a symbol. Each time you need a happy face, you can use the symbol instead of redrawing the image. Figure 3-9 shows the same happy face image with different backgrounds.

Modified symbol instances

Figure 3-9   Using symbols to save file size

After you create a symbol, you can drag it from your symbol library, as shown in Figure 3-10. By doing so, you create an instance, or copy, of that symbol. Use symbols anytime you are required to show one object in many frames. You can change a symbol instance by rotating, expanding, reducing, or recoloring it.

Figure 3-10   Using instances to reuse symbols from a library

When you change the attributes of a symbol, you change the attributes of all instances of that symbol. When you change an instance of a symbol, you change only that instance.

When creating symbols, you need to define a name and a behavior for the symbol. A name should be descriptive and unique, such as "Top Logo Symbol." Figure 3-11 shows a symbol name in the Symbol Properties dialog box and the document's Library panel.

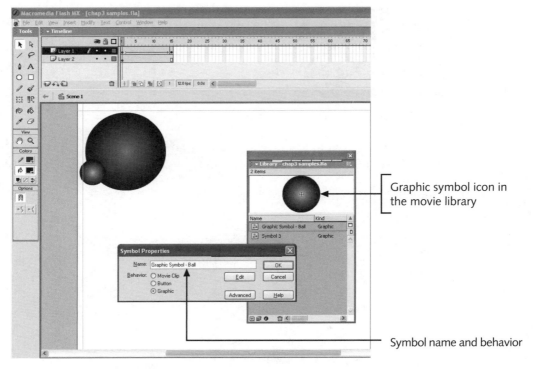

Graphic symbol icon in the movie library

Symbol name and behavior

Figure 3-11   Naming symbols

A symbol can be one of three behavior types: graphic, button, or movie clip. Each symbol type behaves differently on the document Timeline. Table 3-2 describes each type of symbol.

Table 3-2   Types of Symbols

Type of symbol	Description
Graphic	Static images, which are instances that can be animated to change their shape, rotation, and position.
Button	Interactive images that respond to mouse events, such as clicking. Button symbols have four conditions or states: up, over, down, and hit. You can assign different images and sounds to each state.
Movie clip	Reusable animations that have their own Timelines, and play independent of the main document Timeline.

Graphic Symbols

Graphic symbols are ideal for frame-by-frame animation and are essential for tweened animations. Graphic symbols are commonly used in frame-by-frame and tweened animation, and because they have their own Timeline and layers, they can have their own animation. However, the animation stops when the main Timeline stops. In addition, graphic symbols are commonly added to button or movie clip symbols. For example, a button symbol's animation can include several graphic symbols, as shown in Figure 3-12.

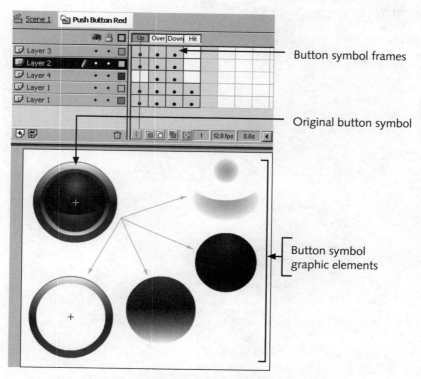

Figure 3-12 Graphic symbol used in a button symbol

Creating Button Symbols

You use button symbols to create graphic elements that viewers can interact with by using their mouse, such as pointing to the button (called a mouse-over) or clicking the button to trigger an action. Buttons that are used for interface design or individual push button controls have a Timeline with distinctive frames. When creating a button, Flash creates a special Timeline with frames corresponding to four possible states: Up, Down, Over, and Hit. You use this Timeline to place a different image or sound on each frame. For example, the button can appear raised in the Up frame and depressed in the Down frame. The Up frame appears when the user's mouse is not on the button, the Over state is what the button will look like as the user rolls the mouse over it, the Down frame appears when the user clicks the button, and the Hit frame triggers an action. For example, the Hit frame of a button determines which pixels in the button are active for clicking. See Figure 3-13.

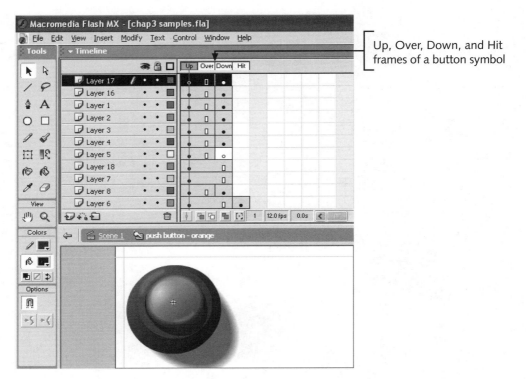

Up, Over, Down, and Hit frames of a button symbol

Figure 3-13   Timeline for a button symbol

You create three versions of a button, one showing the Up, Down, or Over state. Then you define the Hit state, the area of the button that responds when clicked. Table 3–3 describes each button state.

Table 3-3   Button Symbol Frame States

Button state	Description
Up state	The button's natural state with no mouse activity
Over state	The button's state when a mouse rolls over it
Down state	The button's state when a mouse clicks it
Hit state	The button's active area that determines which parts of the button can be clicked

You can test the button symbol in movie-editing mode by clicking Control on the menu bar, and then clicking Enable Simple Buttons. Each of the button states then works as if you tested or published your document. In order to move or edit the button, click to toggle off the Enable Simple Buttons command.

In the following steps, you create a button symbol that changes appearance when a user rolls the mouse over and then clicks the button.

To create a button symbol:

1. In Flash, open **ButtonSymbol.fla** in the Chapter3 folder of your FlashSamples folder. Save the document as **myButtonSymbol.fla** in the same location.

2. Use the **Arrow** tool to select the entire button image by dragging a marquee around it. Convert the existing button image into a symbol by pressing the **F8** shortcut key to open the Convert to Symbol dialog box.

3. In the Name text box, type **myButton**. Click the **Button** option button, if necessary, and then click **OK**.

4. Use the **Arrow** tool to double-click the **button symbol** to open its Timeline, shown in Figure 3-14.

Figure 3-14   Defining the button states

5. In the Timeline, click the **Over frame**, and then press **F5** to copy the frame from the preceding Up frame. Copying the previous frame saves time when you want to use the same object with minor changes in the next frame.

6. Click the **Down frame**, and then press **F6** to insert a keyframe. You insert a keyframe here to simulate clicking. You'll do the same for the Hit frame.

7. Click the **Hit frame**, and then press **F6** to insert a keyframe. Now you're ready to edit the graphic objects to create the appearance of a button that responds to user action.

8. Click the **Down frame**, click a blank part of the Stage to deselect the shadow, and then select the button part of the symbol (not the shadow).

9. To rotate the button 180 degrees to give the appearance of a pressing action, click **Modify** on the menu bar, point to **Transform**, and then click **Scale and Rotate** to enter a precise number. The Scale and Rotate dialog box opens. See Figure 3-15.

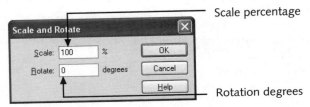

Figure 3-15   Rotating the button with the Scale and Rotate dialog box

10. In the Rotate text box, type **180**, and then click **OK**.

11. To increase the effect of a pressed button, click to select only the shadow under the button.

12. Nudge the shadow image 5 pixels up and 5 pixels right using the keyboard arrow keys. The symbol and frames should look like Figure 3-16.

13. Click the **Scene 1** link to return to your main document Stage.

14. To test your newly created button, click **Control** on the menu bar, and then click **Test Movie**. Click the button to see the effect. Then click the **Close** button to close the test movie.

15. Save and close **myButtonSymbol.fla**, but leave Flash open.

You can design your own button graphics or use the ones that Flash provides. To access the button library, click Window on the menu bar, point to Common Libraries, and then click Buttons. The button library has a variety of button styles organized in library folders.

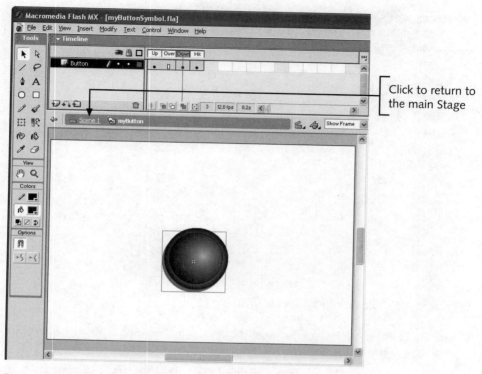

Click to return to the main Stage

Figure 3-16   Completed button symbol and Timeline

Creating Movie Clip Symbols

Use movie clip symbols to create pieces of animation you can reuse in your documents. Unlike graphic symbols, movie clip symbols play continuously on the main document Timeline. A movie clip is an independent Timeline that plays by itself. Movie clips can play like mini-movies inside a main document. For example, you could constantly play a movie clip of an animated logo to promote a product. Movie clips can also contain interactive controls, sounds, and other movie clip instances. To create an animated button, for example, you can place a movie clip instance in the Timeline of a button symbol.

By using ActionScript, you can dictate when to stop, start, or move a frame's object. Movie clip symbols are represented by the icon in Figure 3-17, also shown in the library.

Using Symbols and Instances

Recall that symbols are reusable versions of graphics you've already created or that Flash supplies. When you use a symbol in a document, you are using an instance of the symbol. Instances are created from master symbols stored in a library, which is a collection of folders, imported images, and symbols. Because you can store images as symbols and

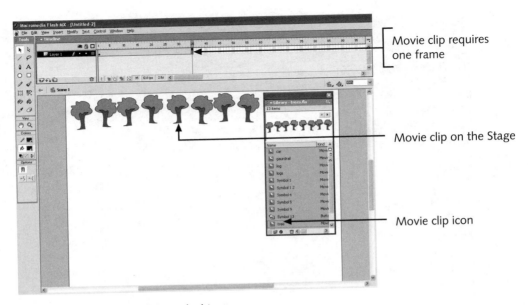

Movie clip requires one frame

Movie clip on the Stage

Movie clip icon

Figure 3-17   Movie clip symbol icon

reuse their instances on the Stage, symbols save download time, disk space, and memory by reducing the Flash file size.

To create an instance, you drag a symbol to your Stage from its symbol master located in the Library panel, as shown in Figure 3-18.

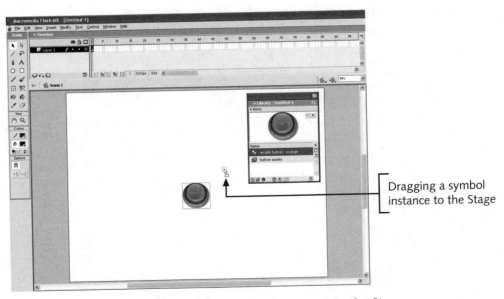

Dragging a symbol instance to the Stage

Figure 3-18   Creating a symbol instance by dragging it to the Stage

Modifying a Symbol Instance

When you place the symbol instance on your Stage, Flash recreates it with the same properties as the master symbol, such as size, shape, and color. When you edit an instance, or copy, of a symbol, you do not affect the symbol or other instances of that symbol that you use in your document. (When you double-click a symbol, however, you can edit the symbol and all of its instances.) After dragging an instance to your Stage, you can modify it with menu commands and the toolbox. You can also use the Info and Transform panels to manipulate instances, as shown in Figure 3-19. Use the Info panel to change the height and width values and position of an instance relative to the top-left corner of the Stage. Use the Transform panel to change the instance size and shape by changing the scaling, rotate, and skew values.

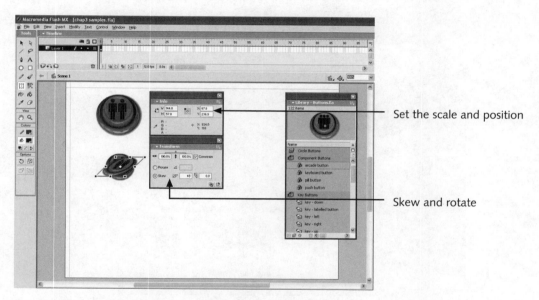

Figure 3-19   Info and Transform panels for modifying a symbol instance

Modifying the Symbol Master

Although editing an instance does not affect the symbol or other instances, when you edit a symbol, you also change all instances of that symbol. You can edit a symbol with two different methods: with the other objects on the Stage, called **Edit in Place**, or in a separate window.

When you edit a symbol, Flash dims other objects on the Stage to distinguish them from the symbol you are editing, although you can still see the other objects.

To edit a symbol in place:

1. In Flash, open the file **EditingSymbols.fla** from the Chapter3 folder of your FlashSamples folder. Save the document as **myEditingSymbols.fla** in the same location.

2. Scroll to the upper-left corner of the Stage, if necessary. Right-click the **ball symbol**, and then click **Edit In Place**. (You can also double-click a symbol to edit in place.) Notice the links listed just above the Stage. The symbol opens in an interim scene named Symbol 1, as shown in Figure 3-20, to separate the symbol you're editing from the rest of the document.

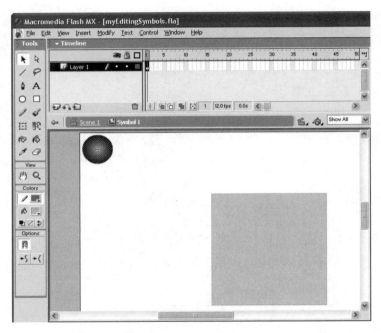

Figure 3-20   Editing a symbol in place

 In any steps that instruct you to right-click, you should Ctrl+click on the Macintosh.

3. Use the **Fill Color** tool to change the ball's color from red gradient to green gradient.

4. Click the **Scene 1** link to return to the main Stage. Note that you have made changes to the symbol master, not just a copy or instance of the symbol.

5. Save **myEditingSymbols.fla**, and leave it open in Flash.

Besides editing a symbol in place, you can edit a symbol in its own window. This is also called symbol-editing mode, and lets you see both the symbol and its Timeline, although not any other objects, as editing it in place does. The Flash window changes from Stage view to a view where only the symbol can be edited. In addition, the Instance panel (and associated Effects, Frame, and Sound panels) are dimmed and inactive. This avoids any unintentional changes to the symbol's behavior, name, color effects, tweening, and sound effects, but does allow you to modify the shape, color, and other properties.

To open a symbol in an editing window:

1. With myEditingSymbols.fla still open in Flash, use the **Arrow** tool to right-click the ball symbol, and then click **Edit In New Window** on the shortcut menu. The symbol opens in a separate window. See Figure 3-21. Notice that the name of the symbol appears above the Stage, replacing the scene name.

Figure 3-21 Window for editing symbol

2. Enlarge the ball symbol by selecting it, clicking the **Free Transform** tool in the toolbox, and then holding down the **Shift** key as you drag a corner handle. The Shift key allows you to maintain the proportion of the circle as you resize it.

3. To exit symbol-editing mode and return to the main Stage window, click **Edit** on the menu bar, and then click **Edit Document**. (Alternatively, click

the **Edit Scene** button in the upper-right corner of the document window and choose **Scene 1** from the menu.) See Figure 3-22.

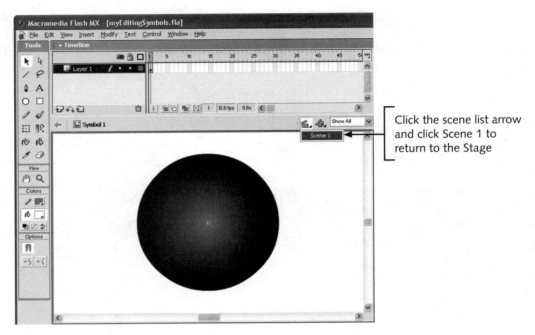

Click the scene list arrow and click Scene 1 to return to the Stage

Figure 3-22   Returning to the Stage after editing a symbol

4. Save and close **myEditingSymbols.fla**, but leave Flash open.

At this point, editing in place or using symbol-editing mode changes the symbol and all instances of the symbol.

Working with the Library Panel

You use the Library panel to view and organize the symbols you are using in the current document. Open the Library panel by clicking Window on the menu bar and then clicking Library, or by pressing Ctrl+L (F11 on the Macintosh). Every time you add an object or create a new symbol to the Stage, Flash adds it to the library for the current document, even while the Library panel is closed. You can use the tools at the bottom of the Library panel and the commands on the Options menu to create, delete, and rename folders in the library to store and organize its objects. See Figure 3-23.

Bitmap image
Button symbol
Library folder

Graphic symbol
Movie symbol
Audio file

Figure 3-23   Library panel for a document

CREATING ANIMATIONS WITH TWEENING

As mentioned earlier, one way to animate objects is to use the tweening method. Tweening is less tedious and time consuming than frame-by-frame animating, although you don't have control over every frame and its content. Flash performs two types of tweening: motion tweening and shape tweening. Both methods can change motion and shape to some degree. Shape tweening changes an object's shape from its initial keyframe to the next. This type of tweening creates the appearance of morphing one shape to another by changing its location, color, shape, and other properties. Recall that with tweening, you define the starting and ending image and keyframes. When you play the animation, Flash redraws the object and does all of the calculations to create the changes between keyframes. These changes are smooth transitions from frame to frame, which are called **tweened frames** or **in-between frames**. Figure 3-24 shows an example of an object and the tweened frames on the Timeline.

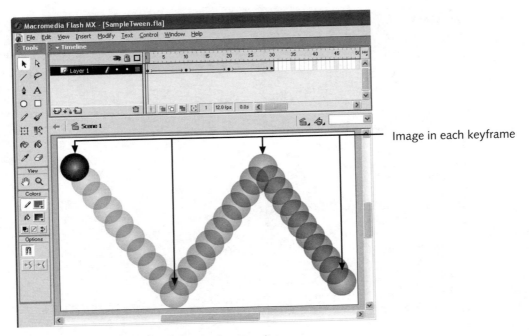

Figure 3-24   Tweened frames on the Timeline

Before you create a tweened animation, you can examine a Flash animation that has already been tweened. As you perform the following steps, note how the appearance of the Timeline and the objects on the Stage change.

To review a tweened animation:

1. Open the file **SampleTween.fla** in the Chapter3 folder of your FlashSamples folder to review working with tweened animations. Scroll to the upper-left corner of the Stage, if necessary. Click **frame 1**. See Figure 3-25.

2. Note that the frames on the Timeline with the black dots are the beginning and ending keyframes. The arrow displayed between the keyframes indicates a successful tween. Drag the **playhead** from left to right, and notice the object move across your Stage and change shape.

3. Drag the **playhead** back to frame 1, click **Control** on the menu bar, and then click **Test Movie** to see the tweened animation in full view.

4. Click the **Close** button to close the test movie.

5. Close SampleTween.fla without saving it.

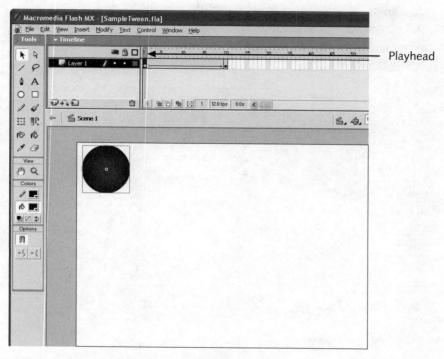

Figure 3-25   Object in SampleTween.fla

Motion tweening is applied to instances of symbols, groups, and text blocks. You can change an object's location, size, rotation, and other properties with motion tweening. The SampleTween.fla animation you viewed in the previous steps uses motion tweening. See Figure 3-26 for the completed Timeline and Stage, with the Onion skin button selected on the Timeline.

Now that you've seen the effect of a tweened animation, you're ready to create one yourself. The following section explains the types of objects that you can animate with motion tweening, and the two methods you can use to create a tweened animation.

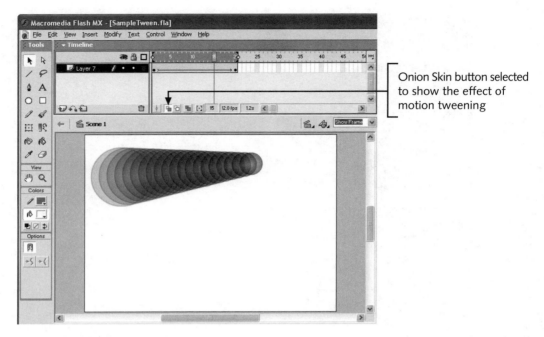

Onion Skin button selected
to show the effect of
motion tweening

Figure 3-26   Motion tweening

Creating Motion-Tween Animations

Depending on what you select on the Stage, you can animate certain types of objects with motion tweening, such as instances of symbols, a grouped object, or a block of text. You can use motion tweening to make one or more objects seem to move across the Stage. You can also use motion tweening to change the size of a group or symbol or to make it rotate.

You can create any of these types of motion-tween animation in one of two ways. One method is to create an object in the first keyframe for the animation, choose Create Motion Tween on the Insert menu, and then move the object to the new location on the Stage. Flash automatically creates the ending keyframe and fills in the tweened frames with the appropriate objects. Another way to create a motion tween is to create the starting and ending keyframes for the animation and then use the Motion Tweening options in the Property inspector to define the properties of the tweened frames.

The motion-tween properties on the Property inspector shown in Figure 3-27 can range from simple movement and changes in size to complex animations that rotate, change color and transparency, or define various levels of speed. To change the size of a symbol as it animates, you need to check the Scale check box in the Frame panel, and then you can place symbols of various sizes on keyframes to simulate size or fading effects. To control the speed or rate of change between keyframes, use the options in the Easing list to control either beginning or ending velocity. Use the options in the Rotate list to control the direction and quantity of rotations for an object.

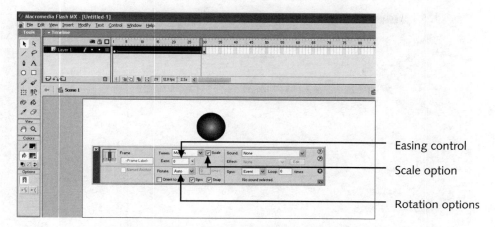

Figure 3-27   Motion-tween options on the Property inspector

Now you can create a motion-tween animation using the Create Motion Tween command on the Insert menu. In this animation, you create a simple motion-tween animation with a bouncing ball. To do this, you create a motion tween with two additional keyframes placed in locations to simulate bouncing, thus creating a total of three segments to one tween.

To create a motion-tween animation using the Create Motion Tween command:

1. In Flash, open the file **MotionTween.fla** in the Chapter3 folder of your FlashSamples folder. Save the document as **myMotionTween.fla** in the same location. Scroll to the upper-left corner of the Stage, if necessary, to see the ball symbol. You will move the ball symbol to the bottom half of the Stage, to the top half, and then once more to the bottom to simulate a normal bounce.

2. Use the **Arrow** tool to click the **symbol** in frame 1 and select it. Note that the playhead in the Timeline indicates you are working in frame 1. Next, you will select a frame later in the Timeline, and then define it as a keyframe.

3. Click **frame 20** on the Timeline.

4. Click **Insert** on the menu bar, and then click **Keyframe**. Specifying frame 20 as a keyframe means that Flash will tween the frames between frame 1 and frame 20. See Figure 3-28.

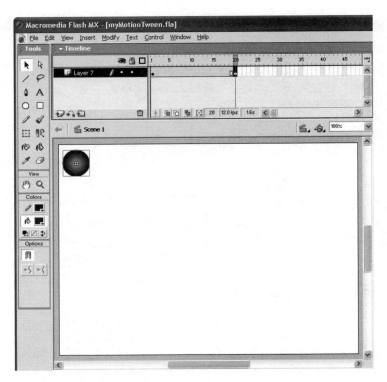

Figure 3-28   In-between frames prior to tweening

5. With keyframe 20 selected, drag the ball to the lower part of the Stage.

If you click elsewhere on the Stage, the object becomes unselected. Drag a marquee around the entire object with the Arrow tool to select it again.

6. Click to select any frame you just created between the two keyframes.

7. Click **Insert** on the menu bar, and then click **Create Motion Tween**. Notice the solid arrow and the light blue background of the in-between frames, as in Figure 3-29. This indicates that you successfully created a motion tween. Select the object, if necessary, and then drag it to another location on the Stage.

You can also right-click the in-between frames and click Create Motion Tween on the shortcut menu, or click the Tween list arrow on the Property inspector and then click Motion.

Now you can insert keyframes at frames 40 and 60, and position the ball symbol in opposite positions on the Stage to complete the act of ball movement.

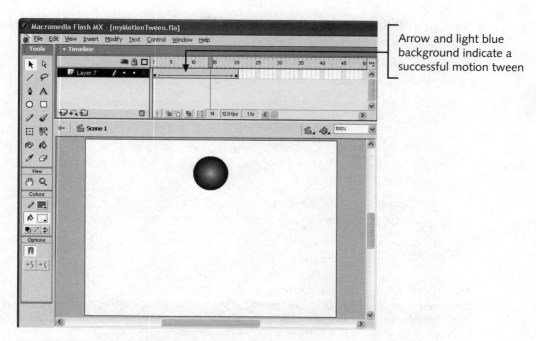

Arrow and light blue background indicate a successful motion tween

Figure 3-29   Successful motion tween

8. Click **frame 40**, click **Insert** on the menu bar, and then click **Keyframe** to make frame 40 a keyframe.

9. Click **frame 60**, click **Insert** on the menu bar, and then click **Keyframe** to also make frame 60 a keyframe.

10. Click **frame 40** again, if necessary, to select it. Then drag the ball to the upper-right corner of the Stage.

11. Click **frame 60** again to select it. Then drag the ball to the lower-right corner of the Stage.

12. In the Timeline, click anywhere between frames 20–39.

13. Click **Insert** on the menu bar, and then click **Create Motion Tween**.

14. In the Timeline, click anywhere between frames 40–59.

15. Click **Insert** on the menu bar, and then click **Create Motion Tween**.

16. Drag to place the playhead on frame 1, click **Control** on the menu bar, and then click **Test Movie** command to see the tweened animation in full view. The ball symbol should move from top to bottom simulating a bounce.

17. Close the test movie window.

18. Save **myMotionTween.fla**, and leave it open in Flash.

You can use this motion-tweening method to quickly achieve effects like fading text, rotating logos, and bouncing balls.

When you want to create an effect such as changing colors or the amount of transparency, use the options in the Effects panel.

To display the motion-tween options in the Property inspector:

1. Expand the Property inspector, if necessary.

2. Select the **ball symbol** on the Stage, if necessary, and then click **frame 1** in the Timeline. The Property inspector shows the properties of the selected frame.

3. On the Property inspector, click the **Tween** list arrow, and then click **Motion**, if necessary, to display the motion-tweening options in the panel.

The motion-tween options in the Property inspector let you animate the objects on the Stage. Table 3-4 describes the options and their purposes.

Table 3-4   Motion-Tween Options on the Property Inspector

Option	Description	Purpose
Frame Label text box	Enter a label to identify the selected frame. This descriptive text will appear on the Timeline on the appropriate layer. To make the text a comment, enter two slashes (//) at the beginning of each line of the text.	Labels describe the contents of frames and remain attached to their frames even if you add or remove frames. Labels are also exported with the published document. Comments are useful for design notes to yourself and others working on the Flash project, and are not exported with the published document. Comments are also widely used in ActionScript commands to document code.
Tween list box	Click the Tween list arrow to select a tween type, including Motion, Shape, or None.	Choose Motion to create a motion tween in the selected frame, choose Shape to make the selected shape appear to change into another shape over time, or choose None if you do not want to tween objects on the frame.
Scale check box	Click the Scale check box to change the size of the selected object during the animation.	When designing an object to change size as it animates, check this box.
Ease list box	Click the Ease list arrow and then drag the slider, or type a value to adjust the rate of change between tweened frames.	By default, the rate of change between tweened frames is constant (or 0 for no ease). Select a positive value between 1 and 100 to begin the tween rapidly and gradually slow at the end. Select a negative value to begin the tween slowly, and then speed up towards the end.

Table 3-4   Motion-Tween Options on the Property Inspector (continued)

Option	Description	Purpose
Rotate list box and times text box	To rotate the selected item while tweening, click the Rotate list arrow and then choose an option from the list: None, Auto, CW (clockwise), or CCW (counter-clockwise).	Use rotation in animations to spin shapes and text across the Stage. Choose None to apply no rotation. Choose Auto to rotate the object once, using the least amount of motion in the last frame of the object. Choose CW or CCW to rotate the object in the specified direction, and then enter a number in the times text box to specify the number of rotations.
Orient to path check box	When using a motion path (explained later in the chapter), select the Orient to path check box to orient the baseline or midpoint of the tweened element to the motion path.	Select this option to specify how an object appears as it follows its path. For example, you can move a golf ball shape across a set of angles and distances. See "Animating Objects on Paths with Guide Layers" later in this chapter.
Sync check box	Select the Sync check box to ensure that an object loops properly in the main document.	Select this option if the number of frames in the animation sequence inside the symbol is not an even multiple of the number of frames the graphic instance occupies in the document.
Snap check box	If you are using a motion path, select the Snap check box to attach the tweened element to the motion path by its center or registration point.	When using a motion path, an object is placed near the path's registration point; the snap option will bring the object to the beginning or end of the path.

Motion tweens are commonly used in Flash animations for any type of movement in an animation such as sliding, moving an object along a path, or spinning objects.

In the following steps, you'll animate a block of text reading "Text Animation." You set the text to slow down as it approaches the end of the animation as it spins or rotates three times across the Stage. To create this motion–tween animation, you use the Frame options in the Property inspector.

To create a motion-tween animation using the Property inspector:

1. Save and close **myMotionTween.fla** and then open **MotionTweenText.fla** in the Chapter3 folder of your FlashSamples folder. Save the document as **myMotionTweenText.fla** in the same location. This document includes a movie clip instance, "Text Rotation," which is placed on frame 1 as a keyframe. See Figure 3–30.

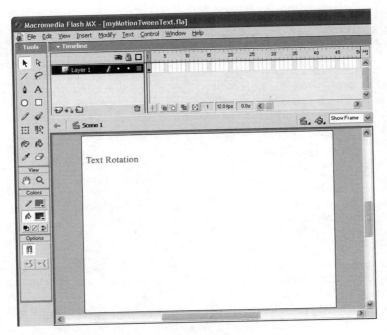

Figure 3-30   Text Rotation movie clip

2. Make sure the Property inspector is open and expanded. (Click **Window** on the menu bar, and then click **Properties** to open and expand the Property inspector. If the Property inspector is open but collapsed, click its title bar to expand it.)

3. Click **frame 20**, which will be the last frame of the tween. Click **Insert** on the menu bar, and then click **Keyframe**.

4. Drag the text block to another location on the Stage, such as the right edge. Then click **frame 1** in the Timeline. (Note that the tween would work if you clicked any frame from 1 to 19.)

5. On the Property inspector, click the **Tween** list arrow and then click **Motion**. The options for a motion tween appear in the Property inspector.

6. In the Ease text box, type **50**. Using a value less than 100 causes the text block to move more slowly as it approaches the end of the tween.

7. Click the **Rotate** list arrow, click **CW** for clockwise, and then type **3** in the times text box if necessary. These settings mean that Flash will rotate the text block three times as it eases from one location to another on the Stage. Figure 3-31 shows the Property inspector and its settings for this animation.

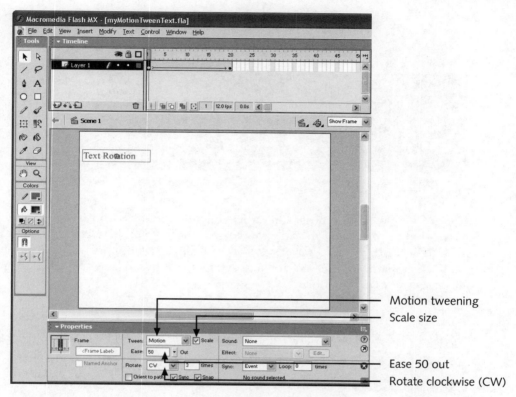

Figure 3-31   Property inspector settings for rotating and easing a motion tween

8. Click **Control** on the menu bar and then click **Play** to view your animation. The text block spins three times clockwise, and slows down as it approaches the end of the animation.

9. Save and close **myMotionTweenText.fla**, but leave Flash open.

Animating with Mask Layers

Mask layers allow you to create a window to other layers beneath the masked layer. Figure 3-32 shows the relationship of background layers to a mask layer.

Figure 3-32   Using a mask layer

A mask layer is superimposed on layers containing objects you want to show through the mask. The objects on the Stage appear only where you have transparent areas on the mask. You create a masked layer by placing a filled shape on a layer. The objects under the filled shape show through the mask, while the other objects are hidden. Figure 3-33 illustrates the masking concept.

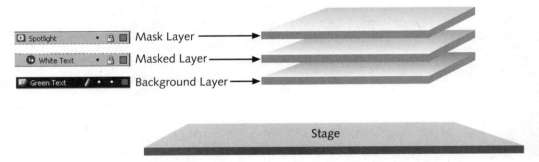

Figure 3-33   Masking concept

You can achieve effects such as a spotlight moving in the dark and shining on certain objects by using a motion tween with masked layers. Figure 3-34 shows how to use a spotlight mask to achieve this effect. You can also preview the completed sample file MaskedAnimation.swf.

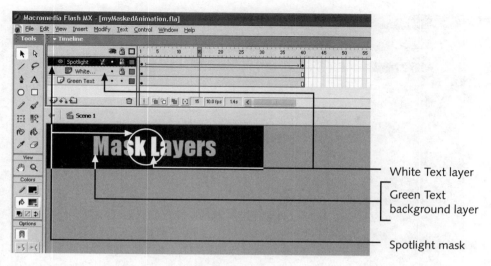

White Text layer

Green Text
background layer

Spotlight mask

Figure 3-34 Masked and background layers

 You cannot mask layers within a button, or use motion paths to give the mask movement. However, you can control masks and mask movement with ActionScript. See Chapter 6, "Introduction to ActionScript."

To create a motion tween with masked layers:

1. In Flash, open the file **MaskedAnimation.fla** in the Chapter3 folder of your FlashSamples folder. Save the document as **myMaskedAnimation.fla** in the same location. As shown in Figure 3-35, this Flash document contains several objects and layers already created for you, a white Stage, a masking layer named Spotlight, a masked layer named White Text—a layer the mask is applied to and will show through the spotlight layer—and a background layer named Green Text that appears where there is no spotlight layer. This document also contains keyframes, with a motion tween set up between them to move the spotlight layer from left to right.

2. Click **Modify** on the menu bar and then click **Document** to display the Document Properties dialog box.

3. Click the **Background Color** text box to open a color palette. Click the **black** color box (first column, first row, with value #000000) to use a black background for this document, and then click **OK** to close the dialog box.

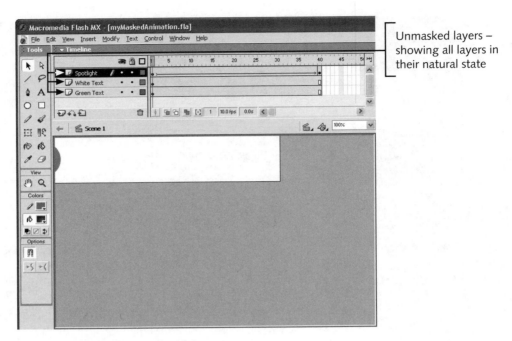

Figure 3-35   Using masked layers

 With a multi-layered scene, make sure you select the layer you will use as the mask layer before you add a filled shape to it. Otherwise, the masking will not appear on the proper layer or at all, because a mask layer always masks the layer beneath it. Therefore, keep your mask layer on top of the layers it affects.

 On masked layers, Flash disregards bitmap fills, gradients, transparency, colors, and line styles. The filled masked object will be transparent, and nonfilled areas are opaque.

4. Right-click the **Spotlight** layer, and then click **Mask** to check that option. The layer becomes a mask layer, as indicated by the mask icon. The mask icon replaces the standard layer icon with a small oval, showing that this layer is now a mask layer. A mask layer always masks the layer immediately beneath it. In this document, the Spotlight layer masks the White Text layer. See Figure 3-36. The Green Text layer will show through the Spotlight layer.

5. Click **Control** on the menu bar and then click **Play** to view the animation. The circle should move from left to right appearing as a spotlight, showing the white text through the green text.

6. To stop the movie, click **Control** on the menu bar, and then click **Stop**.

7. Save and close **myMaskedAnimation.fla**, but leave Flash open.

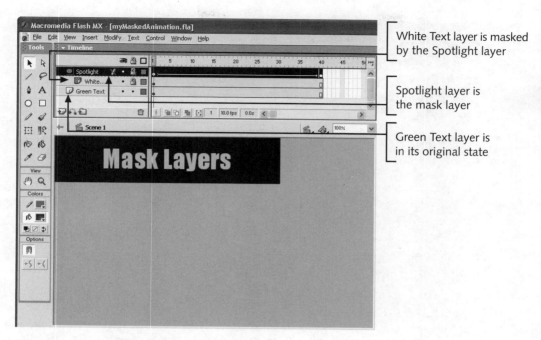

Figure 3-36   Masked layers

Animating Objects on Paths with Guide Layers

On **motion guide layers**, you draw paths along which you can animate tweened objects. The object follows the path when it moves. You draw a path with the Pen, Pencil, Line, Circle, Rectangle, or Brush Tool, and objects connect to the beginning point and follow through the ending point as shown in Figure 3-37. (The path will not appear in the resulting published SWF file.)

In the following steps, you create a motion guide layer from a normal layer, draw a motion guide, and position the already tweened object to the guide.

To create an animation with a motion guide layer:

1. In Flash, open the file named **MotionGuide.fla** in the Chapter3 folder of your FlashSamples folder. Save the file as **myMotionGuide.fla** in the same location. The tweening steps and objects are already prepared for you. See Figure 3-38.

2. Click **frame 1** in the tween (the selected area on the Timeline) to display the motion-tween options in the Property inspector.

3. Click the **Orient to path** check box to select it, if necessary. The middle of the symbol will curve to the motion path.

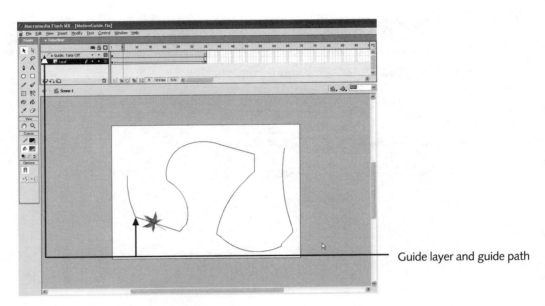

Figure 3-37   Path on the guide layer

Guide layer and guide path

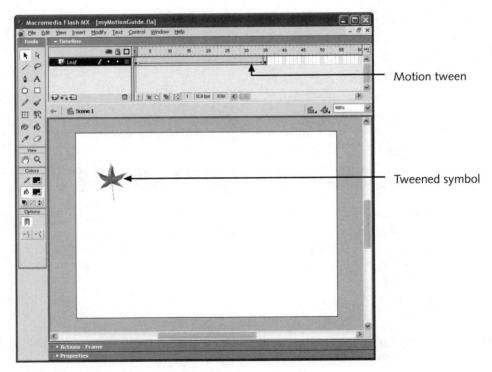

Motion tween

Tweened symbol

Figure 3-38   Object in MotionGuide.fla

4. Click the **Snap** check box, if necessary, to select it. The midpoint of the symbol will snap to the motion path beginning and end points.

5. In the Timeline, click the **Leaf** layer to select it. You will change this to a motion guide layer and then draw a path on it.

6. To insert a motion guide, click **Insert** on the menu bar and then click **Motion Guide**. Alternatively, you can insert a motion guide by clicking the Add Motion Guide icon, shown in Figure 3-39.

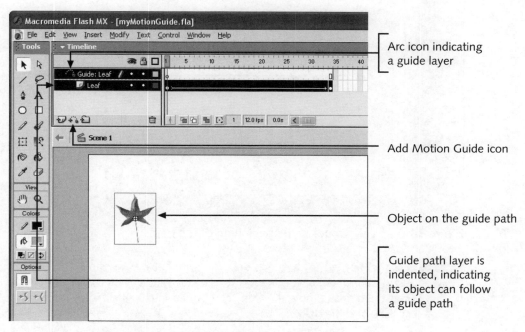

Figure 3-39   Add Motion Guide icon

7. Draw a half figure-eight path with the Pencil tool. (See Figure 3-40 for an example of a half figure-eight shape.) The leaf symbol will follow this path during the animation. Flash snaps the leaf symbol to the beginning of the path for you. See Figure 3-40.

8. Select the last keyframe (frame 35). The leaf object moves toward the end of the path. Because you selected the Snap check box in the Property inspector, Flash also automatically snaps the leaf object to the end of the path. If your guide path extends past frame 35, Flash might snap the leaf object to another part of the path. In this case, use the Arrow tool to drag the leaf symbol to the end of the motion path.

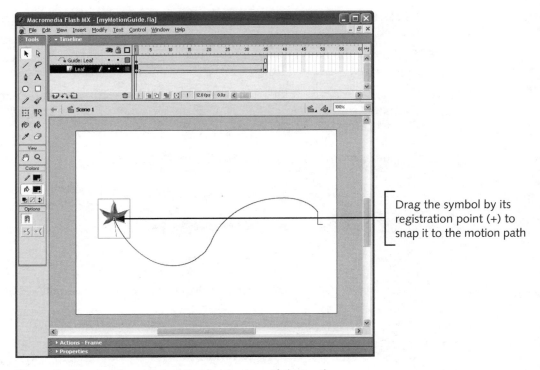

Figure 3-40   Leaf symbol at the beginning of the path

For the best snapping effect, drag the symbol by its registration mark. The registration mark of a symbol is the crosshair in its center. As you drag the registration mark, note the crosshair changes into a small ring and has more stickiness to the snap.

9. To test the animation path, click **Control** menu and then click **Test Movie**. Then close the test movie window.

10. Save and close **myMotionGuide.fla**, but leave Flash open.

Is the path in your way? Click in the Eye column on the motion guide layer to hide the guide layer and the line so that only the symbol's progress is noticeable.

Creating Shape-Tween Animations

Shape tweening changes an object's shape, location, and color. Use shape tweening to change a shape's location on the Stage and to morph, or transform, one shape into another. As with motion tweening, you determine the starting and ending state of the object and Flash creates all the intermediate steps of the shape changes that you can see during the document, giving the appearance of morphing. You can use text that you've divided with the Break Apart command, generic Flash shapes, or imported bitmap images, also divided with the Break Apart command. All objects must be separated into ungrouped, editable components before you can tween them.

Shape tweening works only with shapes, not symbols. For predictable results, you should have only one shape tween per layer.

In the following steps, you complete a shape tween that transforms a common rectangle into the text "Shape Tweening."

To use shape tweening:

1. In Flash, open **ShapeTween.fla** from the Chapter3 folder of your FlashSamples folder. Save the document as **myShapeTween.fla** in the same location. Scroll to the upper-left corner of the Stage, if necessary, to see a blue rectangle. Both the rectangle and text objects are already placed in keyframes for you. The text box has already been broken apart with the Break Apart command on the Modify menu.

2. On the Timeline, drag to select the frames **1** to **19**. Make sure that frames 1–19 are selected, and frame 20 is not selected, as shown in Figure 3-41.

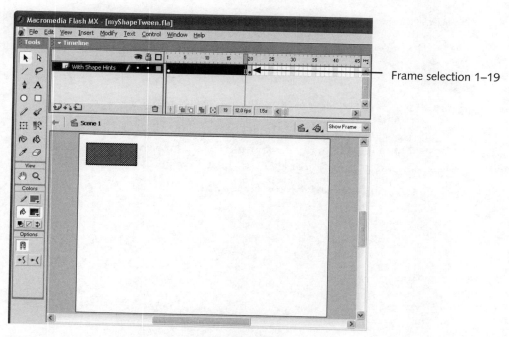

Figure 3-41   Frame selection prior to shape tweening

3. In the Property inspector, click the **Tween** list arrow, and then click **Shape**. Click **frame 1** in the Timeline. The frames between 1 and 19 turn green and frame 20 remains gray, as in Figure 3-42. This means that the shape tween was successfully accomplished.

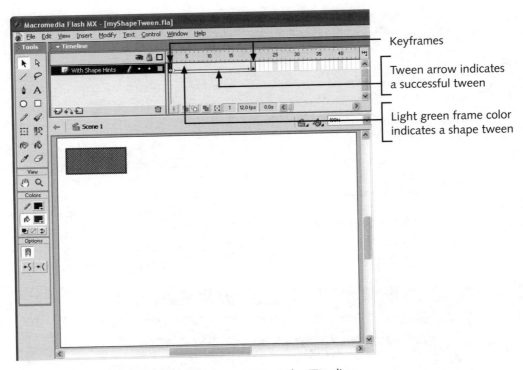

Figure 3-42 Proper shape tweening result on the Timeline

4. To play the animation, click **Control** on the menu bar and then click **Play**. The rectangle gradually morphs, or transforms, into the text, as shown in Figure 3-43. You can also play ShapeTween.swf to see this shape tweening.

5. Save and close **myShapeTween.fla**, but leave Flash open.

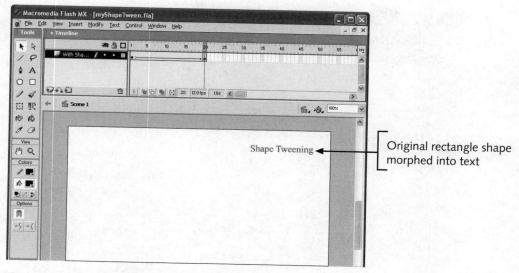

Figure 3-43   Resulting shape tween

Viewing Shape Tweens with Shape Hints

You can add **shape hints** with shape tweening to gain more control over the points that Flash changes. Usually when you shape tween, Flash uses the most effortless logic to transform one shape into another. If you want to control how the image looks as it transforms, you can use shape hints. Shape hints synchronize the points on both beginning and ending keyframes, and are used to control the morphing effect as the object changes in the in-between frames.

Shape hints appear as circled letters with a yellow background on the starting frame and a green background on the ending frame, as in Figure 3-44. Place shape hints on the parts of a tweened shape that are similar, such as an upper corner or edge. You can have up to 26 shape hints, which remain red until you move or snap them to a point on a shape at both beginning and ending shape locations. To remove a shape hint, you drag it off the Stage; to remove all shape hints, click Modify on the menu bar, point to Shape, and then click Remove All Hints. This affects all frames containing hints.

You can apply shape hints only to a tweened shape. Figure 3-45 shows both examples of morphed shapes, with and without using shape hints.

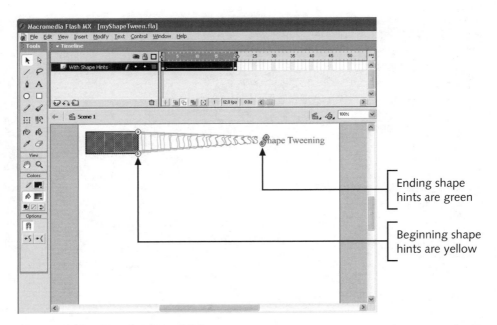

Figure 3-44   Sample shape hints

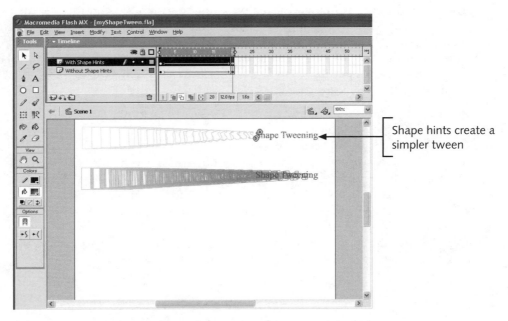

Figure 3-45   Morphed shapes with and without using shape hints

Shape hints work best if you place them beginning at the top-left corner of the shape in a counterclockwise order. For intricate shape tweens, create transitional shapes between your starting and ending shapes.

In the following steps, you complete a shape tween by adding shape hints, and comparing the results to a shape tween without shape hints.

To use shape hints with shape tweening:

1. In Flash, open **ShapeHints.fla** from the Chapter3 folder of your FlashSamples folder. Save the document as **myShapeHints.fla** in the same location. This document has two shape-tween layers, one named "With Shape Hints" and one named "Without Shape Hints," which include a rectangle and text, as shown in Figure 3-46.

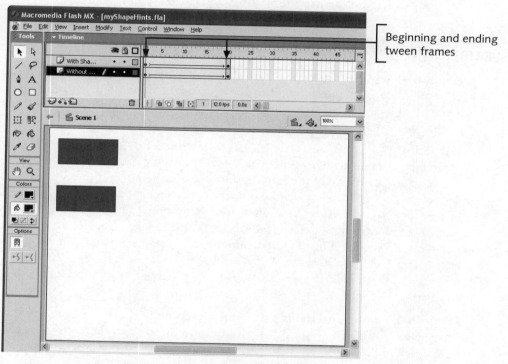

Figure 3-46   Tweened shapes ready for shape hints

2. Click **Control** on the menu bar and then click **Play** to see how this shape currently transforms. Notice that the transitional shapes between the first and last frames are distorted or rough.

3. On the Timeline, click **frame 1** of the With Shape Hints layer.

4. Click **Modify** on the menu bar, point to **Shape**, and then click **Add Shape Hint**. A shape hint (a circled "a" with a red background) appears in the middle of the rectangle.

5. Drag the shape hint to the upper-right corner of the shape.

6. On the Timeline, click **frame 20** of the With Shape Hints layer. Another shape hint appears on the Stage. Drag the new shape hint to the upper-right corner of the text shape, the same location on this shape as the shape hint in the rectangle that appears in the first frame. When you place the shape hints on any edge of the image, the color of the shape hint changes. The beginning objects have yellow shape hints, and the ending objects have green ones.

7. Test the movie by clicking **Control** on the menu bar and then clicking **Play**.

8. Save and close **myShapeHints.fla**, but leave Flash open.

ASSEMBLING FRAME-BY-FRAME ANIMATIONS

Frame-by-frame animation gives you full control over the objects you want to animate. Use the frame-by-frame method to show complex animations requiring specific placement of objects on the Timeline. When you create a frame-by-frame animation, you place a new image on each frame of the whole animation.

A traditional animator creates 24 images for each second of film. Flash uses 12 frames per second, by default, which means you need to create 12 images for each second of animation. You can illustrate the same actions without redrawing them by creating a cycle. A **cycle** is a set of shape or symbol objects that create an entire action, and starts and ends in the same position. Cycles are used frequently by traditional animators to reduce the number of unique objects they need to create. You can create cycles for a variety of reproducible actions including walking, running, and jumping; hand and body gestures; and changes in facial expressions. Any movement with a recurring characteristic has the potential to be an animation cycle; this will be discussed further in Chapter 5, "Advanced Animation Techniques."

Figure 3-47 shows an example of frame-by-frame animation in onion-skinning view. Notice the playhead in Figure 3-47; it indicates the current frame in the document. Also note the dots that appear on each frame, a clue that those particular keyframes are populated.

 Because each frame has its own separate image, the frame-by-frame method also requires the most time and memory of any animation type. It should be used only when the desired effect cannot be accomplished with the tweening method. For an example, open and review FrameByFrame.swf in the Chapter3 folder of the Flash Samples folder.

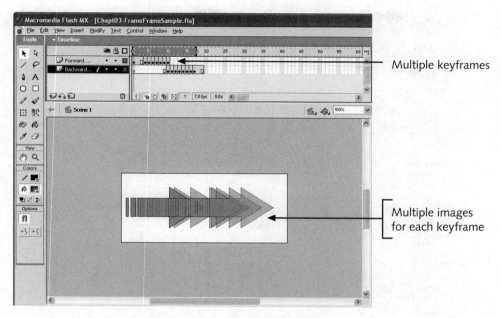

Multiple keyframes

Multiple images for each keyframe

3

Figure 3-47   Example of frame-by-frame animation

Creating the Animation Sequence

You can create a frame-by-frame animation by using images drawn in Flash or by importing images already created. To create the effect of movement or change over time, you must vary the images in each frame in a logical sequence. To achieve this, you must first plan and create, or import the artwork. A good practice is to establish an animation workflow to organize and prepare your images and storyboard. For the following steps, all the artwork has been provided, and a Flash FLA file is already started for you. You will create the appearance of an arrow that changes color from green to blue to red to yellow. To do so, you need four arrow images, one of each color. You start with a green arrow on one keyframe, add a blue arrow to another keyframe, and then red and yellow arrows to other keyframes. (These colors might vary, depending on your monitor and graphics card.)

To create a frame-by-frame animation:

1. Open the sample file **FrameByFrame.fla** in the Chapter3 folder of your FlashSamples folder. Save the document as **myFrameByFrame.fla** in the same location. In the Timeline, frame 1 is already set for you as a keyframe, and a green arrow is placed on the Stage.

2. In the Timeline, click **frame 2**, as shown in Figure 3-48.

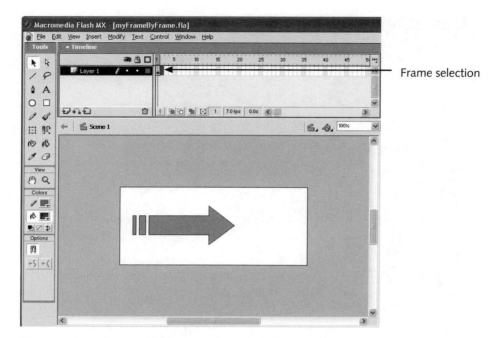

Figure 3-48   Frame selection on the Timeline

3. Click **Insert** on the menu bar, and then click **Keyframe** to insert a keyframe in frame 2. (Or you can press the **F6** key.) Press **Ctrl+L** (**Command+L** on the Macintosh) to open the Library panel, which shows Arrow1.gif, the only object in this document. When you import other graphics in the following steps, they also appear in the Library panel. Now you are ready to import an image of a blue arrow on this keyframe.

4. Click **File** on the menu bar, and then click **Import**.

5. In the Import dialog box, navigate to the Chapter3 folder in your FlashSamples folder, and then double-click **Arrow2.gif** to import it. When a message appears asking if you want to import all of the images in the sequence, click the **No** button. Use the Arrow tool to place it precisely on top of the green arrow if necessary. The blue arrow should completely cover the green arrow.

6. In the Timeline, click **frame 3**, and then press the **F6** key to insert the third keyframe.

7. Repeat Steps 4 and 5 to import **Arrow3.gif**, which contains an image of a red arrow. Place the red arrow on the blue arrow.

8. In the Timeline, click **frame 4**, and then press the **F6** key to insert the fourth keyframe.

9. Repeat Steps 4 and 5 to import **Arrow4.gif**, which contains an image of a yellow arrow. Place the yellow arrow on the red arrow.

10. Test the movie by clicking **Control** on the menu bar and then clicking **Play**. The movie should animate the arrow through green, blue, red, and yellow colors. See Figure 3-49.

Your basic animation is now in place. After reviewing the movie, you can change it by modifying the animation sequence, for example.

11. Save and close **myFrameByFrame.fla**, but leave Flash open.

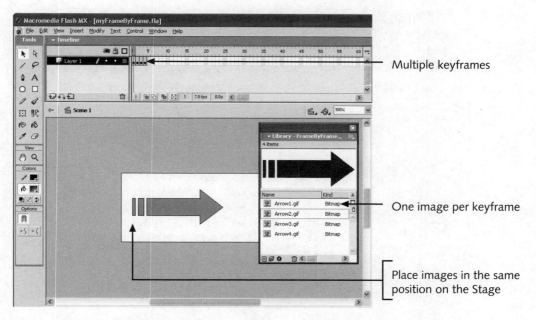

Multiple keyframes

One image per keyframe

Place images in the same position on the Stage

Figure 3-49   Completed frame-by-frame animation and the Timeline

Modifying the Animation Sequence

After you place images and insert frames, you can move them to create different effects, change the sequence of images, and vary the speeds in your document. You can edit only keyframes, although you can delete any type of frame.

 You can delete keyframes, but doing so will also delete from your Stage any images or other objects such as sound files associated with that frame.

Editing animations may also involve using multiple layers, as discussed in Chapter 2, "Creating the Groundwork." Adding layers to a frame-by-frame animation is a good practice; doing so keeps each animation object separate from the others. With single or multi-layer animations, you can modify the Timeline frames with the techniques outlined in Table 3-5.

Table 3-5   Frame Techniques to Modify the Animation Sequence

Frame modification	Frame technique
Move a keyframe	Drag the keyframe or sequence to the new position. The pointer is a standard black arrow when you move a single frame, and it changes to a hand pointer when moving a tweened series (Windows only).
Lengthen the duration of a keyframe	Increasing the duration of a keyframe increases the amount of frames in that animation sequence, and therefore the time that keyframe is performing. Alt+drag (Windows) or Option+drag (Macintosh) the last keyframe to the new location on the Timeline.
Copy a keyframe	To copy a keyframe or frame sequence by dragging, select the keyframe or sequence, Alt+click (Windows) or Option+click (Macintosh), and then drag the keyframe to the new location. Note the pointer changes from a standard black arrow to a hand when you press the Alt or Option key, and a closed hand with a plus sign as you click (Windows only).
Select a frame	Click to select a single frame (when the pointer is a standard black arrow) or a sequence of tweened frames (when the pointer takes the shape of a hand). To select a series of frames (not keyframes), drag from one frame to the next.
Copy and paste a frame	Select the frame, keyframe, or sequence. Click Edit on the menu bar, and then click Copy Frames. Choose the frame or sequence where you want to paste the frame, click Edit on the menu bar, and then click Paste Frames.
Delete a frame	Select the frame, keyframe, or sequence. Press Delete, or click Insert on the menu bar, and then click Remove Frames.
Convert a keyframe to a frame	Select the keyframe, click Insert on the menu bar, and then click Clear Keyframe. The converted keyframe and all frames up to the next keyframe are replaced by the objects in the previous frame.
Change the length of a tween	Drag the beginning or ending keyframe to the left or right.
Reverse an animation sequence	Select the entire tweened sequence, click Modify on the menu bar, point to Frames, and then click Reverse.

CONTROLLING ANIMATIONS WITH BASIC FRAME ACTIONS

Using basic frame actions, you can allow viewers to interact with your document. An **action** is a command you assign to various elements in a document. You can assign an action to a frame, button, or movie clip symbol. For example, a movie loops until it receives a command to stop. You can use the stop action on a keyframe to tell the movie to stop. You can also let the user control when the movie should stop by using the stop action with a button. The Actions panel contains these actions. You use the Actions panel to create and edit actions for an object or frame by selecting prewritten actions from the list and adding actions to the Action list. To have greater control over animations and add interactivity, you use **ActionScript**, Flash's internal scripting facility.

You can create interactive movies for your users by assigning actions to an object or frame on the Timeline. Then you specify an event that triggers the action. For example, you could specify that when the user clicks a button or when the playhead reaches a designated frame, a certain action, such as the movie stopping or restarting will take place. You will learn how to program ActionScript in Chapter 7, "Using Built-In Functions and Expressions," and Chapter 8, "Using ActionScript in Flash." In this chapter (Chapter 3), you will learn how to use the Movie Control actions in the Actions panel to preview Movie Control actions, navigate and add actions to the Action list, and supply the actions with parameters. The first category of actions in the Actions panel is the Movie Control category. See Figure 3-50. You can place actions on frames, buttons, or movie clips at the key places in the document described in the following list.

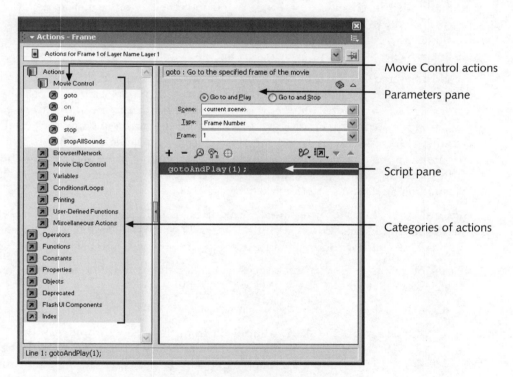

Figure 3-50 Movie Control actions in the Actions panel

- Frame actions execute when the playhead arrives at the frame that contains the action and do not require input from the user.

- Button actions execute when the user participates, normally in the form of a mouse click or keyboard entry.

- Movie clip actions execute in one of two ways depending on how you construct the action—by an event in the movie such as a frame displaying another frame out of sequence based on user input, or by user input such as a button click.

Using the Actions Panel

The **Movie Control actions** are the simplest and most common ActionScript statements you use in a document. For example, you can use a Movie Control action to stop an animation, move to another frame in the Timeline, and play another animation. In the Actions panel, the **Action list** contains all the action statements you can use and edit. As you enter parameters in the lower section of the Actions panel, called the **Script pane** and the **Parameters pane**, they also appear in the Action list. The **parameters** are options or arguments in an action that specify how it should complete a task. For example, you can use the goto action to move the playhead to another frame, and supply the frame number as the parameter.

As mentioned in Chapter 1, you can work with the Actions panel in Expert mode or Normal mode. In Expert mode, you create actions by using ActionScript syntax, as you would write programming code in a text editor or development environment. See Chapters 6 and 8 for more instructions on using Expert mode.

To add an action, such as a frame, a button instance, or a movie clip instance action, you must first select the element in the document to which you want to attach the action. You can attach actions to a frame or object. If you select a frame, the Actions panel displays the title Actions - Frame; if you select a button or movie clip, the panel is titled Actions - Object. Certain aspects of ActionScript vary depending on whether you are assigning actions to a frame or to an object. For example, you can cause the document to do something when it reaches a certain frame number, or give a button interactivity by assigning an action to perform when it is clicked.

Actions are organized into eight categories: Movie Control, Browser/Network, Variables, Conditions/Loops, Printing, User-Defined Functions, and Miscellaneous Actions. You will learn more about these categories as you work with the actions.

In the following steps, you open an existing document with an animation, and use a Movie Control action to play and to stop two buttons.

To assign an action with the Action panel:

1. Open sample file **ActionPanel.fla** from the Chapter3 folder in the FlashSamples folder. Save the document as **myActionPanel.fla** in the same location. Collapse the Property inspector, if necessary, by clicking its title bar.

2. This document contains a motion tween and two button symbols ready to be assigned an action. Right-click the **Play** button, and then click **Actions**. The Actions panel opens. Make sure the panel is in Normal mode.

3. Click **Actions**, if necessary, click the **Movie Control** category to display its actions, and then double-click **play** to add it to the script, or click the plus sign (+) button (also called the Add button) above the Action list and navigate through the Actions and Movie Control menus. See Figure 3-51.

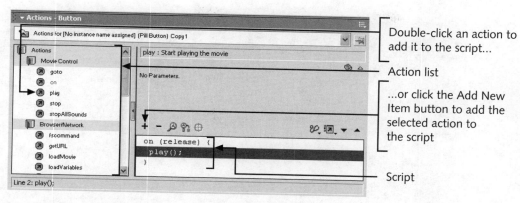

Figure 3-51 Adding actions to the Actions panel

4. Click the **Stop** button and make sure the Actions panel is open. Click the **Movie Control** category to display its actions, if necessary, and then double-click **stop** to add it to the script.

5. Close the Actions panel, and then test the movie by clicking **Control** on the menu bar, and then clicking **Test Movie**. Notice the movie plays automatically.

6. Click the **Stop** button to halt the animation.

7. Click the **Play** button to resume the animation.

8. Close the test movie window, and then save and close **myActionPanel.fla**, but leave Flash open.

Some actions need additional parameters, which are optional or required commands that describe how the action will perform. Enter parameters in the Parameters pane of the Actions panel, located above the Script area on the right pane of the Actions panel.

Movie Control and Browser/Network actions can either automate navigation or let the user control the movie's navigation. You can use these actions to perform processes such as those described in Table 3-6.

Table 3-6   Movie Control and Browser/Network Actions

Action	Action name	Action syntax
Skips to another frame or scene	gotoAndPlay	`gotoAndPlay();`
Plays and then stops the movie	gotoAndStop	`gotoAndStop();`
Stops all sounds in the movie	stopAllSounds	`stopAllSounds();`
Links to another Web address or URL (similar to an HTML Hyperlink), the "_blank" parameter opens the URL in a new browser window	getURL	`getURL();`
Controls any Flash Player that's playing a movie by sending it commands	fscommand	`fscommand();`
Loads or switches other movies without closing the current movie	loadMovie	`loadMovie();`
Unloads a movie clip that was loaded with the loadMovie action	unloadMovie	`unloadMovie();`
Reads data from an external file, such as a text or XML file or text generated by a CGI script, Active Server Pages (ASP), PHP, or Perl script	loadVariables	`loadVariables();`

Opening a URL in a New Browser Window

Launching a new browser window is a common technique in Web design. When you assign the getURL action to a button in your Flash document, the action communicates with the Web browser and instructs it to open a new window. In most cases, you assign the getURL action to a button instead of a frame.

In the following steps, you will assign an action to a button in a Flash document. The action is to open in a separate window the Web page at the URL you specify. Flash uses the getURL action with the _blank option to open a specified Web page in a new browser window. The event that triggers this action is a mouse click. Users can then click the button to open a Web page in a separate browser window.

To assign the getURL action to open an additional browser window:

1. In Flash, open **BasicActions1.fla** from the Chapter3 folder in your FlashSamples folder. Save the document as **myBasicActions1.fla** in the same location. Scroll to the upper-left corner of the Stage, if necessary, which is already set with a layer, frame, and a button symbol labeled "Open Web Page." Close the Actions panel, if necessary, to see more of the Stage. See Figure 3-52.

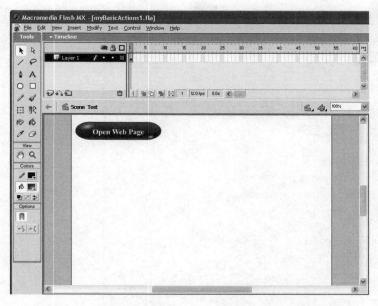

Figure 3-52   myBasicActions1.fla with Open Web Page button

2. First you assign the getURL action to the button. Click to select the **Open Web Page** button, if necessary, right-click the **Open Web Page** button, and then click **Actions** on the shortcut menu to open the Actions panel.

3. In the Actions panel, click the **Browser/Network** category, if necessary, to expand its list of actions. Double-click the **getURL** action, if necessary. The code for the action appears in the right pane of the Actions panel. See Figure 3-53.

4. Click the getURL line to select it, and then type **http://www.FlashTrainingDesign.com** in the URL text box.

5. Click the **Window** list arrow, and then click **_blank**. See Figure 3-54. This command indicates that the Web page you specified in the URL text box should open in its own window.

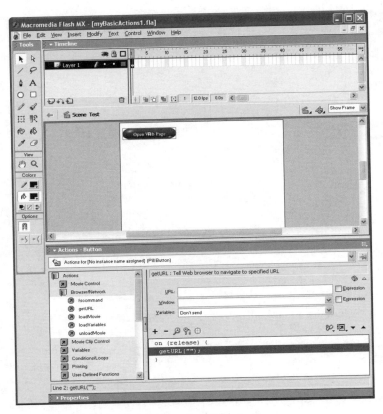

Figure 3-53   Assigning an action to a button

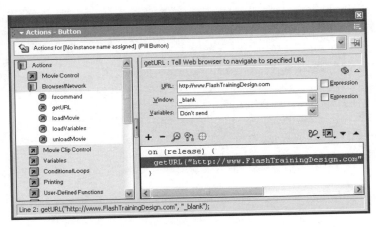

Figure 3-54   getURL actions to open a new browser window

6. Test the movie by clicking **Control** on the menu bar, and then clicking **Test Movie** command. Click the **Open Web Page** button to open the new browser window.

7. Close the browser window and stop playing the movie, if necessary.

8. Click the title bar on the Actions panel to minimize the window. Save and close **myBasicActions1.fla**, but leave Flash open.

 Use the getURL action when you don't want to control the new window's location, size, and ability to show or hide toolbars, menu bars, scroll bars, and the status bar. In Chapter 8, "Using ActionScript in Flash," you will learn to control these browser options by calling a JavaScript function.

Preventing a Movie from Looping

The Flash Player is designed to play a movie from beginning to end and then start again, a process called **looping**. If you want a movie to play from beginning to end and then stop, you can use the stop action to prevent the movie from looping. You assign the stop action to a keyframe; the movie then stops playing when it reaches that keyframe.

 It's a good idea to place all of your frame actions in one layer to make it easier to track them. Frames with actions display a small "a" in the Timeline.

In the following steps, you preview an existing animation to observe it looping, stop playing the movie, and then add the stop action to provide looping control.

To use the stop action to limit looping:

1. Open sample file **StopAction.fla** from the Chapter3 folder in the FlashSamples folder. Save the document as **myStopAction.fla** in the same location.

2. First, test the movie to watch it loop the animation continuously. Then stop the test and close the test window.

3. Click to select **frame 20** in the Timeline.

4. Expand the Actions panel. (Click its title bar.)

5. To assign the stop action to the selected keyframe, double-click **stop** in the Movie Control category. Your Actions panel should resemble Figure 3-55.

6. Click **Control** on the menu bar, and then click **Test Movie** to test the stop action. Now the animation stops at frame 20 instead of replaying the animation.

7. Close the test window, and then save and close **myStopAction.fla**. Exit Flash.

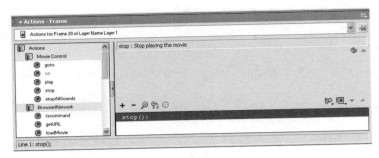

Figure 3-55   Stop action syntax

 You can assign a stop action only to a single keyframe. If you select a frame other than a keyframe, Flash assigns the stop action to the preceding keyframe.

Chapter Summary

❏ You can use any of three methods to create animation: frame-by-frame, motion tweening, and shape tweening. In frame-by-frame animation, you create the image for every frame. In motion- or shape-tweened animation, you create keyframes at significant positions on the Timeline; Flash creates the frames in between, varying the object's properties evenly between the starting and ending frames to create the appearance of gradual movement.

❏ Flash documents generally have small size files, a benefit when distributing and playing documents in a browser.

❏ Flash designers use different types of frames, including keyframes, blank keyframes, and unused frames. Flash frames are similar to the frames professional animators use to draw individual cells of a cartoon animation.

❏ Flash provides three types of symbols: graphics, buttons, and movie clips. Each has its specific purpose and properties. Graphic symbols are ideally used in frame-by-frame and tweened animation; button symbols are interactive images that respond to mouse events, such as clicking. Button symbols have four conditions or states: Up, Over, Down, and Hit, which can have different images and sounds assigned to them. Movie clips are reusable animations that comprise their own Timeline and play independent of the main document Timeline.

❏ You create interactive documents by assigning actions to an object or frame. Then you specify an event that triggers the action. To assign an action to a frame, button, or movie clip, you can work with the Movie Control actions on the Actions panel.

❏ Frame actions execute when the playhead arrives at the frame that contains the action and do not require input from the user.

❏ Button actions execute when the user participates, normally in the form of a mouse click or keyboard entry.

❏ Movie clips are executed in one of two ways depending on how you construct the action: by an event in the movie such as a frame jumping to another frame, or by user input such as a button click.

REVIEW QUESTIONS

1. _____ is the gradual movement or change of an image over time.

2. Which of the following is an element created by the artist that can be used over and over without having to reload it into memory?

   a. image

   b. symbol

   c. action

   d. frame

3. Symbols are largely responsible for the small file sizes in Flash documents. True or false?

4. A symbol cannot be used within another symbol. True or false?

5. Which of the following characteristics do all three types of symbols share?

   a. Timeline

   b. action capabilities

   c. Alpha property

   d. all of the above

6. Which of the following are types of animation methods in Flash?

   a. motion tween

   b. movie tween

   c. frame–by–keyframe

   d. shape frames

7. Which of the following animation techniques is the most similar to manual animation?

   a. motion tween

   b. movie clips

   c. frame–by–frame

   d. shape tween

8. You can use symbols with a motion–tween animation. True or false?

9. You can use symbols with a shape–tween animation. True or false?

10. Motion tweening can perform the following effects:

    a. rotating

    b. movement

    c. changes in size

    d. all of the above

11. The name of the language Flash uses to interact within a Flash document is called:

    a. VBScript

    b. JavaScript

    c. ActionScript

    d. none of the above

12. A mask layer is a special type of layer that lets you draw a path for a symbol. True or false?

13. Mask layers cannot be animated. True or false?

14. An action can be programmed in which of the following elements (choose all that apply):

    a. button

    b. movie clip

    c. graphic

    d. frame

    e. layer

15. A Mouse over event is exclusive to frame properties. True or false?

16. Which type of symbol do you use to enter comments into a frame?

    a. //

    b. < !-- >

    c. < // >

    d. *

17. You can assign actions to a frame and a button that enable them to stop a movie. True or false?

18. Which of the following is *not* true?

    a. A button has a Timeline separate from the main Timeline.

    b. A movie clip can have an instance name.

    c. A graphic should be used for animation.

    d. The Test Movie command plays the current animation with no looping.

19. To use a guide layer you must ensure that the _____ command is checked on the View menu.

20. When using a masked layer, the _____ layer masks the _____ layer.

21. An animation with a guide path is used for attaching objects to follow a path. True or False?

22. You must vary images in each frame to create the effect of movement in _____ animation.

HANDS-ON PROJECTS

Project 3-1

In this project, you begin creating an animated map of the Salt Lake City 2002 Olympic torch relay route. You create a graphic symbol from a bitmap of the torch relay map, and then modify the symbol instances. Start by importing an image file of a U.S. map. Then edit two instances of a single symbol as individual objects to use one symbol as two different Stage objects.

1. In Flash, open **Torch01.fla** from the Chapter3\Projects folder in your FlashSamples folder. Save the document as **myTorch01.fla** in the same location.

2. Adjust the frame rate to 10 frames per second to slow the animation. Click Modify on the menu bar, and then click Document. In the Document Properties dialog box, type 10 in the Frame Rate text box, and then click OK.

3. To make the visible area of the Stage larger, click Window on the menu bar, and then click Close All Panels. Open the Library panel, which is where you will store the symbols you create. To do so, click Window on the menu bar, and then click Library. Drag the Library panel to the lower-right of the Flash window.

4. Click the Large Map layer in the Timeline to select it, and then import the map image. Click File on the menu bar and then click Import. In the Import dialog box, navigate to the Chapter3\Projects folder in your FlashSamples folder, and then double-click map.gif. Flash adds map.gif to the Library panel.

5. Convert the map image into a graphic symbol by clicking anywhere on the map to select it. Click Insert on the menu bar, and then click Convert to Symbol. The Convert to Symbol dialog box opens.

6. Type Map Graphic Symbol as the name, click the Graphic option button, and then click OK. Flash adds the map to the library as a graphic symbol.

7. Click Window on the menu bar and then click Transform to open the Transform panel. To use the Transform panel to precisely scale the large map symbol, type 56.1 in the Width text box, and then press Enter to accept that change. Make sure the Constrain check box is selected. This sets the Height scale option to the same percentage as the Width.

8. Click Window on the menu bar and then click Info to open the Info panel. Use the Info panel to precisely position the large map symbol in the upper-left corner of the Stage. To do so, type 5 in the Info Panel X text box and 5 in the Y text box, and then press Enter. This sets the position of the large map symbol to 5 pixels from the top and 5 pixels from the left of the Stage.

9. Click the Small Map layer to select it, and then drag another instance of the map symbol from the Library window to the Stage. You place this map symbol in a different layer to keep all of your document assets organized.

10. Use the Transform panel to reduce the size of the new map symbol. Make sure the Constrain check box is checked. Then change the height and width of the map from 100% to 25% of its original size. Press Enter, and then close the Transform panel.

11. Use the Info panel to enter an X location value of 5 and Y location value of 285 pixels and set the position of the smaller map instance to the lower-left corner of the Stage. Close the Info panel.

12. Save and close **myTorch01.fla**, but leave Flash open.

Project 3-2

In this project, you continue working with the Olympic torch relay map, and create an animated visual route with a motion tween and a guide path. You create a new layer called Red Icon, and use this as a starting point for the torch.

1. Open **Torch02.fla** from the Chapter3\Projects folder in your FlashSamples folder. Save the document as **myTorch02.fla** in the same location.

2. Right-click the Large Map layer and then click Insert Layer to add a new layer to the image. The new layer should appear above the Large Map layer. Double-click the new layer and type Red Icon as the new name. This layer will contain the motion tween for the red icon to move through the map along the torch route.

3. With the Red Icon layer selected, click Insert on the menu bar, and then click Motion Guide to insert a guide layer. Notice that the Red Icon layer is now indented, indicating it is part of the new guide layer. Rename the guide layer to Guide: Torch Route.

4. Select frame 1 on the Red Icon layer, and use the Oval tool to draw a red ball slightly larger than the blue ones on the map. Place the ball by the torch near Georgia, which indicates the starting point of the icon. Use the Zoom tool, if necessary, to enlarge your view of the map.

5. Next, create a motion tween to give the ball movement. With the Arrow tool, select the red ball, and convert the image into a symbol by pressing the F8 key. Name the symbol Red Icon, select the Graphic behavior, and then click OK. Click frame 96 on the Red Icon layer, and then press the F6 key to insert a keyframe. With the Arrow tool, move the Red Icon symbol next to the Olympic logo in Utah, which is the ending point of the icon. Right-click the in-between frames between frame 1 and 96, and then click Create Motion Tween on the shortcut menu.

3

6. Now create the guide path. Click the Guide:Torch Route layer, and then click the Pen tool. (The Pen tool is a good choice for this path because of the angles in the route.) Start by clicking the first blue oval near the torch image in Georgia, and then continue clicking each bend in the line that forms the torch route. Use the Zoom tool as necessary to enlarge your view of the map. When you reach the last blue oval next to the Olympic icon, double-click to complete the route with the Pen tool.

7. Now you connect the two symbols to the beginning of the guide path. Click frame 1 in the Red Icon layer. Use the Arrow tool to drag the red icon symbol to the beginning of the guide path, if necessary. As you drag, look for a small circle in the middle of the symbol, indicating that the symbol's registration point will snap to the line end. Stop dragging when you see the small snap circle. Click the end frame and drag your symbol to the end of the guide path, snapping the registration point to the line end as it turns into a small circle.

8. Test your movie by clicking Control on the menu bar, and then clicking Play. The red icon should follow along the guide path you created.

9. Click Control on the menu bar, and then click Stop to stop playing the movie. Save and close **myTorch02.fla**, but leave Flash open.

Project 3-3

In this project, you enhance the Olympic torch relay map by highlighting the starting point. You do this by animating the torch to create the appearance that it is lit continuously. You accomplish this by creating a frame-by-frame animation, which you will later integrate with a movie symbol. The files you import are stored in the Chapter3\Projects folder.

1. Open **Torch03.fla** from the Chapter3\Projects folder in your FlashSamples folder. Save the document as **myTorch03.fla** in the same location.

2. Using techniques you learned in Projects 3-1 and 3-2, create a new layer called Animated Torch above the Large Map layer.

3. Create a new symbol by clicking Insert on the menu bar, and then clicking New Symbol. In the Create New Symbol dialog box, type Torch F-F in the Name text box to indicate that this is a frame-by-frame animation for the torch. Click the Graphic option button, if necessary, and then click OK to close the dialog box and enter the symbol-editing mode.

4. Import the bitmap image **Torch-1.gif**, and place it in the center of the Stage. A dialog box asks if you want to import one file or the sequence of files. Import only the file. Do this each time you import during this project. Also note that importing bitmaps automatically centers them in the symbol.

5. Click frame 2, and then press the F6 key to insert a keyframe.

6. Import the bitmap image **Torch-2.gif**, and place it in the center of the Stage.

7. Click frame 3, and then press F6 to insert a keyframe.

8. Import **Torch-3.gif**, and place it in the center of the Stage.

9. Click frame 4, and then press F6 to insert a keyframe.

10. Import the bitmap image **Torch-4.gif**, and place it in the center of the Stage.

11. Click Scene 1 to return to the main document Stage.

12. Save and close **myTorch03.fla**, but leave Flash open.

The frame-by-frame animation now has four slightly different images of the torch flame. Next, you will use this animation in a movie symbol to have it loop continuously, independent of the main document Timeline.

Project 3-4

In Project 3-4, you complete the animated torch by creating a movie clip symbol with the previous frame-by-frame animation graphic symbol.

1. Open **Torch04.fla** from the Chapter3\Projects folder in your FlashSamples folder. Save it as **myTorch04.fla** in the same location.

2. Click the Animated Torch layer, and then create a new symbol by pressing Ctrl+F8 (Command+F8 on the Macintosh).

3. Name the symbol Animated Torch, choose Movie Clip as its Behavior, and then click OK.

4. Press Ctrl+L to open the Library panel, if necessary, and then drag the graphic symbol Torch F-F from the library to the Stage.

5. Click frame 10, and then press F6 to insert a keyframe.

6. Right-click the in-between frames, and then click Create Motion Tween on the shortcut menu. Doing so means the Torch F-F symbol can move within the main document Timeline.

7. Click Scene 1 to return to the main document Stage.

8. Drag the new Animated Torch movie clip symbol onto the Stage.

9. Use the Transform panel to scale the torch symbol to 50% in each of the X and Y dimensions, which is the approximate size of the torch already on the map, and drag the symbol on top of the original torch image. If the torch symbol is not visible, drag to move the Animated Torch layer above the Large Map layer. Use the Zoom tool as necessary to enlarge your view of the Stage.

10. The animated torch symbol is now complete. Click Control on the menu bar, and then click Test Movie. The flame in the torch should look like it's burning.

11. Save and close **myTorch04.fla**, but leave Flash open.

Project 3-5

In this project, you add to the Olympic torch document by displaying a message reading "Support the Torch." You do so by creating a motion tween and a mask.

1. Open **Torch05.fla** from the Chapter3\Projects folder in your FlashSamples folder. Save the document as **myTorch05.fla** in the same location.

2. Create three new layers called Spotlight, White Text, and Red Text and then arrange them in that order, if necessary, above the Large Map layer.

3. Select the Red Text layer, and then use the Text tool to insert a text box directly above the small map. Choose red for the text color. Click Text on the menu bar, point to Font, and click Impact for the font. Click Text on the menu bar, point to Size, and click 14 points for the size. Click Text on the menu bar, point to Style, and make sure no styles are checked. Then type Support the Torch.

4. Select the White Text layer, and insert a text box almost on top of the red text. Use the arrow keys to move the text box about one pixel to the right of the red text. Choose white for the text color, Impact for the font, 14 points for the size, and no style. Type Support the Torch. You can adjust the location by nudging the text box with the arrow keys.

5. To animate the spotlight, select the Spotlight layer and then click frame 1 in that layer. Draw a green circle with no border, slightly larger than the height of the text near the beginning of the text. Using techniques you learned in this chapter and previous projects, convert the green spotlight to a graphic symbol and name it Spotlight.

6. Click frame 1 in the Spotlight layer. Delete the green circle on the Stage. Click frame 1 again to make sure it's selected. Open the Library panel, and then drag the Spotlight symbol from the Library to the left of the text, slightly overlaying the text.

7. Click frame 96 in the Spotlight layer, and then press F6 to insert a keyframe. With only frame 96 selected, delete the green circle on the Stage. Then drag the Spotlight symbol from the Library to the right of the text, slightly overlaying the text.

8. Right-click any frame between frames 2-95, and then click Create Motion Tween on the shortcut menu. The spotlight is now animated and will move across the text.

9. Right-click the Spotlight layer, and then click Mask. The Spotlight layer is now a mask, as indicated by the Mask icon on the layer. The White Text layer is also indented, indicating that the layer above it—the Spotlight Layer—is masking it. Notice both the mask and masked layers (Spotlight and White Text layers) are locked.

10. You can test the masking effects by clicking Control on the menu bar, and then clicking Play. Then stop playing the movie.

11. Save and close **myTorch05.fla**, but leave Flash open.

3

Project 3-6

In Project 3-6, you enhance the Olympic torch relay movie by creating an animated text box that morphs into an Olympic logo. To do this, you create a shape tween.

1. Open **Torch06.fla** from the Chapter3\Projects folder in your FlashSamples folder. Save the document as **myTorch06.fla** in the same location.

2. Create a new layer named Torch Shape Tween as the last layer.

3. Select frame 1 in this new layer, and on the stage, add the text Support the Torch in blue, using Impact for the font, 14 points for the size, and Italic for the style.

4. Use the Arrow tool to select the text box, if necessary, and move it below Florida on the large map. Ungroup the text by clicking Modify on the menu bar and then clicking Break Apart. Break the ungrouped text into pixels by clicking Modify on the menu bar and then clicking Break Apart again. Before you can create a shape tween, you must break apart the beginning and ending shapes.

5. Select frame 96 in the Torch Shape Tween layer, and then press F6 to insert a keyframe. Import the bitmap image **Torch-6.gif**. Scale the torch image so it is about 70 × 70 pixels, and move it to the right of Florida.

6. Select the logo, and then press Ctrl+B to break it apart.

7. Ensure that the text does not appear on the last frame and the logo image does not appear on the first frame; if so, select and delete the text on the last frame and the logo on the first frame.

8. Click to select an in-between frame, and choose Shape as the tweening method on the Property inspector.

9. You can test the shape tween by clicking Control on the menu bar, and then clicking Play. The text should morph into the logo.

10. Save and close **myTorch06.fla**, but leave Flash open.

Project 3-7

In this project, you create a button symbol from a text box and use an instance of the button symbol to link to an e-mail address. You can then click the button to open a new e-mail message.

1. Open **E-mail.fla** from the Chapter3\Projects folder in your FlashSamples folder. Save the document as **myE-mail.fla** in the same location.

2. Add a new layer named Email Link above the Large Map layer.

3. With the Text tool, place your e-mail address on the Stage in black, Arial, 12-point text in the lower-right corner of the stage. If you don't have an e-mail address, you can visit Web sites such as *www.Hotmail.com* or *www.Yahoo.com* for a free e-mail address.

4. Use the Arrow tool to select the e-mail address, and then press F8 to convert the text into a button symbol. Name the symbol Email Link, and select the Button behavior. Click OK to close the convert to symbol dialog box.

3

5. Double-click the Email Link button to open the button in Edit mode. In the button's Timeline, click the Hit frame, and then press F6 to add a keyframe. Notice the Over and Down frame automatically fill with blank keyframes. With the Hit frame still selected, use the Rectangle tool to draw a white filled rectangle with no border to cover the e-mail text. This allows users to click the e-mail address more easily. Click the Scene 1 link to return to the main Stage.

6. Use the Arrow tool to right-click the button symbol, and then click Actions. The Actions panel opens.

7. In the Actions panel, expand the Browser/Network actions, if necessary.

8. Double-click the getURL action to insert the command syntax into the text pane.

9. In the URL parameter, type your e-mail address with the following format: mailto:info@FlashTrainingDesign.com

10. Close the Actions panel.

11. You can test the link to your default e-mail application's new message by clicking Control on the menu bar, and then clicking Test Movie.

12. Save and close **myE-mail.fla**, but leave Flash open.

Project 3-8

In this project, you complete the Olympic torch document by providing a link to a Web site where viewers can find more information about the Olympics. You will do this by creating a button symbol to link to the official International Olympic Committee Web site at *www.olympic.org*.

1. Open **Olympics.fla** from the Chapter3\Projects folder in your FlashSamples folder. Save the document as **myOlympics.fla** in the same location.

2. Create a new layer called More Info above the Large Map layer.

3. Create a button link by using the Flash button library. Click Window on the menu bar, point to Common Libraries, and then click Buttons.

4. Double-click the Push Buttons category, and then drag push button-blue onto the Stage. Move the button to the left of your e-mail address.

5. Right-click the button and then click Actions on the shortcut menu to open the Actions panel.

6. In the Actions panel, double-click the getURL action to insert the command syntax into the text pane.

7. In the URL parameter, type the Olympic Web address with the following format: http://www.olympic.org

8. In the Window list box, select the _blank option. This will cause the Olympic Web site to open in a new browser window.

9. Close the Actions panel, and then test the movie.

10. Save and close **myOlympics.fla**, and then exit Flash.

Case Projects

Case Project 3-1

An art gallery has commissioned you to create a presentation showcasing its most prestigious pieces. The presentation should organize and display the art works, which include paintings and sculptures. It should also let viewers click one button to visit the gallery's Web site and another button to send an e-mail message to the Fundraising department. Use Flash to create an appropriate presentation. Find three to four pieces of clip art on the Web to represent the gallery's art works. Make sure the clip art is in the public domain. For the buttons, use instances of symbols from the Flash Button library. For the links, use the URL of a Web site for an existing art gallery or museum and your own e-mail address.

Case Project 3-2

Use motion tweening to animate a logo using Flash's drawing and painting tools, and then applying movement to the various elements of the logo. Also create or import an appropriate object or image for the logo. For example, if you are using the logo of a shoe manufacturer, import an image of a shoe. Use shape tweening to morph the object or image into the logo. For ideas on logos, visit *www.LogoFusion.com*, or visit various popular name brands, such as Nike, Sony, or Microsoft. You can also search the Web for clip art that is in the public domain.

Case Project 3-3

Your job is to animate a cartoonist's illustrations. You accomplish this project by using frame-by-frame animation. Insert a keyframe for each illustration. You can place each illustration in the same place on the Stage or in different places, depending on the effect you want to create. Then create a motion tween between each keyframe. Be sure to test your movie to make sure it creates the correct effect. For cartoon images, browse to *www.aaugh.com*.

Case Project 3-4

For this case project, design a series of Flash animations for your portfolio or fictional business. The animations should showcase the three Flash animation techniques: motion tweening, shape tweening, and frame-by-frame animation. The animations should portray yourself, your interests, or products and services related to your fictional business. You can create each animation on separate layers in the same Flash movie, or use different Flash movies to display each animation.

4

DESIGNING WITH OTHER MEDIA FILE TYPES

*Enhancing Macromedia Flash Documents
with Image and Media Resources*

In this chapter, you will:

♦ Import vector images from Adobe Illustrator and Macromedia Freehand
♦ Import bitmap files
♦ Use sound media to enhance movies
♦ Integrate QuickTime videos with Macromedia Flash movies
♦ Edit Macromedia Flash native video

In addition to creating images and animations in Macromedia Flash, you can import bitmap and vector images, music and other audio, and animations created in other programs. Recall from Chapter 2 that bitmap images, also called raster images, consist of an array of pixels. You create bitmap files by using a paint program, such as Adobe Photoshop, or a scanner. Because bitmap files can support millions of colors, bitmap images are generally of high quality. The vector graphic file format, on the other hand, was originally designed for print, not the computer monitor, and is best for simple images, such as line drawings and graphs. Recall that the benefit of using vector images is that they retain their form when scaled and they produce small files. You create vector files by using a drawing program such as Adobe Illustrator or Macromedia Freehand. Flash lets you integrate both raster and vector formats in a single file that conserves file size while providing brilliant quality.

Besides using bitmap and vector images from other programs, you can also use sound, music, and video from other programs. Add these types of media to include spoken words, video clips, sound effects, and music in your Flash movies. In this chapter, you will import bitmap and vector images, add sound to button events, synchronize music with the Timeline, and integrate QuickTime movies with your Flash documents.

IMPORTING VECTOR IMAGES FROM ADOBE ILLUSTRATOR AND MACROMEDIA FREEHAND

Adobe Illustrator and Macromedia Freehand are sophisticated drawing programs that create vector images. These programs are common tools of choice for graphic illustrators, who often provide vector images for designers and developers. Although you can use Flash to create vector images, you might prefer to work with the more powerful tools in Illustrator or Freehand, and then import those images into Flash.

When you import a Freehand image file, Flash preserves its vectors and layers, as shown in Figure 4-1. When you import an Illustrator image file, however, Flash can maintain only the vectors. Because of its compatibility with Flash, you can most effectively import vectors from Freehand.

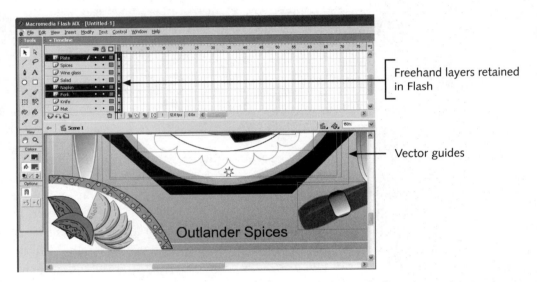

Freehand layers retained in Flash

Vector guides

Figure 4-1　Macromedia Freehand vector file imported into Flash

Note that Flash provides import filters for Macromedia Freehand versions 10 or earlier (*.fh or *.ft files). In the following steps, you import a Freehand vector file that contains layers and multiple pages. When you import, Flash preserves the layers and vector points and converts the pages into frames. **Vector points** are the beginning and ending points on a line or curve segment. Vector graphic files use vector points to define the shape properties.

To import a Freehand vector file into Flash:

1. Start Flash MX, if necessary, and then create a new file. Save the file as **myImportFreehand.fla** in the Chapter4 folder in your FlashSamples folder. The Stage is currently blank.

4

2. To import a Freehand vector file, click **File** on the menu bar, and then click **Import**. The Import dialog box opens.

3. Click the **Files of type** list arrow (click the **Show** list arrow on the Macintosh), and then click **FreeHand**, as shown in Figure 4-2.

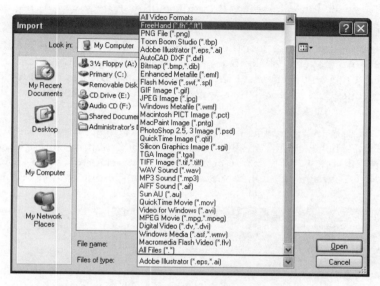

Figure 4-2   Selecting the FreeHand file type

4. Navigate to the Chapter4 folder in your FlashSamples folder, and then double-click **ImportFreehand.fh9**. The FreeHand Import dialog box opens, as shown in Figure 4-3.

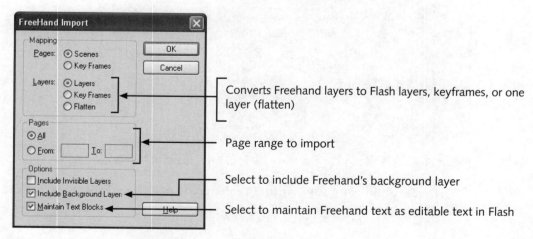

Converts Freehand layers to Flash layers, keyframes, or one layer (flatten)

Page range to import

Select to include Freehand's background layer

Select to maintain Freehand text as editable text in Flash

Figure 4-3   FreeHand Import dialog box

5. In the Mapping – Pages section, click the **Key Frames** option button to convert each Freehand page into a Flash keyframe.

6. In the Mapping – Layers section, click the **Layers** option button, if necessary, to convert each Freehand layer into a Flash layer.

7. In the Pages section, click the **All** option button, if necessary, to import all Freehand pages.

8. In the Options section, select the **Include Invisible Layers** and **Include Background Layers** check boxes, if necessary, to import these layers with the layered file; and then select the **Maintain Text Blocks** check box, if necessary, to import text blocks that you can edit. All three check boxes should contain check marks.

9. Click **OK** to import the file. Click any imported object to select it. You can also double-click a group of objects to open that group in editing mode. The Freehand file opens with vector points and layers retained, as shown in Figure 4-4. Your image might appear larger than the one shown in the figure.

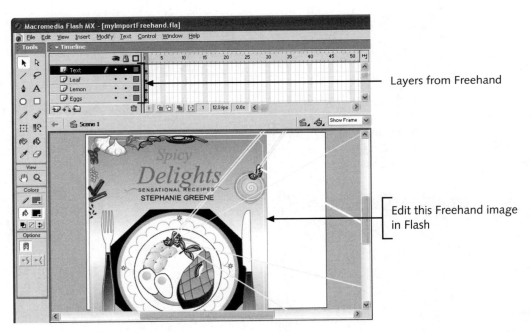

Figure 4-4   Freehand file retaining its vector points and layers

10. Save and close **myImportFreehand.fla**, but leave Flash open for the next set of steps.

You can also import vector files created with Adobe Illustrator version 10 and earlier. When importing Illustrator files, Flash retains the vectors, but not the layers. After importing an Illustrator file, you must ungroup it before you can edit it.

To import and ungroup an Illustrator vector image:

1. Start Flash MX, if necessary, and then create a new file. Save the file as **myImportIllustrator.fla** in the Chapter4 folder in your FlashSamples folder. The Stage is currently blank.

2. To import an Illustrator vector file, click **File** on the menu bar, and then click **Import**. The Import dialog box opens.

3. Click the **Files of type** list arrow (click the **Show** list arrow on the Macintosh), and then click **Adobe Illustrator**.

4. Navigate to the Chapter4 folder in your FlashSamples folder, if necessary, and then double-click **ImportIllustrator.ai**.

5. The Illustrator Import dialog box opens, as shown in Figure 4-5. Use the Convert options to specify what you want to do with the Illustrator file's layers in Flash. You can maintain them as layers, convert the layers into keyframes, or flatten the image so no layers exist. The Include Invisible Layers option allows you to import all layers, including hidden ones, from the Illustrator file. Ensure the **Layers** and **Include Invisible Layers** options are selected, and then click **OK**.

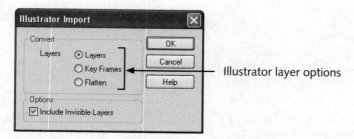

Illustrator layer options

Figure 4-5   Importing an Illustrator file

6. If a message appears indicating that the Flash filter may not understand the entire Illustrator file when importing an EPS file of that format, click **OK**.

   If a dialog box opens indicating that the fonts on your computer don't match those in the Illustrator file you are importing, click the **Use Default** button.

   The Illustrator vector image opens on the Stage as a grouped vector file. See Figure 4-6.

7. You should ungroup the image so you can edit its independent parts. With the vector image still selected, click **Modify** on the menu bar and then click **Ungroup**.

8. Save and close **myImportIllustrator.fla**, but leave Flash open for the next set of steps.

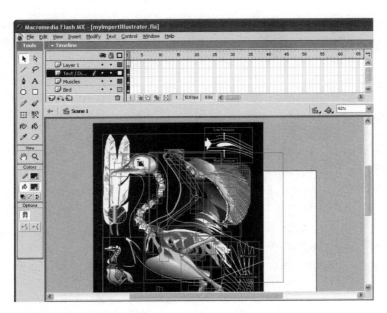

Figure 4-6   Imported grouped Illustrator vector image

IMPORTING BITMAP FILES

In contrast to vector images, bitmap images are generally larger in file size because they contain more visual information. You can use compression tools provided in programs such as Adobe Photoshop or JASC PaintShop Pro to reduce the file size of the image before importing it into Flash. When you **compress** an image, you decrease its file size by removing or replacing data. If you are familiar with HTML, resizing raster images in Flash is much like using the HEIGHT and WIDTH attributes of the HTML <IMG> tag to resize images; the results usually have poor resolution. Flash supports a wide range of bitmap images including bitmap (.bmp), GIF (.gif), JPEG (.jpg, .jpeg), PNG (.png), and PICT (.pct, .pic). The GIF format supports interlacing, transparency, and animation, while the other formats do not. **Interlacing** allows an image to gradually appear in a browser as it downloads. The image is rendered a few fragments at a time, creating an effect of fading in. (Note that interlaced GIF files only appear interlaced in a browser, not in the Flash player.) **Transparency** allows you to see through images or portions of an image, such as the background of a logo. You can place an image with transparent areas on a colored or textured image in Flash or on an HTML page so that the color or texture shows through. **Animation sequences** are much like frame-by-frame animation— they show a sequence of images, with each image slightly different from the one before it, creating an illusion of movement. The most popular image formats used today are described in Table 4-1.

Table 4-1   Popular bitmap image file formats

Format name	Extension	Description
Bitmap	.bmp	Provides an uncompressed Windows format
GIF	.gif	Pronounced "JIF," the Graphics Interchange Format supports 256 colors, interlacing, transparency, and animation sequencing.
JPEG	.jpg or .jpeg	The Joint Photographic Experts Group format supports millions of colors and good compression methods.
PNG	.png	Pronounced "PING," the Portable Network Group format supports 8-bit and 24-bit color and good compression, making it suitable for both line art and bitmap (raster) type of images.
PICT	.pct or .pic	PICT images are for the Macintosh platform only and support 32-bit color and no compression, making them suitable for both line art and bitmap images.

To import a bitmap image:

1. In Flash, create a new file. Save the file as **myImportBitmap.fla** in the Chapter4 folder in your FlashSamples folder. The Stage is currently blank.

2. To import a JPEG bitmap image, click **File** on the menu bar and then click **Import**. The Import dialog box opens.

3. Click the **Files of type** list arrow (click the **Show** list arrow on the Macintosh), and then click **JPEG Image**.

4. Navigate to the Chapter4 folder in your FlashSamples folder, if necessary, and then double-click **JPEGImport.jpg**. The file opens on the Stage as a bitmap file. Press **Ctrl+L** (or **Cmd+L** on the Macintosh) to open the Library panel, if necessary, and note that the bitmap also appears there. Click the **JPEGImport** icon in the Library panel. See Figure 4-7.

5. Save **myImportBitmap.fla**, and leave it open in the Flash window.

Before importing bitmapped images, make sure you first save the file in the size you want. For example, a bitmap image that was produced from a scanned photograph with many colors and variations can be a complex file to import and manipulate. Resizing and optimizing the file in a bitmap-editing program such as Adobe's Photoshop prior to importing it into Flash can improve import and conversion performance, decrease file size, and enhance the quality of the final vector image. If you do not optimize a bitmap image before importing, the image quality might be distorted and the file larger than it needs to be.

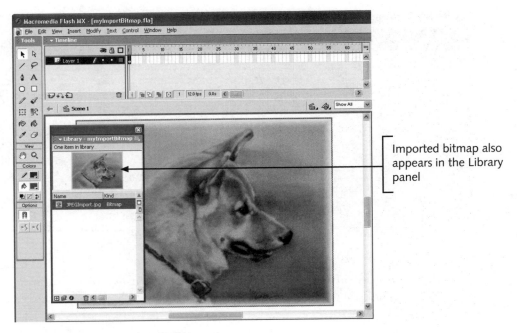

Imported bitmap also appears in the Library panel

Figure 4-7   Imported JPEG file

Adjusting Bitmap Properties

Note that the bitmap of the dog that you just imported is of high quality and has a large file size. You can improve the image size, however, by adjusting the image properties within Flash. After you import a bitmap, you can use the Bitmap Properties dialog box to control the following properties:

- *Allow Smoothing*—Set this option to smooth out the edges of the bitmap. This feature is also known as **anti-aliasing**.

- *Compression*—Use this option to select a file format that compresses images. You can choose the Photo (JPEG) format or the Lossless (PNG/GIF) format. The JPEG option is the best choice for photographs or images with many colors or tones, whereas the PNG/GIF option is best suited for images with line art or fewer colors.

- *Use default document quality*—Select this check box to use the compression setting associated with the file type shown in the Compression list box. To specify a different compression setting, deselect this check box and enter a value from 1 to 100 in the Quality text box, where 1 is the lowest quality but highest compression, and 100 is the highest quality but lowest compression. The larger the quality value, the greater the file size.

In the following steps, you change the properties of the bitmap image of the dog that you imported in the previous section.

4

To set the bitmap properties:

1. With myImportBitmap.fla open in Flash, right-click (Ctrl+click on the Macintosh) **JPEGImport.jpg** in the Library panel, as shown in Figure 4-8, and then click **Properties** on the shortcut menu.

Right-click the file whose properties you want to set

Figure 4-8 Imported JPEG file in the Library panel

2. In the Bitmap Properties dialog box, select the **Allow smoothing** check box, if necessary, to use the anti-aliasing technique to soften the edges of the image. Also verify that the compression option is Photo (JPEG). See Figure 4-9.

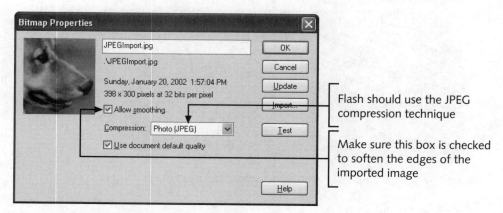

Flash should use the JPEG compression technique

Make sure this box is checked to soften the edges of the imported image

Figure 4-9 Bitmap Properties dialog box

3. Click the **Use document default quality** check box to remove the check mark, if necessary. When you do, the Quality text box appears so you can enter a value to modify the image resolution quality. Type **25** as the value to reduce the image quality and lower the file size.

4. Click the **Test** button. Flash displays both the original size and the compressed size of the file in kilobytes and shows a preview of the image with the current settings.

When you click the Test button to see a preview of the image, you can drag the image in the preview window to see the complete image.

5. Click **OK** to apply the changes to the image.
6. Close the Library panel, and then click a blank area of the Stage to deselect any selected objects. Save **myImportBitmap.fla**, and leave it open in Flash.

Converting to a Vector Object (Animating a Bitmap)

To edit a bitmap image, you first need to convert it to a vector image within Flash by using the Trace Bitmap command. The bitmap retains its original detail, but is broken into separate areas of color. You can then use the Flash editing and coloring tools such as the Brush, Pen, and Pointer tools to modify the image.

Tracing a Bitmap

While converting a bitmap to a vector image lets you edit the image in Flash, it also distorts the image, creating a posterized look, where the range of colors is reduced. A bitmap image contains much more color information than a vector image. When Flash converts a bitmap to a vector, it compares the number of colors and matching pixels to produce the vector representation. This process divides the image into fragments of similar colors. You can then edit these fragments. Figure 4-10 shows an example of an original bitmap and a traced bitmap.

Traced bitmap

Original bitmap (jpg)

Figure 4-10 Comparing an original and a traced bitmap image

To trace a bitmap image:

1. With myImportBitmap.fla open in Flash, save the file as **myTraceBitmap.fla** in the Chapter4 folder in your FlashSamples folder.
2. Click the bitmap to select it on your Stage.
3. Click **Modify** on the menu bar, and then click **Trace Bitmap**. The Trace Bitmap dialog box appears, as shown Figure 4-11. Your values might be different from the ones shown in Figure 4-11.

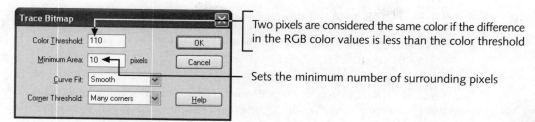

Figure 4-11 Trace Bitmap dialog box

4. In the Color Threshold text box, type **25**. This option sets the accuracy of selecting pixels in the bitmap. Flash compares the pixels in the bitmap and converts them to the same color if the variation is less than the Color Threshold value. You can set this value between 1 and 500; the lower the value, the greater the number of colors in the converted image and the larger the file size.

5. In the Minimum Area text box, type **10**. You can use a value between 1 and 1000 to set the number of surrounding pixels that Flash should consider when assigning a color to a pixel. Choose 10 to set a small amount of pixels to use in the color selection.

6. Click the **Curve Fit** list arrow, and then click **Smooth**. The Curve Fit options control how smoothly Flash draws the resulting vector image area outlines. The options range from pixels (jagged outline) to very smooth (even outline).

7. Click the **Corner Threshold** list arrow, and then click **Many corners**. This will smooth out sharp edges instead of retaining them. See Figure 4-12.

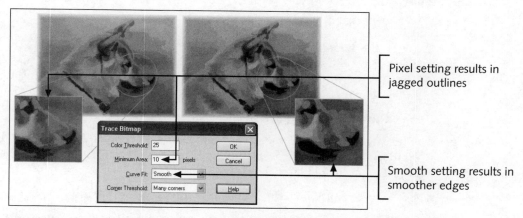

Figure 4-12 Comparing the Trace Bitmap Curve Fit option results

8. Click **OK** to apply the changes and close the Trace Bitmap dialog box.

9. Save and close **myTraceBitmap.fla**, but leave Flash open for the next set of steps.

After the Trace Bitmap process converts a bitmap image into a vector, you can use the Flash drawing tools to manipulate the image by dragging points of vectors, recoloring or moving selected areas, or adding lines and simple shapes to the image. If you need to move or treat the image as one component again, you can group it. If you are grouping the image after deselecting or editing it, select all the vector elements by using the Arrow tool to drag a marquee selection box around them. Then choose the Group command on the Modify menu to group the elements.

 Remember that increasing the quality and size of an image also increases file size. Depending on the bitmap you are converting to vector, you may want to experiment with several value settings in the Trace Bitmap dialog box to find a balance between file size and image quality.

 Importing a bitmap also specifies it as a symbol. If you trace a bitmap and then delete it, the symbol is still stored in the library for that document. If you no longer use the symbol, delete it from the library to reduce file size.

Using the Break Apart Command

The Break Apart command also gives you the ability to modify bitmap images. Breaking apart a bitmap segregates the pixels of the image into discrete areas. You can then select and modify the image elements separately using the Flash drawing and painting tools.

To break apart a bitmap:

1. Open the **BreakApart.fla** file from the Chapter4 folder in your FlashSamples folder. Save the file as **myBreakApart.fla** in the same location. This document contains the imported bitmap of a dog that you have been working with in previous steps.

2. Click to select the bitmap image, if necessary.

3. Click **Modify** on the menu bar, and then click **Break Apart**. The selection border around the image disappears. Figure 4-13 compares the original image to the same image after it has been broken apart.

4. Save **myBreakApart.fla**, and leave it open in the Flash window.

After using the Break Apart command, you can change the colors and shape of the bitmap image elements, or use the bitmap as a fill for other objects. You will learn more about using the bitmap as a fill in "Applying Bitmaps as Fills" later in this chapter.

Original image

Broken apart image, with
sections you can select
and edit

4

Figure 4-13   Comparing original and broken apart images

Selecting Like Colors with the Magic Wand Tool

Selecting colors in a bitmap allows you to recolor or otherwise modify those colors. Because a bitmap may contain many similar shades of the same color, Flash lets you specify which shades are similar, and then lets you select all those shades at the same time to edit them more easily. Flash calls these similar shades "like colors." You use the Lasso tools and the Magic Wand and Magic Wand Properties options to specify and select like colors and to change the fill of selected bitmap areas that have been broken apart. Use the Arrow and Subselection tools to change a selection's shape or vector points.

To select a selection:

1. With myBreakApart.fla still open in Flash, and the broken apart image still selected, click the **Lasso** tool on the toolbox. The Lasso tool options appear in the Options area, as shown in Figure 4-14.

2. Click the **Magic Wand** button to select it, if necessary, and make sure that the Polygon Mode button is not selected. (If it is, click to deselect it.)

3. Click the **Magic Wand Properties** button to open the Magic Wand Settings dialog box, shown in Figure 4-15.

4. In the Threshold text box, type **20** to select a moderate selection of values. You can enter values between 0 and 200; the smaller the number, the more closely the color of adjacent pixels must match to be included in the selection. Choosing 20 means that you set a small amount of pixels to include in the color selection.

5. Click the **Smoothing** list arrow, and then click **Pixels** to define how much the edges of the selection will be smoothed. The Smoothing option determines how the borders of the selection will look; you can choose Pixels (roughest), rough, normal, and smooth. The exact amount of smoothing that occurs depends greatly on the individual image.

6. Click **OK** to accept your settings, and then click the bitmap. The pointer changes to a Magic Wand.

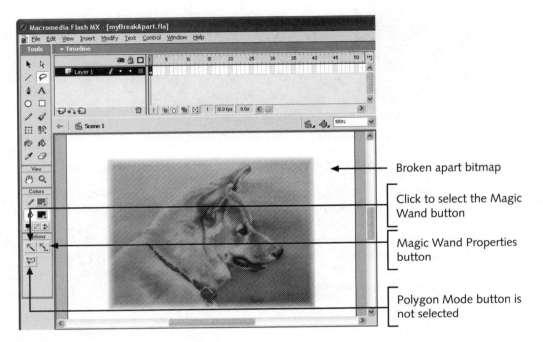

Figure 4-14   Lasso tool options

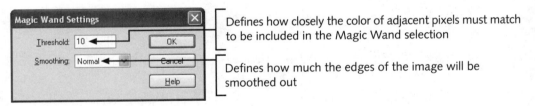

Figure 4-15   Magic Wand Settings dialog box

7. Click to select a like color range. For example, you can select the darker brown areas of the dog's nose. You select similar colors so you can modify them all at once.

8. Save **myBreakApart.fla**, and leave it open in the Flash window.

As Figure 4-16 illustrates, you can also use the Arrow and Subselection tools to select fill areas and move the vector points. You can also recolor those selections with the Paint Bucket tool.

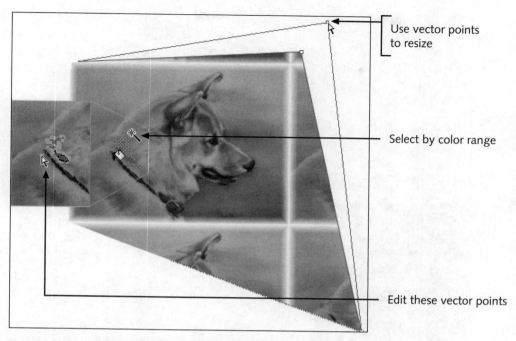

Use vector points
to resize

Select by color range

Edit these vector points

4

Figure 4-16   Dragging and coloring selected areas of a bitmap

Applying Bitmaps as Fills

Using bitmaps as fills is a creative way to fill other shapes or objects with textures and patterns. After breaking apart a bitmap, you can select one part with the Eyedropper tool and fill another object with tiles of the bitmap image. Figure 4-17 shows an example of what a bitmap fill can look like.

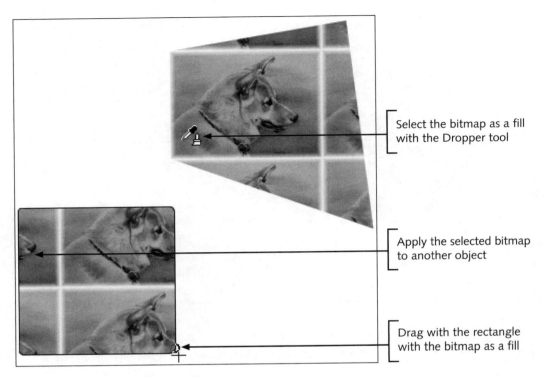

Select the bitmap as a fill with the Dropper tool

Apply the selected bitmap to another object

Drag with the rectangle with the bitmap as a fill

Figure 4-17   Sample bitmap fill

Creating a Bitmap Fill

To fill an object with a bitmap, you first click part of a bitmap with the Eyedropper tool. Doing so selects the bitmap image as a fill. Then you can apply the bitmap to an object using one of the techniques described in the following list and shown in Figure 4-18.

- Select the Brush tool, and paint the tiled bitmap pattern on the Stage. This creates an object that you can further select, manipulate, or delete.

- Use the Paint Bucket tool to fill an existing object.

- Use the Paint Bucket tool to create a new shape with the bitmap as its fill. Choose the Rectangle or Oval tool, and drag on the Stage as you normally would.

To create the bitmap fill:

1. With myBreakApart.fla still open, click the **Eyedropper** tool in the toolbox, and then click the bitmap. A miniature picture appears in the Current Fill icon, representing the selected bitmap.

2. With the Rectangle tool, draw a square on the Stage. As you draw, notice that the square fills with the selected bitmap.

3. Save **myBreakApart.fla**, and then close the file.

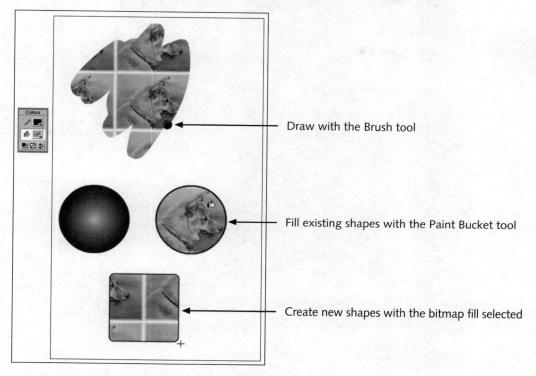

Draw with the Brush tool

Fill existing shapes with the Paint Bucket tool

Create new shapes with the bitmap fill selected

Figure 4-18   Three methods to use a bitmap as a fill

Editing a Bitmap Fill

After you fill an object with a bitmap, you might want to edit the results. Flash lets you edit the bitmap fill by scaling, rotating, moving, or skewing the fill pattern. This is accomplished by using the Free Transform tool to select one tile of the patterned fill. When you use the Free Transform tool to click a tile, the center point of the tile appears. You can drag the center point to move the entire image within the fill. A border with editing handles called a **bounding box** also appears around the tile. You use the bounding box and the Free Transform tool modifiers to resize, rotate, or skew the fill. To scale a fill, you drag a square editing handle on the bounding box. To rotate or skew a fill, you drag a circular handle on the bounding box. To create a wavy border, you use the **Envelope** modifier, which lets you adjust straight and curved segments to create a wave effect, for example.

Figure 4-19 shows the tools and pointers you can use to edit a bitmap fill.

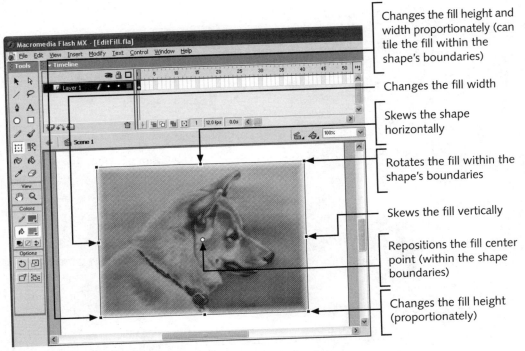

Changes the fill height and width proportionately (can tile the fill within the shape's boundaries)

Changes the fill width

Skews the shape horizontally

Rotates the fill within the shape's boundaries

Skews the fill vertically

Repositions the fill center point (within the shape boundaries)

Changes the fill height (proportionately)

Figure 4-19   Bitmap fill and associated tools and pointers

To edit a bitmap fill:

1. Open the **EditFill.fla** file from the Chapter4 folder in your FlashSamples folder. Save the file as **myEditFill.fla** in the same location. Note that the bitmap in EditFill.fla is already broken apart.

2. Click the **Free Transform** tool in the toolbox. The image's bounding box and editing handles appear, as shown in Figure 4-20.

3. Click the **Rotate and Skew** button in the Options section of the toolbox. Use the circular arrow pointer to click the image's upper-right handle, and then drag to freely rotate the entire image.

4. Click the **Scale** button. Drag the lower-left corner sizing handle to scale the fill proportionally; drag the bottom or left sizing handles to scale only the height or width. Depending on the image, this may distort the height and width ratio and the resulting image.

5. Click the **Distort** button, and then drag a corner handle. That part of the image extends to where you dragged the corner handle. Distorting an image allows you to click a handle, and drag it to any position. For example, you can drag a handle toward the center of an image, independent of the other handles.

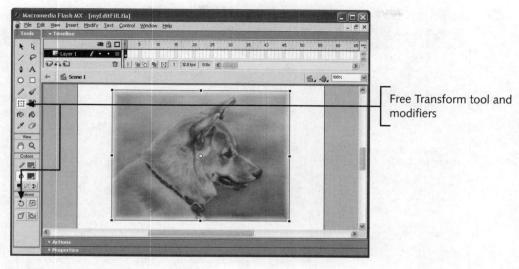

Free Transform tool and modifiers

4

Figure 4-20   Free Tranform tool

6. Click the **Envelope** button. Notice the intermediate circular handles on the bounding box. They are used to create straight and curved segments for a variety of wavy effects. Drag the upper-left and upper-right circular handles toward the image to create a wavy border.

7. Click the **Arrow** tool and then click an empty area to deselect the fill.

8. Save and close **myEditFill.fla**, but leave Flash open for the next set of steps.

Editing a bitmap fill with the Free Transform tool changes every instance of that bitmap in the library, not only the selected bitmap.

USING SOUND MEDIA TO ENHANCE MOVIES

Adding sound files to your movies can make them more appealing and informative. Flash efficiently compresses sound files while preserving quality, as it does with graphics. This means that you can use sound in a Flash movie without significantly increasing the file size. You can also import and coordinate sounds within your animation to provide feedback to your audience, such as with button clicks; and import uninterrupted streaming music and audio clips orchestrated on a frame in the Timeline.

Flash works with the sound file formats listed and described in Table 4-2.

Table 4-2   Sound file formats in Flash

Sound format	Description
WAV (Windows)	A wave file, also know as WAV, is a standard uncompressed raw audio data file created by Microsoft. A WAV file is identified by a file extension of .wav and is used primarily in PCs, although it has been accepted as a viable interchange medium for other computer platforms, such as Macintosh (QuickTime 4 required). The WAV format stores information about the number of tracks (mono or stereo), sample rate, and bit depth in a sound file.
AIFF (Macintosh)	AIFF (Audio Interchange File Format) is a common audio file format used on the Apple Macintosh. An AIFF file contains the raw audio data, channel information (mono or stereo), bit depth, and sample rate. The extension for this file type is .aif. QuickTime 4 is required to import AIFF files in the Windows version of Flash.
MP3 (both platforms)	MP3 (Moving Picture Experts Group, Audio Layer III) is a compression format that shrinks audio files without sacrificing sound quality by stripping out frequencies that are in the outer range of what the human ear recognizes.

If you have QuickTime 4 or later installed on your system, you can import and use these additional sound file formats or multiple platforms in Flash:

- Sound Designer II (Macintosh only)
- Sound Only QuickTime Movies (Windows or Macintosh)
- Sun AU (Windows or Macintosh)
- System 7 Sounds (Macintosh only)
- WAV (Windows or Macintosh)

You can use the audio files provided in the Flash Sounds Common Library, or you can import a compatible file just as you would a graphic file. When you import a sound file, Flash displays it in the Library panel for that document. When you add a sound to a Flash document, and then select a frame in the Timeline that contains the sound, the Property inspector displays the properties of that sound. You can then use the Property inspector to select or edit a sound and choose a synchronization method.

Sound files can use considerable amounts of disk space and RAM if they are not compressed. MP3 sound data, however, is compressed and smaller than WAV or AIFF sound data. Generally, when using WAV or AIFF files, use 16-bit 22 kHz mono sounds (stereo uses twice as much data as mono), although Flash can import either 8- or 16-bit sounds at sample rates of 11 kHz, 22 kHz, or 44 kHz. Flash can convert sounds to lower sample rates when you export.

You can find and download MP3 and other sound files on a variety of Web sites. However, unless an audio file is clearly marked as in the public domain, it is probably protected under copyright law. Recent legal actions have limited the free distribution of MP3 files. Make sure you purchase or otherwise have a legal right to use sound files you download from Web sites.

Insert Streaming Sound on a Timeline

When you access sound files on a Web site, they play only after they are completely downloaded. **Streaming sound**, on the other hand, starts playing as soon as enough sound data has been downloaded to the first few frames in a Flash movie. Streaming sound is associated with specific frames on the Timeline and is designed for playback over the Internet via a Web browser. Playing sound over the Internet is affected by your viewers' connection and computer speed. Flash coordinates images and sounds, but passes over frames if the animation cannot keep up with the audio, most likely causing a stutter in the animation.

In the following steps, you open a Flash file, import a WAV file, add it to the Timeline, and modify its effects. The sound file is designed to play as a sound effect during an animation.

To insert streaming audio:

1. Open the **StreamingAudio.fla** file from the Chapter4 folder in your FlashSamples folder. Save the file as **myStreamingAudio.fla** in the same location. This file contains a sample animation.

2. To import StreamingSample.wav, click **File** on the menu bar, and then click **Import**. In the Import dialog box, click the **Files of type** list arrow (click the **Show** list arrow on the Macintosh), click **All Sound Formats**, navigate to your Chapter4 folder, if necessary, and then double-click **StreamingSample.wav**. Press **Ctrl+L** (**Cmd+L** on the Macintosh) to open the Library panel, if necessary, to see that the StreamingSample.wav file is added to the movie's library.

3. Create a new layer for the sound. Click the **Insert Layer** icon on the Timeline. Double-click the new layer and rename it **Audio**.

4. With the Audio layer selected, drag the **StreamingSample.wav** file from the Library panel to the Stage. The Timeline shows a sound wave icon on the current frame, as in Figure 4-21.

5. Click the **title bar** of the Property inspector, if necessary, to open it. In the Audio layer, click **frame 1**, the frame with the sound wave icon. The Property inspector lists the sound effects, synchronization methods, and looping options, as shown in Figure 4-22.

6. Make sure that StreamingSample.wav appears in the Sound text box. (If it does not, click the **Sound** list arrow, and then click **StreamingSample.wav**). Note that the Sound list contains imported sounds and any other sounds included in the Sound library for the current document.

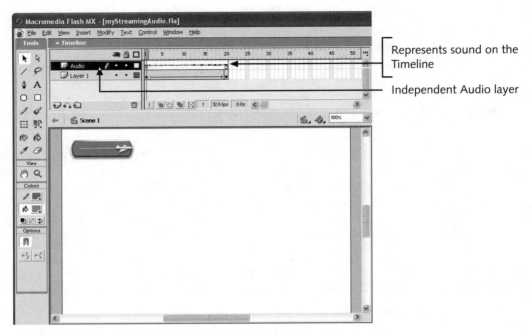

Figure 4-21   Sound represented on the Timeline

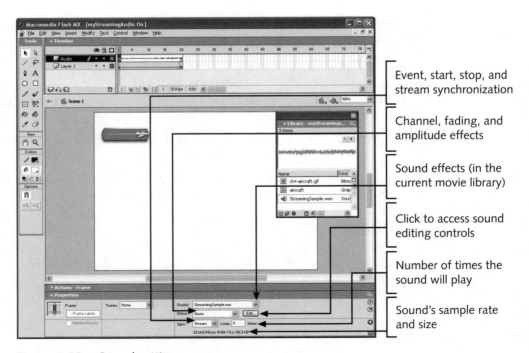

Figure 4-22   Sound settings

7. Click the **Effect** list arrow. These effects let you manipulate the channels to play on, fading options, and custom options that you define yourself:

   ■ None applies no effects, and removes any effects previously applied.

   ■ Left Channel/Right Channel plays sound in the left or right channel only.

   ■ Fade Left to Right/Fade Right to Left shifts the sound from one channel to the other.

   ■ Fade In gradually increases the amplitude of a sound over its duration.

   ■ Fade Out gradually decreases the amplitude of a sound over its duration.

   ■ Custom lets you create your own In and Out points of sound using the Edit Envelope.

8. Click **Fade Out**.

9. Click the **Sync** list arrow. These options allow you to specify the following synchronization settings:

   ■ Event coordinates the sound to respond to an event, such as a user clicking a button. It plays at its starting keyframe to its end, independent of the Timeline, even if the movie stops.

   ■ Start is the same as Event, except that if the sound is already playing, a new instance of the sound is started.

   ■ Stop silences the specified sound.

   ■ Stream synchronizes the sound specifically for playing on a Web site and stops if the animation stops. Flash forces animation to keep pace with stream and skips frames if Flash can't animate the frames quickly enough.

10. Ensure Stream is selected in the Sync text box.

11. In the Loops text box, type **2**. This value determines how many times you want to play the sound.

12. To test the movie, click **Control** on the menu bar and then click **Test Movie**. To hear the sound, you must have a sound card or adapter and speakers already operating on your computer. To stop testing the movie, close the test window.

13. Save and close **myStreamingAudio.fla**, but leave Flash open for the next set of steps.

 Adding sound to its own layer is a good practice because it allows you to easily select and modify your sounds.

Button Event Sounds

In addition to streaming sound, you can also add event sounds in Flash. An **event sound** plays when an event occurs, such as a user clicking a button. Adding sounds to button events is more than an appealing feature in Flash. Usability expert Jakob Nielson, in his book, *Designing Web Usability* writes, "The main benefit of audio is that it provides a channel that is separate from that of the display. Audio can be used to provide a sense of place or mood, as done to perfection in the game Myst. Non-speech sound effects can be used as an extra dimension in the user interface to inform users about background events. Good-quality sound is known to enhance the user experience substantially."

Sound events provide feedback to your audience about their selections. For example, you can add sounds to a button's Over and Down frames. The Over frame plays the sound when a user points to the button without clicking. The Down frame plays a sound when a user clicks the button. Though less common, you can also add sounds to your button's Up and Hit frames. When a user moves the mouse pointer from the button, the Up frame plays the sound; the Hit frame plays a sound when the user releases the mouse button.

In the following steps, you add sound from the Flash sounds Common Library to a button's Over and Down frames.

To add a sound to button events:

1. Open the **ButtonSound.fla** file from the Chapter4 folder in your FlashSamples folder. Save the file as **myButtonSound.fla** in the same location. A button symbol is already created and placed on the Stage and in the Library panel for you, as shown in Figure 4-23. (Press **Ctrl+L**—**Cmd+L** on the Macintosh—to open the Library panel, if necessary.)

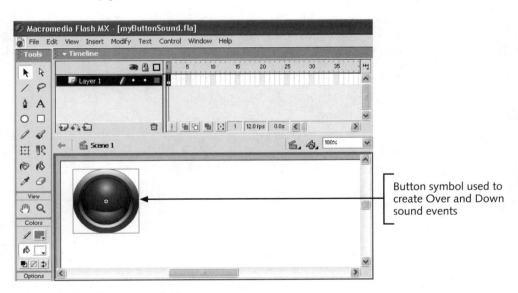

Button symbol used to create Over and Down sound events

Figure 4-23   Button symbol

2. Right-click the button in the Library panel (Ctrl+click on the Macintosh), and then click **Edit** to open the button in symbol-editing mode. In editing mode, four special frames are available to you in the Timeline: Up, Over, Down, and Hit.

3. Click the **Over** frame in Layer 1.

4. Open the Flash Sounds Common Library. Click **Window** on the menu bar, point to **Common Libraries**, and then click **Sounds**.

5. In the Flash Sounds Common Library, expand the Library-Sounds panel, if necessary, drag **Stick Hit** to the Stage to associate this sound with the button event.

6. Click the **Over** frame again in Layer 1 to examine the properties of the Stick Hit sound. In the Property inspector, the Effect list box should show None, the Sync list box should show Event, and the Loop text box should show zero.

7. Click the **Down** frame on Layer 1.

8. From the Flash Sounds Common Library, drag **Brick Drops** to the Stage. Click the **Down** frame again on Layer 1. Your frame and sound properties should resemble those shown in Figure 4-24.

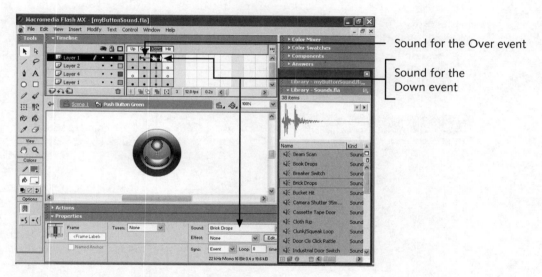

Figure 4-24 Frame and sound settings

9. Click the **Scene 1** link to leave editing mode and return to the main Stage.

10. Test the button by clicking **Control** on the menu bar and then clicking **Test Movie**. Point to and click the button to hear the sounds associated with those events. Close the test window when you're finished.

11. Save **myButtonSound.fla**, and leave it open in Flash for the next set of steps.

If you intend to assign sound to your button's Hit frame, you must also have an image in the Hit frame, even if it is transparent. Without the image, your button will not play the sound.

Customizing Sound Export Settings

Flash compresses audio to save file size, but may degrade sound quality while doing so. As with graphic images, you must balance the tradeoff between sound file size and quality. The compression settings you choose depend on your audience, their connection and computer speed, and the type of Flash movie you are designing. Obviously, the quality degradation for shorter sounds like button clicks is minor compared to streaming audio or looping sound tracks. You can take one of two approaches to modifying compression settings: Change the individual sound setting in the current movie's Library panel, or change sound settings all at once in the Publish Settings dialog box. In this section, you can explore changing the individual sound settings. Using the Publish Settings dialog box is covered in more detail in Chapter 9, "Optimizing and Publishing Flash Movies."

You use the Export Settings area of the Sound Properties dialog box to choose the sound compression preferences. The options change depending on the compression method you select. In this section, you examine the library's sound settings with the following compression methods: ADPCM, MP3, Raw, and Speech. The Publish Settings dialog box uses the default compression settings when you export your movie if you select no changes, or keep the Default compression option. For sounds in the Library panel for the current document, double-click the sound icon in the library to open the Sound Properties dialog box, as in Figure 4-25.

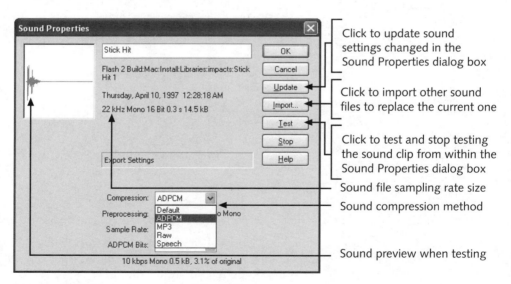

Figure 4-25   Sound Properties dialog box

ADPCM Compression

Adaptive differential pulse-code modulation (ADPCM) is a method for translating analog information to binary information (a string of 0s and 1s). This is performed by taking frequent samples of the sound and expressing the value of the sampled sound modulation in binary terms. Practically, the ADPCM compression option sets compression for 8-bit or 16-bit sound data and is most useful when you are exporting shorter event sounds such as button clicks.

In the following steps, you examine the Sound Properties dialog box for a button click in the Library panel.

To set the ADPCM options:

1. With **myButtonSound.fla** open in Flash, double-click the **Stick Hit** sound icon in the Library-Sounds panel to open the Sound Properties dialog box.

2. Click the **Compression** list arrow, and then click **ADPCM**. The related sample and bit rate options appear in the dialog box. See Figure 4-26.

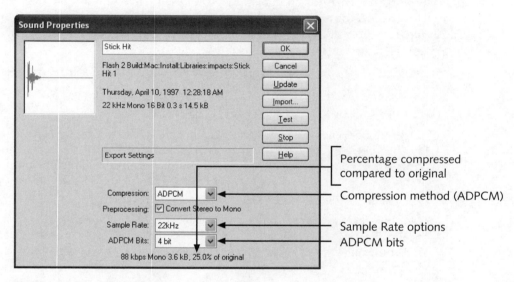

Figure 4-26   ADPCM compression settings

3. Click the **Convert Stereo to Mono** check box to select it for the Preprocessing option, if necessary. Choosing this option conserves file size.

4. Click the **Sample Rate** list arrow, and then click **5kHz** to minimize the file size, which is appropriate for short sounds. Ideally, you should experiment with different sounds and formats to balance the sound quality and file size. The other rate options are as follows:

   - 11 kHz is the lowest recommended quality for a short segment of music.
   - 22 kHz is a popular choice for streaming Web playback.
   - 44 kHz is the standard CD audio rate.

5. Click the **ADPCM Bits** list arrow, and then click **2 bit** to reduce the file size.

6. Click **OK** to save your settings.

7. To test the quality of your changes, click the **Play** button on the Library panel.

8. Save and close **myButtonSound.fla**, but leave Flash open for the next set of steps.

Double-clicking a library symbol name lets you rename the symbol instead of opening its Properties dialog box.

MP3 Compression

MP3 is a standard format for compressing a sound sequence into a very small file (about one-twelfth the size of the original file) while maintaining the original level of sound quality when it is played. Using the MP3 format is a very good choice when you are exporting longer stream sounds such as music sound tracks.

In the following steps, you set MP3 options by opening the Sound Properties dialog box for a sound loop.

To set MP3 options:

1. Open the **StreamingSound.fla** file from the Chapter4 folder in your FlashSamples folder. Save the file as **myStreamingSound.fla** in the same location. An MP3 file is already imported and placed on the Timeline and in the Library panel for you. (Press **Ctrl+L—Cmd+L** on the Macintosh—to open the Library panel, if necessary.)

2. Double-click the **Intro Music** sound icon in the Library panel to open the Sound Properties dialog box. The MP3 compression format is already selected for you as it was recognized by Flash. Make sure Convert Stereo to Mono is selected for the Preprocessing option.

3. Click the **Bit Rate** list arrow and then click **16 kbps**. Flash supports a bit rate from 8 kbps to 160 kbps. For music loops and sound tracks, select 16 kbps to minimize the file size and preserve the quality of the imported MP3. Ideally, you should experiment with different values, and measure the published file size compared to audible quality. As you select options, the bottom of the Sound Properties dialog box displays kbps and shows how much the sound was compressed.

4. Click the **Quality** list arrow, and then click **Medium**. This option sets the value to determine how fast the sound is compressed as the movie is published. The Quality options are as follows:

   - Fast yields a more rapid compression, but reduced sound quality.

   - Medium compresses more slowly, but creates a higher quality sound.

   - Best compresses the slowest, but provides the best quality.

5. Click the **Test** button to preview the sound.

6. Click **OK** when you are satisfied with your selection.

7. Save and close **myStreamingSound.fla**, but leave Flash open for the next set of steps.

Raw Compression

The Raw compression method is exported with no compression at all and is generally not used over the Internet. This method is suitable for Flash movies delivered on a CD-ROM, for example, and played on a computer with substantial processing power and memory. In the Sound Properties dialog box, you can select Raw from the Compression list and pre-process the file by selecting Convert Stereo to Mono to convert mixed stereo sounds to mono and to minimize file size. For Sample Rate, select an option to control the sound's file size and quality. Rate options are as follows:

- 5 kHz is barely acceptable for speech.

- 11 kHz is the lowest recommended quality for a short segment of music.

- 22 kHz is a popular choice for Web playback.

- 44 kHz is the standard CD audio rate.

Speech Compression

The speech compression method is new to Flash MX and exports with a compression algorithm especially for speech sound. Speech requires less bandwidth overhead, so a sample rate between 5 and 11 kHz is appropriate.

INTEGRATING QUICKTIME MOVIES

Apple is the creator of QuickTime, a multimedia development, storage, and playback technology. QuickTime has become the media standard application for multimedia playback on your computer. QuickTime files combine sound, text, animation, and video in a single file and can be recognized by their filename extensions: .qt, .mov, and .moov. Using a QuickTime player that is already installed in a Web browser or can be downloaded from Apple, you can view and control brief multimedia sequences, shown in Figure 4-27. You can integrate a QuickTime movie into your Flash movie, add animation to it, and then export it again from Flash to a QuickTime format.

Figure 4-27   Apple QuickTime player version 5

 The QuickTime player also provides a way to play WAV files on a Macintosh computer and AIFF files on the Windows operating system.

Importing and Publishing QuickTime Movies

Importing a QuickTime file is similar to importing a graphic file—you use the Import dialog box to locate and select the file. After you import the QuickTime movie and it appears on the Stage in its own layer, you need to find on which frame the movie ends so you can determine the length of any tweens or animation you want to add. To determine where to place additional elements, drag the playhead on your Timeline after the movie sequence, and see where the QuickTime movie stops appearing on your Stage. Flash MX also prompts you to either embed or link the imported video. To integrate any Flash animation techniques into a QuickTime movie and then export it back into a QuickTime medium, you link to an external video file. In the next section, "Editing Macromedia Flash Native Video," you will explore other video techniques. You cannot play a QuickTime movie in SWF format, but you can embed the video inside the Flash movie, where it is converted to Flash video for playback in SWF; when you are finished working with the imported QuickTime movie, you must publish the Flash file as a QuickTime movie.

In the following steps, you import a QuickTime movie. Note that if you are working on a Macintosh, you need the latest version of QuickTime.

To import a QuickTime movie into Flash:

1. Open the **AnimatingQuickTime.fla** file from the Chapter4 folder in your FlashSamples folder. Save the file as **myAnimatingQuickTime.fla** in the same location. A QuickTime layer has already been added to this file, as shown in Figure 4-28.

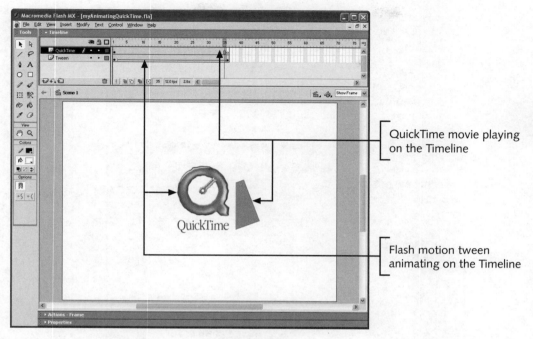

QuickTime movie playing
on the Timeline

Flash motion tween
animating on the Timeline

Figure 4-28   QuickTime movie and tweened layers

2. Click the **QuickTime** layer, click **File** on the menu bar, and then click **Import**.

3. In the Import dialog box, click the **Files of type** list arrow (click the **Show** list arrow on the Macintosh), and then click **All Video Formats**. Locate **AnimateQuickTime.mov** and then click **Open**. The Import Video dialog box appears. Click the **Link to external video file** option button, and then click **OK**. The Link to external video file option allows you to republish the Flash animation and the imported QuickTime video back into the QuickTime format. The embedding option retains the video in the Flash published environment.

4. A dialog box appears indicating the amount of frames the video will take. Click **Yes** to insert the default number of frames. The first frame of the movie appears on the Stage.

 If a rectangle with an "x" appears in place of the QuickTime frame, you know your playhead is on a frame beyond the end of the .mov file.

5. Drag to move the playhead to the last frame in the .mov file, frame 60. Recall that you indicate where the movie ends because you will not want your added Flash animation to exceed the number of frames of your QuickTime movie.

6. Insert or delete frames so that both movies have the same number of frames. Delete any extra frames that exceed any other layers' frames by right-clicking them, and then click the **Remove Frames** command.

7. Test your movie by using the Controller toolbar. Click **Window** on the menu bar, point to **Toolbars**, and then click **Controller** to open the Controller toolbar. Click the **Play** button on the Controller toolbar. The QuickTime movie plays. See Figure 4-29.

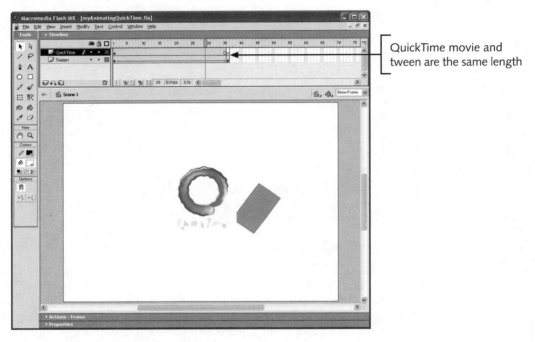

Figure 4-29   QuickTime movie playing

8. To publish your movie, click **File** on the menu bar, and then click **Publish Settings**. The Publish Settings dialog box will look as shown in Figure 4-30.

9. Click the **Formats** tab to display all available formats Flash supports during an export.

10. Click to select only the **HTML**, **Flash**, and **QuickTime** check boxes. (The Flash format is automatically selected when you click the HTML format.)

11. Click the **HTML** tab. Click the **Template** list arrow, and then ensure that **QuickTime** is selected.

12. Click the **Publish** button, and then click the **OK** button. The integrated QuickTime and Flash movie appears in your default browser.

13. Save and close **myAnimatingQuickTime.fla**, but leave Flash open for the next set of steps.

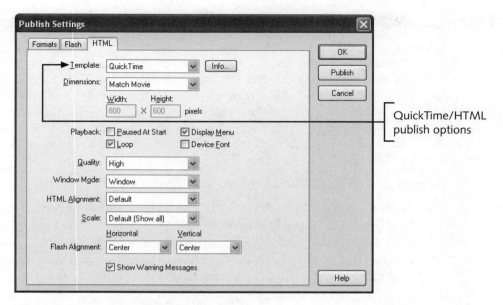

Figure 4-30   Publish Settings dialog box

Testing the integrated movie with the Test Movie command on the Control menu does not display the QuickTime object. You must publish the Flash movie as a QuickTime movie .mov file. You can use the Publish Preview command on the File menu after changing the Publish Settings to preview in the QuickTime format.

EDITING MACROMEDIA FLASH NATIVE VIDEO

With prior versions of Flash, you were able to use video only with QuickTime. Now with Flash MX, you can embed video directly into your Flash MX SWF generated file without needing to use QuickTime or another application. Several video formats are supported for import such as QuickTime (.mov), Motion Picture Experts Group (.mpg and .mpeg), Digital Video (DV), and Audio Video Interleave (.avi). Flash has its own compression with the Sorenson Spark video codec. A **codec** is a **co**mpression/**dec**ompression algorithm that reduces the number of bytes consumed by large files. The Sorenson Spark codec uses both spatial and temporal compression methods. **Spatial** compression is applied to a single video frame compressing it as a single .JPG image would be compressed, affecting the overall video quality. **Temporal** compression recognizes the differences between consecutive frames and stores only those frame differences with the compressed file called **interframes**. This greatly reduces the size of the video file.

For more information regarding Sorenson and the Sorenson Spark codec, visit *www.sorenson.com*.

Importing and Compressing Video in Macromedia Flash MX

To import and compress video with Flash, you import the video file as you do any media type. The imported video file plays in your published SWF file where it appears on the Stage. When importing the video file, the Import Video dialog box lets you choose to embed the video in the Flash document instead of linking to an external QuickTime file. After you embed a video, you can configure it by using the Import Video Settings dialog box to set compression options such as quality, keyframe interval, dimensions, whether to synchronize to Flash frame rates, the number of frames to encode per Flash frame, and whether to import audio as well as video.

The following list describes the options in the Import Video Settings dialog box:

- **Quality** governs the overall image quality of the exported video. The higher the quality setting, the better the video quality, but the larger the file size.

- **Keyframe interval** determines how often a full video frame is preserved on the Flash Timeline. Using a high keyframe interval value is most likely a good practice to reduce file size and overhead, and results in fewer keyframes.

- **Scale** determines the video's dimensions in relation to the imported video file.

- **Synchronize video to Macromedia Flash document frame rate** matches the rate of imported video frames to your Flash frame rate. Without this option, Flash assigns a one-to-one ratio video to Flash frame, which can cause the video to play slower or faster depending on the video's internal frame rate.

- **Number of video frames to encode per number of Macromedia Flash frames** specifies the ratio of imported video frames to Flash frames on the Timeline. By decreasing the number of video frames per Flash frames, you reduce the choppiness of a video that plays faster than a Flash movie.

- **Import audio** allows you to either include or not include the audio track from the video, if one exists.

To import and embed a .mov movie file:

1. Open **EmbedVideo.fla** from the Chapter4 folder in your FlashSamples folder. Save the file as **myEmbedVideo.fla** in the same location.

2. Click **File** on the menu bar, and then click **Import**.

3. In the Import dialog box, locate **EmbedQuickTime.mov** and then click **Open**. The Import Video dialog box appears. Click the **Embed video in Macromedia Flash document** option button, then click **OK**. The Import Video Settings dialog box appears, shown in Figure 4-31.

4. Enter **75** in the Quality text box.

5. Type **24** in the Keyframe interval text box, if necessary.

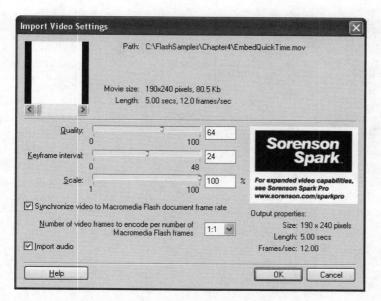

Figure 4-31   Video Import Settings dialog box

6. Make sure the 100 appears for the Scale option, and the Synchronize video to Macromedia Flash document frame rate box is checked. Keep the Number of video frames to encode per number of Macromedia Flash frames option at a 1:1 ratio. Also make sure the Import audio box is checked.

7. Click **OK** to import the video. Then click **Yes** to continue. If a Resolve Library conflict dialog box opens, make sure the **Don't replace existing items** option button is selected, and then click **OK**. Your Stage should resemble Figure 4–32.

8. Test the document and movie by clicking **File** on the menu bar, pointing to **Publish Preview**, and then clicking **Default**. Save **myEmbedVideo.fla**, and then close Flash.

Figure 4-32 Video on the Stage

CHAPTER SUMMARY

❐ Adobe Illustrator and Macromedia Freehand are sophisticated drawing programs that create vector images. These programs are common tools of choice for graphic illustrators, who may often provide vector images for you. Flash lets you integrate both raster and vector formats in a single file that conserves file size while providing high quality.

❐ Bitmap or raster images are generally larger in file size because they contain more visual information. You can use compression tools provided in programs such as Adobe Photoshop or JASC PaintShop Pro to reduce the image's file size before importing it into Flash. Compressing images decreases their file size by removing or replacing image data.

❐ Flash supports a wide range of bitmap images including bitmap (.bmp), GIF (.gif), JPEG (.jpg, .jpeg), PNG (.png), and PICT (.pct, .pic).

❐ You can import and coordinate sounds within your animation to create interactive feedback. Sounds include button clicks, streaming music, and audio clips coordinated on a frame in the Timeline. Flash efficiently compresses sound files while preserving quality, as it does with graphics.

❏ By adding sound files to your movies, you can make your Flash movies more appealing and informative. Flash efficiently compresses sound files while preserving quality, as it does with graphics. This means that you can use sound in a Flash movie without significantly increasing the file size.

❏ QuickTime, and now native Flash video, have become a standard program for multimedia playback on your computer. QuickTime files combine sound, text, animation, and video in a single file. You can view and control brief multimedia sequences with the QuickTime player. You can integrate QuickTime movies into your Flash movies, add animation to them, and then export them again from Flash to a QuickTime format.

❏ Flash MX uses its own compression with the Sorenson Spark video codec with both spatial and temporal compression methods.

4

REVIEW QUESTIONS

1. Flash imports vector images from Freehand while retaining vectors and layers. True or false?

2. You can edit imported Illustrator files only after you _____ them.

3. You _____ a bitmap image to reduce its file size.

4. Which of the following file formats is *not* used for bitmaps?
   a. GIF
   b. bitmap
   c. JIFF
   d. PICT

5. Use the _____ technique to smooth the edges of an image.

6. Bitmap images can be converted into vector objects within Flash. True or false?

7. You can edit imported bitmap images in Flash by using the _____ command first.

8. Which of the following audio formats can Flash import?
   a. AIFF
   b. MP3
   c. WAV
   d. all of the above

9. _____ is a common audio format for streaming music.

10. Streaming audio is downloaded entirely before it plays. True or false?

11. You can work with event sounds and button symbols to give audio feedback to your audience. True or false?

12. Flash can import a QuickTime movie, let you edit it, and then export it again to a QuickTime format. True or false?

13. _____ are the beginning and ending points on a line or curve segment.

14. The Bitmap Properties dialog box controls the following properties:

    a. Allow smoothing

    b. Compression

    c. Use default document quality

    d. all of the above

15. You cannot embed video directly into your Flash MX SWF generated file without the need for QuickTime. True or false?

HANDS-ON PROJECTS

Project 4-1

In this project, you import a vector image of a graph in an Adobe Illustrator format, and edit the grouped object. You recolor all the graph bars and legend symbols to reflect a new color scheme.

1. Start Flash MX, if necessary, and open **Graph.fla** from the Chapter4\Projects folder in your FlashSamples folder. Save the file as **myGraph.fla** in the same location.

2. Import the Illustrator file **Graph.ai**. Choose to convert layers in Illustrator to layers in Flash. Note that the file imports as a grouped vector object.

3. If necessary, click the object to select it. See Figure 4-33.

4. Click Modify on the menu bar, and then click Ungroup. Click a blank spot on the Stage to deselect the objects.

5. Click any bar in the graph to select that group of graph bars. All bars are now selected.

6. Right-click the selected group, and then click Edit Selected on the shortcut menu. The Edit Selected command allows you to edit the group temporarily, without having to ungroup the objects again; the surrounding objects are dimmed, indicating they are not selectable. This is similar to the Edit in Place command for Flash-drawn objects.

7. Click any bar to select the bar and legend group. Click Modify on the menu bar, and then click Ungroup. This ungroups the bars from the legend.

8. Click any bar to select that group of bars. Click Modify on the menu bar, and then click Ungroup. This ungroups the bars, but leaves the bar colors grouped.

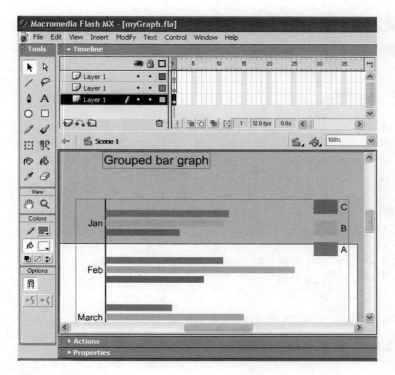

4

Figure 4-33

9. Click the one green bar to select it. Click Modify on the menu bar, and then click Ungroup. This breaks the green bar down to its individual pixels for further editing.

10. Click the Fill Color tool, and then click a dark blue color (hex #333366) as its fill. Click the green bar to fill it with the dark blue.

11. Repeat Steps 8 through 10 for the remaining two bars and the legend key. See Figure 4-34.

12. Notice the Scene 1 area has several groups in edit mode. To return to the Stage, click the Scene 1 link.

13. Save and close **myGraph.fla**, but leave Flash open for the next project.

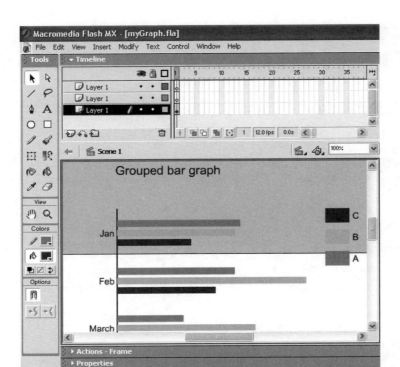

Figure 4-34

Project 4-2

In this project, you import a bitmap image, edit the symbol's properties to compress it, and then compare the image quality and file size of the results. Then you use the Trace Bitmap command and create a textured fill with the bitmap.

1. Open **Bitmap.fla** from the Chapter4\Projects folder in your FlashSamples folder. Save the file as **myBitmap.fla** in the same location.

2. Import the **Bitmap.jpg** image file from the Chapter4\Projects folder in your FlashSamples folder. See Figure 4-35.

3. Use the Property inspector to scale the image to approximately 243 pixels in height and 200 pixels in width.

4. Click Modify on the menu bar, and then click Break Apart so that you can select parts of the bitmap.

5. Use the Eyedropper tool to select the bitmap as a fill.

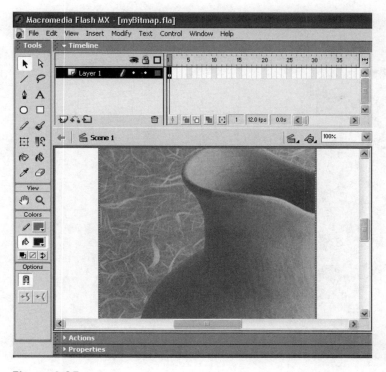

Figure 4-35

6. Click the Rectangle tool and draw a rectangle, using the bitmap as a fill. See Figure 4–36.

7. Save and close **myBitmap.fla**, but leave Flash open for the next project.

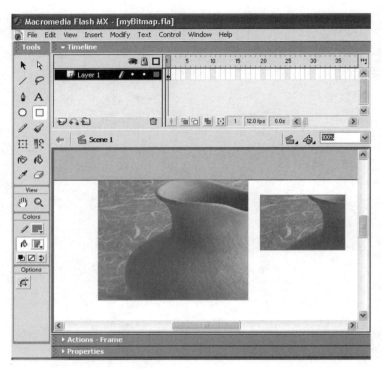

Figure 4-36

Project 4-3

In this project, you assign a sound to a navigation button on its Over and Down frames.

1. Open **NavButton.fla** from the Chapter4\Projects folder in your FlashSamples folder. Scroll to the upper-left corner of the Stage, if necessary, to see a button symbol named myButton on the Stage with its own layer named Navigation. Save the document as **myNavButton.fla** in the same location.

2. Import **ButtonDown.wav** and **ButtonOver.wav** into the movie library with the Import command. See Figure 4-37

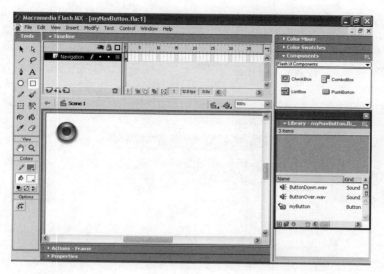

Figure 4-37

3. Use the Arrow tool to double-click the symbol on the Stage, which opens the button in editing mode and shows the button's Timeline.

4. Click the Over frame on Layer 4 to select the frame.

5. Drag the ButtonOver.wav file onto the Stage from the Library panel. Notice the audio symbol on the frame appears, indicating there is sound on that frame.

6. Click the Down frame on Layer 1 to select the frame.

7. Drag the ButtonDown.wav file onto the Stage. Again, notice the audio symbol on the frame appear indicating there is sound on that frame.

8. Click Scene 1 to return to the Stage.

9. Click Control on the menu bar, and then click Enable Simple Buttons. This lets you test the button sounds without publishing the file or using the Test Movie command.

10. Position your mouse over the center of the button. You should hear a clicking sound.

11. Click the button. You should hear another sound similar to popping.

12. Save and close **myNavButton.fla**, but leave Flash open for the next project.

Project 4-4

In this project, you create a streaming sound clip in a Flash movie.

1. Open **SoundClip.fla** from the Chapter4\Projects folder in your FlashSamples folder. Save the file as **mySoundClip.fla** in the same location.

2. Insert a keyframe in frame 1. Use the Import to Library command on the File menu to import the audio file **Techno.mp3** from your Chapter4\Projects folder. Flash adds the file to the library for the mySoundClip.fla file.

3. On the Timeline for Layer 1, scroll to the right until you reach frame 300. Click frame 300.

4. Press the F5 key to insert blank frames on frames 1 through 300. See Figure 4-38.

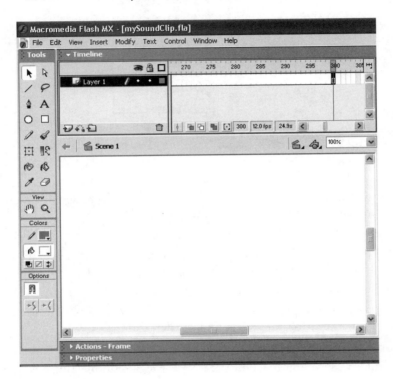

Figure 4-38

5. Scroll back to frame 1, and then click to select it.

6. From the Library panel, drag the audio file to the Stage. The audio appears on all the frames you inserted and will play on those frames until it loops again. (Recall that you can change this setting in the Property inspector.)

7. Test the audio stream by clicking Control on the menu bar and then clicking Play.

8. Save and close **mySoundClip.fla**, but leave Flash open for the next project.

Project 4-5

In this project, you use the Sync option in the Property inspector to start and stop a sound.

1. Open **StartStop.fla** from the Chapter4\Projects folder in your FlashSamples folder. Save it as **myStartStop.fla** in the same location.

2. Import **StartStop.wav** from the Chapter4\Projects folder in your FlashSamples folder.

3. Click frame 10 in the Timeline to select the frame, and then press F6 to insert a keyframe.

4. Drag StartStop.wav from the Library panel to the Stage. Click frame 10 again.

5. In the Property inspector, click the Sync list arrow, and then click Start to start the sound in frame 10 where you inserted the keyframe.

6. Click frame 50 in the Timeline, and then press F6 to insert a keyframe.

7. In the Property inspector, click the Sound list arrow, and then click StartStop.wav.

8. Click the Sync list arrow, and then click Stop to stop the sound in frame 50 where you inserted the keyframe. See Figure 4-39.

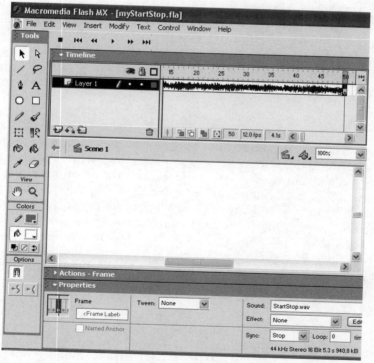

Figure 4-39

9. Test and play your sound frames by using the Controller toolbar. Click Window on the menu bar, point to Toolbars, if necessary, and then click Controller. Use the Play button to start the sound clip.

10. Save and close **myStartStop.fla**. Leave Flash open if you want to complete the Case Projects. Otherwise, exit Flash.

CASE PROJECTS

Case Project 4-1

An engineering firm has hired you to work with their mechanical Computer Aided Design (CAD) department. They have several large CAD files that they use to model a large complex machine in Adobe Illustrator. Import the **Mechanical Part Drawing.ai** file from the Chapter4\Cases folder in the FlashSamples folder, and then break down the large model and segregate it into many smaller pieces in Flash.

Case Project 4-2

A friend's startup band wants to develop a promotional Web site to demonstrate various music clips. You agree to design a Flash Web site with audio streaming to accomplish this. The friend gives you music loops in an MP3 format. Design a small Flash Web site to play the imported MP3 files and see descriptions of the music. You can either create the MP3 samples to stream or visit *www.mp3.com* and *http://launch.yahoo.com/* for MP3 files that are free of copyright.

Case Project 4-3

A small fashion design company asked you to create a Web site displaying a QuickTime video of their new fashion line. The video is in a QuickTime format already, but requires text to be integrated and animated with the videos. Use the Flash importing and editing tools to create a Web page linking to the video. Edit the video with the text and motion tween tools to display and animate the fashion designer's name. Describe and show samples of the clothing line, if possible. For resources and ideas on fashion, visit *www.fashion.net*. For QuickTime resources, go to *www.apple.com/quicktime*. You can link to other sites from these Web sites to find appropriate QuickTime movie files, or you can use AnimatingQuickTime.mov in the Chapter4 folder in the FlashSamples folder.

Case Project 4-4

For this case project, find and import media files for your portfolio or fictional business. Use at least one bitmap file and one sound file. If possible, also use one QuickTime video file. The media files should be related to your interests, or to products and services for your fictional business.

CHAPTER

5

ADVANCED ANIMATION TECHNIQUES

Enhanced Design and Interface Features

> **In this chapter, you will:**
> ◆ Work with complex movies
> ◆ Design movie preloaders
> ◆ Create advanced movie clips and complex buttons
> ◆ Develop animation effects
> ◆ Design and customize interfaces

In Chapters 3 and 4, you learned the basics of designing Macromedia Flash movies with symbols, animation, imported images, audio, and video. In this chapter, you will learn advanced design techniques to make your movies more sophisticated and interactive.

As you design larger and more complex Flash movies, their structure and organization becomes more important. You have already worked with Timelines that have multiple layers; now you will learn how to design and manage more complex movies, called multi-scene and multi-level movies. You create a **multi-scene movie** by adding and managing more than one scene, which often demands careful choreography. As you already know, a movie has one scene by default (Scene 1). Adding new scenes can help you overcome problems such as managing large storyboards, dealing with complex content, and handling frequent changes.

In a **multi-level movie**, you load one movie into another movie's Timeline. You can load a new movie into any frame of the main Timeline, and then layer it on top of the existing movie to create a series of movie segments. This means that you can construct a three-movie Web site, for example, with buttons that allow your audience to load one movie at a time without opening another HTML page. This saves time and memory because the user's browser does not have to request or reload another page, and it creates an efficient design for changes and updates to content and structure.

You can also use a movie preloader to enhance your Flash presentations. A **preloader** contains a few frames that Flash loads into the user's browser before the entire movie loads. The user can then watch the preloader instead of waiting for the main Flash movie to load. You can include text and images in a preloader that display a message to introduce the site and its content. To determine if a preloader will be beneficial, use the Bandwidth Profiler to simulate performance, and view three important factors: the movie playing, movie statistics, and a graph showing your movie as streaming frames or in a frame-by-frame view.

Creating **advanced movie clips** and complicated buttons can make your movies more engaging and provide sophisticated navigation. You have already created simple movie clips when you animated a button in Chapter 3. You can also create advanced movie clips that users can move around the Stage by dragging, and that you control from the main movie. You will also learn how to design complex buttons that have animated states and morphing effects, such as rollover buttons that display different content depending on where the user's mouse points.

To create a more engaging and interactive movie, you can use dynamic animation effects such as blurring effects, fade or dissolve transitions, easing motions, and objects that users can drag. You can also design the interface, the look and feel, of a Flash movie to make movies easier to use. For example, you can use consistent navigation devices, structure information logically, and use color and image effectively to help your audience quickly access your movie's content.

WORKING WITH COMPLEX MOVIES

One way to organize a complex movie is to work with scenes. All Flash movies have one scene by default. To organize a movie thematically, you can use more than one scene. For example, you could use separate scenes for an introduction, the main content, and a summary.

You can manage multiple scenes in three ways. You can use the Scene panel to add, rename, move, copy, and delete scenes. You can navigate scenes by using the Go to command on the View menu, or you can manage scenes using the Edit Scene button, located above the upper-right corner of the Stage. Figure 5-1 shows the Scene panel, Go to Scene menu commands, and the Edit Scene button.

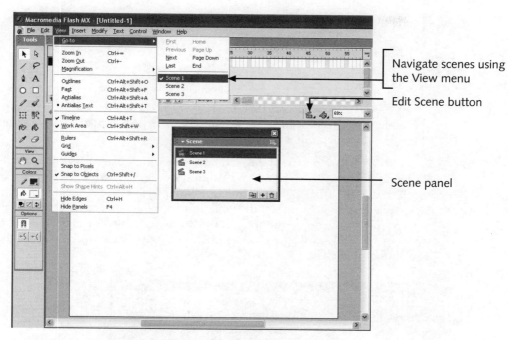

Navigate scenes using the View menu

Edit Scene button

Scene panel

Figure 5-1   Tools for working with scenes

Setting Up Multi-Level Scenes

The best time to use more than one scene is when a movie has a large amount of content or a very long Timeline. Then you can organize the content into scenes. For example, a travel presentation could have scenes named Main, Back Roads, Mountains, Expeditions, and For More Information. When you publish a multi-scene movie, Flash plays the scenes in the order they are listed in the Scene panel. You can also use the actions in the Actions panel to control when scenes play. Each scene has its own Timeline so you can create separate animations and layers, for example, and assign actions to particular frames.

In the following steps, you work with a movie that provides information about Adventure Travel, a fictitious company that provides guided expeditions around the world. The movie already contains two scenes, Main and Whitewater. The Main scene includes a graphic of a mountain and animated topic images for each category of travel—Whitewater, Underwater, Adventure, and Rockclimbing—and also contains a goto action that determines when the Whitewater scene plays. The Whitewater scene includes the same mountain graphic and an animated image of a kayak. You will add a scene to this movie to show rock climbing information, rename the new scene, and then add a rock climbing image to it.

If you receive a Missing Font Warning message in any steps in this chapter, click the "Don't warn me again" check box, and then click the Use Default button.

To add a scene to a movie:

1. Open **AdventureTravel-Scene.fla** from the Chapter5 folder in your FlashSamples folder. Save the document as **myAdventureTravel-Scene.fla** in the same location.

2. Click **Window** on the menu bar, and then click **Scene** to open the Scene panel, which lists the Main and Whitewater scenes, with the Main scene selected. A text label appears in the Timeline in the Actions layer, indicating the purpose of the gotoAndPlay action in the Main scene. Drag the playhead to frame 100 to view the images in this document. See Figure 5-2. (You might need to scroll the Stage and close some panels to see all the images in this document.)

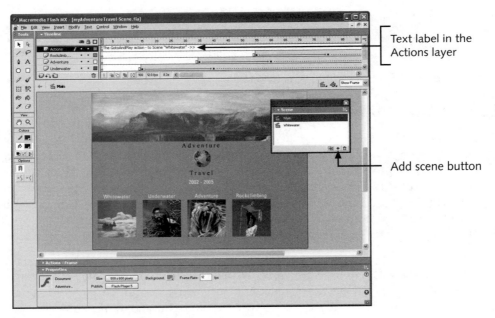

Text label in the Actions layer

Add scene button

Figure 5-2   AdventureTravel-Scene.fla with two scenes

3. In the Scene panel, click **Whitewater** to view its contents. Note that this scene includes the same graphic image of mountains as the Main scene.

4. Add a new scene by clicking the **Add scene** button on the Scene panel. (Point to the buttons on the bottom of the Scene panel to see their names.)

5. A new scene appears in the Scene panel. Double-click the new scene name in the Scene panel, and then type **Rockclimbing** and press **Enter** to rename it.

The Rockclimbing scene currently contains only a gold background, the same background as in the other two scenes.

6. To add the graphic image of mountains to the Rockclimbing scene, open the Library panel by pressing **Ctrl+L** (**Command+L** on the Macintosh). With the Rockclimbing scene selected in the Scene panel, drag the **TopImage** graphic symbol from the Library to the Stage and center it on the top of the Stage, as in the other two scenes.

7. Drag the JPG image **chapter5_rockclimbing_mountain.jpg** to the lower-left corner of the Stage.

8. Save **myAdventureTravel-Scene.fla** and leave it open for the next set of steps.

Now you can add the goto action to the Rockclimbing scene so that when the movie reaches a specified frame, it returns to the Main scene.

To add actions to the new scene:

1. In the Rockclimbing scene Timeline, click **frame 35**, and then press **F6** to add a keyframe. You will add an action to this frame so that the Rockclimbing scene plays until frame 35.

2. To create a layer for the actions in the Rockclimbing scene, click the **Insert Layer** button to add a new layer. (Point to the buttons below the layers to find the Insert Layer button.) Then double-click the new layer and type **Actions** to rename it.

3. In the Actions layer, click **frame 35**, and then press **F7** to insert a blank keyframe.

4. With frame 35 selected, open or expand the Actions panel, if necessary. Make sure the panel is in Normal mode by clicking the **View Options** button—Normal mode should be selected.

5. In the Actions panel, click to expand the Actions and Movie Control categories, if necessary and then double-click **goto** to add the gotoAndPlay command to frame 35. Make sure the Go to and Play option button is selected.

6. Click the **Scene** list arrow, and then click **Main**. Make sure Frame Number appears in the Type text box, and 1 appears in the Frame text box. See Figure 5-3.

7. In the Scene panel, click the **Whitewater** scene. Click **frame 50** in the Actions layer, which contains the Stop action. Because you are adding a new scene, delete the Stop action by clicking **stop();** in the script and then pressing **Delete**.

8. Double-click the **goto** action to add the gotoAndPlay command to frame 50.

9. In the Actions panel, click the **Scene** list arrow, and then click **Rockclimbing**. Make sure Frame Number appears in the Type text box, and 1 appears in the Frame text box.

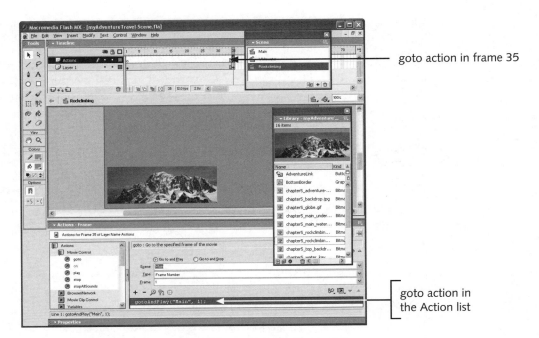

Figure 5-3   Setting the gotoAndPlay action on frame 35

10. To test your movie and the flow of your scenes, click **Control** on the menu bar, and then click **Test Movie**. First the Main scene plays, and images for Whitewater, Underwater, Adventure, and Rockclimbing slide in from the edges of the screen. Then the Whitewater scene plays and the kayak image slides in from the left. Finally, the Rockclimbing scene plays and the rock climbing image appears. Close the test window.

11. Save and close **myAdventureTravel-Scene.fla**, but leave Flash open for the next set of steps.

Designing Multi-Level Movies

Similar to a multi-scene movie, a multi-level movie is separated into logical sections. However, the sections are longer than a scene—they are usually as long and complex as a complete movie. When you create a multi-level movie, you can play additional movies without closing the Flash Player, or switch movies without loading another HTML page. To do so, you use the **load** and **unload** movie actions to start and stop playing a specified movie. You usually assign the load and unload movie actions to navigational buttons in the main movie. The **main movie** is considered the first movie in a series of levels, and is known as level 0. Other movies are loaded on top of level 0 in any order you specify. You layer movies to identify which movie plays when, as illustrated in Figure 5-4. The main movie, however, always remains at level 0.

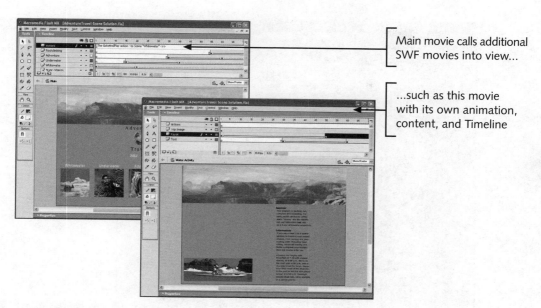

Main movie calls additional SWF movies into view...

...such as this movie with its own animation, content, and Timeline

Figure 5-4   Layering in multi-level movies

You use the load movie action to load SWF files into the current movie level 0. The main movie is considered the **parent** that governs several Stage settings of the **child** movies in the hierarchy of loaded movies. The main movie's Stage determines the following properties of the other movies you load:

- Size
- Background color
- Frame rate
- Registration point

Note that the parent movie defines the registration point of all loaded movies. The **registration point** is the upper-left corner of the parent movie and acts as the focal point for positioning other objects. For example, if you load a child movie that is smaller than the main movie, Flash places the upper-left corner of both movies on top of one another, as shown in Figure 5-5. Suppose you want to show longer, more complex movies in the Adventure Travel presentation. Instead of adding scenes to the movie, you could load other movies from the Main movie.

If you load a child movie that is larger than the main movie, Flash crops the child movie to fit on the smaller Stage of the main movie. To avoid cropping a movie, keep the Stage size the same for all movies.

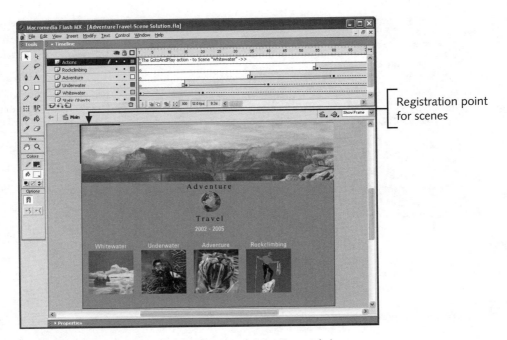

Registration point for scenes

Figure 5-5   Parent and child movies' registration points

Before you can load and unload a movie, you must create a movie in Flash and then publish it to produce an SWF file. When loading movies, you should know where they are located, so be sure to establish and use an organized folder structure for your SWF files. A good practice is to keep all associated HTML and SWF files within one folder. When you use the load movie action, you specify the Uniform Resource Locator (URL). You can specify a full Web server path beginning with http:// followed by the host name, and, finally, the folder structure leading to the HTML and SWF file. This is called the **absolute path** because it begins from the topmost level to identify the location of the files. Figure 5-6 defines each section of a URL that uses an absolute path.

Figure 5-6   Parts of a URL

Instead of an absolute path, you can use a **relative path**, which omits the protocol and domain name, and specifies where the files are in the current working folder. For example, a relative path to the rockclimbing.swf file in the rockclimbing folder of the current folder would be /rockclimbing/rockclimbing.swf. You should use a relative path in the commands for the load movie and unload movie actions because users will play the main movie on a computer different from the one you use when you create the movies. If you use an absolute path to a file on your computer, and users have a folder structure different from yours, Flash won't be able to find the child movies.

In the following steps, you continue to use the Adventure Travel presentation to work with a multi-level movie. Like the AdventureTravel-Scene movie you worked with earlier, the file AdventureTravel-Levels.fla is already set up for you, but is structured to use buttons and multiple SWF files, not automated scenes. The main movie uses the topic images (for the Whitewater, Underwater, Adventure, and Rockclimbing travel categories) as buttons that users can click to load and unload a SWF movie. The Whitewater button loads AdventureTravel-Levels01.swf, and the Underwater button loads AdventureTravel-Levels02. swf. You start by examining the actions associated with these buttons. In the next set of steps, you set up the Adventure and Rockclimbing buttons to load and unload the remaining movie files, AdventureTravel-Levels03.swf and AdventureTravel-Levels04.swf, respectively.

To examine a multi-level movie:

1. Open **AdventureTravel-Levels.fla**, and then save it as **myAdventureTravel-Levels.fla**. (If a dialog box appears warning you about missing fonts, click the "Don't warn me again" check box, and then click the **Use Default** option button.) Notice that this movie has only one scene.

2. Start by examining an action already assigned to a button. Click **frame 100** in the Whitewater layer, and then use the **Arrow** tool to click the **Whitewater** button symbol located on the Stage under the "Whitewater" text. Expand the Actions panel, if necessary.

3. In the Actions panel, click the **loadMovieNum** line of code. See Figure 5-7.

   This action specifies that when the Whitewater button is clicked and released, Flash loads the movie named AdventureTravel-Levels01.swf. The number at the end of the loadMovieNum("AdventureTravel-Levels01.swf", 2); statement, in this case 2, indicates that Flash will play this as a child movie of level 1, the main movie.

4. To examine the action associated with the Underwater button symbol, click **frame 100** in the Underwater layer, click the Underwater button symbol, and then examine the Actions panel. See Figure 5-8.

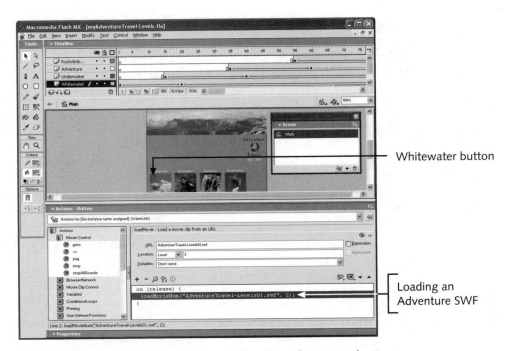

Figure 5-7   Examining the load action for the Whitewater button

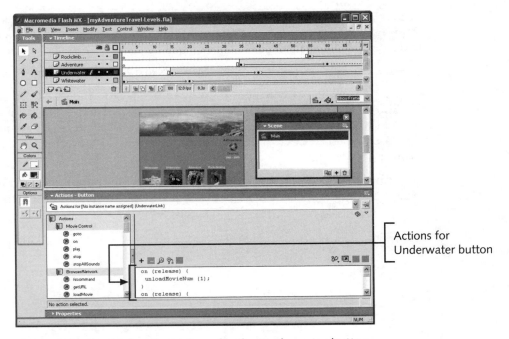

Figure 5-8   Examining the actions for the Underwater button

This action specifies that when the Underwater button is clicked and released, Flash unloads the movies playing at levels 1, 3, and 4 (AdventureTravel-Levels01.swf) and loads AdventureTravel-Levels02.swf (a level 2 child movie) into level 1.

Now you can assign actions to the Adventure button so that when users click and release this button, Flash unloads other movies and loads AdventureTravel-Levels03.swf. Because you will set AdventureTravel-Levels03.swf to play at level 3, you must first unload any movies playing at levels 1, 2, and 4.

To assign unload and load actions to the Adventure button:

1. Click **frame 100** on the Adventure layer, press **F6** to insert a keyframe, and then click the **Adventure** button symbol on the Stage.

2. In the Actions panel, click the **Browser/Network** category to expand it, if necessary, and then double-click the **unloadMovie** action. Flash first inserts the on (release) event for you. The unloadMovieNum action is also selected.

3. Make sure the Location is specified as Level 1 so that Flash unloads the movie playing at level 1. (If necessary, type **1** in the text box next to the Location list box.) After you unload all the movies that could be playing at other levels (that is, levels 1, 2, and 4), you can load the appropriate movie in level 3.

4. In the Actions panel, double-click the **unloadMovie** action. In the second Location text box, type **2** so that Flash unloads any movies playing at level 2.

5. In the Actions panel, double-click the **unloadMovie** action. In the second Location text box, type **4** so that Flash unloads any movies playing at level 4. Now you can load the movie you want to play when the Adventure button is clicked.

6. In the Actions panel, double-click the **loadMovie** action. In the URL text box, type **AdventureTravel-Levels03.swf**, the name of the movie that should play when the Adventure button is clicked.

7. To specify at which level this movie should play, make sure Level is selected in the Location text box, and then type **3** into the second Location text box.

   Now you can set the actions for the Rockclimbing button. First, you unload movies playing at levels 1, 2, and 3, and then load the Rockclimbing movie so it plays at level 4.

8. Click **frame 80** in the Rockclimbing layer, and then click the **Rockclimbing** button symbol on the Stage. In the Actions panel, insert three unloadMovie actions to unload movies playing at levels 1, 2, and 3. (See Steps 3-4 for details.) Then double-click the **loadMovie** action. In the URL text box, type **AdventureTravel-Levels04.swf**, the name of the movie that should play when the Rockclimbing button is clicked, and specify that this movie plays at level **4**.

9. Save **myAdventureTravel-Levels.fla**, close the Actions panel, and test the movie by clicking **File** on the menu bar, pointing to **Publish Preview**, and then clicking **Default-(HTML)**, which opens the movie in your default browser. Click each button to make sure each movie loads properly, unloading any movies that are playing first.

10. Close your browser and **myAdventureTravel-Levels.fla**, but leave Flash open for the next set of steps.

It is not always necessary to unload the movies prior to loading new ones. Organizing your movies as in the previous steps involves working with many actions. Instead of unloading the three possible movies, and then loading the one desired, you could have used only two levels, 0 and 1. By using two levels, Flash unloads the previous movie in level 1 and replaces it with another movie. For example, you could load level 2 into your movie, and then load level 3 on top of that, and so on. The disadvantage to this is that the file size increases every time you load a movie, and the organization of your movie becomes complex. The advantage of loading one movie without unloading another is that you can save programming and development time.

Designing Movie Preloaders

Usability studies have shown that the first reason users leave a Web site is download time. If you do not address bandwidth resolution by streaming efficiently, users could have longer than anticipated delays when downloading your Flash movies. In efficiently designed movies, the speed of playback is typically slower than that of the downloading frames. As the beginning frames appear, more frames and scenes of the movie can download in the background. These beginning frames are commonly called the movie **preloader**, which can serve two purposes: A preloader gives your audience something interesting to view as they wait for the rest of the movie to download; a preloader can also indicate the download progress.

Recall that unlike standard images and HTML files, a streaming Flash SWF file loads its Timeline one frame at a time. For example, suppose your latest Flash movie for the Web loaded a large movie clip symbol near the beginning of the Timeline. Any frames before that will play and then halt until the frame with the large movie clip symbol loads. Flash works around this delay by providing the MovieClip._framesloaded property, which checks whether the content of a frame has loaded. If the specified frame is not loaded, Flash can play a movie preloader. Figure 5-9 is an example of the _framesloaded actions used with the preloader frames, the frames that appear before the actual movie starts.

In the example shown in Figure 5-9, Flash checks to see if frame 275, the last frame in the movie, has loaded. If it has, Flash plays the movie. If frame 275 has not loaded, Flash plays only the preloader frames.

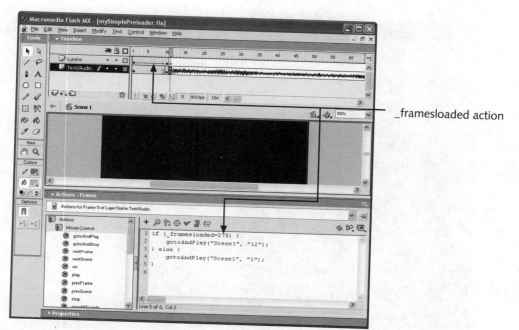

_framesloaded action

Figure 5-9 _framesloaded action

To analyze the efficiency of your movie, you can use both the Bandwidth Profiler and the Size Report. The Size Report is covered in detail in Chapter 9, "Optimizing and Publishing Flash Movies." You can use the **Bandwidth Profiler** while testing your movies to display detailed information about your movie, including how much data Flash sends for each frame according to the modem speed you specify. In this way, you can determine whether the movie must wait for some frames to load. See Figure 5-10.

The Bandwidth Profiler is divided into two panes. The left pane displays the following information:

- Movie attributes, such as Stage dimensions, frame rate, size in bytes, movie duration by frames, and amount of frames being preloaded

- Settings for the current bandwidth or modem speed (which you set using the Debug menu)

- State of the current frame and its size, the percentage and quantity of frames loaded, and the total size of what is loaded

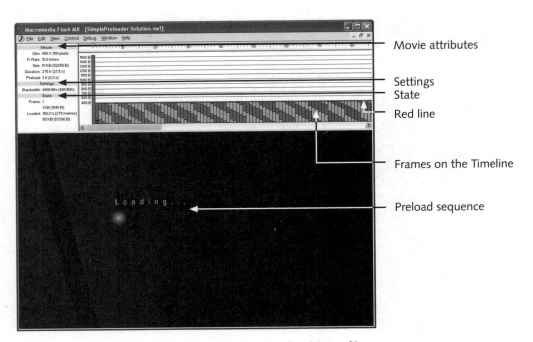

Movie attributes

Settings
State

Red line

Frames on the Timeline

Preload sequence

Figure 5-10   Information displayed in the Bandwidth Profiler

The right pane of the Bandwidth Profiler shows the Timeline header and graph. Each bar in the graph represents a frame of the movie. The size of the bar corresponds to the size of the frame in bytes. A red line in the graph indicates whether a frame streams in real time with the current modem speed set in the Control menu. If a bar extends above the red line, the movie must wait for that frame to load. This indicates that your movie will produce distorted sound as it plays in the user's browser.

Creating a Simple Preloader

A simple preloader displays a message or graphics to notify your audience they need to wait for more content. The notification can use sound, images, animation, or a combination of each. For example, the preloader can include a small sound file that plays the message "Loading," or it can provide a more interactive preload sequence, as in Figure 5-11.

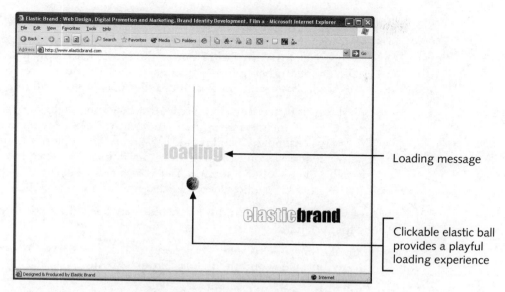

Figure 5-11   Interactive preloader at *www.elasticbrand.com*

To use a movie preloader, set up the first few frames in the movie to play a preload sequence, such as a "Loading" message with a simple animation. Immediately after the preload sequence, insert two keyframes. The first keyframe should use the ifFrameLoaded and gotoAndPlay actions. When the movie reaches the first keyframe, Flash checks whether a specified frame (usually the last frame or close to it) and all frames prior to it have loaded. If that frame has loaded, Flash plays the frame specified in the gotoAndPlay action, which is usually the frame that starts the movie. The second keyframe should have only the gotoAndPlay action, which specifies which frame should play only if the frame specified in the ifFrameLoaded has not loaded. The second keyframe usually specifies that the preload sequence should replay.

In the following steps, you open a file containing a preloader sequence that displays a "Loading" message and a simple animated graphic while Flash downloads two audio files. You add the proper actions to the keyframes that come just after the preload sequence to test whether the last frame (275) has loaded into your browser. If it has, Flash begins playing the first audio file. You also use the Bandwidth Profiler to help identify when it is best to use preload sequences depending on the amount of frames, size of content on the frames, and various modem speeds.

To complete a movie preloader:

1. Open **SimplePreloader.fla** from your Chapter5 folder in your FlashSamples folder. Save the file as **mySimplePreloader.fla**. Note that the first 10 frames in the Timeline contain the preload sequence, frames 11 and 12 are keyframes, and the Text/Audio layer contains two audio files that play after frame 12.

2. Drag the playhead from **frame 1** to **frame 10** to view the preloader. (Drag in the ruler part of the Timeline, not in the frames.) In the Text/Audio layer, point to any frame between frame 12 and frame 125 to see the name of the first audio file—Ambient.wav. Point to any frame after frame 125 to see the name of the second audio file—Coffee Shop.wav. You want Flash to play the preloader— frames 1 to 10—until the audio files are loaded into frames 13 to 275.

3. Click **frame 11** on the Text/Audio layer, and then open the Actions panel to set actions for that frame.

4. Ensure your Actions panel is in Expert mode. (Click the **View Options** button on the Actions panel, and then click **Expert Mode**.)

5. Type the following code in the code pane:

```
if (_framesloaded=275) {
    gotoAndPlay("Scene1", "12");
} else {
    gotoAndPlay("Scene1", "1");
}
```

6. In the Actions panel, click the **View Options** button, and then click **Normal Mode**. Click the first gotoAndPlay line. If necessary, click the **Scene** list arrow, and then click **<current scene>**; click the **Type** list arrow, and then click **Frame Number**. This means that at frame 11, Flash checks whether frame 275 has loaded into your browser. Figure 5-12 shows what the Actions panel should look like at this point.

7. Click the **gotoAndPlay("Scene1", "1");** line. This line follows the "else" condition in the ActionScript, and sets what Flash should do if frame 275 has not loaded, which means that both sound files have not yet loaded. Click the **Scene** list arrow and then click **<current scene>**, if necessary. Click the **Type** list arrow and then click **Frame Number**. Type **1** in the Frame text box, if necessary. See Figure 5-13.

   These settings mean that if frame 275 has not loaded, Flash should go to frame 1 in the current scene and start playing the animation. In this case, it plays the pre-load sequence again. When the playhead reaches frame 11, Flash checks whether frame 275 has loaded yet. If it has, it plays frame 12, which is the beginning of the first sound file.

8. Save **mySimplePreloader.fla**, and leave it open in Flash for the next set of steps.

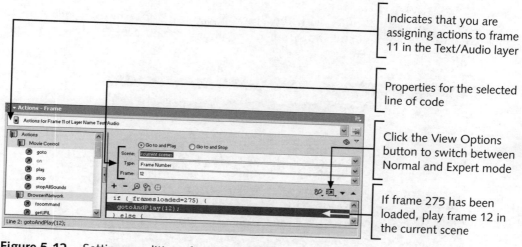

Figure 5-12   Setting conditions for the preloader

Figure 5-13   Playing the preloader again if frame 275 has not loaded

Testing with the Bandwidth Profiler

Using the Bandwidth Profiler, you can view both the movie playing in the Flash SWF player and a streaming or frame-by-frame graph. When you select the Show Streaming command on the View menu, the movie plays as it will in the Flash Player. If you uncheck the Show Streaming command to turn streaming off, the movie starts over without simulating a Web connection. You can set the graph to appear in Streaming or in Frame-by-Frame view. In Streaming view, the graph shows which frames will pause the playback. In Frame-by-Frame view, the graph shows the size of each frame—if a frame extends above the red line in the graph, the Flash Player halts playback until the entire frame downloads.

When you play the movie, Flash uses the current speed and quality settings, simulating how your audience will view the movie. The Bandwidth Profiler also shows the frame currently playing, the size of that frame, the percentage of total frames loaded, the number of frames loaded, and the total size of data loaded. When analyzing and testing for load delays, you can contrast the modem speeds and playback quality. Figure 5-14 shows the Bandwidth Profiler with the Show Streaming command selected. This movie distributes its content and animation across all of the frames, so the download and playback speed do not fluctuate.

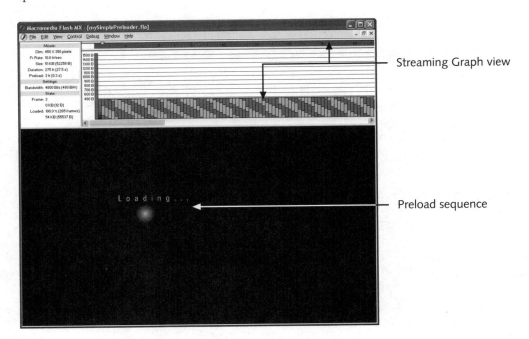

Streaming Graph view

Preload sequence

Figure 5-14   Bandwidth Profiler in Streaming Graph view

In the following steps, you continue working with the SimplePreloader.fla file and use the Bandwidth Profiler to analyze and test the preload sequence and frames that have loaded. You will toggle from Frame-by-Frame view to Streaming view, and use the Show Streaming command to show the load time details, such as percent loaded, download time, and what frames are troublesome and can be optimized. You will also test various modem speeds and playback qualities.

To analyze and test the preload sequence:

1. With **mySimplePreloader.fla** still open in Flash, click **Control** on the menu bar, and then click **Test Movie**. The preload sequence starts playing. To open the Bandwidth Profiler, if necessary, click **View** on the menu bar, and then click **Bandwidth Profiler**.

2. To help you test, display the **Controller** toolbar; click **Window** on the menu bar, point to **Toolbars**, and then click **Controller**.

3. Stop the movie and then rewind it by clicking the **Stop** and **Rewind** buttons on the Controller toolbar so you can alter the modem speed.

4. To select the lowest speed your audience could use to view your movie, click **Debug** on the menu bar, and then click **14.4 (1.2 KB/s)** modem speed, if necessary.

5. Besides the lowest speed, you should also test using the highest quality to determine where your movie would have the most delays. Click **View** on the menu bar, point to **Quality**, and then click **High**, if necessary.

6. Now you are ready to test the streaming speed set at the 14.4 modem speed. Click **View** on the menu bar, and then click **Show Streaming** to play the movie as your audience will play it in the Flash Player. The preload sequence plays until frame 275 is reached. (Frame numbers appear on the left of the Bandwidth Profiler.) See Figure 5-15.

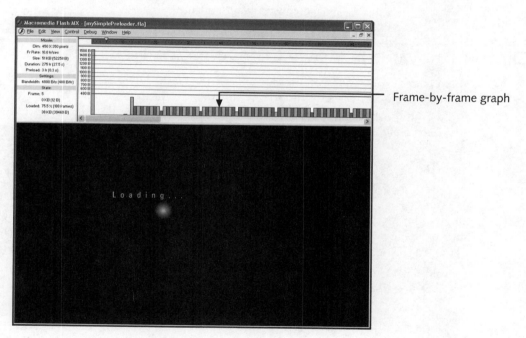

Figure 5-15   Frame-by-frame graph view

7. Use the Controller toolbar to stop and rewind the movie.

8. Now you can reset the movie to test at the 56k modem speed. Click **View** on the menu bar, and then click **Streaming Graph**. (Make sure show streaming remains selected.)

9. Now you can test the movie at a higher download speed, but lower quality. Click **Debug** on the menu bar, and then click **56k (4.7 KB/s)**. Click **View** on the menu bar, point to **Quality**, and then click **Low**.

10. Play the movie to test the performance of the movie at the new settings. The difference in performance might be difficult to see in the Flash Player, although it is apparent when you publish to a Web server.

11. Close the test movie window, and then save and close **mySimplePreloader.fla**. Leave Flash open for the next set of steps.

Besides using the Bandwidth Profiler, you should also test your movie on a Web server connected to the Internet. This way, you can analyze more accurately the quality and download performance.

CREATING ADVANCED MOVIE CLIPS AND COMPLEX BUTTONS

Movie clip and button symbols can make your Flash movie easy to access and navigate for your audience. These symbols should include meaningful text or images, so users quickly understand the purpose of the symbol. For example, Figure 5-16 shows the *www.emerils.com* Web site, which uses Flash movie clips and buttons to simplify navigation.

Besides using text and images that are clearly related to the purpose of a button or movie clip, you can also make buttons interactive by using rollovers. A **rollover** involves replacing one image with another when the user's mouse rolls over an image. For example, you can create a button that changes color or position when a mouse points to it. A button symbol with a rollover effect can provide helpful cues to your audience—if the button changes when a user points to it, that means clicking the button triggers an action. In this section, you learn how to animate buttons using various types of rollovers, including those that play movie clips. For example, you work with a movie clip that also serves as a button rollover.

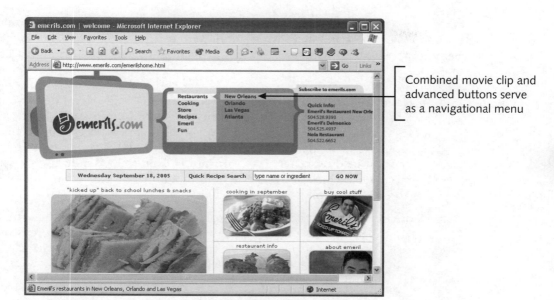

Combined movie clip and advanced buttons serve as a navigational menu

Figure 5-16   Using movie clips and buttons for navigation

Animating Buttons with Advanced Rollovers

A simple button with a rollover effect might change color when the user points to it. Advanced rollover buttons can provide more explicit information. For instance, a button rollover could show a subset of menus or related links. The Sun International Resorts' Flash Web page at *www.Atlantis.com* uses advanced rollovers to help users navigate their site. See Figure 5-17.

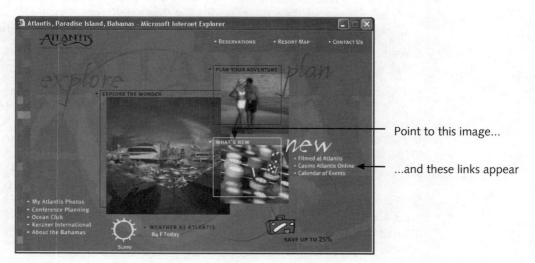

Point to this image...

...and these links appear

Figure 5-17   Advanced rollover buttons

In the following steps, you create the rollover actions for a button symbol using only button and movie clip symbols. (You do not need to use ActionScript.) When users point to the button, text and graphics appear that explain the effects of clicking that button.

To create a rollover for a button:

1. In Flash, open **AdvancedRollover.fla** from the Chapter5 folder in your FlashSamples folder. Save the file as **myAdvancedRollover.fla** in the same location. This document will become a Web site for Visio Training Central, a fictitious company that offers training on Microsoft Visual Studio .NET and other software. Press **Ctrl+L** (**Command+L** on the Macintosh) to open the Library panel, which contains the buttons and movie clip symbols you will use to create the rollover.

2. In the Library panel, click the **Button** movie clip symbol and then the **Text** movie clip symbol to preview these images. The Button movie clip is the normal state of the image—you will assign this image to a button's Up state. The Text movie clip shows what appears when the user rolls the mouse over the Button-Home button symbol.

3. Open the **Button-Home** button symbol in Edit mode by double-clicking it in the Library panel. (Be sure to double-click the icon, not the name of the button symbol.)

4. With the Up frame selected in the Timeline, drag the **Button** movie clip onto the Stage. This sets how the button appears when the mouse pointer is not over the button.

5. Open the Info panel, if necessary, and then use it to position the symbol to the coordinates X="**−69.0**" and Y="**−43.0**".

6. In the Timeline, click the **Over frame** to select it, drag the **Text** movie clip onto the Stage, and then use the Info panel to set X to -69.0 and Y to -128.0. This sets how the button appears when the mouse pointer is over it.

Next, you set how the button looks when you click it. In this case, the button will look the same when you point to it and when you click it.

7. Click the **Down frame** to select it, click **Insert** on the menu bar, and then click **Clear Keyframe** to remove the keyframe for the down frame. In the Down frame, Flash will display the same image as in the Over frame. Click the **Text Symbol** on the Stage to verify its position in the Info panel. Your Stage should appear as in Figure 5-18.

8. Click **Scene 1** to return to the main movie Timeline.

9. Drag the **Button-Home** button symbol onto the Stage. To test the button, click **Control** on the menu bar, and then click **Enable Simple Buttons** if it is not already selected. Point to the button. The descriptive text should appear, as shown in Figure 5-19.

10. Save and close **myAdvancedRollover.fla** and the Info panel, but leave Flash open for the next set of steps.

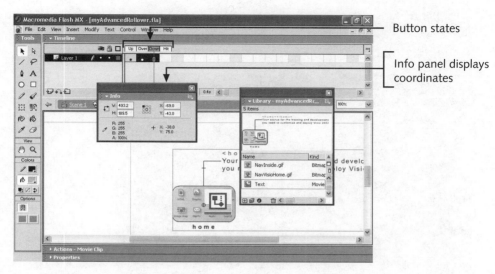

Figure 5-18   Button symbol states

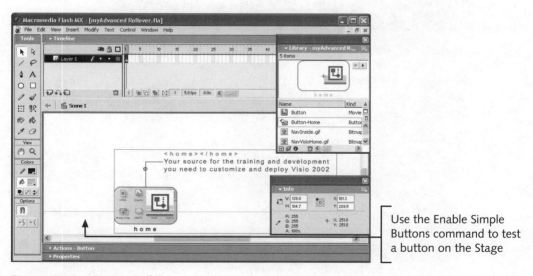

Figure 5-19   Button rollover

Animating Buttons with a Movie Clip Rollover

Adding an animation to a rollover button is an effective way to attract attention to a specific element of your movie. For example, the Spider-Man movie promotion from Columbia Pictures and Sony at *www.spiderman.sonypictures.com* uses navigation buttons that scroll from left to right with a mouse movement. See Figure 5-20.

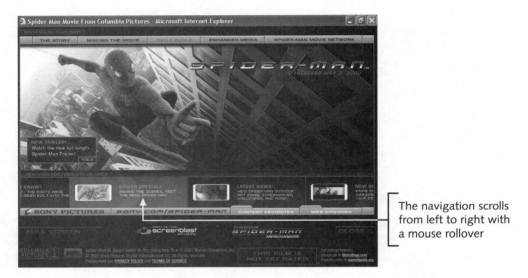

The navigation scrolls from left to right with a mouse rollover

Figure 5-20   Animation on a rollover button

In the following steps, you continue working with the Web site for Visio Training Central. You will add a movie clip symbol to the Home button so that a short animation plays when the mouse points to the button.

To create an animated rollover:

1. In Flash, open **AnimatedRollover.fla** from your Chapter5 folder in your FlashSamples folder. Save the file as **myAnimatedRollover.fla** in the same location.

2. Press **Ctrl+L** (**Command+L** on the Macintosh), if necessary, to open the Library panel, and then double-click the **Text** movie clip symbol to open it in Edit mode, shown in Figure 5-21.

3. Drag the **NavAni** movie clip symbol onto a blank area of the Stage. This movie clip simply plays a sequence of symbols—an X and three asterisks. You will place this movie clip on the Home button to draw attention to that button.

4. Use the Property inspector to scale the symbol to a height and width of **16** pixels each.

5. Position the symbol on the button image, close to the center, as in Figure 5-22.

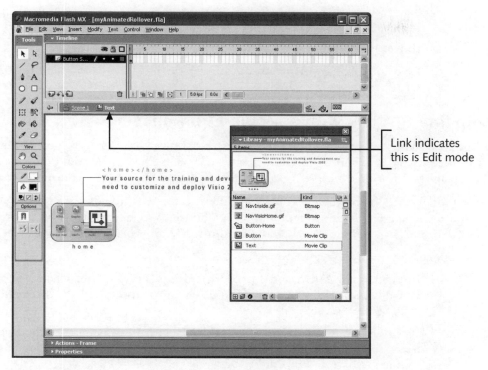

Link indicates
this is Edit mode

Figure 5-21   Text movie clip symbol in Edit mode

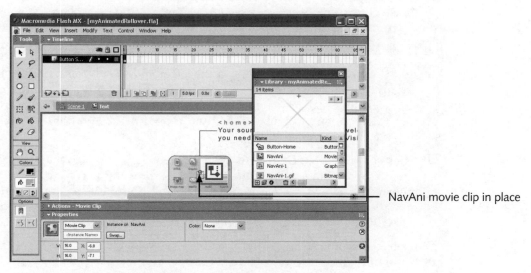

NavAni movie clip in place

Figure 5-22   NavAni movie clip symbol positioned

6. Click **Control** on the menu bar, click **Test Movie**, and then point to the **Home** button. The short animation plays and the descriptive text appears above the button. Close the test movie window.

7. Save and close **myAnimatedRollover.fla**, but leave Flash open for the next set of steps.

Morphing Buttons with a Movie Clip Rollover

Besides adding static and animated rollovers to buttons, you can also morph a button to change its shape when users interact with it. For example, you could create a circular button that morphed into text that described the purpose of the button.

In the following steps, you continue working with the Web site for Visio Training Central. You review and add a morphed symbol to a button symbol that serves as an e-mail link so that users can point to or click the button to see an e-mail address.

To morph a button during a rollover:

1. In Flash, open **AnimatedButtonMorphing.fla** from your Chapter5 folder in your FlashSamples folder. Save the file as **myAnimatedButtonMorphing.fla** in the same location.

2. Press **Ctrl+L** (**Command+L** on the Macintosh) to open the Library panel, if necessary, and then double-click the icon for the **EmailMC** movie clip symbol to open the symbol in Edit mode.

3. Drag the playhead on the Timeline from **frame 1** to **frame 10** to review the movie clip's shape tween, as shown in Figure 5-23. Then click the **Scene 1** link to return to the main Stage.

4. Double-click the icon for the **EmailBT** button symbol to open it in Edit mode.

5. Add the **EmailMC** movie clip to the Over and Down frames of the button. To position the movie clip symbol, click the **Over** frame, place the movie clip over the EmailBT to match the registration points, and then press **Ctrl+C** to copy the symbol. Click the **Down** frame and then press **Ctrl+V** to paste the symbol.

6. Click to select the **Hit frame**. With the rectangle tool, draw a rectangle with a white border and white fill to cover the arrow and text on the EmailBT button. This allows the mouse pointer to roll on top of the entire button, not only the text or arrow. Click the rectangle you drew to select it and make it visible. Then you can adjust its position over the button.

7. Click the **Scene 1** link to return to the main Stage. Drag the **EmailBT** button symbol from the Library to the Stage, as in Figure 5-24.

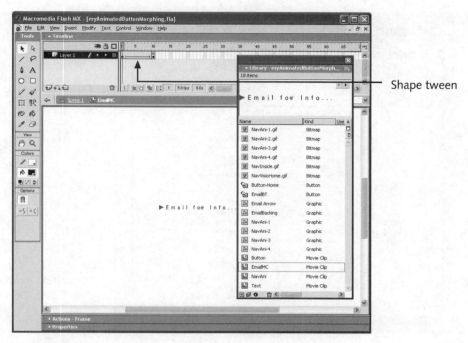

Figure 5-23   Movie clip's shape tween

8. Click **Control** on the menu bar and then click **Test Movie**. Point to the **Email for Info** button to see the Email for Info text morph into "on Visio training" text. Also click the button to test the morphing effect. Close the test movie window.

9. Save and close **myAnimatedButtonMorphing.fla**, but leave Flash open for the next set of steps.

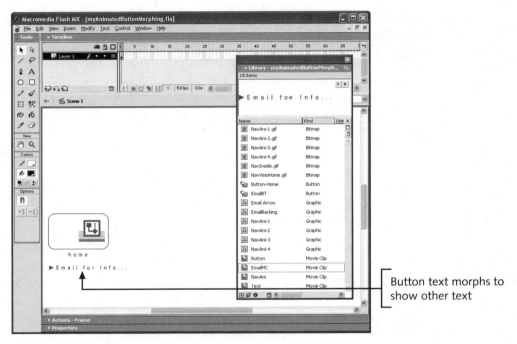

Figure 5-24   Morphed button on the Stage

Button text morphs to show other text

DEVELOPING ANIMATION EFFECTS

Besides playing video and animating rollover effects, you can also add animation effects to your Flash movies. Animation effects such as images that slide in from the edge of the screen, dissolve from one image to another, or break apart are common video techniques that attract attention to parts of your movie and signal a transition, such as from one topic to another. For example, the Fox Sports and Lycos Web site at *foxsports.lycos.com*, shown in Figure 5-25, uses animation effects to provide up-to-date information above the secondary navigation.

In this section, you create a rolling text box that slides into a movie from off the screen, and set up a dissolve effect where one image replaces another.

Creating a Rolling Text Box

You can animate text by creating a rolling text box, which slides a block of text from one area of the Stage to another. Rolling text boxes also draw the viewer's attention, and indicate that the viewer should read the text. This technique is most effective with blocks of text, rather than headings. Text boxes can contain dynamic text that is updated and formatted from an outside file, and then scroll across the screen to focus the movie on the new text.

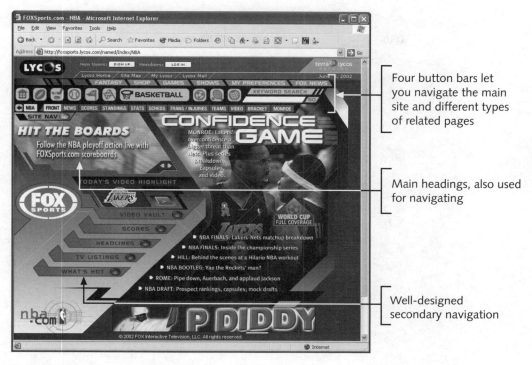

Four button bars let you navigate the main site and different types of related pages

Main headings, also used for navigating

Well-designed secondary navigation

Figure 5-25   Enhanced Flash design

In the following steps, you create a rolling text box that scrolls from off the Stage to the middle of the Stage. The movie elements, including text box, are already in place for you. You animate the text box, and then examine how the Flash document uses a transparent rectangle to show the text scrolling upward.

To create a rolling text box:

1. In Flash, open **DynamicText.fla** from the Chapter5 folder in your FlashSamples folder. Save the file as **myDynamicText.fla** in the same location. In this document, you continue working with the Web site for Visio Training Central.

2. Create a new layer called **Dynamic News Text** (click the **Insert Layer** button, double-click the layer name, type **Dynamic News Text**, and then press **Enter**). Drag the **Dynamic News Text** layer to position it after the Text Background layer. Click any frame in the new layer, expand the Property inspector, and then type **Scroll** in the Frame label text box. This adds a label to the frames that identifies the purpose of the new layer. Click the title bar of the Property inspector to collapse the panel.

3. Press **Ctrl+L** (**Command+L** on the Macintosh) to open the Library panel, and then drag the **Dynamic Text** graphic symbol below your Stage as in

Figure 5-26. The text will scroll from the bottom of the Stage to the lower half of the Stage.

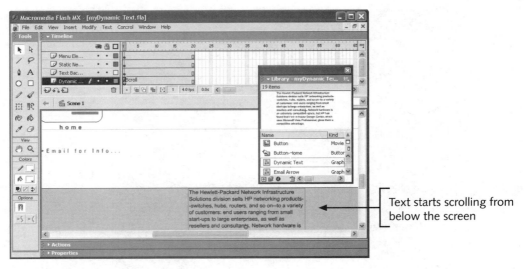

Figure 5-26   Location of text before scrolling

4. To set the text to stop scrolling at frame 20, click **frame 20** on the Dynamic News Text (same layer), and then press **F6** to add a keyframe.

5. To set the position of the text when it stops scrolling, drag the **DynamicText** graphic symbol from below the Stage and place it just below the Visio Training News heading, as in Figure 5-27.

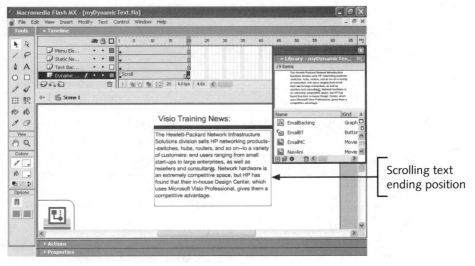

Figure 5-27   Location of text after scrolling

6. To create a motion tween that moves the DynamicText text box from the bottom of the Stage to just below the Visio Training News heading, click **frame 1** in the Dynamic News Text layer. Click **Insert** on the menu bar, and then click **Create Motion Tween**.

7. Click **Control** on the menu bar, and then click **Test Movie**. The text should scroll from the bottom of the screen to the heading. Notice the scroll speed is slow (the movie's frame rate is set to 4 frames per second) to avoid creating an abrupt effect. Close the test movie window.

   So that the text only appears in a designated area, this document specified this area with the Rectangle tool on the Text Background layer. This layer is positioned above the Dynamic News Text layer, and, therefore, appears first. You examine this rectangle and its properties in the following steps.

8. Click the **Text Background** layer. Double-click the **rectangle** that includes the Visio training News heading. This breaks up the rectangle into four parts—bottom and top parts with a white fill, hiding the text box as it scrolls behind it; a top blue bar to separate the text from the heading; and a middle section with a transparent fill.

9. Click **Window** on the menu bar, and then click **Color Mixer**, if necessary, to open the Color Mixer panel. This displays all the colors in the current movie, called the movie's swatch. (If necessary, click the title bar of the Color Mixer panel to see the full panel.)

   Note that the author of this document added transparent fill to the swatch by using 255 for all the RGB values, clicking Color Mixer panel's menu, and then clicking Add Swatch, as shown in Figure 5-28.

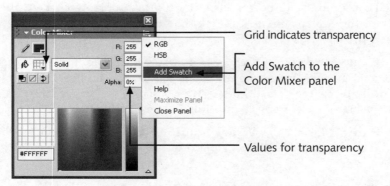

Figure 5-28   Adding transparent values to the swatch

10. Save and close **myDynamicText.fla**, but leave Flash open for the next set of steps.

Simulating Transitions

A common and effective animation technique is a dissolve effect, in which an image appears to fade in or out. By using two motion tweens on one layer, and manipulating the Alpha values, you can create a dissolve transition in Flash. Another effect is a slide, or wipe, where parts of an image are hidden, and then appear one part at a time, as if someone were wiping away a layer to reveal an image under it.

In the following steps, you add a dissolve effect to the Visio Training Central Web site by using two motion tweens for one graphic symbol located on one layer. You will edit the Alpha settings for a graphic so that it appears to dissolve and then fade back in.

To create a dissolve effect:

1. In Flash, open **TransitionsDissolve.fla** from the Chapter5 folder in your FlashSamples folder. Save this file as **myTransitionsDissolve.fla** in the same location. Press **Ctrl+L** (**Command+L** on the Macintosh) to open the Library panel.

2. The layer Transition – Dissolve is already added for you. In this layer, click **frame 1**, and then drag the **Visual Studio .NET** graphic symbol from the Library panel to the upper-left corner of the Stage, centered below the Visio Training Central.com logo. Figure 5-29 shows the correct placement. You will insert keyframes on this layer to define where the book begins to dissolve and then reappear.

3. In the Transition – Dissolve layer, click **frame 10** and then press **F6** to add a keyframe. Do the same for frames 20, 30, and 40.

4. Click **frame 1**, click the **Visual Studio .NET book** graphic symbol, expand the Property inspector, click the **Color** list arrow, click **Alpha**, and then edit the Alpha value to **0**. Click the title bar of the Property inspector to collapse the panel.

5. Add a motion tween from frames 1 to 10. Click **frame 1** in the Transition – Dissolve layer, click **Insert** on the menu bar, and then click **Create Motion Tween**. This sets the Visual Studio .NET instance to change from transparent (Alpha value of 0) in frame 1 into full color in frame 10.

6. Click **frame 30**, click the **Visual Studio .NET book** graphic symbol, and edit the book instance's Alpha value to **0** in the Property inspector. (Refer to Step 4 for details.)

7. Refer to Step 5 to create a motion tween from **frame 20** to **30**. This sets the book to change from full color in frame 20 to transparent in frame 30. The graphic remains in full color from frames 10 through 19, and transparent from frames 30 to 39. Collapse the Property inspector again. See Figure 5-29.

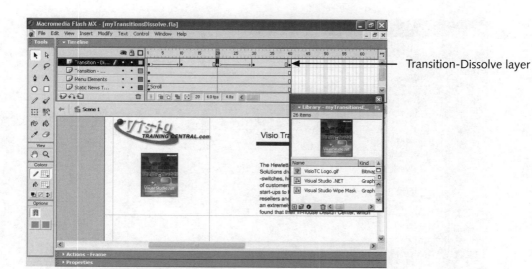

Transition-Dissolve layer

5

Figure 5-29   Timeline for dissolve transitions

8. Click **Control** on the menu bar, and then click **Test Movie**. The Visual Studio .NET book graphic fades in and out as the movie plays.

9. Save and close **myTransitionsDissolve.fla**, but leave Flash open for the next set of steps.

You can also use Flash to create a wipe or slide transition effect, which temporarily hides an object, and then displays it at specified moments in your Timeline.

In the following steps, you create a sliding transition that combines a motion tween and a mask. You continue working with the Web site for Visio Training Central. The symbols are already set for you on the Stage. You will complete the movie by adding the mask elements to the layers so that the Visual Studio .NET book is hidden and then revealed.

To create a wipe effect:

1. In Flash, open **TransitionsWipe.fla** from the Chapter5 folder in your FlashSamples folder. Save the file as **myTransitionsWipe.fla** in the same location. Note that the Transition – Mask layer already include a tween to move the mask.

2. Right-click the **Transition – Mask** layer, and then click **Mask** on the shortcut menu. By default, the two layers are locked to hide them from view except when the masked layer tweens behind the masking layer. Figure 5-30 shows how your Stage should look at this point.

3. Click **Control** on the menu bar, and then click **Test Movie**. The Visual Studio .NET book should now slide in a little at a time from the right, and then slide back out. Close the test movie window.

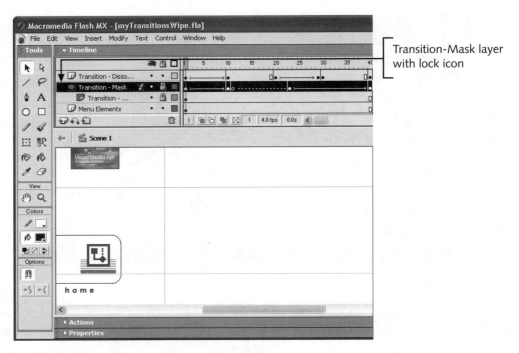

Transition-Mask layer
with lock icon

Figure 5-30 Masked layer on the Timeline

4. Save and close **myTransitionsWipe.fla**, but leave Flash open for the next set of steps.

DESIGNING AND CUSTOMIZING INTERFACES

In addition to using Flash to create navigation buttons and animation effects on a Web site, you can use Flash to create the complete interface. The interface includes all the elements the user interacts with on a Web site: graphics, color, organization, navigation devices, and use of sound and video. For example, the FAO Schwarz online toy store at *www.fao.com* was designed with Flash. See Figure 5-31.

Visitors can use the FAO Schwarz Web site to shop for toys and to contact customer service, and its design reflects this usage. The typeface, images, and organization also signal that this is a business-oriented site, one that parents can trust while making purchases.

In contrast, the Barbie Web site (*www.barbie.com*) shown in Figure 5-32 is designed to attract children. This award-winning Flash production reflects the identity of Barbie by the use of color, theme, and fun graphics, and by offering games, toys, and some features for parents as well.

Effective Flash navigation

Figure 5-31   FAO Schwarz Web site

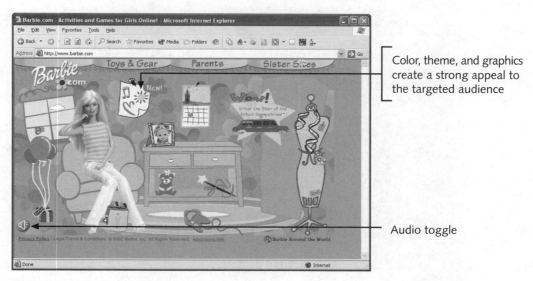

Color, theme, and graphics create a strong appeal to the targeted audience

Audio toggle

Figure 5-32   Barbie Web site

Images and color are more than combinations of red, green, and blue or cyan—they are nonverbal communication. Colors are natural signs with which users have strong associations, and images can represent ideas or actions. Intuitive design takes advantage of nonverbal communication by linking visual messages with meaning. For example, e-commerce sites typically use a shopping cart to represent where users store purchases.

Besides using color and graphics to express meaning and create appeal, these design elements can help make your Flash interface accessible. An accessible interface can be used by all people without the need for adaptation or specialized design. Tim Berners-Lee, World Wide Web Consortium (W3C) director, says, "The power of the Web is in its universality. Access by everyone regardless of disability is an essential aspect."

Using Color Effectively

Colors and images have symbolism and meanings as well as visual appeal. Color can send a message to your visitors, and even create a physical reaction. For example, red can be a signal for danger and can increase blood pressure. Other times color has cultural associations. For example, in America, white is for weddings, while in some Eastern cultures, white is the color of mourning.

The use of color in a Flash movie should be integrated with the purpose and identity of the Web site. The color should enhance brand identification, corporate identity, and cultural sensitivity. For example, the official United Nations' Web site (*www.un.org*) uses color and imagery that is not offensive to any cultural group or nation. See Figure 5-33.

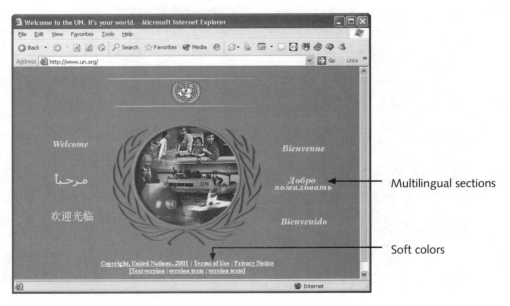

Figure 5-33   United Nations Web site

Color on the Web is specified in terms of the amount of red, green, and blue in the color. Black is defined as no light or low intensities of red, green, and blue, whereas white is the brightest color and full intensity of red, green, and blue. In Flash and other design applications, these amounts of red, green, and blue are specified with numbers from 0-255 called the **RGB model**. Red, green, and blue pixels are assigned brightness values 0 to 255, where 0 is dark and 255 is bright. In order for your computer to understand these numbers, they are translated into six-digit **hexadecimal** (hex) numbers; for instance, the colors red 255, green 255, and blue 0 becomes hex FFFF00. The first pair (FF) is red, the second pair (FF) is green, and the last pair is blue, where FF is the hexadecimal equivalent of 255 and 00 is the hexadecimal equivalent of 0.

Primary colors are red, blue, and yellow and are the source of all other colors. **Secondary colors** are created when equal parts of two primary colors are combined, such as green from blue and yellow; they lie midway between the primary colors on the color wheel and are less strong than primaries. Figure 5-34 shows a color wheel. **Intermediate colors** are formed when primary color is mixed with an adjacent secondary color, such as when blue (a primary) and violet (a secondary) combine to make blue-violet, an intermediate. **Complementary colors** lie opposite each other on the color wheel. For example, red and green are complements, as are blue and orange, and yellow and violet.

Tertiary and quaternary colors are subtle blends of pure color which are richer hues than shades made by adding black. **Tertiary** colors are formed when two secondary colors are mixed. They add depth and sophistication to a color scheme. **Quaternary** colors are formed when two tertiary colors are mixed, such as when brick and slate become eggplant.

When designing for the Web, you should use Web-safe colors, which are colors that appear as designed on all browsers and computer platforms. Different browsers, such as Microsoft Internet Explorer and Netscape Navigator, interpret colors with slight differences. In addition, the same color does not appear identical on all computer screens. As a cross-platform environment, colors on the Web are limited to the lowest common capacity of 216 colors on 72 dpi monitors.

To improve the quality of your images, use anti-aliasing and transparency techniques with your movie elements. **Aliasing** is how monitors show images and text in a raster mode, where you can see the pixels that make up the image and curves appear jagged instead of smooth. Aliasing is caused by not enough **sampling**, or SPI (samples per inch), which is a measurement of image resolution. **Anti-aliasing** takes advantage of how your eyes work. An anti-aliased curve has squares of color along the curve that are shaded darker or lighter so that your eye fills in the color to see a smooth curve. See Figure 5-35.

5

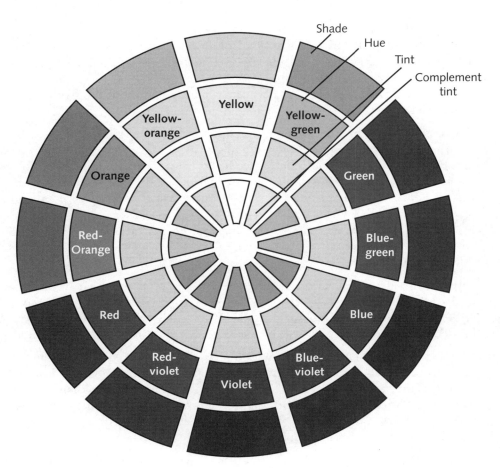

Figure 5-34 RGB color wheel

Figure 5-35 Comparing anti-aliasing to aliasing

Flash supports the alpha channel or opacity to enhance your capacity to design. The alpha channel in an object means the pixel value is invisible so you can see through the image to whatever is in the background. You can also maintain the transparency of imported PNG and GIF89a images, and dictate the level of opacity for Flash drawn objects, as in Figure 5-36.

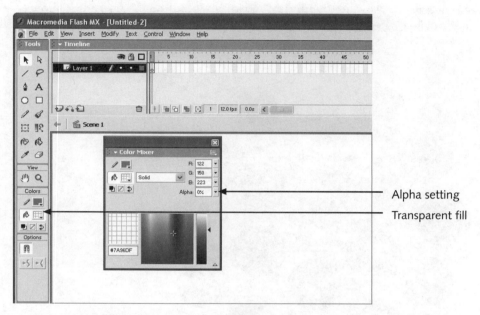

Figure 5-36   Setting alpha transparency

The way color and images are identified is how they appear to viewers. There are no color thermometers or other measuring devices. Colors can look different when they are features of physical surfaces, films, volumes, or light sources. Edward R. Tufte, the author of *Visual Explanations*, writes, "In the study of perception, just noticeable differences measure the very limits of human abilities to detect the faintest of differences between, say, two adjacent colors almost exactly alike in a continuous spectrum of 1,000,000 colors."

Certain conditions are better than others for identifying colors; certain people are better than others at identifying colors. Colored objects can appear differently when viewed using different distances, illuminations, and backgrounds. For example, colors can be warm or cool. In general, colors have the following qualities.

- Cool colors, such as blue, green, and white, can calm

- Warm colors, such as red, yellow, orange, and black, can excite

- Mixed cool and warm colors, such as purple and light green, are pleasing to the eye

- Neutral colors, such as brown, tan, beige, gray, silver, black, and white, are good for backgrounds

Color popularity is subject to trends, especially with products such as home furnishings and clothing. For a while, hunter green or mauve is popular, and then the trend shifts to apricot, for example. While using trendy colors can date a movie, they can also add appeal or represent a period of time. You can take your movie visitors back to the 60s with avocado or fluorescent colors. Turquoise and yellow are reminiscent of the 50s. Sepia tints are associated with times of long ago, although good color choices are appealing outside of any trend. Complementary colors in general provide the best combination of colors. See Figure 5-37 for a complementary color chart.

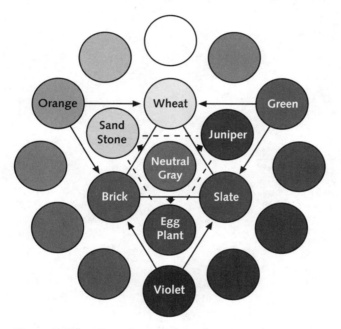

Figure 5-37   Complementary colors

The age and experience of your viewers also determine the colors you can use in a Flash movie. For example, children like bright, happy colors. Obviously, black or tan would not be an appropriate primary color for a Web presentation with school-age children as the target audience. The color preferences of adults are influenced by learned responses and are usually more conservative than those of younger people.

The most important aspect of color in daily life is probably the one that is least defined and most variable. It involves aesthetic and psychological responses to color and influences art, fashion, commerce, and even physical and emotional sensations. Psychologists have suggested that color impression can account for 60 percent of the acceptance or rejection of a product or service.

Figure 5-38 shows the Web site for Eerdmans Publishing Company on the right (*www.eerdmans.com*); the page uses a muted color scheme consistent with Eerdmans' primary business of publishing religious and academic texts. The page on the left (*www.eerdmans.com/youngreaders/*) is also from the Eerdmans Publishing Web site, but is designed for their young readers, and uses a brighter color scheme with more white space. Symbolism in color prevails here over consistency.

5

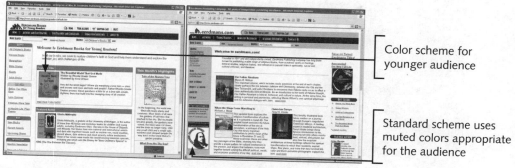

Color scheme for younger audience

Standard scheme uses muted colors appropriate for the audience

Figure 5-38   Eerdmans Publishing Company Web site

Designing for Ease of Use

Interface design has been an important topic for decades, forged by pioneers like Jacob Nielsen. Your goal when creating movies is to blend the design and the content. As you know, design involves more than arranging colored text and animation, and content is more than text. Your design uses images, movie elements, and other objects to reflect the content, which is the message of your movie and the information it provides. In Figure 5-39, the Salomon Nordic Web site (*www.salomonnordic.com*) combines functionality, content, and appearance in an effective way.

To design effective navigation, consider the content of the site and its overall design. For example, Figure 5-40 shows the Surreal Sketch Gallery Web site (*www.studiomagic.com*), which includes a portfolio of drawings. A navigation bar that includes thumbnails—miniature versions of the drawings—provides an effective way to move from one drawing to another, and to inform viewers about other content on the site.

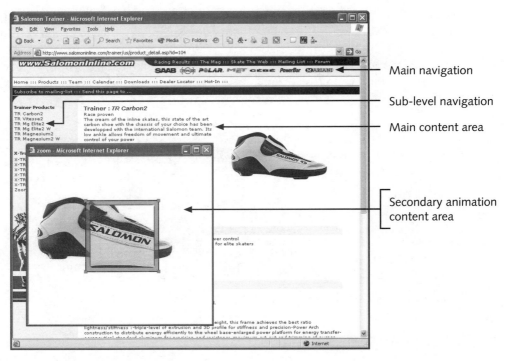

Figure 5-39   Salomon Nordic Web site

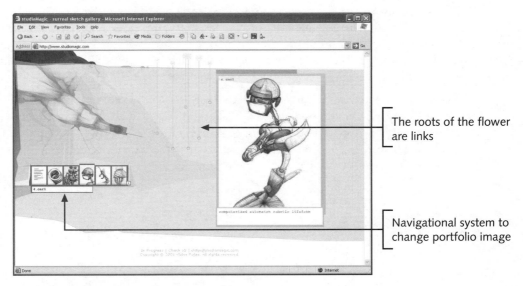

Figure 5-40   Using thumbnail drawings in a navigation bar

Drop-down menus are ideal for navigating large hierarchies of information. This style of design can provide many links without using a lot of screen space, as shown in Figure 5-41.

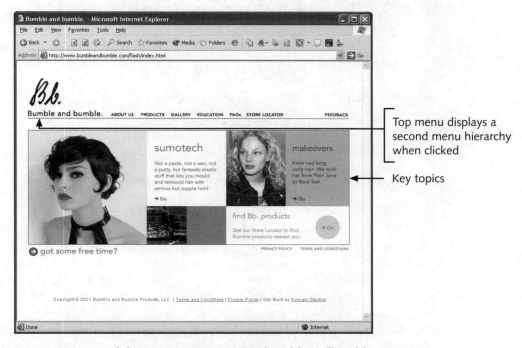

Figure 5-41   Usability in navigation (*www.bumbleandbumble.com*)

Design Principles for the Designer and Developer

Designing Flash movies is both a technical and creative process. You must be able to envision something abstract that does not yet exist, and apply technical skills to create a design based on a vision. Your goal is to create a useful and visually pleasing product that balances content and design. The design is the first and last impression that users have of your presentation or Web site. Many Web sites use poor design, yet are technically functional, while others look pleasant but serve as nothing more than a digital canvas. The Web sites shown in Figure 5-42 (*www.joannagebhardt.com* and *www.cantcryhardenough.com*) combine design, content, and technical function. Joanna Gebhardt's site on the left combines art, content, and technology, while the Can't Cry Hard Enough site on the right provides only animated images, which reinforces its content.

Form reflects
artistic content

Site provides only audio
and visuals appropriate for
the content

Figure 5-42   Combining form and function

Vincent Flanders, author of the book, *Web Pages That Suck: Learn Good Design by Looking at Bad Design* as well as the Web site *www.webpagesthatsuck.com*, ironically points out good design principles by reviewing bad ones.

Part of the design process is considering your audience. Knowing the gender or age group of your viewers, for example, can help you determine style, color, and audio and video elements. The effective balance and use of images guides viewers toward the focal points of the page. For example, most viewers' eyes are accustomed to starting at the upper-left point on the screen, then moving down toward the right. Take advantage of this tendency by putting important or identifying information and images in the upper-left corner of a movie. Intentionally, key headlines in a newspaper are located in the top half of the page "above the fold." If a Flash presentation forces viewers to scroll down to a second screen of information, viewers expect that the most important information appears before they have to scroll. This point might be different for viewers with monitors of different sizes and screen resolutions. A good rule of thumb is to test your movies using the settings your viewers are likely to use. For most Web users, this means 800 × 600 and 1027 × 768 screen resolutions, 15-inch and 17-inch monitors, and both Windows and Macintosh platforms. Recognize, however, that this no longer includes users with 680 × 460 screen resolution, 14-inch monitors, or platforms other than Windows and Macintosh, such as Unix, or browsers that don't support the Flash player.

Your design can force users to scroll up and down depending on the content, but left to right scrolling is generally regarded as taboo. Figure 5-43 shows the Cable News Network Web site (*www.cnn.com*), which displays the main headings, search links, and news stories on the first screen, before viewers have to scroll. This information would appear on the first screen on both 15-inch and 17-inch monitors and at 800 × 600 and 1027 × 768 screen resolutions.

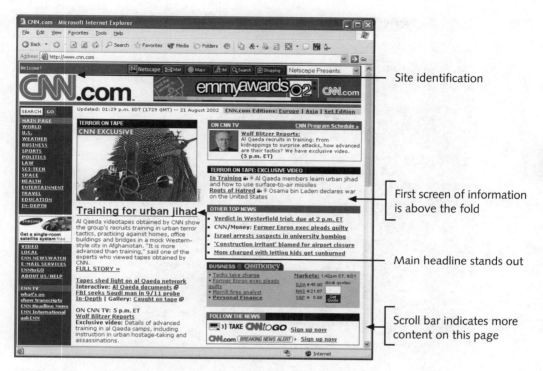

Site identification

First screen of information is above the fold

Main headline stands out

Scroll bar indicates more content on this page

Figure 5-43 Placing important information above the fold

When designing movies, you should balance quality and speed. Be sure to design for moderate modem speeds (33.6k–56k) as well as higher speeds. Zona Research reports that "Two-thirds of Web users abandon sites after just eight seconds of waiting." Flash supports fast downloading by using scalable vector graphics, reusable symbols, audio compression algorithms, and a portable SWF animated display format. Macromedia, Inc. statistics claim that over 98.3 percent of all Web users have the Macromedia Flash Player installed. OptiView Technologies, a Web optimization and rating firm, measures Disney's Web site at *www.disney.go.com*, largely designed in Flash, in the top five for download efficiency, and number one in their entertainment industry. OptiView (*www.optiview.com*) accelerates Web content by optimizing graphics and HTML without visual degradation, and provides a free 56K modem simulator that compares download times both with and without optimization. Figure 5-44 shows a page on the Disney Web site.

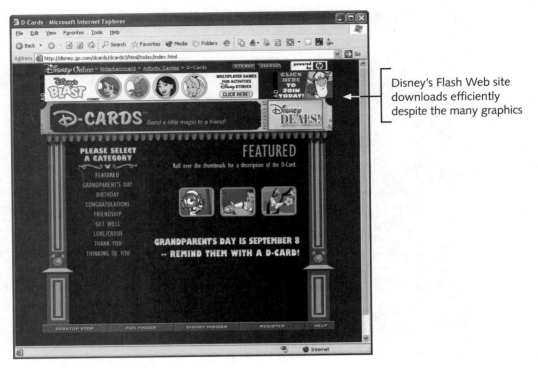

Disney's Flash Web site downloads efficiently despite the many graphics

Figure 5-44 Disney Web site

One way to balance quality and speed is to use a design that is well integrated with the product the Web site features. For example, you could use a design that reflects the product itself. Palm, Inc.'s Web site (*www.palm.com*) uses a Palm Pilot (see Figure 5-45) as a part of the Flash movie interface.

Designing Macromedia Flash Usability

Fierce competition for online visibility and recognition means designers must make their Web sites appealing and easy to use. For instance, most sites include navigation devices on the sides or the top edges of the browser window to make them easy to find. This design technique makes the Web site easier to use and access. Usability also refers to providing understandable and retrievable content that is presented in a clear and simple manner, and is easy to navigate within a page and from one page to another.

To make your Web site easy to use, test the site with focus groups, which are groups of typical users. The destination most users want to reach is the most important part of your Web site. For example, after user analysis, you could change a shopping cart experience to reduce the steps required to complete a purchase, as the RedEnvelope Web site (*www.RedEnvelope.com*) has achieved. See Figure 5-46. To accomplish this, consider multiple routes or group similar tasks together to remove steps.

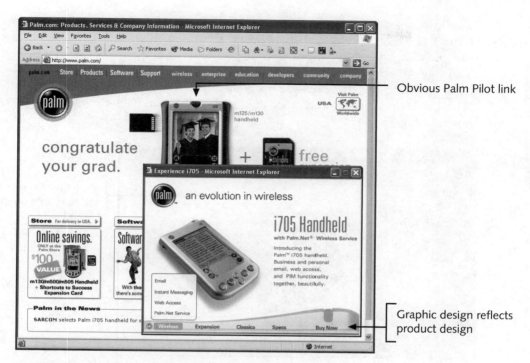

Obvious Palm Pilot link

Graphic design reflects product design

Figure 5-45   Palm.com's metaphoric design

Figure 5-46   RedEnvelope Web site

Usability expert Jacob Nielsen (*www.useit.com*) holds 16 usability patents, mainly on ways to make the Internet easier to use. Nielsen says the Web is a functional but ill-used database due to the quantity and frivolous use of images and media that designers tend to use. Flash designers must be good citizens of the Web. Although Flash allows you to create dozens of animated effects and use many interactive techniques, some of the best Web sites are the ones that keep it simple. See the Jumpman23.com Web site (*www.jumpman23.com*), shown in Figure 5-47.

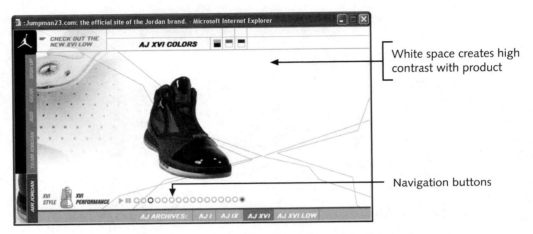

Figure 5-47   White space focuses viewer's eye on the product

In addition to designing for simplicity, you should also design for the user by providing useful sources of information and helpful navigation. For example, the FranklinPlanner beta Web site (*www.FranklinPlanner.com*), shown in Figure 5-48, was created entirely as a Flash movie application. The design here is effective due to the use of space, features, and workflow provided to the users.

Designing in Support of User Goals

Because technology can be intimidating, users like to feel they are in charge of the technology, and can turn it off and on at will. You should give users some control to turn off video or music loops, for example. The Web site shown in Figure 5-49 (*www.flashsound.com /*) provides tools for playing or stopping a variety of sounds. Giving users the option to play or skip an animated introduction or splash screen also lets users control their experience of a Web site.

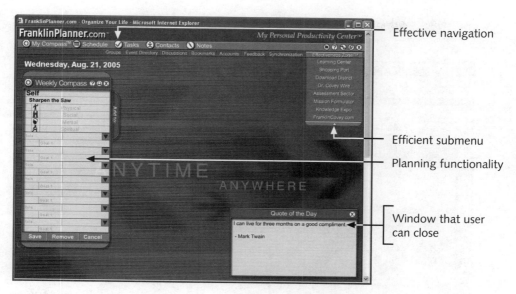

Figure 5-48   Online planning system at the FranklinPlanner Web site

The Salomon Sports Web site shown in Figure 5-50 combines HTML and Flash, and lets users control their path through the Web site.

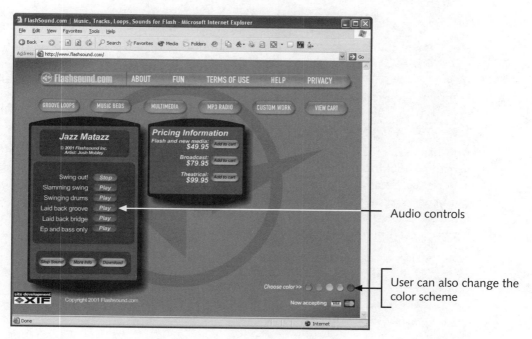

Figure 5-49   User controls music playback

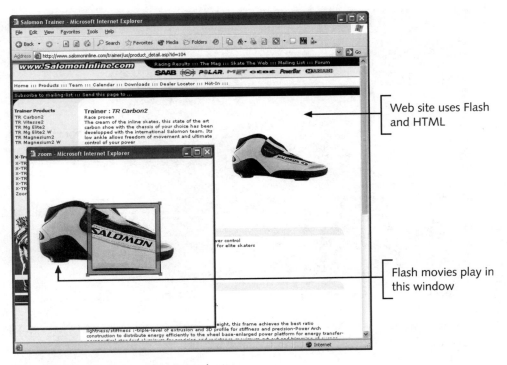

Web site uses Flash and HTML

Flash movies play in this window

Figure 5-50   Salomon Sports Web site

How much content your viewers want is another factor to consider when designing a Flash movie. If your viewers demand a lot of content, consider using HTML pages with your Flash movie. The National Hockey League's Web site (*www.NHL.com*), shown in Figure 5-51, uses a Flash movie as the main source of navigation and is combined with HTML to handle information that changes frequently, such as scores and statistics. This is one way to provide a lot of content without using too much bandwidth.

Another user goal is ease of use. Because users navigate and experience a Web site primarily by clicking buttons and images, the design of these elements is critical to a user's experience. Small navigational target areas with gaps between buttons, or a button that can be clicked only on its label create poor target areas. Consider the calendar shown in Figure 5-52. Not only are the buttons small, but the target areas leave dead zones between each button. This makes the act of navigating much harder.

Links to information that changes frequently

Figure 5-51   NHL Web site

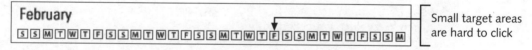

Small target areas are hard to click

Figure 5-52   Example of a poor target area

Selecting a specific day of the month is difficult on this calendar because the design does not follow what Fitt's Law teaches. **Fitt's Law** is the relationship between movement time, accuracy, and size of target. Figure 5-53 shows a Web site that provides a simple clicking task to which Fitt's Law can be applied. Place the mouse pointer inside the starting object (red circle), and then move the mouse to the target area (blue rectangle). Timing begins as soon as the mouse pointer leaves the starting object and ends when the mouse is inside the target area. The time is displayed at the bottom of the window along with the width and amplitude for the trial. The lower the time, the better the design. You can use ActionScript to improve the target area of buttons as the mouse approaches, such as with an animated site map or button that enlarges or divides obvious links with rollovers actions.

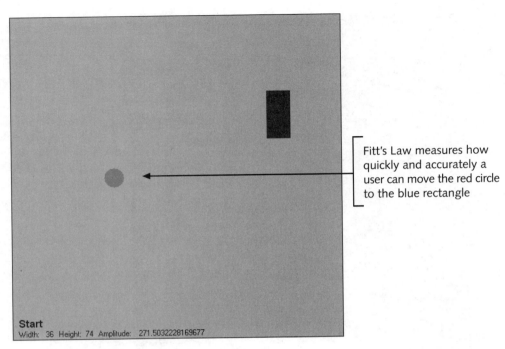

Fitt's Law measures how quickly and accurately a user can move the red circle to the blue rectangle

Figure 5-53   Sample of what Fitt's Law can measure

You can find more information about Fitt's Law and a design quiz to assist user measurement at *AskTOG.com*, a searchable Web site with articles and reports on design issues by Bruce Tognazzini, a recognized leader in human and computer interaction design.

Performing Usability Heuristics

Usability heuristics is evaluating design with focus on the needs and wants of users. This increases your understanding of usability, making your job easier and the end product better. Other than testing performance, browsers, resolutions, platforms, and bandwidths, how can you determine how performance and stability meet user requirements? One testing methodology is to design two comparison sites. These are small versions of the site to use for testing expert users on timed tasks such as answering factual and task-oriented questions, and providing observations and survey feedback.

Visit *www.usablenet.com* to take advantage of free and paid services to evaluate your design and simplify the process of understanding and complying with Section 508 and the Web Accessibility Initiative (WAI) standards, both of which are covered in the next section, "Designing for Accessibility."

Designing for Accessibility

You can create a visually rich Flash movie, but some viewers may not be able to experience the movie as you designed it. For example, they might use a portable device with a small screen or a text-to-speech renderer to navigate Web sites by sound rather than sight.

In some cases, it may be useful to create a single page for a site, intended to function in all these devices. For instance, you can use the NOEMBED HTML tag to provide text descriptions of your Flash movie for browsers that do not support the SWF format. In other situations, it may be more effective to provide different versions of your movie in one file, where one section is optimized for text, another for small screens, and another for spoken delivery. This approach allows visitors to choose a page that suits their needs.

You can take advantage of Flash features such as content magnification, mouse-free navigation, sound synchronization, and custom color palettes to deliver accessible Web content. To address individuals who use assistive technology products such as screen readers, Flash MX must be used with the Flash Player 6, the appropriate screen reader software, and an operating system that supports Flash accessibility. The Macromedia Flash Accessibility Kit contains a template you can use to create accessible movies. You can also download examples with source code at *www.macromedia.com/software/flash/productinfo/accessibility*.

Web Accessibility Initiative (WAI)

The Web Accessibility Initiative (WAI) of the World Wide Web Consortium (W3C), in association with global organizations, promotes Web accessibility by providing technology, guidelines, tools, education, and research and development. To follow the WAI guidelines with your Flash movies, you can create and distribute captions and transcripts of audio, descriptions of video, and auditory descriptions of the key visual elements in a multimedia presentation to your users. Key visual elements include actions, settings, body language, graphics, and displayed text.

The following list describes resources you can use to find tools, checklists, and guidelines to validate your Flash designs and movies:

- The W3C has a guideline to help you produce accessible content at *www.w3.org/TR/WCAG*.

- Macromedia has an accessibility resource center at *www.macromedia.com/macromedia/accessibility*.

- Microsoft provides accessibility resources at *www.microsoft.com/enable*.

- The Center for Applied Special Technology (CAST) uses technology to expand opportunities for those with disabilities. The Bobby Validator was created by CAST to help Web page authors identify and repair significant barriers to access by individuals with disabilities. Visit *www.cast.org/bobby*.

- Dave Raggett's HTML TIDY is a free utility for cleaning hard-to-read markup language generated by specialized HTML editors and conversion tools. TIDY identifies where you need to make your pages more accessible to people with disabilities. Visit *www.w3.org/People/Raggett/tidy*.

Section 508 Compliance

Section 508 (*www.section508.gov*) of the Federal Rehabilitation Act requires that the electronic and information technology produced by federal agencies be accessible to people with disabilities. The criteria for Web-based technology and information are based on access guidelines developed by the WAI of the W3C. Many of these provisions ensure access for people with vision impairments who rely on assistive products to access computer-based information, such as screen readers, which translate computer screen information into automated audible output. Certain conventions, such as verbal identification of images and technologies such as frames, are necessary so that these devices can interpret them for the user in a logical way.

The standards intend to ensure that identification information is also available in an accessible format and do not prohibit the use of images or animation. The standards address the use of text labels or descriptors for graphics and certain format elements, and the usability of multimedia presentations and animation.

Designing for a Global Presence

Global accessibility means providing information so that users around the world can understand it in the context of their own culture. Doing business online means your Web site has a global presence, and requires an understanding of customers who reside in other cultures and have their own currencies, languages, customs, and laws. Making your Flash movies accessible around the world means they are relevant to a customer's language and culture regardless of origination. For example, cultural differences appear in the use of currency symbols, date formats, calendars, numerical separators, and sort orders.

Localizing a Flash movie involves translating the text and using appropriate terminology and images for a particular culture. To successfully localize a global product, you need to work with professional translators and localizers. For example, you can translate the English word "download" into German as "herunter laden," but the usage is incorrect. In the German, *herunter laden* means to "unload," as in unloading boxes from a truck. An experienced translator should be aware of the nuances and will use each word in its proper context.

A nonprofit association, **Localization Industry Standard Association (LISA)**, is the leader for Globalization, Internationalization, and Localization (GIL) business communities. LISA identifies the differences between **localization** and **translation**: "In scope, it is certainly true that localization involves translation. On the content side, programs often have to be changed to conform to national and cultural norms. In multimedia applications the color, size, and shape of objects such as coins and notes, taxis, telephones and mailboxes, and buses and ambulances, traditionally vary from country to country." LISA continues to define **internationalization** as, "the process of designing and implementing a product which is as culturally and technically 'neutral' as possible, and which can therefore easily be localized for a specific culture or cultures."

Recognize that when you use Flash as a design and delivery tool on the Web, you are engaging a global audience of viewers. Flash supports localization by helping you document your movie, manage movie content, and include localized text in your movies.

Documenting Flash movies involves analyzing and recording the meta-data or internal elements, such as font attributes, color, ActionScript syntax and variables, library objects, scenes, references to external files, and elements that promote navigation and interactivity. You can document your movies with the help of the Flash Movie Explorer, which is covered in the next section, "Using the Movie Explorer." You can also create a Project Specification Report to structure your movie elements that need to be translated or modified in some form. If you are using HTML to display your Flash products, you need to translate the <META> tags for site keywords and descriptions, the <TITLE> tag that appears on the browser title bar, and any <ALT> text attributes that provide text descriptions of images.

Managing content involves categorizing your library and symbols; allocating room for translated text for design objects; preparing for cultural diversity; commenting and translating any ActionScript code variables; and testing for usability, errors, and cross-browser compatibility.

To integrate multiple languages into your movies, you should understand the character encoding that Flash uses to display characters and to deliver SWF files to a browser. Flash uses the ISO 8859-1 (Latin-1) character set for both Windows and Macintosh platforms, and displays the characters in SWF files. The Latin-1 standard character set is becoming popular, and may replace the standard ASCII character set in Europe and Latin America. Table 5-1 lists the languages that the Latin-1 character set supports.

Table 5-1   Languages Supported by Latin-1 Character Set

Afrikaans	Finnish	Italian
Basque	French	Norwegian
Catalan	Galician	Portuguese
Danish	German	Scottish
Dutch	Icelandic	Spanish
English	Irish	Swedish
Faeroese		

Flash also supports the Shift Japanese Industrial Standard (Shift-JIS), which is a format for Japanese multibyte-encoded characters. You can use any version of Japanese Windows above 3.1 and the Flash Player where Japanese is the active language.

Delivering SWF files in a wide range of possible character sets is a goal because Latin-1 is an extension of the 7-bit ASCII set, which means it's supported by Transmission Control

Protocol/Internet Protocol (TCP/IP). **TCP/IP** is a suite of networking protocols that computers on the Internet use to communicate with one another. These protocols are also referred to as the U.S. Department of Defense (DOD) or Arpanet protocol suite because their early development was funded by the Advanced Research Projects Agency (ARPA). Besides being used on the Internet, TCP/IP protocols are used to build local area networks (LANs) within a small geographic area, such as a building. TCP/IP is also used on private networks called virtual private networks (VPNs), sometimes called intranets, that can span global distances and are used exclusively by one organization. Because the TCP/IP protocol itself transfers 8-bit data correctly, authoring Flash movies based on TCP/IP delivery does not lead to any loss of information due to its SWF format.

By using external text files to load data into your design elements using dynamic text, you can integrate other Latin-1-based languages, and you can safeguard your FLA files with language experts. You can call the files into dynamic text fields with the loadVariables action without sacrificing the expression of style and color.

Using the Movie Explorer

In previous chapters, you used the movie Library panel to organize objects. As you add complexity to your movies, you can use the Movie Explorer to organize your movie objects. You can use the Movie Explorer to assist in production and troubleshooting of more intricate tasks in Flash.

The Movie Explorer is a Flash tool that organizes the objects of your movie in a hierarchy, starting with the scene as its top level. Each scene is broken down into layers and then into various frames. Where a frame contains content, it can display the objects within it, including button symbols and actions for that button, for example. See Figure 5-54.

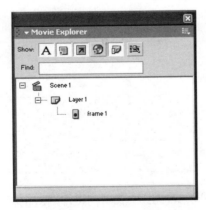

Figure 5-54   Movie Explorer

Using a naming convention for scenes, layers, frames, and objects can make it easy to identify the parts of your movies. The conventions here are adopted from the Reddick VBA (RVBA) Naming Conventions, which were developed for use in Visual Basic for

Applications (VBA). The goal of the RVBA is to use a name for an object that conveys information about the meaning of that object. For instance, a movie symbol name should always include a mov prefix, as in the generic name movSymbol, or the more descriptive movSymbolMenuTop. Another example could be for a movie's dynamic text field for data entry, txtNameFirst. You can create your own system for naming objects, but be sure to write guidelines that have the most meaning for your work. The RVBA conventions are based on the Hungarian conventions for constructing object names, developed by Charles Simonyi. The general format of an object name is [prefixes]tag[BaseName[Suffixes]]. Table 5-2 describes each part of this naming convention.

Table 5-2   RVBA Naming Convention

Component	Description
Prefix	Modifies the Tag component to indicate supplemental information, lowercase
Tag	Short set of characters, usually mnemonic for ease of memory, indicating the type of the object, all lowercase
BaseName	One or more words that indicate what the object represents; capitalize the first letter of each word in the BaseName
Suffixes	Additional information about the meaning of the BaseName; capitalize the first letter of each word in the Suffix

Integrating HTML into Macromedia Flash Movies

The Property inspector for a text box has an option for using HTML within Flash. This selection gives you the opportunity to use common HTML tags within your movie for formatting purposes. In many cases, you use this option when you are loading an external text file into Flash. Then you can easily update text objects and maintain the look and feel of your movie at the same time.

Flash supports the following HTML tags, and lets you edit these tags in standard text boxes:

- <A> – anchor tag for linking to a URL
- <B> – bold text
- <FONT COLOR> – changes the font color
- <FONT FACE> – changes the font face, for example, Arial or Verdana
- <FONT SIZE> – changes the font size
- <I> – italicizes text
- <P> – separates paragraphs
- <U> – underlines text

Dynamic Text Fields and HTML

Dynamic text refers to a change in the content of a text box. The text can be a single line or a wrapped paragraph of text. For example, suppose you are designing a Web site with Flash, and you want to include a News page that is updated daily. Instead of updating and republishing the Flash .FLA file every day, you could update the News page's text with an ASCII text file.

With the loadVariables action, you can change the contents of a text box with an external text file. In addition, using the HTML option on the Text Options panel, you can embed the HTML tags in the preceding list into the text file to preserve the formatting of a Web page when you publish the SWF file.

In the following steps, you use the loadVariables action to load an external generic text file into a dynamic text box. A text file named load_text.txt is already created for you; it contains text about running the New York City marathon and is formatted with HTML tags. You can open the text file in an editor such as Notepad or WordPad in Windows, or Simple Text on the Mac. The contents and HTML formatting will load into the dynamic text box, replacing the current contents.

To load text from an external file:

1. Open **load_text.txt** in Notepad to examine the text and the HTML tags. See Figure 5-55. Then close Notepad.

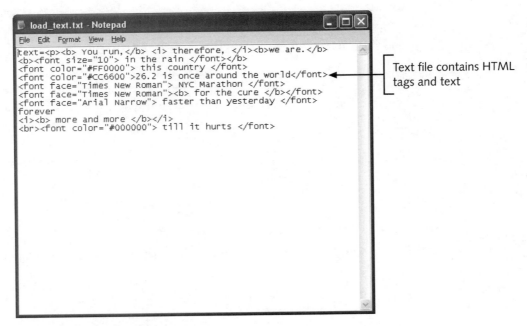

Text file contains HTML tags and text

Figure 5-55 Contents of the text file

2. In Flash, open **LoadTextFile.fla** from the Chapter5 folder in your FlashSamples folder. Save the file as **myLoadTextFile.fla** in the same location. Notice the text box already in place for you on the Stage.

3. Click the text box on the Stage, open the Property inspector, if necessary, click the **Text type** list arrow (this is the text box that contains "Input Text"), and then click **Dynamic Text**. Close the Property inspector.

4. Click **frame 1** on the Actions layer, and then expand the Actions panel. Switch to Normal Mode, if necessary.

5. Click to expand the **Browser/Network** folder, if necessary, and then double-click the **loadVariables** action to add it to the Action list.

6. In the URL text box, type **load_text.txt**. Be sure you have the text file in the same folder as the LoadTextFile.fla file, or Flash will not be able to find the file.

7. Keep the remaining parameters as their default settings, as in Figure 5-56. These settings mean that when this movie plays frame 1, Flash displays the contents of the load_text.txt because you set the text box type to dynamic.

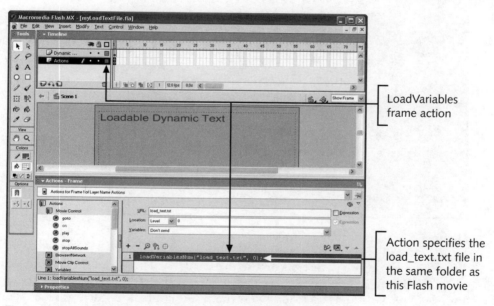

Figure 5-56   The loadVariables action calling a text file

8. Click **Control** on the menu bar, and then click **Test Movie**. Notice that Flash replaces "Loadable Dynamic Text" with text from the load_text.txt file, which is about the New York City marathon and is formatted using HTML tags.

9. Close the Test Movie window, and then save and close **myLoadTextFile.fla**, but leave Flash open for the next set of steps.

Customizing the Mouse Pointer

Customizing your mouse pointer or its trailers, which are images that appear under or behind the pointer as you move it, makes the pointer easier to see when you are moving it. Customized mouse pointers and trailers can add diversity to your movie and are common in games or entertainment Web sites, such as the Barbie Web site, which uses floral mouse trailers, as shown in Figure 5-57.

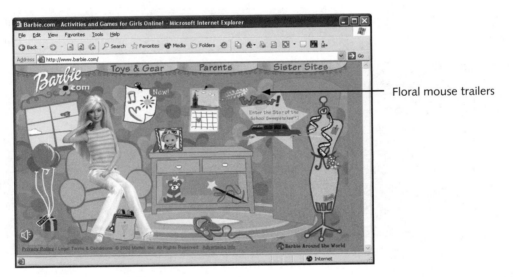

Floral mouse trailers

Figure 5-57   Custom mouse trailers

To customize mouse pointers, you use the startDrag action and the Mouse.hide method with a movie clip symbol. This symbol contains the shape and appearance of the new mouse. The startDrag action gives the user control of dragging a symbol. The Mouse.hide method hides the default mouse until a Mouse.show method is used to make it visible again.

To customize a mouse pointer:

1. In Flash, open **NewMousePointer.fla** from the Chapter5 folder of your FlashSamples folder. Save the file as **myNewMousePointer.fla** in the same location. The new mouse movie clip symbol is already placed on the Stage

for you, and the Timeline already includes an Actions layer. Press **Ctrl+L** (**Command+L** on the Macintosh) to open the Library panel. Click the **New Pointer** icon in the Library panel.

2. Click **frame 1** on the Actions layer, and then open the Actions panel.

3. First, you will hide the default mouse pointer in order to use the new one. Scroll down the Action list and open the **Objects** folder.

4. Open the **Movie**, **Mouse**, and then **Methods** folders to access the hide and show methods. Double-click **hide** to add the Mouse.hide action to the Action list.

5. Next, you need to drag and use the movie clip symbol instead of the default mouse. Scroll up to and open the **Movie Clip Control** folder in the Actions folder, and double-click the **startDrag** action to add it to the Action list.

6. In the Target text box, type **arrow** to give it a reference name, and then click the **Lock mouse to center** check box to select it. These settings mean the movie clip will function like a mouse pointer and will appear in the center of the screen because "arrow" refers to the link identifier. See Figure 5-58.

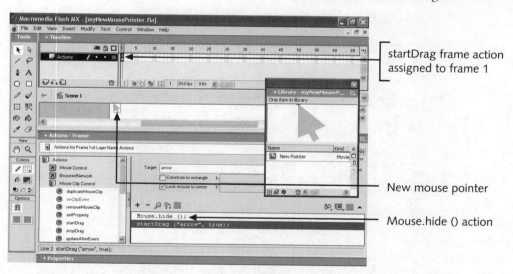

Figure 5-58   Actions panel with Mouse.hide action

7. Close the Actions panel, and then test your movie. (Click **Control** on the menu bar, and then click **Test Movie**.) Move the mouse—the green arrow now appears as the pointer instead of the default black pointer. Close the Test Movie window.

8. Save and close **myNewMousePointer.fla**, but leave Flash open for the next set of steps.

Creating Mouse Trailers

The startDrag action is the power behind a mouse trailer. Once you have created the movie clip for the mouse pointer, setting up how to move it with the mouse is straightforward. In the following steps, you use the startDrag action with an existing movie clip. The movie clip shows a spinning target, which appears as the mouse trailer for the default mouse pointer.

To create mouse trailers:

1. In Flash, open **MouseFollow.fla** from the Chapter5 folder of your FlashSamples folder. Save the file as **myMouseFollow.fla** in the same location. The movie clip symbol of a target is already in place for you as is an Actions layer.

2. Double-click the **movie clip symbol** (named Follow Mouse) on the Stage to open it in Edit mode to view the tween, and then return to **Scene 1**.

3. Click **frame 1** on the Actions layer, and then open the Actions panel.

4. In the **Actions**, **Movie Clip Control** folder, double-click the **startDrag** action.

5. In the Target text box, type **/follow** to have the symbol follow the default mouse pointer.

6. Click the **Lock mouse to center** check box to select it. Your Actions panel should resemble Figure 5-59.

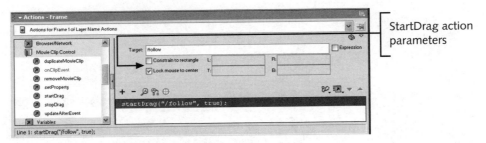

Figure 5-59   Actions panel with startDrag parameters

7. Collapse the Actions panel, and then test your movie. A spinning target should appear under your mouse pointer as you move it. Close the Test Movie window.

8. Save and close **myMouseFollow.fla**, and then exit Flash.

CHAPTER SUMMARY

❑ You can organize larger and more complex movies using more than one scene and more than one movie level. Adding new scenes can help you organize a movie that has a lot of content or a very long Timeline. Similar to a multi-scene movie, a multi-level movie is separated into logical sections, although these sections are usually as long and complex as a complete movie. When you create a multi-level movie, you can play additional movies without closing the Flash Player, or switch movies without loading another HTML page. A new movie can be called from any frame of the main Timeline and layered on top of the existing movie.

❑ To avoid having users leave a Web site because of download time, you can use a movie preloader, which is a set of frames that appears quickly to indicate that a movie is loading. A preloader gives your audience something interesting to view as they wait for the rest of the movie to download and can also indicate the download progress.

❑ Movie clip and button symbols can make your Flash movie easy to access and navigate for your audience. These symbols should include meaningful text or images so users quickly understand their purpose.

❑ Besides playing video and animating rollover effects, you can also add animation effects to your Flash movies. Animation effects such as images that slide in from the edge of the screen, dissolve from one image to another, or break apart are common video techniques that attract attention to parts of your movie and signal a transition, such as from one topic to another.

❑ In addition to using Flash to create navigation buttons and animation effects on a Web site, you can use Flash to create the complete interface, which includes all the elements the user interacts with on a Web site. The graphics, color, organization, navigation devices, and use of sound and video are all part of the interface.

❑ Your goal when creating movies is to blend the design and the content. Designing the interface involves more than arranging colored text and animation. Your design should use images, movie elements, and other objects to reflect the content, which is the message of your movie and the information it provides.

❑ Three interface elements that you can design with Flash are drop-down menus, dynamic text, and customized mouse pointers and trailers. A drop-down menu is a button or other link that users click or roll over to display a list of related options, and it is ideal for navigating a large hierarchy of information. Dynamic text appears in a standard Flash text box, but changes depending on the content of an external file. You can include HTML tags in the external file to maintain consistent formatting. Customizing your mouse pointer or its trailer, which are images that appear under or behind the pointer as you move it, makes the pointer easier to see when you are moving it.

5

REVIEW QUESTIONS

1. The most appropriate time to use multi-level movies is when your main movie is short. True or false?

2. For which of the following purposes do you use movie preloaders?

   a. indicate the amount of time to wait before the movie downloads

   b. entertain viewers as they wait for the movie

   c. load the entire movie effectively

   d. all of the above

3. Use the _____ for analyzing movie optimization.

4. You should avoid testing movies to estimate download time from a Web server because it is too time-consuming. True or false?

5. Animated buttons are used with what type of symbol?

   a. graphic symbol

   b. Action symbol

   c. movie clip symbol

   d. none of the above

6. You must know how to use ActionScript to create dynamic animations such as transitions. True or false?

7. Assessing user preferences can help determine choices of color and design for your movie. True or false?

8. You should test movie output on systems that use the fastest download speed and highest monitor resolution. True or false?

9. Which of the following movie elements cannot be used as content in a design effectively?

   a. font style

   b. color

   c. Stage speed

   d. graphic symbols

10. The use of style and color can affect a viewer's mood. True or false?

11. Usability analysis can help which of the following features?

   a. Web site functionality

   b. an online shopping experience

   c. use of color and style

   d. all of the above

12. Animation is useful for attracting the attention of users. True or false?

13. You should avoid integrating Flash with HTML; this can create performance problems. True or false?

14. Flash movies can be designed for accessibility by which of the following?

    a. mouse-free navigation

    b. custom color palettes

    c. content magnification

    d. all of the above

15. A _____ is a button or other link that users click or roll over to display a list of related options.

16. Interpreted content with computer-based translating is always the best method. True or false?

17. Text boxes can contain _____ text that is updated and formatted from an outside file.

18. When integrating an HTML file with a text box, which of the following tags can you *not* use?

    a. <A> – anchor tag for linking to a URL

    b. <include> – to use another HTML file

    c. <FONT COLOR> – change the font color

    d. <B> – use bold text

19. Hiding the standard mouse uses the _____ method.

20. You can use a _____ symbol to customize the mouse pointer.

HANDS-ON PROJECTS

Project 5-1

In this project, you create an advanced rollover button that displays a description of the button and related service when the user points to it. The series of symbols in the middle of the Stage also serve as rollover buttons to display more information about the topic heading. The first button is already created for you. You will create the rollover effect for the Coaching Courses button under the coaching services heading.

1. In Macromedia Flash, open **WebCoach01.fla** from the Chapter5\Projects folder in your FlashSamples folder. Save the file as **myWebCoach01.fla** in the same location.

2. Test the movie with the Test Movie command on the Control menu, and point to the first button in the Coaching Services column called Personal Coaching.

Text appears to the right of the button, describing the related coaching service. Close the Test Movie window and return to the Stage.

3. Open the Library panel, if necessary. Be sure the Button Nav layer is selected in the Timeline. Click Insert on the menu bar, and then click New Symbol to create a button symbol. Type btCoachingCourses as the name of the new button symbol, click the Button option button, and then click OK.

4. The Up frame of this button will show the mcCoachingCourse symbol. Add a keyframe to the Up frame by pressing the F6 key, and then click the Up frame again to make sure it's selected. Drag the mcCoachingCourses movie clip symbol onto the Stage.

5. Open the Property inspector, if necessary, and position the mcCoachingCourses movie clip symbol to −50.0 on the Stage for both the X and Y axes.

6. The Over frame will show the mcCoachingCoursesText movie clip, and work as a mouse rollover to display the descriptive text, just as the Personal Coaching button does with its descriptive text. Click to select the Over frame, and add a keyframe to it by pressing the F6 key. Click the Over frame to make sure it's selected. Drag the mcCoachingCoursesText movie clip symbol onto the Stage.

7. Position the mcCoachingCoursesText symbol to −50.0 on both the X and Y axes. This ensures that the two movie clips appear in the same place during the rollover.

8. Click to select the Down frame on the Timeline. From the Insert menu, click the Clear Keyframe command. This will insert a clear keyframe to simply use the prior Over frame's content.

9. Return to Scene 1 by clicking on the Scene 1 command just below the main Timeline. You need to delete the existing mcCoachingCourses movie clip symbol from the Stage, as it was used as a visual placeholder. Note the position of the mcCoachingCourses movie clip symbol (the one with the man in a floating yoga position) was 219.0 for the X axis value and 375.9 for the Y axis value.

10. Click to select the mcCoachingCourses movie clip symbol on the Stage, and delete it. Ensure the Button Nav layer is selected, and drag the new btCoachingCourses button symbol to the Stage in the same position as the symbol you just deleted, 219.0 for the X axis value and 375.9 for the Y axis value.

11. Test the movie by clicking the Test Movie command on the Control menu. Descriptive text appears to the right when you point to the btCoachingCourses button symbol in test mode.

12. Return to the Stage by closing the Test Movie window, and then save and close **myWebCoach01.fla**.

Project 5-2

In this project, you continue working with the Web Coach Central movie to create a text box that displays the text from a standard text file, such as Windows Notepad or Macintosh SimpleText. You incorporate HTML tags to format the text in the text editor, and use this as a fictitious weekly news column.

5

1. Start a text editor such as Notepad (click Start, point to All Programs, point to Accessories, and then click Notepad) or SimpleText for the Macintosh. Open **coaching_tips.txt** in the Chapter5\Projects folder in your FlashSamples folder. Review the text and the HTML tags, and then close the text editor.

2. In Macromedia Flash, open **WebCoach02.fla** from the Chapter5\Projects folder in your FlashSamples folder. Save the file as **myWebCoach02.fla** in the same location.

3. Select the text box on the upper left area of the Stage, containing the "Coaching Tips & Techniques, loaded from coaching_tips.txt" text, and then open the Property inspector if necessary.

4. In the Property inspector, click the first list arrow (named "Text type" when you point to it), and click the Dynamic Text option. Ensure that the Multiline option is selected in the Line type list arrow, and then ensure the Selectable, Render text as HTML, and Show Border Around Text buttons are selected.

5. In the Var or Variable text box, type the word "text" (without the quotation marks). This word is referenced in the text file, and is used as a link from the text box on the Stage to the text file.

6. Click frame 1 on the Dynamic Text layer, and then open the Actions panel. Ensure the Actions panel is in Normal mode.

7. In the Actions panel, expand the Browser/Network folder, and double-click the loadVariables action. Enter "coaching_tips.txt" (without the quotation marks) in the URL text box. The loadVariables action loads the text file into the text box on the Stage.

8. Close the Actions panel. You need to resize the text box after making it dynamic. Do this by clicking the Text tool on the toolbox, and dragging the sizing handle to increase the length of the text box to the bottom of the symbols on the Stage.

9. Test the movie by clicking the Test Movie command on the Control menu and verify the content of the text box is from the external text file, not the placeholder text you see on the Stage in design mode.

10. Return to the Stage by closing the Test Movie window, and then save and close **myWebCoach02.fla**.

Project 5-3

In this project, you continue working with the Web Coach Central movie to create a series of dissolve effects. This will create an eye-catching design in the heading area of the presentation with text and images that fade in and out. Three new layers, tweens, and objects are already placed on your Stage and the Timeline.

1. Open **WebCoach03.fla** from the Chapter5\Projects folder in your FlashSamples folder.

2. Save the file as **myWebCoach03.fla** in the same location.

3. Click to select frame 25 of the Stepping Stones layer. In the Property inspector, type 75 in the Ease text box. With frame 25 still selected, use the Arrow tool to click the "grTopHeader-Rocks" symbol on the Stage. (This is the image of a hand placing stones on a slab.) The Property inspector changes to reflect that selection. Click the Color list arrow, and select the Alpha option. In the Alpha text box, type 25 and press Enter. This creates a gradual dissolve effect to frame 25, then back to a normal image to frame 50.

4. Click to select frame 30 of the Planning layer. In the Property inspector, type –75 in the Ease text box. With frame 30 still selected, click to select the "grTransitionPlanning" symbol on the Stage. (This is the image that shows a pen, phone, graph, and computer.) The Property inspector changes to reflect that selection. Click the Color list arrow, and select the Alpha option, if necessary. In the Alpha text box, type 25 and press Enter. This creates a gradual dissolve effect to frame 30, then back to a normal image to frame 50.

5. Click to select frame 35 of the Stepping Stones layer. In the Property inspector, type 25 in the Ease text box. With frame 35 still selected, click to select the "grHabitText" symbol on the Stage. (This is the Habit 1 Be Proactive text.) The Property inspector changes to reflect that selection. Click the Color list arrow, and select the Alpha option, if necessary. In the Alpha text box, type 35 and press Enter. This creates a gradual dissolve effect to frame 35, then back to a normal image to frame 50.

6. Click the Test Movie command from the Control menu to test the movie, to verify that the dissolve effects appear in the heading area. Close the Test Movie window, and save and close **myWebCoach03.fla**.

Project 5-4

In this project, you create a multi-level movie. The main navigational button has a rollover, but you need to set the button so that a click loads an appropriate movie. A new SWF file should load on top of the main movie for each movie section. The only change that occurs, is the text describing the section replaces the News text box.

1. Open **WebCoach04.fla** from the Chapter5\Projects folder in your FlashSamples folder. The WebCoach04a.swf file is already placed in the same location for you. Save the file as **myWebCoach04.fla** in the same location.

2. In this step, you will add a button click sound to the Personal Coaching (btCoachingServices) button symbol (the blue symbol with a satellite). Double-click the btCoachingServices button symbol on the Stage to open it in Edit mode. Open the Library, if necessary. Click to select the Over frame in the Timeline, and drag the Switch Small Plastic sound from the document library to the Stage. It is automatically added to the Over, Down, and Hit frames due to the structure of the keyframes in that button.

3. Click the Scene 1 button to return to the main scene's Stage. Test the sound effect by clicking the Test Movie command in the Control menu. Then, roll your mouse over the Personal Coaching (btCoachingServices) button symbol to hear the sound effect. Close the Test Movie window to return to the main Stage.

4. Right-click the Personal Coaching (btCoachingServices) button symbol on the Stage, and then click Actions on the shortcut menu to display the Actions panel for that button symbol.

5. Ensure you are working in Normal mode. Open the Actions and the Browser/Network folders, double-click the loadMovie action, and type "WebCoach04a.swf" (without the quotation marks) in the URL property of the loadMovie action. Leave the remaining properties with their default setting. Close the Actions panel.

6. Click the Test Movie command from the Control menu to test the movie, and then click the personal coaching image to verify that the WebCoach04a.swf loads in the main movie.

7. Close the Test Movie window, and save and close **myWebCoach04.fla**.

CASE PROJECTS

Case Project 5-1

A nonprofit association has commissioned you to design a Flash Web site. The association's objectives are to provide education and outreach for disabled people. The Web site must comply with the Section 508 and WAI standards. First do the necessary research to produce a general set of requirements, write a two- to three-page report describing the requirements, and then sketch your design.

Case Project 5-2

The sponsors of an automotive Web site have asked you to create an interactive Web site that presents an online catalog of automotive products and lets users display detailed information about a selected product. The intended audience for this design are other automotive businesses. Write two or three product descriptions in separate text documents. Then use dynamic text boxes to create a basic interactive form. Include two or three movie clips and rollover buttons. Use the loadMovie techniques to display detailed product information when users point to a movie clip or rollover button.

Case Project 5-3

Create a Flash movie presenting your interests or showcasing the products and services of your fictitious company. The movie should involve at least two of the advanced animation techniques you learned in this chapter, such as using multiple scenes, loading movies, using a movie preloader, and using rollover effects with movie clips and buttons.

6

INTRODUCTION TO ACTIONSCRIPT

Scripting in Macromedia Flash

In this chapter, you will:

♦ Understand ActionScript

♦ Learn what's new in Macromedia Flash MX ActionScript for developers

♦ Work with the Macromedia Flash MX scripting environment

♦ Learn ActionScript techniques and uses

♦ Work with ActionScript structures and commands

♦ Troubleshoot and debug ActionScript syntax

In previous chapters, you learned the basics of designing Macromedia Flash movies with symbols, animation, imported images, audio, and video. In this chapter, you begin learning advanced design techniques to make your movies more sophisticated and interactive. One powerful technique is a scripting tool called ActionScript. A scripting tool is a programming language you use to manipulate, customize, and automate an application. ActionScript provides a full range of scripting capabilities for automating Flash movies.

UNDERSTANDING ACTIONSCRIPT

ActionScript is the scripting language that Flash provides to create interactive movies that users can control by clicking objects and entering information. A scripting language is a way to communicate with a program; you can use scripts to tell Flash what to do and to find out what is happening as a movie runs. This two-way communication lets you create interactive movies. ActionScript provides elements, such as actions, operators, and objects, that you use in scripts to tell your movie what to do. You set up your movie so that events, such as button clicks and key presses, trigger these scripts. **Events** are programming statements that give instructions to movie elements to react to user commands. An event can be as simple as a user clicking a button or pressing a key, or as involved as loading a movie clip or moving to another frame on your Timeline. For example, you can use ActionScript to create navigation buttons for your movie.

You are already familiar with using the Actions panel in Normal mode to write scripts with ActionScript. In Normal mode, you build scripts by choosing options from menus and lists and entering customized information in text boxes. In this way, you can write simple scripts without becoming an advanced ActionScript user. Once you have a script, you can attach it to a button, movie clip, or frame to create the interactivity you need. Recall that you can also use the Actions panel in Expert mode, where you enter text directly into the Script pane. If you have worked with a script editor for another scripting language, such as JavaScript or Active Server Pages (ASP), you will see that Expert mode lets you work the same way. You edit actions, enter parameters for actions, or delete actions directly in the Script pane. See Figure 6-1.

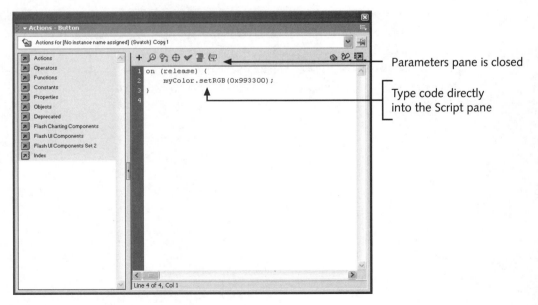

Figure 6-1   Actions panel in Expert mode

In Expert mode you can also check script syntax for errors, automatically format code, and use code hints to help you complete syntax. In addition, the punctuation balance feature helps you correctly pair parentheses, braces, or brackets in the script. You'll examine these features later in this chapter. Although Flash provides these features to make creating scripts easier, when you use the Actions panel in Expert mode, you must have a clear understanding of ActionScript.

Like other scripting languages, ActionScript follows its own rules of syntax, reserves keywords, provides operators, and allows you to use variables to store and retrieve information. You can use the objects and functions built into ActionScript, or you can create your own objects and functions. See the "Working with ActionScript Structures and Commands" section for a detailed explanation of ActionScript basics and syntax.

ActionScript is a combination of predefined actions and other programming syntax. This syntax can include variables; conditional statements such as looping and if-then-else structures; operators such as arithmetic or comparison (<=) operators; predefined functions such as the getVersion() function to report the current Flash player version; object properties such as the height and width of a button; and a list of deprecated objects that are being phased out of ActionScript.

In the following steps, you use ActionScript to set the visible property of a button to zero (0). This property causes the button itself to become invisible when it is clicked. The standard Flash movie elements do not allow you to achieve this effect; you must use ActionScript to make a button invisible.

To use ActionScript to make a button invisible:

1. Open **ActionScriptSample.swf** from the Chapter6 folder in your FlashSamples folder.

2. Click the button to test the effect. Then close ActionScriptSample.swf.

3. Open the **ActionScriptSample.fla** from the Chapter6 folder in your FlashSamples folder.

4. Open the Actions panel and switch to Expert mode, if necessary. (Click the **View Options** button; if **Expert Mode** is not checked, click this option to select it.) Also turn on line numbers, if necessary, by clicking the **View Options** button and then clicking **View Line Numbers** to select this option.

5. Click to select the **button** on the Stage, and then review the ActionScript code in the Actions panel. See Figure 6-2.

   The `on (release)` line determines when the next statement occurs. `On release` is an event that Flash performs when the mouse button is released after clicking the object that is selected on the Stage. The `setProperty` line sets the visible property of the selected object, in this case the button on the Stage, to zero, which makes the button invisible.

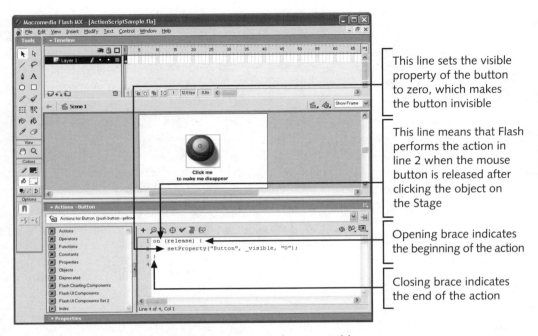

Figure 6-2   ActionScript code for making an object invisible

6. Close the Actions panel. Then close ActionScriptSample.fla without saving it, but leave Flash open for the next set of steps.

Now that you see how a simple script works, you're ready to learn about what is new in Flash MX ActionScript. In the following sections, you also work with the ActionScript programming environment, and learn more about ActionScript techniques and uses. You work with the various ActionScript command structures and syntax, and troubleshoot and debug ActionScript syntax.

WHAT'S NEW IN MACROMEDIA FLASH MX ACTIONSCRIPT FOR DEVELOPERS

If you are familiar with ActionScript in Flash 5, this section describes some of the new features in ActionScript, including dot notation syntax and several new commands.

ActionScript and the Dot Notation Syntax

As with any programming language, you need to learn and understand the rules for writing statements. Flash 5 was the first Flash version to use the dot notation syntax and the first to comply with the ECMA-262 standard, the specification written by the European Computer Manufacturers Association. Some ActionScript elements in Flash 5 and earlier have been deprecated, or are being gradually phased out of use. These elements are replaced by new ActionScript elements that correspond to the ECMA Standard.

Dot notation syntax is the programming convention that ActionScript uses to combine commands into statements the script can execute by separating the commands with periods, or dots. Dot notation syntax replaces the slash syntax used in Flash before version 5, and makes it easier to program with ActionScript. For example, if you want to reference a movie clip and program it to play in earlier versions of Flash, you would need three lines of code using the older Tell Target action and its slash notation.

```
Begin Tell Target ("/mcBall")
                    Play
End Tell Target
```

With the dot notation, you need only one line, as in the following code for the following "ball" movie clip.

```
mcBall.play();
```

For more information on the ECMA standard, visit the following Web links:
- ECMA – Standardizing Information and Communication Systems: *www.ecma.ch*
- Standard ECMA-262 – ECMA Script Language Specification: *www.ecma.ch/ecma1/STAND/ECMA-262.HTM*
- Sun and Netscape's JavaScript guide, JavaScript Developer Central: *developer.netscape.com/tech/javascript/index.html*
- International Organization for Standardization: *www.iso.ch*
- Netscape's JavaScript guide: *wp.netscape.com/eng/mozilla/3.0/handbook/javascript*
- Microsoft's ECMA C# and Common Language Infrastructure Standards: *msdn.microsoft.com/net/ecma/default.asp*

New ActionScript Commands

Flash MX builds on an already powerful ActionScript tool by adding several new commands, including those that let you control the layout of the Stage, use a Switch statement to test conditions in ActionScript code, and control text field and button objects.

You can use the new Stage object in Flash MX to change the information that sets the boundaries of a Flash movie. For example, you can use ActionScript to control the alignment of the Flash movie in a user's browser, set the height and width of the Stage in pixels, and manage the scale properties of the Stage. Figure 6-3 shows the properties of the Stage.

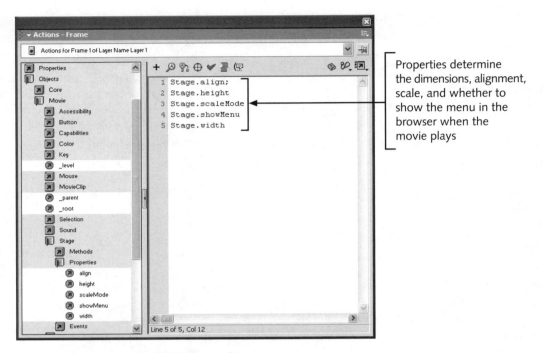

Properties determine the dimensions, alignment, scale, and whether to show the menu in the browser when the movie plays

Figure 6-3   Properties of the Stage object

You can use ActionScript to set the following properties of the Stage:

- *Align*–Sets the vertical and horizontal alignment of the Flash movie in the browser

- *Height*–Sets the height of the Stage in pixels

- *ShowMenu*–Determines whether to show the browser menu when the Flash movie plays

- *ScaleMode*–Sizes the Stage to fit exactly within the browser window, to show all the objects on the Stage, to omit a border, or not to scale in the browser window

- *Width*–Sets the width of the Stage in pixels

In addition to setting the properties of the Stage, you can also use ActionScript to set the properties of some objects. All text field and button symbols in a Flash MX movie are instances of their respective object. You can use ActionScript to manipulate the methods and properties of an object. For example, you can control the rotation, visibility, and scale of an object with ActionScript.

WORKING WITH THE MACROMEDIA FLASH MX SCRIPTING ENVIRONMENT

Flash MX provides a sophisticated environment for you to work with ActionScript. An **environment** is the set of available tools, editors, and conditions you use in a program. Recall that as in prior versions, Flash MX comes equipped with a movable and dockable Actions panel, with both Normal and Expert modes.

One part of the scripting environment makes it easier to write scripts for specific objects. The Flash MX Actions panel now supports pinning. **Pinning** the Actions panel allows you to restrict all of your scripting to one frame; otherwise, the Actions panel changes its contents as you select frames on the Timeline. For example, Figure 6-4 shows the Pin current script command to lock the Actions panel to the currently scripted object.

6

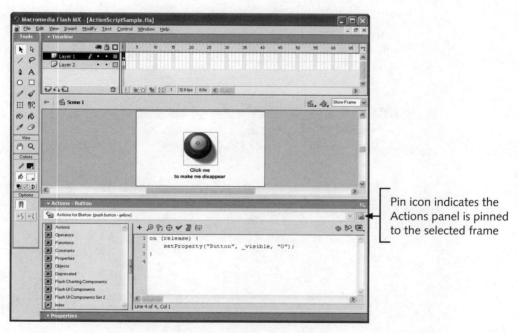

Pin icon indicates the Actions panel is pinned to the selected frame

Figure 6-4   Using the Pin current script command

Using the Find and Replace Commands

Find and **Replace** are useful commands that allow you to quickly search for and replace text within a script. As in a text document that you edit with a word processor, you can make mass replacements of a text entry and match the case of searched text. For example, suppose you create several buttons that will respond to the release of the mouse, write the code for those actions, and later realize that instead of the release event, you need to use the rollout event, which performs an action when the mouse points to a button. You can use the Replace command to search for every instance of the `on (release) {` line of code and replace it with the `on (rollOut) {` line of code.

In the following steps, you work with a block of stamp symbols in a Flash movie. When users point to a stamp and then move the mouse pointer away, the stamp symbol is supposed to disappear from the Stage. To create this effect, the Flash movie uses a script that begins with `on (rollOut) {` for each stamp instance. However, the scripts for some stamps start with `on (release) {` instead. You will use the Replace command to replace script text so all the stamps follow a script that begins with `(rollOut) {`.

To use the Replace command:

1. Open the **FindAndReplace.fla** file in the Chapter6 folder in your FlashSamples folder. Save the file as **myFindAndReplace.fla** in the same location.

2. Right-click (press Ctrl + click on the Macintosh) the **top left stamp**, which is an instance of the stamp button named "stamp1," and then click **Actions** on the shortcut menu. The Actions panel opens, displaying ActionScript code associated with frame 1. See Figure 6-5.

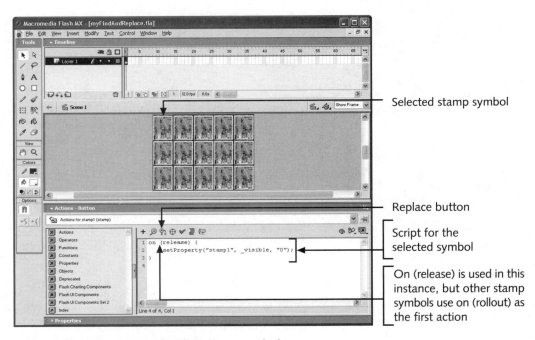

Figure 6-5 ActionScript for the stamp symbol

3. Click the **Replace** button on the Actions panel.

4. Type **release** in the Find what text box.

5. Type **rollOut** in the Replace with text box. The Replace dialog box should look like the one in Figure 6-6.

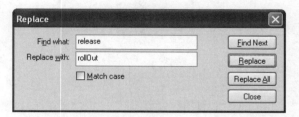

Figure 6-6   Replace dialog box

6. Click the **Replace All** button to replace the text as you specified. Flash replaces all instances of "release" with "rollOut." The instance of the stamp symbol "stamp1" now matches the code for all of the other 14 stamp instances. Click **OK**, then click the **Close** button.

7. Test the movie and watch the stamp instances disappear as you point to each stamp and then move your mouse pointer away from the stamp.

8. Click the **Close** button and then close the Actions panel.

9. Save and close **myFindAndReplace.fla**, but leave Flash open for the next set of steps.

Alternatively, you can select the Find and Replace commands in the Actions panel menu (located in the upper-right corner of the Actions panel) or press Ctrl+F and Ctrl+H (Option + F and Option + H on the Macintosh), respectively. You can click the Find Next and Replace or Replace All buttons to find and replace the next or all instances of the words you specified in that page of code.

Customizing ActionScript with Preferences

You use **preferences** to customize the appearance of the Actions panel. For example, you might want to change the syntax coloring or prevent lines of code from automatically indenting. You can access these preferences by using the Actions panel menu or by clicking Edit on the menu bar and then clicking Preferences to open the Preferences dialog box. The ActionScript Editor tab in the Preferences dialog box contains all of the options relevant to the Actions panel and ActionScript customization, as shown in Figure 6-7.

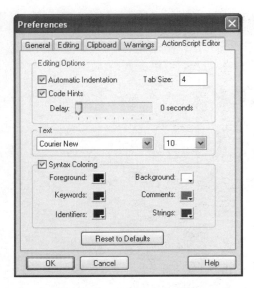

Figure 6-7   Setting preferences for the ActionScript Editor

Table 6-1 describes the ActionScript Editor preferences. Some of the most common and beneficial features are the syntax coloring, text style and size, and code hint delay. The code hint delay is useful for setting the amount of time Flash waits before displaying a code hint.

Table 6-1   ActionScript Editor Preferences

Preference	Description
Automatic Indentation	Click this check box to automatically indent ActionScript code when you are working in Expert mode
Tab Size	Enter the tab size for the indentation; the default is four character spaces
Code Hints	Click this check box to use code completion tips in both Expert and Normal modes
Delay	Set the delay time in seconds for a code hint to appear
Text	Select the font style of the text within the Actions Editor
Text Size	Select the size of the text within the Actions Editor
Syntax Coloring	Check this box to set the color of ActionScript syntax, and then select the color you want to use for foreground and background text, keywords, comments, identifiers, and strings
Reset to Defaults	Click this button to restore all settings to the default settings, as if Flash MX had just been installed

Flash MX provides other ActionScript features to assist any novice or experienced Flash designer. Some of these tools are covered in the following sections.

Using Auto Format and Auto Complete

Code formatting helps you read and interpret ActionScript code. Use the **Auto Format** feature to arrange your code in the ActionScript formatting style; for example, place braces ({ }) around your code and space it so you can clearly see where one action begins and ends. An Auto Format Options dialog box with several options and a pre-view pane is also available, as shown in Figure 6-8. Each option in this dialog box is described in the following list. To open the Auto Format Options dialog box, click the menu icon on the Actions panel, and then click Auto Format Options.

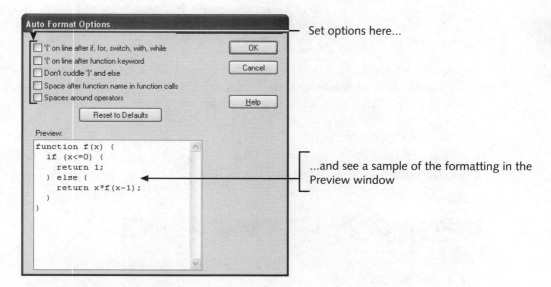

Set options here...

...and see a sample of the formatting in the Preview window

Figure 6-8   Auto Format Options dialog box

- *'{' on line after if, for, switch, with, while*—Inserts the brace after these statements of code, instead of under them

- *'{' on line after function keyword*—Inserts the brace after a function statement of code, instead of under it

- *Don't cuddle '{' and else*—Within an if-then-else statement, inserts the brace above an else statement of code, instead of before and after the else statement

- *Space after function name in function calls*—Inserts a character space after a function

- *Spaces around operators*—Inserts a character space around logical and arithmetic operators

In the following steps, you turn on and off the various Auto Format options and view the results in the Preview window.

To test the Auto Format options:

1. Open a new Flash document.

2. Open the Actions panel, if necessary.

3. Click the **menu** icon in the upper-right corner of the Actions panel, and then click **Auto Format Options**. The Auto Format Options dialog box opens.

4. Click an option to select it, view the results in the Preview window, and then click the option again to deselect it. Repeat for each option.

5. Click the **Space after function name in function calls** check box to select it. This makes it easier to interpret your code. Then click **OK**.

6. Close the Flash document without saving it.

ActionScript commands that carry out actions and are assigned to a movie object are called **methods**. The **Auto complete** feature helps you finish ActionScript methods by listing all the possible options you can use to complete the command. The options appear in a list box directly in your code window. This feature is very useful when you don't remember a command.

For example, you may be writing code for the Stage object, and want to change some of its size properties. Auto complete can assist you in doing this by providing the list of all possible methods and allowing you to select a method from that list. See Figure 6-9.

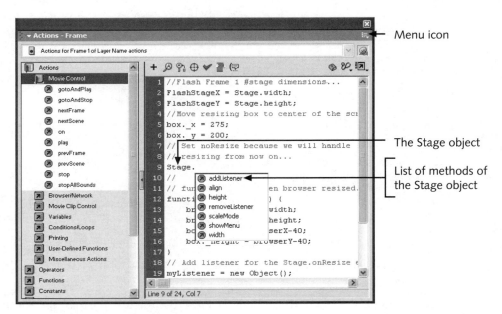

Figure 6-9 Auto complete list box commands

Code Hinting and Completion

Code hints are useful when you are working with various ActionScript commands and action names. **Code hints** are small pop-up windows that look like a Windows ScreenTip; they provide hints and options for completing your line of code. The options are highlighted in bold as you move through the series of hints, as shown in Figure 6-10. The completed option appears in brackets, indicating the last hint.

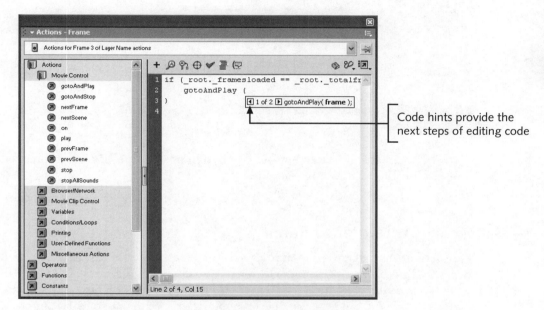

Code hints provide the next steps of editing code

Figure 6-10   Editing ActionScript code with a code hint

To use code hints, you open the Preferences dialog box to the ActionScript Editor tab, and select the Code Hint check box.

To use Auto complete, Auto format, and code hints:

1. Open **CodeHint.fla** from the Chapter6 folder in your FlashSamples folder. Save the file as **myCodeHint.fla** in the same location.

2. Open the Actions panel, if necessary. Click the **menu** icon on the upper-right corner of the Actions panel, and then click **Preferences**. In the Preferences dialog box, click the **ActionScript Editor** tab, if necessary. Make sure the **Code Hints** check box is selected. Then click **OK** to close the Preferences dialog box.

3. Type the following line of code on line 2 of the Actions panel, including the period:

   myCircle_mc.

4. When you type the period after the command, the methods appear because Auto complete is toggled on. Scroll to the **gotoAndPlay** method, click it, and press the **Tab** key to accept the method. The code hint appears, as shown in Figure 6-11.

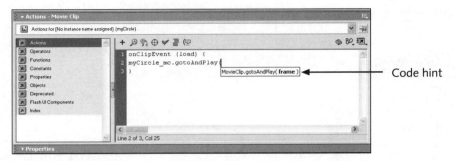

Figure 6-11   Code hint to help you complete a statement of code

5. Complete the statement of code by typing **1);**. The code hint disappears, and your line of code is complete.

6. Save and close the file, but leave Flash open for the next set of steps.

ActionScript Reference Panel

The ActionScript **Reference panel** is a quick reference to detailed descriptions and usage of all ActionScript commands. The Reference panel is a two-sided scalable window that is much like the ActionScript Editor. The left side is the entire ActionScript dictionary; the right side shows the referenced actions, the current Flash player version for which the action is available, syntax usage, any applicable parameters, any applicable values it returns, a description, and an example. See Figure 6-12.

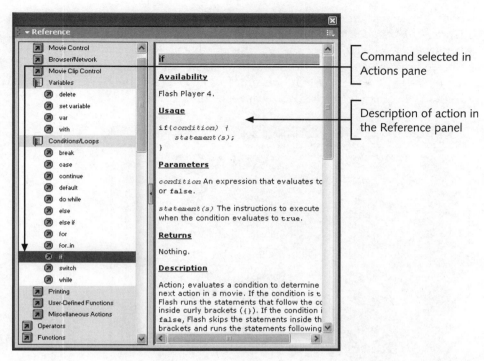

Figure 6-12   ActionScript Reference panel

ACTIONSCRIPT TECHNIQUES AND USES

ActionScript can affect all parts of your Flash movie. The central logic of a movie's ActionScript is based on the Timeline or a movie clip's Timeline or button. You assign ActionScript code to the frames on the Timeline. You can also place ActionScript on a button or movie clip instance. As you already know, buttons are an important aspect of any movie because they control navigation for your user. Movie clips can perform many functions, such as running on their own Timelines independent of the main Timeline, and controlling the behavior of other movie clips.

In the following sections, you will explore several uses for ActionScript that enhance a movie. In some instances you will play a Flash MX SWF file, and in others you will examine ActionScript code to walk through the programming flow.

Controlling the Browser

ActionScript in Flash MX can now take advantage of the Back button in browsers to navigate a movie. In prior versions, Flash developers were required to use JavaScript code to navigate to previously accessed Web pages. In addition to using the Back button, you can extract information from the browser, such as its x and y values and its height and width. You can then use this information to precisely position your Flash movie. See Figure 6-13. The text boxes must be dynamic in order to accept the value, and they are referenced in code by their variable name, FlashStageX for example. The variable name is then referencing the Stage dimensions using the `Stage.width;` and the `Stage.height;` methods. This becomes a valuable technique when you need to get the values of the Stage to further resize or reposition it.

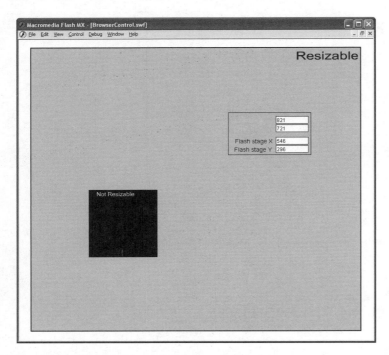

Figure 6-13   Displaying browser values

Scratch-Art Masking

With Flash MX, you can design creative masked effects. You have already worked with masks in Chapters 4 and 5. This section introduces an example of what you can do by combining masking with ActionScript. You set up a mask as you did in Chapter 4. Then you create a script that erases the top simulated clay mask, revealing the next image also as a mask, and then finally displaying the second picture.

In the following steps, you explore a scratch-art mask that reveals one image under another image. Traditional **scratch-art** consists of a black or white clay-textured board coated with a colored layer. You use a pointed tool to scratch into the board, revealing the colored layer beneath. An electronic scratch-art mask reveals an image under a black coating with a custom cursor that contributes an appropriate look and feel. As you drag to scratch and reveal the underlying image, the masking effects are removed in a gradual fade, as shown in Figure 6-14. Once the entire masking layer is removed, a second image is revealed.

Figure 6-14   Gradual fade of masking effect

To work with an example of scratch–art masking:

1. Open **ScratchArtMask.swf** from the Chapter6 folder in your FlashSamples folder. The Flash SWF file opens in the Flash 6 Player. Notice the black outer layer and the airbrush pointer.

2. Drag the mouse to "scratch" away the black covering and reveal the underlying image. You can reveal the entire image or experiment with an abstract design, as shown in Figure 6-15.

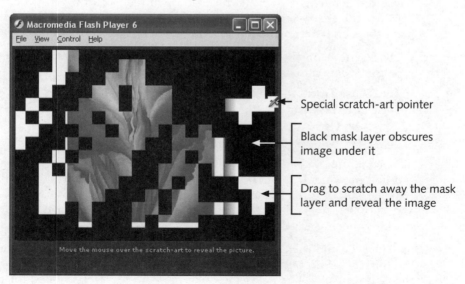

Figure 6-15   Scratching black coating mask to reveal first image

When the complete image is revealed, another image appears, which you can also scratch away to reveal the image underneath it, as shown in Figure 6-16.

Figure 6-16 Second image appearing after first image is removed

3. Click **Control** on the menu bar, and then click **Step Forward** to walk through the layers and actions used in the ScratchArtMask.swf file without using the pointer.

4. Close the ScratchArtMask.swf file, and open the **ScratchArtMask.fla** file. Save the file as **myScratchArtMask.fla**. Now you can examine and complete the ActionScript that creates the scratch-art effect.

5. Click **frame 1** on the Actions layer, open the Actions panel, click line 17, and type the following code to complete the ActionScript code:

```
if (curMaskTotal == maskTotal) {
    curMaskTotal = 0;
    play();
    trace("The mask has been cleared.");
```

This code uses a conditional **if** statement to test whether the movie clip has finished masking. If the condition is true, then the current mask total (curMaskTotal) is reset to zero, and the movie continues to play. An additional and optional step is the trace action, used to display a message box once the mask has been cleared.

6. Save the file and then test it by publishing it and opening the swf file. (To test the file, click **File** on the menu bar, and then click **Publish Preview**.) Close the Actions panel. Then close all open files, but leave Flash open for the next set of steps.

For more information on scratch-art and where to research scratch-art products, go to *www.scratchart.com*.

Manipulating Information

Flash lets you change the attributes of various objects on your Stage. For example, you can change the location, scale, or even the color of a movie clip dynamically. When you are presented with information or data, and you want to change that data, you are essentially manipulating information. Information comes in many forms; the color scheme as described below, a person's demographic information and financial statistics are all forms of information that can be manipulated or changed with the use of ActionScript.

In the following steps, you use a Flash MX SWF file to change the color of a movie clip, as shown in Figure 6-17.

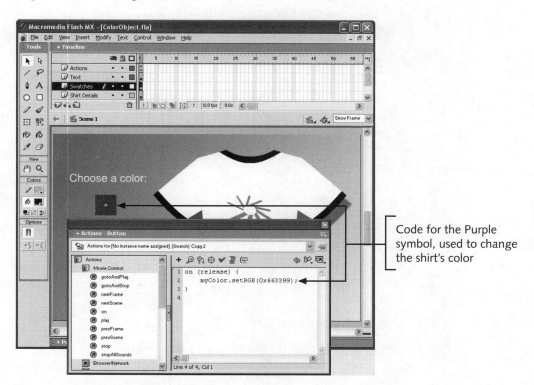

Figure 6-17   Changing the color of a movie clip

To dynamically change a movie clip's color:

1. Open **ColorObject.swf** from the Chapter6 folder in your FlashSamples folder. The Flash SWF file opens in the Flash 6 Player.

2. Click each color choice in the Choose a color list. Observe the movie clip change as you select particular colors. See Figure 6-18.

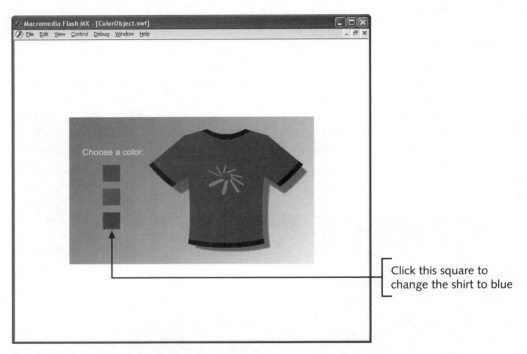

Figure 6-18   Movie clip changing colors

3. Close **ColorObject.swf**, and then open the **ColorObject.fla** file from the Chapter6 folder in your FlashSamples folder to explore the color object's attributes and properties. Save the file as **myColorObject.fla** in the same location.

4. Right-click (Ctrl + click on the Macintosh) **frame 1** on the Actions layer, and then click **Actions** to open the Actions panel. Make sure you are working in Expert mode.

5. Note the following line of ActionScript syntax:

```
"myColor = new Color(_root.myShirt);"
```

The variable named myColor changes the shirt's color based on the button symbols on the Swatches layer ActionScript syntax.

6. Click the **purple** swatch on the Stage to show its ActionScript code, and type the following on line 2, as shown in Figure 6-19:

myColor.setRGB(0x663399);

Figure 6-19   Swatch ActionScript syntax

6

7. Save and close **myColorObject.fla**, but leave Flash open for the next set of steps.

WORKING WITH ACTIONSCRIPT STRUCTURES AND COMMANDS

A scripting language is a programming language that you use to manipulate, customize, and automate an application. Such functionality is already available in Flash through a user interface and basic commands; the ActionScript language exposes the same functionality to program control.

ActionScript enhances your movie by communicating with the movie's various components, performing computations, and manipulating computational objects (movie clips, buttons, and Timeline frames) within a host environment (the Stage). Because it is based on ECMA Script, ActionScript does not contain proper classes such as those in C++, Smalltalk, or Java; ActionScript instead supports constructors, which create objects by executing code that allocates storage for the objects and initializes all or part of them by assigning initial values to their properties. ActionScript therefore has qualities of object-oriented programming, but is not totally object-oriented. Objects are collections of methods and properties. By defining these properties, such as the color of an object, or the position of a movie clip, you can change each instance of an object on your Stage. Properties are the attributes such as size or color that define an object, and methods are the functions that are assigned to an object to carry out a specific task, such as the gotoAndPlay method.

Planning ActionScript Movies

Taking the time to plan and create storyboards for your ActionScript structures increases the effectiveness of your project and shortens your design cycle. It also provides a forum for you and your client or stakeholder to agree on your design and make changes to it. A storyboard can be broken into manageable sections and help you structure your ActionScript accordingly. By devising a plan, you can write down ideas and decide what form your ActionScript will take.

Build and design your storyboards from the bottom up; this approach gives you the most flexibility for making changes or debugging code. A bottom-up design helps you look at individual objects and build solutions for them instead of focusing on top-level problems or requirements.

A good way to plan movies with ActionScript is to list the different deliverables you will provide the project stakeholder. You might provide the following items from an informal discussion or group of ideas:

- A storyboard, prototype, or rough sketch of each scene in the Stage. You can draw these items by hand or use software such as Microsoft Visio or Adobe Photoshop. A hand-drawn sketch is shown in Figure 6-20.

- A functional flowchart that documents how a movie clip or a button will perform. A flowchart can also document the movie's flow through the Timeline, as shown in Figure 6-21.

- A site map provides a hierarchical view of the main movie elements structured in scenes. Figure 6-22 illustrates how a site map can function well in a scene-by-scene flow.

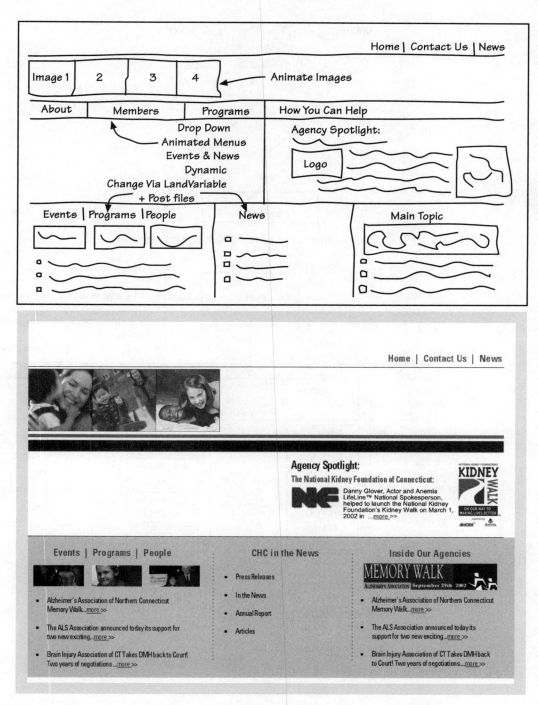

Figure 6-20   Hand-drawn sketch and Visio sketch of a home page storyboard

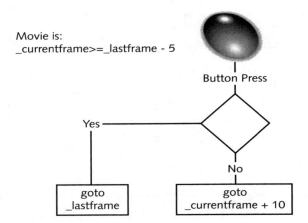

Figure 6-21   Functional flowchart of a movie's button function

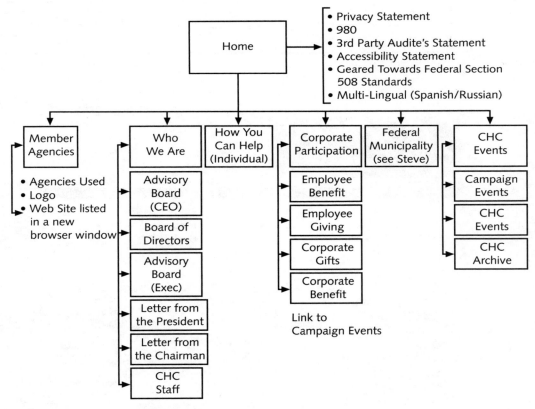

Figure 6-22   Site map of movie scenes

Overview of ActionScript Syntax

ActionScript is quite flexible. Depending on how you structure your movie's contents and what functionality you need, you can place code on the main Timeline, within a movie clip or movie clip instance, on buttons, on Flash user interface components, within an external SWF file, or an external script.

Like other scripting languages, ActionScript follows its own rules of syntax, reserves keywords, provides operators, and allows you to use variables to store and retrieve information. Flash MX will also understand ActionScript that was written in any previous version of Flash. Table 6-2 lists and describes some of the most common syntax rules.

Table 6-2 ActionScript Rules and Punctuation

ActionScript	Description	Example
Dot (.) syntax	Dot (.) is used to indicate the properties or methods related to an object or movie clip. It is also used to identify the target path to a movie clip, variable, function, or object. A dot syntax expression begins with the name of the object or movie clip followed by a dot, and ends with the element you want to specify.	For example, the _x movie clip property indicates a movie clip's x-axis position on the Stage. The expression ballmc._x refers to the _x property of the movie clip instance ballmc.

Curly braces	ActionScript statements are grouped together into blocks with curly braces ({ }).	`On(release) {`
		`    Mydate = new Date();`
		`    Currentmonth =`
		`        mydate.getmonth();`
		`}`

Semicolons	An ActionScript statement is terminated with a semicolon, as shown in the example statements at right. If you omit the terminating semicolon, Flash still compiles your script successfully. However, using semicolons is good scripting practice.	`Column =`
		`    passeddate.getday();`
		`Row = 0;`

Parentheses	When you define a function, place any parameters inside parentheses.	`Function myfunction`
		`(name, age,reader){`
		`...`
		`}`

Table 6-2   ActionScript Rules and Punctuation (continued)

ActionScript	Description	Example
Uppercase and lowercase letters	Only keywords in ActionScript are case sensitive; with the rest of ActionScript, you can use uppercase and lowercase letters interchangeably. For example, the statements at right are equivalent. Because ActionScript is not case sensitive, you must not use variable names that match built-in ActionScript objects. Therefore, the two statements shown at right are not allowed.	`Cat.hilite = true;` `CAT.hilite = true;`

Comments	In the Actions panel, use comments to add notes to scripts. Comments are useful for keeping track of development requirements, and for passing information to other developers if you work in a collaborative environment or need to provide samples.	`On(release) {`
		`    // create new Date object`
		`    Mydate = new Date();`

Keywords	ActionScript reserves words for specific use within the language, so you can't use them as variable, function, or label names. The column at right lists all ActionScript keywords.	Break, else, instanceof, typeof, case, for, new, var, continue, function, return, void, default, if, switch, while, delete, in, this, with

Constants	A constant is a property whose value never changes. For example, the constants BACKSPACE, ENTER, QUOTE, RETURN, SPACE, and TAB are properties of the Key object and refer to keyboard keys.	`If(Key.getcode() ==`
		`Key.ENTER){`
		`    Alert = "Are you ready`
		`        to play?";`
		`    Controlmc.gotoand`
		`stop(5);`
		`}`

Data types	A data type describes the kind of information a variable or ActionScript element can hold.	`String, Number, Boolean,`
		`Object, Movieclip,`
		`Null, Undefined`

String	A string is a sequence of characters such as letters, numbers, and punctuation marks. You enter strings in an ActionScript statement by enclosing them in single or double quotation marks. You can use the addition (+) operator to concatenate, or join, two strings.	`Greeting = "Welcome,"` `+ firstname;`

Table 6-2 ActionScript Rules and Punctuation (continued)

ActionScript	Description	Example
Number	The number data type is a double-precision floating-point number. You can manipulate numbers using the arithmetic operators addition (+), subtraction (–), multiplication (*), division (/), modulo (%), increment (++), and decrement (--).	`Math.sqrt(100);`

Boolean	A Boolean value is one that is either true or false. ActionScript also converts the values true and false to 1 and 0 when appropriate.	`OnClipEvent(enterframe) {`
		`    If (username == true &&`
		`       password == true){`
		`            Play();`
		`        }`
		`}`

Object	An object is a collection of properties. Each property has a name and a value. The value of a property can be any Flash data type, even the object data type, which allows you to arrange objects inside each other, or "nest" them. To specify objects and their properties, you use the dot (.) operator.	`Employee.weeklystats.` `hoursworked`

Movieclip	Movie clips are symbols that can play animation in a Flash movie. Clips are the only data type that refers to a graphic element. The movieclip data type allows you to control movie clip symbols using the methods of the movieclip object. You call the methods using the dot (.) operator.	`Myclip.startdrag(true);`
		`Parentclip.geturl`
		`("http://www.macromedia`
		`.com/support/"`
		`+ product);`

Null	The null data type has only one value, null. This value means "no value" —that is, a lack of data.	Null indicates that a variable has not yet received a value or no longer contains a value. It can also be used as the return value of a function, to indicate that no value was available to be returned by the function, as a parameter to a function, or to indicate that a parameter is being omitted.

6

ActionScript Structures

ActionScript uses if, else, else if, for, while, do while, for in, and switch statements to perform an action depending on whether a condition exists. This section explains several sample statements for your review.

The **if statement** is a conditional expression used in a special block of statements called a decision structure. The expression controls whether the other statements in your structure execute and in which order. If the condition specified in the if statement is false, you can complete the structure with else or else if statements. The **else statement** executes a series of statements other than the false if statement. The **else if statement** evaluates an additional condition to test before executing another group of statements. Here is an example:

```
If (condition1) {
      Statements execute if condition1 is true;
} else if (condition){
      Statements execute if condition1 is true;
} else
      Statements execute if no condition is true;
}
```

The if statement and related statements are widely used with ActionScript, and are a good choice to help determine a movie's navigational flow.

Like the if statement, the **while loop** handles repeated tasks for you. For example, a series of movie clips named ball_1 through ball_4 repeat the same task. Within the while loop, the three statements in the body of the loop structure execute over and over again until the expression in parentheses equals false. The test represented by the expression known as the loop condition is executed at the start of the loop. In this example, the condition turns to a false value at the fifth loop:

```
ball_counter = 1;
num_balls = 4;
while (ball_counter <= num_balls) {
      this ["ball_" + ball_counter]._x += xSpeed
      this ["ball_" + ball_counter]._x += ySpeed
      ball_counter++;
}
```

The **For loop** repeats consistently until a condition is met at the end of the loop structure, and will initialize a counter variable, describe a conditional test based on that variable, and increment that variable on one line of code. The three arguments or parts to this loop are within the parentheses and separated by semicolons: the start value (initialization), end value (condition), and iteration that will increment the variable called ball (increment).

```
For (ball = startValue; ball <= endValue; Ball++) {
      ...some actions
}
```

In order to get a better understanding of this loop, you create a small FLA file and test it to review its success.

To use a For loop:

1. Start Flash and open a blank new document.

2. Click **frame 1**, and then open the Actions panel, if necessary.

3. In Expert mode, type the following lines of code:

```
for (var movieElement=0; movieElement <5;
    movieElement ++){
       trace(movieElement);
}
```

4. Test the code by clicking **Control** on the menu bar and then clicking **Test Movie**. You should see the Output window display five numbers (0–4).

5. Close all open windows.

This code uses the For loop to initialize a variable named movieElement to zero, testing to see whether it is less that 5, and using the ++ operator to increment the values.

TROUBLESHOOTING AND DEBUGGING ACTIONSCRIPT SYNTAX

While designing and publishing your movies, you may run into difficulties viewing them on a supported browser or platform. By testing your movies according to the following simple guidelines, you can prevent problems from becoming obstacles.

Troubleshooting ActionScript Syntax

You should start testing your movie early in the design process. This helps you discover and fix problems while they are still minor, before you add other interdependent features to your movie. If you wait to test a feature until you implement another interdependent feature with it, and one of these features exhibits a problem, you'll have a more complex set of possibilities to evaluate. An important part of the testing process is determining the minimum system requirements for your users' computers.

The Actions Panel Code Debugger

The Flash MX Debugger can show your code while showing you the individual lines of ActionScript. You can open the Debugger window in the Flash Player while you are testing a movie. The Debugger allows you to step through code and find any syntax errors that may be generated.

To open the Debugger window, click Control on the menu bar and then click Debug Movie. As shown in Figure 6-23, the Debugger window is divided into two sections. The right side contains the code view pane and the debugging commands. The left side has the status bar, display list, several tabs (which are covered in detail in Table 6-3), and the call stack pane. You can resize the window and the intermediate panes within it to fit your viewing needs. The Debugger also has **breakpoints**, which allow you to stop a movie running in the Flash Player at a specific line of ActionScript.

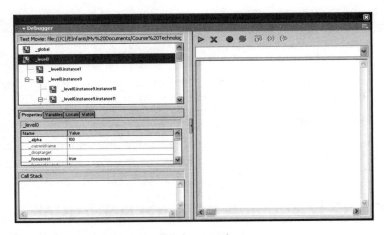

Figure 6-23   Debugger window tools

Table 6-3 describes the full suite of debugging tools in the Debugger window.

Table 6-3 Flash MX Debugging Tools

Debugging tool	Description
Status bar	Displays the URL or local file path of the movie and tells you whether the Debugger is running in Test mode or from a remote location.
Display list	Displays and updates automatically as the movie plays. If a movie clip is removed from the movie at a specific frame, the clip is also removed from the display list in the Debugger, along with its variable and variable name. However, if you mark a variable for the Watch list, that variable is not removed.
Properties tab	Displays all the properties of any movie clip on the Stage, and allows you to change a value and see its effect in the movie while it runs.
Variables tab	Displays the names and values of any global and Timeline variables in the movie.
Locals tab	Allows you to see the values of all local variables.
Watch tab	Displays the absolute path to the variable as well as the value.
Call stack pane	Informs you of nested or hierarchical function calls. The stack of function calls lets you see the calling and referenced functions.
Continue button	Continues playing the movie script until a breakpoint is reached.
Stop debugging button	Stops the Debugger without quitting, then allows you to continue.
Toggle breakpoint button	Adds or removes a breakpoint for the selected lines of code.
Remove all breakpoints button	Removes all breakpoints from the script pane.
Step over button	Executes the current line of code and stops at the next line in the script.
Step in button	Executes the current line of code. If the current line is a function call, it steps through every line of the function. If not, it performs just like the Step over command.
Step out button	Executes all lines up to the end of the current code block. This command is efficient in debugging loops that carry out several iterations of code.
Horizontal and vertical splitters	Let you adjust the Debugging window.
Code view	The pane where all ActionScript code is located.

6

In this next exercise, you will debug and correct a structure of code that duplicates a movie clip on your Stage.

To debug ActionScript code:

1. Open **DoDuplicate.swf** from the Chapter6 folder in your FlashSamples folder. Notice the staircase effect of the circles. Except for the original circle on the

Stage, the others are in a perfect formation and equidistant from each other, staggering from top left to bottom right of the Stage as shown in Figure 6-24.

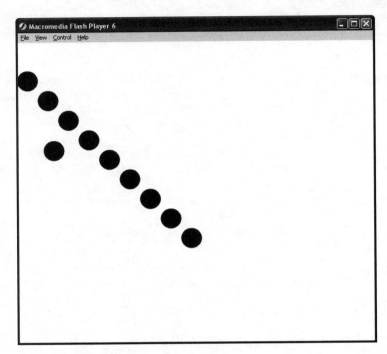

Figure 6-24 DoDuplicate.swf file

2. Close DoDuplicate.swf, and open **DoDuplicate.fla** from the Chapter6 folder in your FlashSamples folder. Save the file as **myDoDuplicate.fla** in the same folder. This file contains errors, and you will use the debugging tools to find and then correct the errors.

3. Click **Control** on the menu bar, and then click the **Debug Movie** command. The file opens in Test mode, with the Debug window open and active. See Figure 6-25.

4. The VCR-style toolbar above the code view pane is lit up to indicate it is active, and the movie is currently started and paused, waiting for your interaction. Click the **Properties** tab, if necessary, and resize the Debugger window to make it longer. Click the **Script** list arrow (in the list box above the script pane), and then click **Actions for Scene 1: Frame 1 of Layer Name Layer 1** to open the script for scene 1, frame 1. See Figure 6-26.

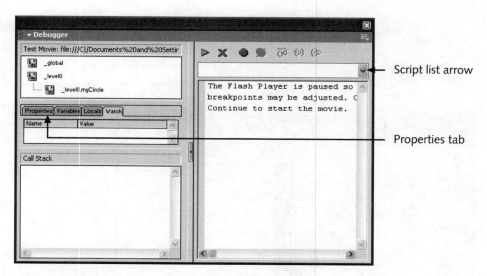

Figure labels (right side):
- Script list arrow
- Properties tab

Figure 6-25   Debug window in action

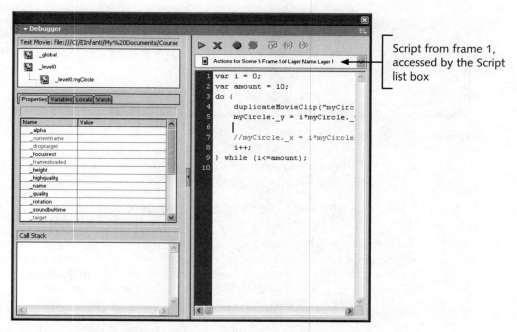

Figure labels (right side):
- Script from frame 1, accessed by the Script list box

Figure 6-26   Selecting a script

5. To toggle on a breakpoint on line 5, right-click **line 5** (Ctrl+click on the Macintosh), and then click **Set breakpoint** on the shortcut menu. Notice the red dot that appears to the left of the line of code, indicating that a

breakpoint is set for that line. Setting the breakpoint helps you determine where the error is in your code. See Figure 6-27.

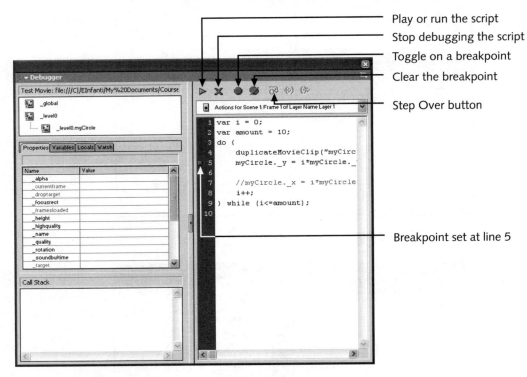

Figure 6-27   Breakpoint set for the line of code

6. Click the **Play** button to move the movie forward. Notice the circles appear on the Stage, but are not staggered.

7. Click the **Continue (Play)** button to continue running your code. Notice the movie stops playing at the line of code you set as a breakpoint.

8. To continue troubleshooting, you can step over that line of code to see your movie code run. Click the **Step Over** button, once for each time your loop is set to run. This executes the entire module of code, helping you determine that the error is not in the code in line 5, but the code in line 7.

9. Close the Debug window and the SWF file, and return to the movie.

10. In the Actions panel, click **line 7** in your code, and type the following line of code to fix the problem:

    myCircle._x = i*myCircle._width;

    A comment is also inserted for your convenience.

11. Save myDoDuplicate.fla, and test the movie without debugging it to make sure it runs correctly. Then close the file.

The debugging process can also take place online, so your code can be exposed through the SWF file. For many Flash designers, this is a unique opportunity to share ActionScript in the public domain. As for commercial development, a client or stakeholder may not want to share this information, especially after paying for it. To help make your debugging process more secure, the Debugger creates a new file format, a Shockwave Debug (SWD) file. This file contains all of the ActionScript code and breakpoint data.

Naming Conventions and Formatting Code

ActionScript has a growing user base and is now widely used in commercial Web applications. As in any development environment, ActionScript conforms to accepted programming standards. If you have ever edited another programmer's code, then you realize the need for standards and neatly formatted code. For example, there is no way to tell if the following statement references a variable or a movie clip:

```
gotoAndPlay ( current );
```

In Chapter 5, you learned about Hungarian notation, where a unique, three-character prefix is used to assign each data type to each type of control. For example, in the code fragment **myColor = new Color(_root.clpShirt);**, the clpShirt indicates that this is a movie clip, not a button symbol.

Formatting code helps to make it appear complete and easy to read. Keep your code understandable by organizing it into functional pieces, and document it with comments as much as possible. The following list provides some formatting conventions and examples to remember:

- Avoid placing multiple statements on one line.

- Use indentation to show structure.

```
if (getTimer()<timePressed+300) {
    // if the condition is true,
    // the object was thrown.
    // what is the new location of this object?
    xNewLoc = this._x;
    yNewLoc = this._y;
    }
```

- Use white space to group related tasks.

```
if (condition){
    statement(s);
} else if (condition){
    statement(s);
}
```

- Comment on the purpose of the ActionScript, statement, or module of code with comment headers.

- Comment on any important changes in the code over time.
- Comment on what errors may be expected.
- Comment on inline notations for code processes.

```
while(ball < 5) {
    duplicateMovieClip("_root.flower", "mc" + ball, ball);
// Duplicated movie clip
    }
```

- Comment on variables with end-of-line notation.

```
while(ball < 5) { // Execute while the variable is
  less than 5
    duplicateMovieClip("_root.flower", "mc" + ball, ball);
// Duplicated movie clip
        }
```

Modular Programming

Efficient and reusable ActionScript provides an ideal model for debugging code. By structuring your code in a modular way, you can use code components over and over again. You can organize your code, SWF files, scenes, and movie elements to solve a portion of a larger problem, or to behave as a piece of a more complex task. If a similar problem occurs elsewhere, you can more readily reuse working modules of Flash elements to help solve the problem. Figure 6-28 illustrates how modular programming can break down large, complex tasks into more manageable and reusable code.

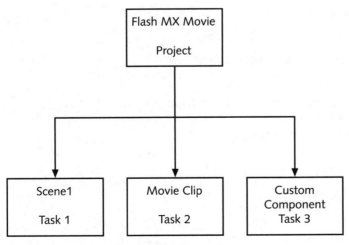

Figure 6-28   Modular programming

CHAPTER SUMMARY

❑ ActionScript is the scripting language that Flash provides to create interactive movies that users can control by clicking objects and entering information. A scripting language is a way to communicate with a program; you can use scripts to tell Flash what to do and to find out what is happening as a movie runs.

❑ In general, ActionScript lets you add interactivity in your Flash movies by using events. Events are programming statements that give instructions to movie elements to react to user commands. An event can be as simple as a user clicking a button or pressing a key, or as involved as loading a movie clip or moving to another frame on your Timeline.

❑ When you work with the Actions panel in Expert mode, you can check script syntax for errors, automatically format code, and use code hints to help you complete syntax. In addition, the punctuation balance feature helps you correctly pair parentheses, braces, or brackets in the script. Although Flash provides these features to make creating scripts easier, when you use the Actions panel in Expert mode, you should have a clear understanding of ActionScript.

❑ Dot notation is the programming convention that ActionScript uses to put commands together into statements. It replaces the slash syntax used in Flash before version 5. The dot notation makes it easier to program with ActionScript.

❑ Flash MX builds on an already powerful ActionScript tool by adding several new commands, such as the Stage object, the Switch statement, text field, and button symbols.

❑ Flash MX provides a more sophisticated environment for you to work with ActionScript. As in prior versions, Flash MX comes equipped with a movable and dockable Actions panel, with both Normal and Expert modes.

❑ ActionScript has many uses that can affect all parts of your Flash movie. Most central logic of a movie's ActionScript is based directly on the Timeline. The Timeline's frames act as placeholders for code and function as directors orchestrating elements on your Stage. You can also place ActionScript on a button or movie clip instance. Buttons are an important aspect of any movie because they control navigation for your user. Movie clips can perform a wide array of functions, such as running on their own Timelines independent of the main Timeline, and controlling the behavior of other movie clips.

❑ While designing and publishing your movies, you may run into difficulties viewing them on a supported browser or platform. By testing your movies according to a few simple guidelines, you can prevent problems from becoming obstacles. The Flash MX Debugger can show your code while showing you the individual lines of ActionScript. Efficient and reusable ActionScript provides an ideal model for debugging code. By structuring your code in a modular way, you can use code components over and over again.

REVIEW QUESTIONS

1. ActionScript can extend the capabilities of your Flash movie. True or false?

2. On which of the following is ActionScript based?

   a. XML Script

   b. Apple Script

   c. ECMA JavaScript

   d. all of the above

3. The _____ is a good analogy for ActionScript objects.

   a. Verb

   b. Adjective

   c. Noun

   d. none of the above

4. The ActionScript dot syntax is more efficient than the slash syntax. True or false?

5. The Actions panel can be used in which of the following modes?

   a. Expert mode

   b. Programmers' mode

   c. User mode

   d. Advanced mode

6. Although it is good programming practice to include the semicolon to terminate an ActionScript statement, it is not necessary. True or false?

7. Supplementing your code with _____ is a good way to document your movie.

8. ActionScript can test for logical conditions and make decisions by using conditional statements. True or false?

9. ActionScript variables are a useful place in memory to store _____.

   a. movie clips

   b. Flash preferences

   c. data

   d. keyframes

10. The use of conditional statements such as _____ can control your movie flow.

11. Which of the following has properties and methods, and provides a way of grouping information so you can use it in a script?

  a. ActionScript

  b. variables

  c. objects

  d. all of the above

12. ActionScript cannot control the Stage dimensions. True or false?

13. The Actions panel can be customized by color-coding the script. True or false?

14. The Actions panel can be referenced one frame at a time by using which of the following?

  a. pinning

  b. glue

  c. tagging

  d. none of the above

15. Using _____ arranges your code in Flash's formatting style.

16. ActionScript cannot display hints for completing a statement of code. True or false?

17. You can quickly reference a detailed description of all ActionScript actions with the _____.

18. ActionScript can now control the browser's Back button. In prior versions of Flash, which application was needed to manipulate the Back button?

  a. HTML

  b. XML

  c. Cascading Style Sheets (CSS)

  d. JavaScript

19. Dynamic text boxes can display changing content in a Flash movie. True or false?

20. The process of _____ is used to troubleshoot and find ActionScript errors.

HANDS-ON PROJECTS

In these projects, you work with actions and ActionScript statements to build on what you learned in this chapter.

Project 6-1

In this project, you design an entry form that requires a user to enter a password to go to the proper scene. You program the ActionScript syntax to validate the user password, and then route to the proper scene if the password is authenticated or route back to the Password field if it is not.

1. Open the **Password.fla** file from the Chapter6\Projects folder in your FlashSamples folder. Save the file as **myPassword.fla** in the same location. The scenes, button, and text object are in place for you. You only need to configure the text box object and create the ActionScript.

2. Right-click (Ctrl + click on the Macintosh) the blank text box object, and then click Properties on the shortcut menu to open the Property inspector.

3. In the Property inspector, click the first list arrow (identified as Text type when you point to it), and then click Input Text. This sets the text box to accept text that the user types.

4. Click the Show Border around text box button in the Property inspector. (Point to the buttons to see their names.) If you don't click this button to select this option, the text box appears without a border, making it invisible on a white background. Including a border helps the user see where to type.

5. In the Var text box, type "password" (without the quotation marks). This specifies that the variable name for this text box is "password," so you can reference its name in the `if (password == "flashmx") {` code.

6. Use the Arrow tool to right-click (Ctrl + click on the Macintosh) the button symbol, and then click the Actions command. To ensure that the Actions panel is in Expert mode, click the View options icon on the upper-right corner of the Actions panel. If the Expert mode command is not checked, click it to select it.

7. Enter the following code exactly as it appears below:

```
on (release) {
  password = password.toLowerCase();
  if (password == "flashmx") {
        gotoAndPlay ("Scene 2", 1);
  } else {
        gotoAndPlay ("Scene 3", 1);
  }
}
```

Briefly, this script means that the button to accept the password controls the flow of the code on the release of the mouse. Once that is done, the password is set to lowercase to avoid any case-sensitive conflicts, and then the button checks for the validity of the password. If the password is accurate, then you are routed to scene 2, otherwise; you are routed to scene 3, and you are required to again enter the accurate password.

8. Close the Actions panel, and then test the movie, first by entering a false password, then by entering flashmx, the correct password. Scene 2 should open when you enter the correct password.

9. Return to the Stage when you finish. Save and close **myPassword.fla**, but leave Flash open for the next project.

Project 6-2

In this project, you create an advanced preloader that checks whether the SWF file has already been loaded into cache. If so, it opens the main page; if not, it plays the preloader. The preloader displays a status message of the percentage of loading completed. While you can only see the full effect of a preloader when you publish a Flash movie to a Web site, in this project, you can see how a preloader works.

1. Open the **Preloader.fla** file from the Chapter6\Projects folder in your FlashSamples folder. Save the file as **myPreloader.fla** in the same location. The scenes and movie elements are already in place, as well as some of the code.

2. Select frame 1 in the Actions layer, and then open the Actions panel in Expert mode.

3. Type the following code exactly as it appears below:

```
if (_root._framesloaded == _root._totalframes) {
        gotoAndPlay("main", "startmain");
} else {
        loadMovieNum("intro.swf", 1);
}
```

This code checks to see if the total frames of the movie have loaded. If they have, Flash loads the main movie. If they have not, Flash loads intro.swf.

4. Click Window on the menu bar, and then click Movie Explorer to open the Movie Explorer and use it to browse and investigate the other movie components.

5. Test the movie, which shows the preloader briefly then loads the main movie. Open the Bandwidth Profiler by clicking View on the menu bar, and then clicking Bandwidth Profiler. Use the Bandwidth Profiler to determine the best load time.

6. Click **View** on the menu bar, and then click **Frame-by-Frame Graph** to display a frame-by-frame graph. Click the longest bar in the graph. A "loading essential components" message appears. Web users would see this message as their browsers downloaded the myPreloader Flash movie.

7. Save and close **myPreloader.fla**, but leave Flash open for the next project.

Project 6-3

In this project, you complete the ActionScript programming for a color changer. This Flash file has an object on the Stage, an image of flowers, and several colored circles. The colored circles are used to color a silhouette of the flowers. You complete the programming by adding the code for the colors; gray, black, yellow, and green.

1. Open the **ColorProject.fla** file from the Chapter6\Projects folder in your FlashSamples folder. Save the file as **myColorProject.fla** in the same location. The scenes, button, and text object are in place for you.

2. Right-click (Ctrl + click on the Macintosh) the gray color changer, and then click Actions on the shortcut menu to display the Actions panel.

3. Type the following code exactly as it appears below:

```
on (press) {
    c = new Color (_root.colorTarget);
    c.setRGB (0x9C9C9C);
}
```

4. Click the black color changer, and then click Actions on the shortcut menu to display the Actions panel.

5. Type the following code exactly as it appears below:

```
on (press) {
    c = new Color (_root.colorTarget);
    c.setRGB (0x313100);
}
```

6. Click the yellow color changer, and then click Actions on the shortcut menu to display the Actions panel.

7. Type the following code exactly as it appears below:

```
on (press) {
    c = new Color (_root.colorTarget);
    c.setRGB (0xFFFF00);
}
```

8. Click the green color changer, and then click Actions on the shortcut menu to display the Actions panel.

9. Type the following code exactly as it appears below:

```
on (press) {
    c = new Color (_root.colorTarget);
    c.setRGB (0x00FF00);
}
```

10. Save **myColorProject.fla**, and then test the movie. Click the color changers to see the area around and over the flowers change color. Then exit Flash.

CASE PROJECTS

Case Project 6-1

A vehicle dealership has hired you to build and design a Flash Web site to serve its prospective buyers. Flash will allow the site's visitors to select a vehicle model, select interior and exterior colors, select package options, and display a summary in real time. You can refer to *www.us.landrover.com* and *new.volvocars.com/build/* to get an idea of this Flash model.

Case Project 6-2

A software manufacturing company is requesting a Flash presentation to promote its new release of a Personal Information Manager (PIM). The company wants a complex, capabilities-based presentation that will have many elements and be displayed based on user input. The software demonstration allows the user to try the features of the calendar, address book, and task list; the software is also compatible with different hand-held devices and cell phones through the Wireless Application Protocol (WAP).

Use Flash's ActionScript to enhance the movie flow and control the resulting display features. Provide the user with a simulated PIM demonstration that is easy to use and navigate. For PIM resources and ideas, refer to the following PIM software Web addresses: *www.weblicon.net/html/products.html*, *www.miclog.com/isover.htm*, *www.frontrange.com/goldmine/goldmine_demos.asp*, and *www.microsoft.com/office/outlook/*.

6

Case Project 6-3

The marketing group of a Personal Document Manager (PDA) company has asked you to design a working prototype of its new PDA model. Users must be able to operate the PDA online and discover its features and benefits. You must design functions that will respond to user input via the mouse and keyboard, including turning on the PDA, selecting a feature through the PDA's natural interface, managing settings and preferences, adding a contact, adding a task, and using the calendar to add a dated appointment. Refer to these Web addresses for resources on PDA's: *www.compaq.com/products/handhelds/pocketpc/*, *www.handspring.com*, and *www.palm.com*.

Case Project 6-4

In the Flash movie you created presenting your interests or showcasing the products and services of your fictitious company, use ActionScript to let a user interact with the movie. Use at least one of the ActionScript applications illustrated in this chapter, such as controlling the browser window, adding a scratch-art mask, or letting the user change movie information, such as color.

7

MACROMEDIA FLASH MX COMPONENTS

Application Design with Macromedia Flash MX Components

> **In this chapter, you will:**
> ♦ Learn about Macromedia Flash MX components
> ♦ Work with Macromedia Flash MX components
> ♦ Bring components to life with ActionScript
> ♦ Install additional components in Macromedia Flash MX

In Chapter 6, you learned the basics of integrating Flash movies with ActionScript. In this chapter, you will learn further advanced design techniques by adding user interface (UI) components to your Flash movies. A UI **component** is a reusable, advanced movie clip with parameters and ActionScript methods you can set during your design. Components are like wizards or macros in an Office application; they can save you time as you reuse them to solve common problems.

Understanding Macromedia Flash MX Components

Flash MX components are a collection of movie clips that you can add to a Flash document so that users can make selections or provide information. You typically use components in online forms, where users select information using option buttons, list boxes, or check boxes, and enter text into form fields. When you add a component to a Flash document, you insert a graphic control to the document, such as a button or check box. After you add a component to a Flash document, you configure the component so that it provides the correct information for a user to select. To make some components work, you must also use ActionScript to assign actions to the frame containing the component. For example, suppose you add a "Send more information" check box to a form document. Users click this check box if they want to receive more information via e-mail. You must assign actions to the frame containing the "Send more information" check box so that Flash gathers information about that component—whether or not it is selected—and knows what to do in each case.

You can also customize the appearance of components with a process called skinning. When you **skin** a component, you change its appearance, such as its color, font, or shape. The Skins folder in the Component Skins folder in the Library panel contains the skins used by all types of components in your Flash document. You can edit the skins on the Stage to customize them.

 Components are the successor to Smart Clips in Flash 5. Macromedia developed Flash MX to include a suite of user interface tools that you can add directly to your Flash movies and movie objects.

Components are an ideal tool for you to use to design common and advanced user interfaces. Recall from Chapter 5 that a user interface (UI) includes everything you add to an application, such as an online form, to help a user interact with the application. For example, Figure 7-1 shows several Flash MX UI components, including a series of check boxes that allow a user to select options; a list box of options in a scrollable list; and a scroll bar for reading text.

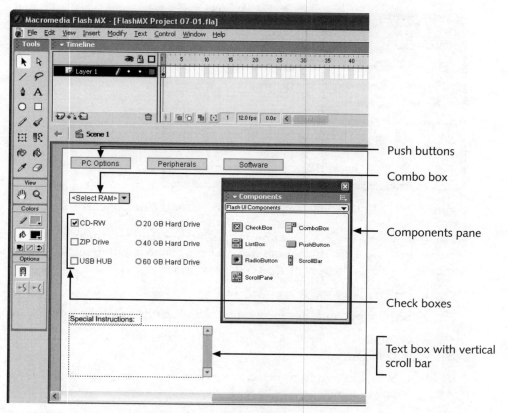

Figure 7-1 Flash MX user interface components

Flash also has an extended set of components called Flash UI Components Set 2, as well as a Charting Components extension with line, pie, and bar charts (see Figure 7–2). Set 2 contains the following components:

- Calendar component for creating a graphical display of a month

- Draggable pane component for enclosing content in a movable, scrollable pane

- IconButton component for creating a button with a custom icon and custom look

- MessageBox component for creating dialog boxes

- ProgressBar component for creating progress sequences

- SplitView component for the layout of complex data or image views

- Ticker component for scrolling data repeatedly through a window

- Tree component for creating a classic tree view of related data elements

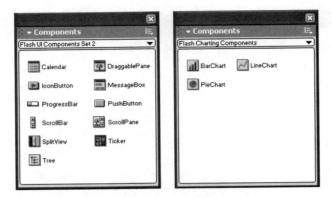

Figure 7-2 Flash UI Components Set 2 and Charting Components

In the following steps, you use the DraggablePane component from Set 2 to create a window that users can drag, minimize, and close. The window displays an image inside a movie clip. This component has the following parameters:

- Pane Title of the draggable pane
- Scroll Content where you type the linkage name of the movie clip
- Close Box to determine whether the draggable pane has a close box (true) or not (false)
- Is Scrolling setting to determine whether the draggable pane has scroll bars (true) or not (false)
- Resizable setting to determine whether users can resize the draggable pane manually (true) or not (false)
- Has Shader setting to include a shader box, which acts as a minimize button to collapse the window (true) or not (false)

To create a draggable pane window:

1. Open **DragPane.fla** from the Chapter7 folder in your FlashSamples folder. Save it as **myDragPane.fla** in the same location.

2. Press **Ctrl+L**, if necessary, to open the Library panel. (Press **Command+L** on the Macintosh to open the Library panel here and throughout the chapter.) In the Library panel, expand the **Flash UI Components Set 2** folder to show its contents, if necessary.

3. Drag the **DraggablePane** component from the library to the Stage.

4. Ensure the component is selected on the Stage, and then open the Property inspector, if necessary.

5. Click the **Parameters** tab, if necessary, to display the parameters for the DraggablePane component. Click **Pane Title**, and then type **Drag Me** in the text box to provide a title for the component.

6. Click **Scroll Content**, and then type **RaftingImage** in the text box. The scroll content is the name the image references to display an image or text in the pane. You must provide Scroll Content information to display content in the pane.

7. To specify the linkage property of the movie clip, right-click the **RaftingImage** movie clip in the library, and then click **Linkage** in the shortcut menu. The Linkage Properties dialog box opens.

8. Click the **Export for ActionScript** check box to select it. Notice that selecting this check box also automatically inserts RaftingImage as the Identifier name and selects the Export in first frame check box. The ActionScript code for the component references the identifier when it constructs the series of movie clips to make up the specific component.

Your Linkage Properties dialog box should resemble Figure 7-3.

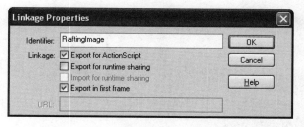

Figure 7-3   Linkage Properties dialog box

9. Click the **OK** button to accept your changes.

10. In the Parameters tab of the Property inspector, make sure the other parameters are set as true.

11. In the Component text box, type **DragMeComponent** to name the component. Your Stage and Parameters panel should resemble Figure 7-4.

12. To test your component, click **Control** on the menu bar, and then click **Test Movie**. Use the component by scrolling the image within the pane; resize to see more of the image by dragging the scale handle located on the lower-right corner of the window pane. Also, collapse and expand the pane by clicking the **down** arrow in the upper-left corner of the pane. Then close the pane by clicking the **Close** button (the white X) in the upper-right corner of the pane, as shown in Figure 7-5.

13. Close the test window, and then save and close **myDragPane.fla**, leaving Flash open for the next set of steps.

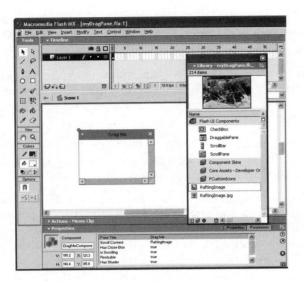

Figure 7-4   Current Stage and Parameters panel

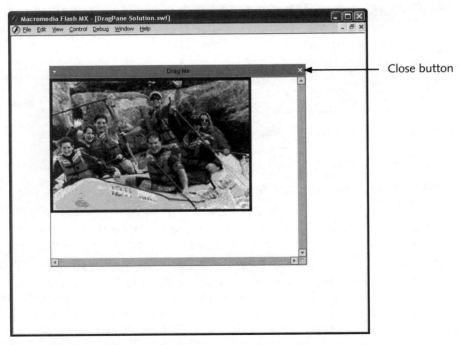

Close button

Figure 7-5   Testing the Drag Page component

Experienced ActionScript developers can create custom components to add to their Flash movies. For example, you can create a component that displays stock market data in a ticker tape format. Then you can customize the component in other movies to display particular stock symbols. Third-party component developers create custom components, such as the Tooltip Mania component. The Tooltip component, shown in Figure 7-6, allows you to add a standard, dynamic, or menu Tooltip to your Flash elements. Macromedia also provides an Extension Manager for Flash 5, Flash MX, and Dreamweaver MX to install and manage third-party and Macromedia extensions.

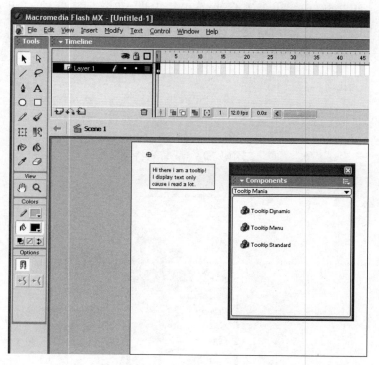

Figure 7-6 Tooltip Mania component

 Macromedia supports a community of Flash designers and developers dedicated to the open exchange of Flash FLA files, custom component extensions, and other resources. For details, see "Installing Additional Components in Macromedia Flash" later in this chapter.

WORKING WITH MACROMEDIA FLASH MX COMPONENTS AND FLASH MOVIES

With the UI components in Flash MX, you can design a user interface with common controls directly in your movie. UI components have their own Components panel, which you can access by clicking Window on the menu bar and then clicking Components (or by pressing Ctrl+F7). Each time you add a component to your Stage, the component and any nested components are also added to your movie's library. A nested component is a component within a component, such as a scroll pane that also uses a scroll bar. You can place a scroll pane directly on your Stage, and the scroll bar will perform as it should, provided there is enough content within the scroll pane for the scroll bar to do its job. The following standard components are available with Flash MX and some are shown in Figure 7-7.

- Scroll bars
- List boxes
- Scroll panes
- Check boxes
- Combo boxes
- Push buttons
- Radio buttons

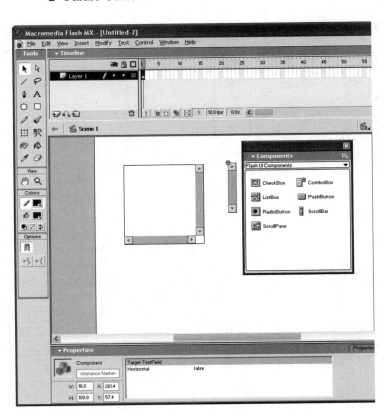

Figure 7-7   UI components

Once you add a component to the Stage and the library, you should not drag the component to the Stage again. If you do, you might accidentally overwrite your existing components. Simply add another instance of your component from the current library.

Working with the Scroll Bar Component

The **scroll bar** component allows you to drag and drop an already functional scroll bar into a dynamic or input text box. You can add a scroll bar to the left, right, top, or bottom of a Flash element. As you drag the scroll bar into your text box, it will snap to the nearest side of the text box. The scroll bar will not be grouped with the text box automatically, so it is a good idea to group them manually. Use vertical and horizontal scroll bars to add long blocks of text to a text field without displaying all of the text simultaneously. Users can drag the scroll box on a scroll bar or click a scroll arrow to see text that doesn't appear in the text field.

In the following steps, you create a text box that displays current news text for a company. In the next set of steps, you design a full user interface with the basic set of user interface components, including the company news text box. Because the news can be long, you add a scroll bar to the text box so that you restrict the amount of space the text box requires while you allow users to read all of the text.

To create a scrollable, dynamic text box with a scroll bar:

1. Open **ScrollBar.fla** from the Chapter7 folder in your FlashSamples folder. Save it as **myScrollBar.fla** in the same location.

2. Use the **Text** tool to create a text box just below the "Special Instructions" text on the Stage. Open the Property inspector, if necessary.

3. Use the **Arrow** tool to select the **text box**, click the **Text type** list arrow (the first list arrow in the Property inspector), and then click **Dynamic Text**, if necessary. Resize the text box so it matches the one shown in Figure 7-8.

4. Enter **TextBox1** in the text box containing "<Instance Name>." Click the **Line Type** list arrow and choose **Multiline**.

5. Click **Window** on the menu bar, and then click **Components** to open the Components panel, if necessary. Click the list arrow and then click **Flash UI components**, if necessary.

6. Drag a **ScrollBar** component onto the right edge of the text field bounding box. See Figure 7-8 for placement.

7. Click the **Text** tool, if necessary, and then enter a few lines of text in the text box—at least one more line than the text box would normally hold.

8. To test the dynamic text box and scroll bar, click **Control** on the menu bar, click **Test Movie**. The resulting movie resembles Figure 7-9. Close the Test Movie window.

9. Save and close **myScrollBar.fla**, but leave Flash open for the next set of steps.

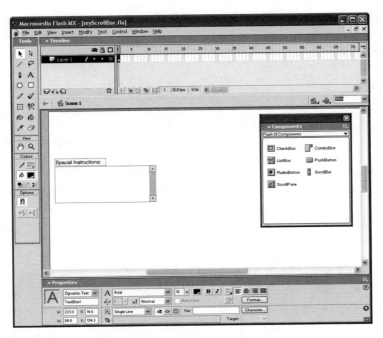

Figure 7-8   Scroll bar and text box properties

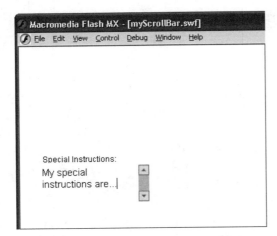

Figure 7-9   Scroll bar and dynamic text box

Working with the Check Box Component

The **check box** is a common interface component that acts as a toggle for your movie options. Check boxes appear as square boxes with identifiable labels and are typically used to select independent and nonexclusive choices. A user can select a check box, which toggles it on, and a user can select multiple or no check boxes. If multiple check boxes are required for a common task, such as selecting several choices of literature to be sent from a Web site's form, then the check boxes are typically grouped in a like area or screen space. The advantage of check boxes is that you can toggle them on or off in any combination, and you can also use them to affect other controls with ActionScript. For example, you can use a check box to filter the contents of a list box, as shown in Figure 7-10. The check box is useful for giving your users the ability to check a series of options in an unrestricted progression, or to check no option with that list.

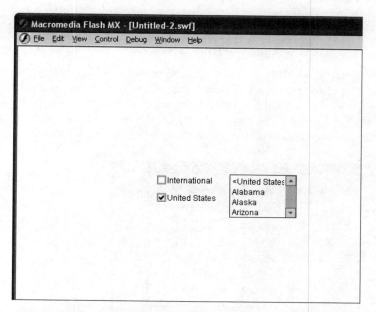

Figure 7-10   Using a check box to filter the contents of a list box

Set the following parameters when creating a check box:

- Instance Name, to name the instance of the check box component on the Stage

- Height and width values of the check box's bounding border, which does not increase the size of the actual check box. (This helps you align a series of check boxes.)

- X and y values to designate the location of the check box on the Stage

- Label name

- Initial Value to set the check mark on or off (true or false)

- Label Placement either left or right of the check box

- Change Handler field, which allows you to add an ActionScript command or function

Placing the check box component is as easy as dragging the scroll bar component to the Stage. In the following steps, you continue creating a user interface by adding a series of check boxes to a Flash document.

To add check boxes to a Flash document:

1. Open **CheckBox.fla** from the Chapter7 folder in your FlashSamples folder. Save it as **myCheckBox.fla** in the same location.

2. Open the Flash UI Components set, if necessary. Drag the **CheckBox** component from the Components panel four times to add four check boxes under the Subscription Options text box. Open the Property inspector, if necessary.

3. Use the **Arrow** tool to click the **first check box** on your Stage to select it.

4. In the Property inspector, click **Label**, and then type **Company News** to add a new label to this check box. Because Company News is the most popular subscription option, click **Initial Value**, click the list arrow, and then click **true**. See Figure 7-11. Setting the Initial Value to true means that this check box appears checked when the user opens this Flash movie.

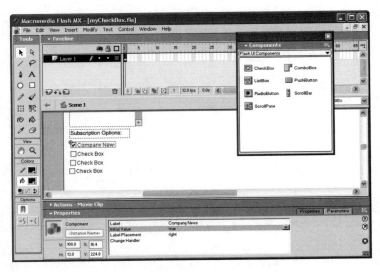

Figure 7-11   Company News check box component

5. Add the following labels to the remaining three check boxes: **Company Events**, **Special Events**, and **Daily Blast**. Leave the Initial Value set to false. Use the **Free Transform** tool, if necessary, to resize the check boxes so they display all of the text, or change the Width attribute in the Property inspector.

6. Test the movie (click **Control** on the menu bar, and then click **Test Movie**), and then check the boxes, noting that you can check one or more. See Figure 7-12.

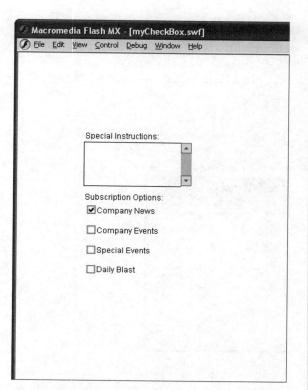

Figure 7-12   Testing the check boxes

7. Close the test window, and then save and close **myCheckBox.fla**, leaving Flash open for the next set of steps.

Working with the Radio Button Component

A **radio button**, also referred to as an option button, requires users to make a single choice from a set of multiple options, as shown in Figure 7-13. You use a radio button when you want to provide a list of options, but want users to select only one. For example, if you used radio buttons to select a shipping method for an online purchase, you would have to select only one method.

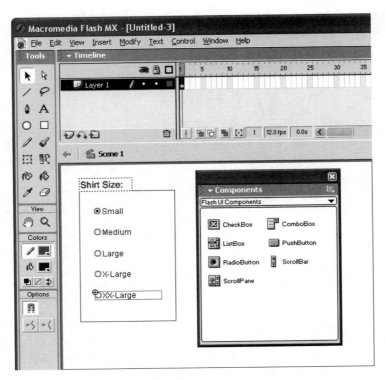

Figure 7-13   Option buttons in Flash

Set the following parameters when creating radio buttons:

- Instance name, to name the instance of the radio button component on the Stage
- Height and width values of the option button's bounding border, which does not increase the size of the actual option button (this is ideal to help align a series of option buttons)
- X and y values to designate the location of the option button on the Stage
- Label name
- Initial state to set the option button on or off (true or false)
- Group Name to give the set of option buttons the ability to select only one in the group
- Data, meaning what value or data the option represents in the group
- Label placement, either left or right of the option button
- Change Handler field, allowing you to add an ActionScript command or function

In the following steps, you create an option group, a series of option buttons designed to provide a set of related choices. In the option group, only one option button can be selected at a time, and one must be selected. These options will determine the delivery format of the subscription e-mail.

To add a group of option buttons to a Flash document:

1. Open **OptionButton.fla** from the Chapter7 folder in your FlashSamples folder. Save it as **myOptionButton.fla** in the same location.

2. Drag the **RadioButton** component from the Components panel four times to add four option buttons under the Delivery Format text box. Use the **Arrow** tool to click the first option button on the Stage to select it, and then open the Property inspector, if necessary.

3. In the Property inspector, click **Label**, and then type **HTML Format** to name this option button. Because HTML is the most popular format for this company's audience, set the Initial State to **true**.

4. Click **Group Name**, and then type **DeliveryFormat** as the name for this group of option buttons. Providing the same group name for each option in the group means that only one option button can be selected in that group.

5. Set the Group Name parameter for the remaining three option buttons to **DeliveryFormat**.

6. Add the following labels to the remaining three option buttons: **Text Format**, **AOL Format**, and **Not Sure**. Your Stage should resemble Figure 7-14.

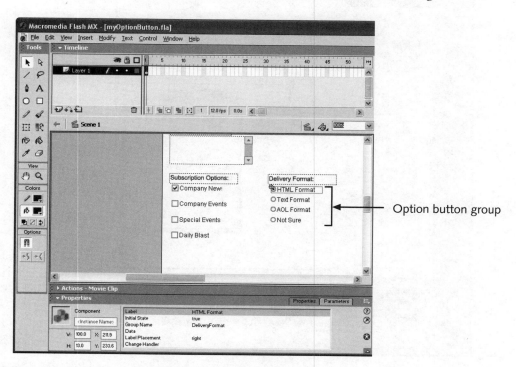

Figure 7-14   Option buttons on your Stage

7. Test the movie, and then click each option button to test how it works.

8. Close the test window, and then save and close myOptionButton.fla, leaving Flash open for the next set of steps.

Working with the List Box Component

The **list box** component allows your users to click and select multiple options. You should display at least three, but no more than eight, items in the list at one time. As Figure 7-15 illustrates, you can select multiple noncontiguous or neighboring items in the list using the Ctrl key (PC/Windows) or Command key (Mac). The list box is ideal for displaying several options within a group without taking up too much screen space. Unlike a check box, however, users can select either one option from the list or many options. For example, in the next set of steps, you define a list box that includes entries describing the frequency of e-mail delivery: Weekly, Daily, Monthly, Bi-Monthly, and Quarterly. Use a list box component when you want to present many entries, commonly three to eight, in a single component.

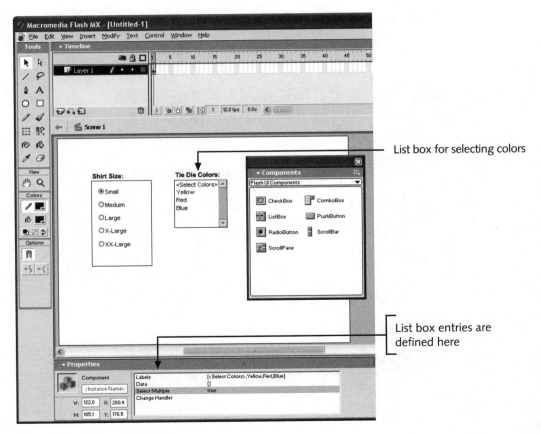

Figure 7-15 Using a list box

The parameters for a list box are:

- Instance Name, to name the instance of the list box component on the Stage
- Height and width values of the list box's bounding border, which does not increase the size of the actual list box. This is ideal to help align a series of list boxes.
- X and y values to designate the location of the list box on the Stage
- Label name
- Labels for the entries in the list box
- Data, the value that the entry represents and that you enter as a label using a Values dialog box, which you open by clicking the entry box for the Label parameter
- Select Multiple specifies whether the user is allowed to select more than one item in the list box; the default setting is false
- Change Handler field, which allows you to add an ActionScript command or function

To add a list box to a Flash document:

1. Open **ListBox.fla** from the Chapter7 folder in your FlashSamples folder. Save it as **myListBox.fla** in the same location.

2. Drag the **ListBox** component from the Components panel to your Stage just below the Delivery Frequency heading. Use the **Free Transform** tool to change the size of the list box, if necessary. Open the Property inspector, if necessary.

3. Click **Labels**, and then click the **Magnifying Glass** button to open the Values dialog box.

4. To add value entries, click the **Add** (+) button, and then type a value, replacing the "defaultValue" text. Add the entries to reflect the following text: **Weekly**, **Daily**, **Monthly**, **Bi-Monthly**, and **Quarterly**.

5. You can rearrange the values you entered; for example, click the **Daily** entry, and then click the **Up arrow** button to move the value upward in the list. Your Values dialog box should match Figure 7-16.

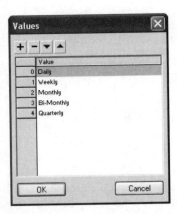

Figure 7-16   Entering list box values

6. Click **OK** to accept your entries. The Labels field in the Property inspector fills with the entries you typed.

7. Make sure the Select Multiple parameter is set to false. If necessary, you could click Select Multiple, and then set it to true to allow users to select more than one item in the list.

8. Test the movie, and then click each of the entries individually. If you had allowed users to select more than one entry, you could hold down the Ctrl key (Command for the Mac) and then click each entry.

9. Close the test window, and then save and close myListBox.fla, leaving Flash open for the next set of steps.

Working with the Combo Box Component

The **combo box**, otherwise known as a drop-down list box, is used to select only one item within a list. The combo box is like an option button, but can more efficiently handle a large number of items, as shown in Figure 7-17. Depending on your movie size, you should display from three to eight items in the list at one time and allow your user to scroll for the remaining items.

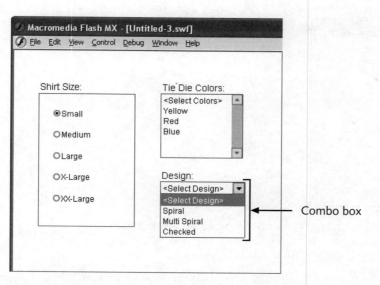

Figure 7-17   Combo box in Flash

Following are the parameters for the combo box:

- Instance Name, to name the instance of the combo box component on the Stage
- Height and Width values of the combo box's bounding border, which does not increase the size of the actual combo box. These values help align a series of combo boxes.
- X and Y values to designate the location of the combo box on the Stage
- Label name
- Labels for the entries your user can select
- Data, which is the value or other data that the entry represents in the group of entries. You enter the label and data using a Values dialog box shown in Figure 7-18, which you open by clicking the entry box for the Label parameter.
- Editable determines whether the combo box is editable or static. Editable combo boxes allow you to enter text in a field to search for the matching item in the scroll list or to scroll through the list and select items. Static combo boxes allow users only to scroll through the list and select items.
- Row Count, which determines the amount of items to display in the list
- Change Handler field, which allows you to add an ActionScript command or function

Figure 7-18 Values dialog box for defining combo box values

To add a combo box to a Flash document:

1. Open **ComboBox.fla** from the Chapter7 folder in your FlashSamples folder. Save it as **myComboBox.fla** in the same location.

2. Drag the **ComboBox** component from the Components panel to your Stage just below the Major Topic of Interest heading.

3. Click the **combo box** on the Stage to select it, and then open the Property inspector, if necessary.

4. Click **Labels** in the Property inspector, and then click the **Magnifying Glass** button to open the Values dialog box. Add entries, as you did for the list box component, by clicking the **Add** (+) button and then typing the entry text into the highlighted field. Add the following list of topics as the combo box entries: **Products**, **Services**, **Events**, **Website**, **General Feedback**, and **Contact Requested**.

5. Click **OK** to accept your entries. Your Stage should resemble Figure 7-19.

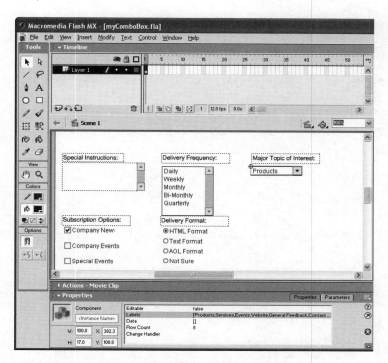

Figure 7-19 Stage and combo box values

6. Test the movie, and then test the combo box by clicking the list arrow in the combo box and clicking a value.

7. Close the test window, and then save and close myComboBox.fla, leaving Flash open for the next set of steps.

Working with the Scroll Pane Component

The **scroll pane** component allows you to view a movie clip as if you were looking through a window. The movie clip does not have to be located on the Stage—you can set parameters to use both horizontal and vertical scroll bars, and you can set an option to scroll or pan the movie clip within the confines of the scroll pane. To **pan** means to drag and navigate to bring another area of the movie clip into view within the scroll pane. You link the movie clip to the scroll pane with the Identifier field in the movie clip's Linkage Properties dialog box, as shown in Figure 7-20. You open the Linkage Properties dialog box by right-clicking the movie clip in your library and clicking Linkage on the shortcut menu. You also need to click the Export for ActionScript option check box in the Linkage Properties dialog box.

Figure 7-20   Specifying the movie clip identifier

The parameters for the scroll pane component are shown in the following list. Figure 7-21 shows both ways you can edit the parameters—using the Component Parameters panel or using the Property inspector.

- Instance Name, to name the instance of the scroll pane component on the Stage
- Height and Width values of the scroll pane's bounding border, which does not increase the size of the actual scroll pane
- X and Y values to designate the location of the scroll pane on the Stage
- Scroll Content
- Horizontal and Vertical scroll options
- Draggable content settings to allow or not allow a movie clip to be panned

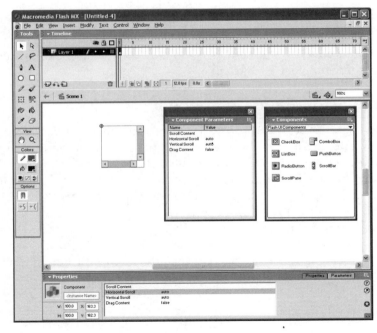

Figure 7-21   Scroll pane component

To add a scroll pane to a Flash document:

1. Open **ScrollPane.fla** from the Chapter7 folder in your FlashSamples folder. Save it as **myScrollPane.fla** in the same location.

2. Drag the **ScrollPane** component from the Components panel to your Stage just below the Our Company Represents heading.

3. Click the scroll pane to select it, and then open the Property inspector, if necessary.

4. Click **Scroll Content** and type **ScrollPaneImage** in the text box. This represents the image that will appear in the scroll pane. This image has already been added to the library for you.

5. Click **Drag Content**, and set the value to **true** so users can move or pan the image within the scroll pane's dimensions.

6. Test the movie, and then drag or use the scroll bar to view more of the image in the scroll pane, as shown in Figure 7-22.

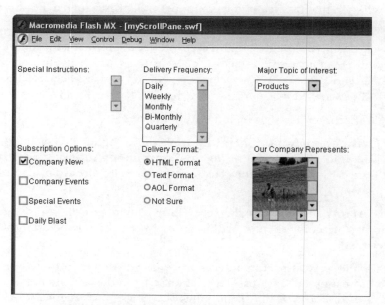

Figure 7-22   Viewing an image in the scroll pane

7. Close the test window, and then save and close myScrollPane.fla, leaving Flash open for the next set of steps.

BRINGING COMPONENTS TO LIFE WITH ACTIONSCRIPT

The components in Flash MX add interaction to your user's Web experience. They help provide immediate feedback, build a user interface, and provide form content to a Web site. With the addition of ActionScript, components become even more functional. You can use the strong scripting capabilities in Flash to create interactive and engaging online experiences that are impossible with HTML.

When a user selects a menu item, option button, or a check box, the corresponding component calls a change handler function to institute the change. The PushButton component calls a click handler function. All components have a Change Handler parameter for specifying a change handler function that is called. You can write change handler and click handler functions in a variety of ways. It is good coding practice to create a single handler function that specifies the actions for the components in your document, and then use the name of this handler function as the Change Handler parameter for the components. This ensures that conflicting actions are not assigned, and makes it easier to update and change the code. A Change Handler or Click Handler function always accepts at least one parameter, which is the instance of the component that has changed. For more information, visit *www.macromedia.com/support/flash/action_scripts _dict.html.*

The following steps help you build a simple user interface and then add ActionScript to the scroll bar component to provide feedback about the scroll bar. The interface will contain a scroll bar and a text box that receives typed text entries. The scroll bar's position is automatically recorded in a dynamic text box below the scroll bar.

To build a simple user interface that includes ActionScript:

1. Open **ComponentActionScript.fla** from the Chapter7 folder in your FlashSamples folder. Save the file as **myComponentActionScript.fla** in the same location. Some of the interface components are already placed on the Stage for you.

2. Use the **Arrow** tool to click the **scroll bar** component on your Stage. Notice that the component is within an input text box, which will be used to enter text.

3. Open the Property inspector, if necessary. Type **ScrollerH** in the Component text box to name the scroll bar. The ActionScript code you enter later can then refer to the scroll bar by this name. Click the Horizontal parameter in the Property inspector and make sure it is set to true, as shown in Figure 7-23. This setting defines the control as a horizontal scroll bar, where a scroll box moves left and right, rather than up and down.

4. Add a small text box below the lower-right corner of the scroll bar.

5. Configure the text box to contain **Dynamic Text** and a single line, if necessary.

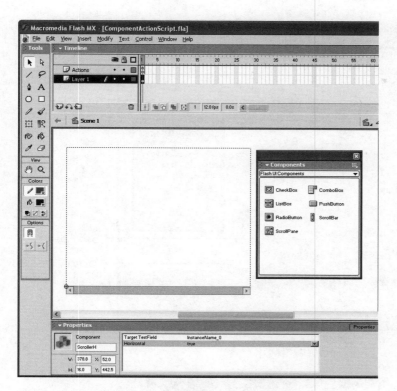

Figure 7-23   Horizontal scroll bar parameters

6. Name the text box **TextFieldH**. The ActionScript code you enter can then refer to the text box by this name. In your var text box, type **scrollValue**. Your screen should resemble Figure 7-24.

7. Right-click (Ctrl+click on the Macintosh) **frame 1** on the Actions layer of your movie, and then click **Actions** on the shortcut menu. The Actions panel opens. Ensure that the window is in **Expert** mode. (Click the **View Options** button on the Actions panel, and then click **Expert Mode**, if necessary, to check that option.) Also view line numbers using the View Options button.

8. Type the following lines of code. When you finish, the Actions window should resemble Figure 7-25.

```
ScrollerH.setScrollProperties(99, 0, 100);
// Arguments: page size, min, and max positions
// (page size, min, max)
ScrollerH.onEnterFrame=function(){
TextFieldH.text=ScrollerH.getscrollPosition();
};
```

This code first sets the size and the minimum and maximum positions of the scroller. Then the code uses an onEnterFrame event action to retrieve the scroll bar's position to display in the text box on the Stage.

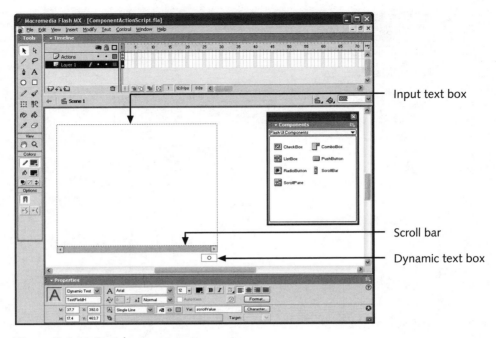

Figure 7-24   Text box parameters

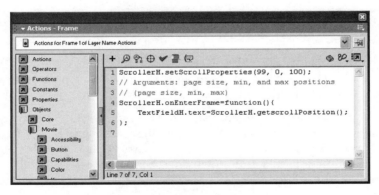

Figure 7-25   ActionScript code for the scroll bar

9. To test the scroll bar's code, click **Control** on the menu bar, and then click **Test Movie**.

10. Drag the **scroll bar** from left to right. Notice that the text box dynamically changes values from 0 to 100, from left to right.

11. Save myComponentActionScript.fla, and then close the file. Leave Flash open for the next set of steps.

INSTALLING ADDITIONAL COMPONENTS IN MACROMEDIA FLASH

Components can come from other sources, such as an experienced ActionScript developer, online forums, and Macromedia. Macromedia offers several components directly from its Application Development Center, *www.macromedia.com/desdev/mx/flash*. You can install these components to work just like the standard Flash MX components discussed earlier in this chapter. Components can be downloaded as MXP files, or Macromedia extension files.

An extension is a piece of software that can be added to a Macromedia application to enhance the application's capabilities. For example, Macromedia Dreamweaver extensions can include HTML code or JavaScript commands. HTML code can be added to the Object panel and Insert menu, and JavaScript commands can be added to the Command menu and floating panels. An extension file is used by the Macromedia Extension Manager, which provides an easy and convenient way to install and delete extensions in Macromedia applications such as Flash MX, Flash 5, and Dreamweaver MX.

The Extension Manager also assists you in submitting and researching components built by third parties on the Macromedia Exchange for Flash Web site, *www.macromedia.com/exchange*. The Extension Manager can toggle extensions on or off; display the extension version, type, and author; and provide details such as installation and usage instructions. The Extension Manager is shown in Figure 7-26.

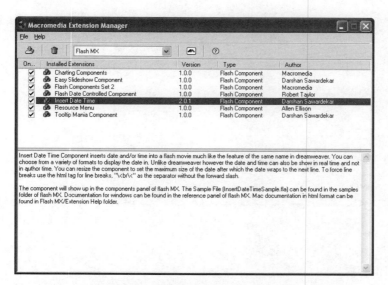

Figure 7-26   Macromedia Extension Manager

In the following steps, you locate and download the Charting Components from the Flash MX Application Development Center.

To locate and download the Charting Components:

1. Start your browser and visit the Macromedia Exchange Login page at *http://macromedia.com/exchange*. Click **Macromedia Flash**.

2. If you have not logged on to the site before, click **Get a Macromedia ID**. Enter the requested information to log on.

3. Click the **Designer & Developer** link. Click the **Development Centers** list arrow, and then click **Macromedia Flash MX**.

4. Click the **Charting Components** link.

5. Click either **PC** or **MAC**, depending on your operating system, as shown in Figure 7-27.

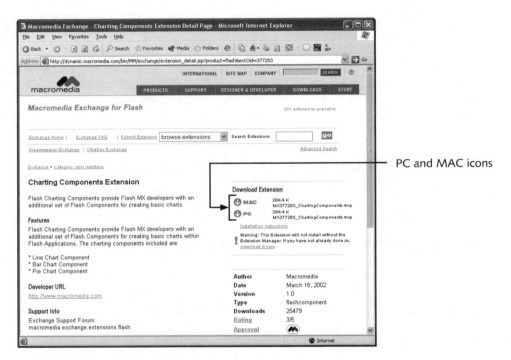

Figure 7-27   Macromedia Exchange for Flash page

6. Click the **Save File As** button and save the file in your Chapter7\ FlashSamples folder.

 If the Macromedia Extension Manager is not already installed on your system, download it by visiting *www.macromedia.com/downloads*. You need the Extension Manager to open MXP files, which you do in Step 7.

7. Navigate to your Chapter7\FlashSamples folder and double-click the **MX377283_ChartingComponents.mxp** file. Click **Accept** after you've read the disclaimer. Click **OK** when the installation is finished. Your Extension Manager should resemble Figure 7-28, which shows the Charting Component details. Your list of Charting Components might differ.

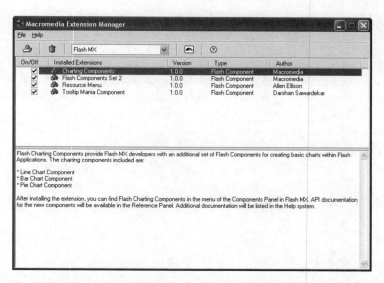

Figure 7-28   Charting Components in Flash MX

8. Open Flash MX, and open a new, blank file. To verify that the components were installed correctly, click **Window** on the menu bar, and then click **Components**. In the Components pane, click the list arrow, and then click **Flash Charting Components**. The BarChart, PieChart, and LineChart components appear.

CHAPTER SUMMARY

❑ Flash MX components are a collection of movie clips that you can add to a Flash document so that users can make selections or provide information.

❑ When you add a component to a Flash document, you insert a graphic control to the document, such as a button or check box. After you add a component to a Flash document, you configure the component so that it provides the correct information for a user to select. To make some components work, you must also use ActionScript to assign actions to the frame containing the component.

❑ Flash MX components are the successor to Smart Clips in Flash 5. Macromedia developed its MX version to include a suite of user interface tools that you can add directly to your Flash movies and movie objects.

❐ With the UI components in Flash MX, you can design a user interface with common controls directly in your movie. Such controls include check boxes, list boxes, and scroll bars. UI components have their own Components panel in Flash MX.

❐ Components add interaction to your user's Web experience. They help provide immediate feedback to your users, help you build a user interface, and provide form content to a Web site. With the addition of ActionScript, components become even more functional.

❐ Components can come from other sources, such as an experienced ActionScript developer, online forums, and Macromedia. Macromedia offers several components directly from its Application Development Center, *www.macromedia.com/desdev/mx/flash.* You can install these components to work just like the standard Flash MX components.

REVIEW QUESTIONS

1. A user interface (UI) includes everything you add to an application to help a user interact with it. True or false?

2. Which of the following is not a standard UI component of Flash MX?
   a. advanced scroll pane
   b. scroll bars
   c. charting components
   d. combo box

3. Flash MX components are the successor to _____ in Flash 5.

4. Flash has an extended set of components called Flash UI Components Set 2. True or false?

5. Macromedia provides an Extension Manager for which applications?
   a. Flash 5
   b. Flash MX
   c. Dreamweaver MX
   d. all of the above

6. Each time you add a component to your Stage, the component is also added to your movie's library. True or false?

7. With the scroll bar component you can add a scroll bar to which part of a text box?
   a. left
   b. right
   c. top and bottom
   d. all of the above

8. Using a component already in use on your Stage, from a new component set in the Components panel, can overwrite the existing components within your document's library. True or false?

9. A parameter for the check box component is _____.
   a. Modify Handler
   b. Change Handler
   c. Checkmark
   d. none of the above

10. The radio button, also referred to as the _____, requires users to make a single choice from a set of multiple options.

11. The radio button's group name allows you to _____.
   a. select several option buttons in a group
   b. select only one option button in the group
   c. select the entire group of option buttons
   d. none of the above

12. The list box component allows your users to click and select multiple options. True or false?

13. You can configure the list box to select multiple noncontiguous or neighboring items in the list by the use of the Ctrl key (PC/Windows) or Command key (Mac). True or false?

14. The combo box, otherwise known as a drop-down list box, is used for selecting _____.
   a. multiple items
   b. one item
   c. every other item
   d. none of the above

15. Using a combo box _____ parameter determines the amount of items to display in the list.

16. The scroll pane's related movie clip is linked via the movie clip's linkage properties identifier. True or false?

17. You can set the scroll pane to drag content or not with the _____ parameter.

18. Components can come from other sources, such as _____.
   a. online forums or Flash communities
   b. experienced ActionScript developers
   c. Macromedia
   d. all of the above

19. An extension is a piece of hardware that can be added to a Macromedia application to enhance the application's capabilities. True or false?

20. The Macromedia Extension Manager provides an easy and convenient way to _____ extensions.

HANDS-ON PROJECTS

The Hands-on Projects in this chapter help you add a set of user interface components to a movie and then install new extensions with the Extension Manager.

Project 7-1

In this project, you design a user interface form to help users select options for a PC purchase.

1. Open the **PushButton.fla** file from the Chapter7\Projects folder in your FlashSamples folder. Save the file as **myPushButton.fla** in the same location.

2. Select three push-button components from the standard set of UI components, and drag them to the upper-left corner of the Stage.

3. Use PC Options, Peripherals, and Check Out as the labels for the buttons. In this project, you work on the PC Options button.

4. Create five text boxes arranged horizontally under the buttons. Enter the following text in the text boxes.

   ❑ Hard Drive:

   ❑ RAM:

   ❑ Monitor:

   ❑ CD Drive:

   ❑ Software Selections:

5. Under the Hard Drive text box, drag three option buttons onto the Stage. Make sure they appear indented under the text box. Label each option button as follows. Make sure all of the option buttons have Hard Drive as the group name.

   ❑ 20 GB

   ❑ 30 GB

   ❑ 40 GB

6. Under the RAM text box, drag three option buttons and label them as follows. Make sure all of these option buttons have the same unique group name, such as RAM.

   ❑ 128 MB

   ❑ 256 MB

   ❑ 512 MB

7. Under the Monitor text box, drag three option buttons and label them as follows. Make sure all of these option buttons have the same unique group name, such as Monitor.

   ❑ 15"

   ❑ 17"

   ❑ 19"

8. Under the CD Drive text box, drag three option buttons and label them as follows. Make sure all of these option buttons have the same unique group name, such as CD.

   ❑ CD-ROM

   ❑ CD-DVD

   ❑ CD-RW

9. Under the Software Selections text box, drag four check boxes and label them as follows:

   ❑ Windows OS

   ❑ Office

   ❑ Encarta

   ❑ Games

10. Create a text box under all of the options you have created on the left side of the stage. Make the text box 223 pixels wide by 88 pixels high, use Special Instructions as the instance name, and choose Input Text for the Text type.

11. Create a single-line text box directly above the Special Instructions text box. Type "Special Instructions" (without the quotation marks) in this text box. This will appear as a label for the text box to the user.

12. Drag a scroll bar into the text box and snap it to the right side.

13. Save and close **myPushButton.fla**.

Project 7-2

In this project, you create a PC comparison modeler. You place check boxes for each of the models in a series of PCs and either compare the series or release all of the check boxes with a set of push buttons.

1. Open the **CheckBox.fla** file from the Chapter7\Projects folder in your FlashSamples folder. Save the file as **myCheckBox.fla** in the same location. The scenes and movie elements are already in place.

2. Add a check box for the series of PCs under the PC Series label name. Use the following labels for the PCs:

   ❑ Home PC

   ❑ Home Office

   ❑ Small Office

   ❑ Enterprise System

3. Add a push button named Compare and another named Select All.

4. Add an option button for the four categories of processors to be selected. Use the following labels for the processors. Assign the option buttons to the same group named Speed.

   ❏ Pentium 4 – 500 mhz

   ❏ Pentium 4 – 800 mhz

   ❏ Pentium 4 – 1.2 ghz

   ❏ Pentium 4 – 2.0 ghz

5. Save and close **myCheckBox.fla**.

Project 7-3

In this project, you extend the PC storefront to provide a Flash demo movie, but allow the user to first select the series and options to be viewed.

1. Open the **OptionButton.fla** file from the Chapter7\Projects folder in your FlashSamples folder. Save the file as **myOptionButton.fla** in the same location.

2. Create check boxes for the following types of PCs for which your user can choose to play the demo.

   ❏ Home PC

   ❏ Home Office

   ❏ Small Office

   ❏ Enterprise System

3. Add three option buttons to allow the user to display the demo in one of the following modes. Assign them to the same group named Demo.

   ❏ Full Screen

   ❏ New Window

   ❏ Same Window

4. Add a Dynamic Input text box to collect the user's name and e-mail address before the demo is allowed to play.

5. Finally, add a push button to play the demo.

6. Save and close **myOptionButton.fla**.

Project 7-4

In this project, you use the list box component and a movie clip together. This component displays a short list of entries and corresponds to a movie clip that holds a series of images to be displayed as you select different list box entries. The list box component and images are already set on the Stage for you. You configure the list box, and write the ActionScript to complete this project.

1. Open the **ListBoxPhotos.fla** file from the Chapter7\Projects folder in your FlashSamples folder. Save the file as **myListBoxPhotos.fla** in the same location.

2. Select the list box on the Stage, and enter the following entries in the Labels parameter through the Values dialog box: Contact, Partner, Employment, and Support. This will fill the list box with these labels when the movie is played.

3. Select the Data field in the Property inspector, and enter the following into the Values dialog box: /contact.jpg, /partner.jpg, /employment.jpg, and /support.jpg

   This entry will reference the images that are stored in the same folder as your Flash project file, and the image referenced in the movie clip.

4. Ensure Select Multiple is set to false.

5. Set the Change Handler value to read "loadImages." This text references the ActionScript code that is located on frame 1, and loads the various images as you select the entries in the list box.

6. Select frame 1 on the Actions layer. Display the Actions panel, if necessary.

7. Type the following line of code on line 2 in your Actions panel:

   ```
   jpgHolder.loadMovie(listBox.getSelectedItem().data);
   ```

   This code references the movie clip, and loads the images as the various list entries are selected from the list box.

8. Test your movie. Click to select different entries, observing that the images load with the entry that is selected.

9. Save and close **myListBoxPhotos.fla**.

Project 7-5

In this project, you use a custom component to serve as a news broadcaster that also provides links to various Web sites. This component displays a short list of entries that correspond to Web addresses. The component is already set on the Stage for you. You configure the component to complete this project.

1. Open the **URLScroller.fla** file from the Chapter7\Projects folder in your FlashSamples folder. Save the file as **myURLScroller.fla** in the same location.

2. Select the component on the Stage, and enter the following entries in the Parameters dialog box:

   Orientation = Horizontal

   Scroll Direction = Decremental

   Speed = 10

   Spacing = 3

   Stop On Focus = true

3. Scroll in the Property inspector and click in the DataArray field to display the Values dialog box. Enter the following entries in order: FlashMX, Dreamweaver, ColdFusion, and Fireworks. These are the entries that users can scroll in the list.

4. Click in the URL field, and display the Values dialog box. Type these entries in order:

   http://www.macromedia.com/software/flash

   http://www.macromedia.com/software/dreamweaver

   http://www.macromedia.com/software/coldfusion

   http://www.macromedia.com/software/fireworks

   These entries link to the text entries you entered in the DataArray field, and will open the browser window with the Web URL that you typed.

5. Test your movie by clicking File on the menu bar, pointing to Publish Preview, and then clicking Default (HTML). Click to select different entries, observing that the pages for the entered Web addresses appear. If an output window appears, close it.

6. Close **myURLScroller.fla** and save any changes.

Project 7-6

In this project, you use a custom component to scroll through a list with either happy or sad faces. This component combines the list and scroll bar, as well as custom elements to insert a face movie clip into the list. You edit the parameters and add entries to fill the list.

1. Open the **CustomList.fla** file from the Chapter7\Projects folder in your FlashSamples folder. Save the file as **myCustomList.fla** in the same location.

2. Select the component on the Stage.

3. In the Property inspector, click the Labels field to display the Values dialog box. Enter the names of ten friends. Click in the Data field to display the Values dialog box. Enter the following entries depending on whether your friend is having a good or bad day; happy or sad are the only acceptable entries. Add only seven entries. (Note that "happy" and "sad" are case sensitive, and should not include any uppercase letters.)

4. Test your movie, and click to select different entries. The happy or sad icon should appear next to your entries.

5. Close **myCustomList.fla** and save any changes.

CASE PROJECTS

Case Project 7-1

A software manufacturing company has commissioned you to design a user interface to gather information from its Web site. Your role is to put together a set of user controls that will assist the audience in filling out a questionnaire. The questions will be a mixture of true/false and multiple choice formats. Use your knowledge of UI components to implement the questionnaire. Design a Flash movie with components to portray this user interface.

Case Project 7-2

Your associate is moving a shareware version of a scheduling application to the Web and has asked for your advice. Your job is to provide a functional layout of a Flash-based calendar program. You will interview the main stakeholders and a small focus group to determine any change in requirements, and design the calendar program with Flash's UI and advanced UI components. Design a prototype of this application, and write a 1- to 2- page report detailing the functionality of each element and component. Use the following resources:

❐ *www.macromedia.com/desdev/mx/flash*

❐ *dynamic.macromedia.com/bin/MM/exchange/main.jsp?product=flash*

Case Project 7-3

An online retailer wants to upgrade its Web site to a Flash-based Web presentation in hopes of attracting a more experienced and loyal consumer base. The Web site has a standard set of user controls to select shirt sizes, shipping methods, and quantities. Your role is to redesign the interface positions with the Flash MX and advanced components to provide a Flash-based e-commerce system. You can review some common online retailers for ideas at *www.landsend.com* and *www.rei.com*. Design a prototype of what you would change within the Flash environment, and write a 1- to 2- page report explaining why you would make these changes.

7

Case Project 7-4

For your personal or fictional business Case Project, design a Flash document containing at least three types of components. For example, you could create an online form for your fictional business, or create a form that lets users select options to match your interests to theirs.

8

USING THIRD-PARTY LANGUAGES WITH MACROMEDIA FLASH MX

Macromedia Flash MX Design Techniques with XML, CGI, and JavaScript

> **In this chapter, you will:**
> ◆ Understand the languages that work with Macromedia Flash MX
> ◆ Work with Extensible Markup Language (XML)
> ◆ Work with Common Gateway Interface (CGI)
> ◆ Work with the JavaScript programming language

In Chapters 6 and 7, you learned the basics of integrating Macromedia Flash movies with ActionScript and the Flash MX components. In this chapter, you will learn more advanced design techniques by integrating Flash MX with other popular and powerful technologies, including Extensible Markup Language (XML), the Common Gateway Interface (CGI), and JavaScript. By using these technologies, you can work outside the limitations of Flash and ActionScript.

XML allows you to use its technology to separate data from the presentation. XML documents contain data only, not formatting instructions, so the programs that process XML documents can determine how to display its information.

CGI is a standard protocol that allows Web users to interact with programs on Web servers. CGI is a protocol, not a programming language, so you create a **CGI script** to process information. You can use scripts that already exist within your Flash movies, working with JavaScript to extend the capabilities of your movies. You use **JavaScript** to enhance the way Web pages look and work, making them more dynamic and interactive.

XML, CGI, and JavaScript let you navigate and control the information that appears in the browser window. For example, an XML document can provide the data for a graphical chart or navigational menu presented in Flash. You can use a CGI script to transfer information from an online form to an e-mail address. Use JavaScript to open new browser windows from your Flash movies and control an optional status bar or address bar. With Flash MX, you can also manage the history of Web pages your users visit when they click the Back button on their browsers.

UNDERSTANDING THE LANGUAGES THAT WORK WITH MACROMEDIA FLASH MX

For years Flash users have wanted an application-based Web tool that could use Flash movies. Beginning with Flash version 3, Macromedia Generator was used for such functions. Flash MX now accomplishes these same tasks, such as communicating with database content via XML, and establishing connectivity through the Macromedia ColdFusion database application server (see Figure 8-1). Macromedia Generator, a server-based application that dynamically updates Flash graphics and animation using external data sources, is being phased out due to the interoperability with application servers such as Macromedia's ColdFusion.

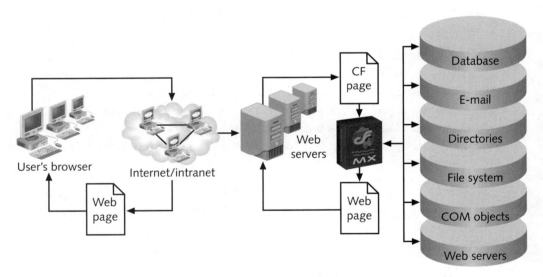

Figure 8-1   Macromedia Flash MX and ColdFusion application server

The language integration in Flash MX provides the foundation for a new generation of tools for Flash designers. Flash can now be a user-interface development tool for Web-based applications while ColdFusion or other servers power the back end. These servers can create real Flash objects and build Flash content without actually using Flash.

Instead, they take advantage of a feature called Flash Remoting, which simplifies the Flash application development life cycle by providing a powerful yet simple programming model. You can now send structured variables, record sets, or arrays from your server to the Flash Player easily and securely.

You can use XML to build applications in Flash such as the slideshow shown in Figure 8-2. However, the syntax used in XML is more complex than that of other markup languages. For example, HTML contains a predefined set of tags; if a tag is missing, Web browsers can make assumptions about any missing tags. However, XML does not include predefined tags. Whereas <p> is always a paragraph tag in HTML, a <p> tag in an XML document could mean anything at all. Programs called **parsers** that read and interpret XML can't make assumptions about the meaning of an XML tag. The rules for creating and formatting XML documents are strictly enforced by XML parsers, like the one in the Macromedia Flash 6 Player. XML can be combined with Flash to render XML data in the Flash Player, and ease the maintenance and updating of the data by segregating the data from the presentation.

Figure 8-2 Flash slideshow application

Using components you have worked with in previous chapters, Flash can communicate with CGI technology. You can use CGI to send Flash form data through a user's browser to send an e-mail message (see Figure 8-3), for example, or to calculate the results of an online poll.

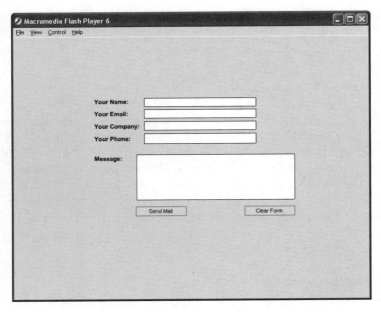

Figure 8-3   Flash e-mail application using a CGI script

A typical Web application first relies on the user to request pages for nearly every HTTP interaction, and then relies on a Web server to process and respond to the requests. The role of a Web-hosting organization's Web server is to respond to these requests and provide appropriate information. This technique, even with a high-speed connection, is slow and resource intensive. By adding basic UI components, which are standard in other interfaces, you can very quickly create powerful applications. For example, Figure 8-4 demonstrates how JavaScript can use a message box to control what the user enters and what the browser displays. Using Flash, you can use JavaScript to control the browser window, enhance the browser environment with color and background images, and control rollover events.

Figure 8-4   JavaScript message box

In the next sections you begin learning about XML and how it works with a Flash movie.

WORKING WITH EXTENSIBLE MARKUP LANGUAGE (XML)

XML is a markup language for documents containing structured information. Structured information includes not only content, such as words and pictures, but indications of what role the content plays. For example, content in a section heading has a different meaning than content in a database table.

XML is a markup language like HTML, and was designed to describe data. Tags are not predefined in XML; you must define your own tag sets, called a Document Type Definition (DTD) or an XML Schema, to describe the data. Once defined, these tags are designed to be self-descriptive. For example, if you are creating an XML document to describe charting data, the XML tags themselves can describe the actual data for a pie chart, as shown in Figure 8–5. This document uses <pie color> as a tag for the data that sets the color of a pie wedge.

8

```
pieData.xml - Notepad
File  Edit  Format  View  Help
<?xml version="1.0"?>
<pieData>
   <pie color="FF0000">
      <value>320</value>
      <text>Item 1</text>
   </pie>
   <pie color="00FF00">
      <value>450</value>
      <text>Item 2</text>
   </pie>
   <pie color="0000FF">
      <value>70</value>
      <text>Item 3</text>
   </pie>
   <pie color="FFFF00">
      <value>150</value>
      <text>Item 4</text>
   </pie>
   <pie color="FF00FF">
      <value>250</value>
      <text>Item 5</text>
   </pie>
   <pie color="00FFFF">
      <value>552</value>
      <text>Item 6</text>
   </pie>
</pieData>
```

Figure 8-5 Self-describing data tags in XML

Understanding the Difference Between XML and HTML

XML is a complement to HTML, not a replacement for it. The two languages were designed with different goals in mind: XML describes and holds data and focuses on what the data represents, while HTML displays data and focuses on how it looks. XML is used as a cross-platform tool for transmitting information, independent of the software and hardware used with it.

The following example shows graphical pie-chart data stored as an XML document.

```
<?xml version="1.0"?>
<pieData>
  <pie color="FF0000">
    <value>320</value>
    <text>Item 1</text>
  </pie>
  <pie color="00FF00">
    <value>450</value>
    <text>Item 2</text>
  </pie>
  <pie color="0000FF">
    <value>70</value>
    <text>Item 3</text>
  </pie>
  <pie color="FFFF00">
    <value>150</value>
    <text>Item 4</text>
  </pie>
</pieData>
```

The following example shows HTML code.

```
<html>
<head>
</head>
<body>
<ul>
<li>This is a bullet with a closing tag</li>
<li>This is also a bullet, with no closing tag
</ul>
</body>
</html>
```

As the previous code indicates, XML tags are not predefined. You must design and code your own tags and document structure.

Understanding XML Rules and Syntax

HTML syntax rules are fairly forgiving, but XML is more rigid. The first line in the document—the XML declaration—defines the XML version and the character encoding used in the document. In the previous example, the document conformed to the 1.0 specification of XML and used the ISO-8859-1 (Latin-1/West European) character set. The next line describes the root element of the document. The next lines describe the child elements of the root, or the subelements. Finally, the last line defines the end of the root element. Table 8-1 describes XML rules and provides examples.

Table 8-1   XML Syntax Rules

XML rule	Rule example
The XML declaration should always be included in the first line of the document. It defines the XML version of the document. In the example at right, the document conforms to the 1.0 specification of XML.	`<?xml version="1.0"?>`
The next line defines the first element of the document (the root element).	`<note>`

The next lines define child elements of the root element (to, from, heading, and body in the example at right).	`<to>To</to>`
	`<from>From</from>`
	`<heading>Reminder</heading>`
	`<body>This weekend</body>`

The last line defines the end of the root element.	`</note>`
All XML elements must have a closing tag.	`<p>This is a paragraph</p>`
XML tags are case sensitive.	`<message>This is` `correct</message>`
All XML elements must be properly nested.	`<b><i>This text is bold and` `italic</i></b>`

All XML documents must have a root tag.	`<root>`
	`  <child>`
	`    <subchild>`
	`    </subchild>`
	`  </child>`
	`</root>`

Attribute values must always be enclosed in quotation marks.	`<?xml version="1.0"?>` `<note date="12/11/99">`

Using XML with Macromedia Flash MX

The number of applications in development that use XML documents in some way is steadily increasing. In the Flash environment, the word "document" refers not only to traditional documents such as ASCII text files, but also to other XML formats, including vector graphics, e-commerce transactions, mathematical equations, object meta-data, and other kinds of structured information.

In the following steps, you use XML to complete a document that represents charting data, and then you view the XML data in a Flash movie.

To edit the XML document and view the Flash movie:

1. Open **3DPieChart.swf** from the Chapter8 folder in your FlashSamples folder. Notice the pie-chart data, which comes directly from an XML file, as shown in Figure 8-6.

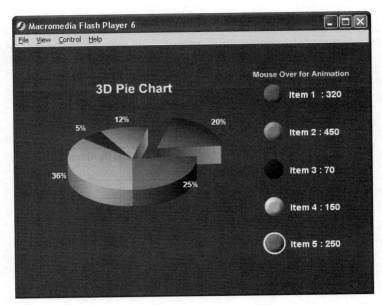

Figure 8-6 XML data providing information to a Flash SWF file

2. Point to each button on the right, and then close the SWF file.

3. Use a text editor such as Notepad or SimpleText to open the XML document **pieData.xml** from the Chapter8 folder in your FlashSamples folder.

4. Directly under the last </pie> tag, add the following lines of syntax to complete the XML data:

```
<pie color="00FFFF">
  <value>552</value>
  <text>Item 6</text>
</pie>
```

This XML code defines the pie-chart color, the numeric value, and the item number. The first line of code provides the color in the common HTML hexadecimal format, a value tag to display the numeric value being represented, a text tax to display the item name, and then closes the code with the ending </pie> tag.

5. Click **File** on the menu bar, and then click **Save** to save pieData.xml with the same filename and in the same location. Then close your text editor.

6. Open the **3DPieChart.swf** file again and notice the additional sixth item. Roll your mouse over the button to test the animation, as shown in Figure 8-7.

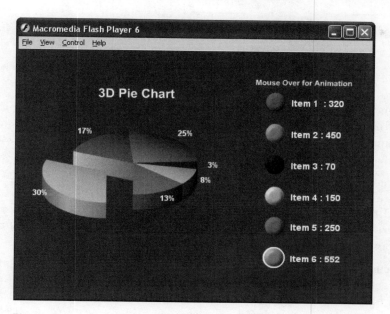

Figure 8-7   Completed SWF file from an edited XML document

7. Close 3DPieChart.swf, but leave Flash open for the next set of steps.

In the next section, you explore different uses and applications with CGI and Flash.

WORKING WITH COMMON GATEWAY INTERFACE (CGI)

CGI permits interactivity between a client (Web browser) and a host operating system (Web server) through the World Wide Web via the Hypertext Transfer Protocol (HTTP). CGI is a standard for external gateway programs or scripts to interact with HTTP servers or Web servers. In other words, a visitor to your Web site can run a program or script from your Web server, which significantly increases the power and flexibility of a Web site. Another advantage CGI offers is that you can use popular CGI scripts in the common Linux Web server platform.

A plain HTML document that the Web server delivers is static, meaning it doesn't change. Alternatively, a CGI program is executed in real time, so it can display dynamic information such as a stock market reading or the latest results from a database query. CGI can be hosted on a Web server or remotely on a CGI provider's server, which handles information requests and then returns the appropriate information or generates a document in real time, as illustrated in Figure 8-8.

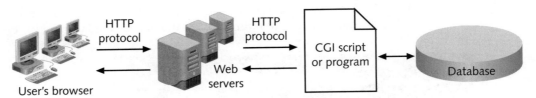

Figure 8-8 CGI protocol for handling requests and providing information

CGI scripts can be used for a variety of purposes, but their most common use is handling HTML form data requests for HTTP servers. The Common Gateway Interface is a convention among Web designers to integrate executable scripts and programs that can run on their own.

Gateways that conform to this specification can be written in a programming language to produce an executable file. Some of the more popular languages to use include C, C++, Perl, and Python. It doesn't matter in which language the program is written, as long as it is written correctly and you have the permission and resources to run it on your Web-hosting provider's server.

In the next section, you use an existing CGI script named FormMail.pl to handle Flash text box form data and send it through to an e-mail. You create the text fields where users enter information, and then assign actions to a button user's click to send the data to the CGI script. Before you do this, however, examine how to integrate CGI with Flash.

Integrating CGI with Macromedia Flash

To integrate CGI with Flash, you primarily use the loadVariables method in ActionScript. The loadVariables method can open and read a text file or XML file, and can reference a variable such as a Web URL. The load variable in the following steps uses a CGI script, the movie's level, and the data transfer method POST. The CGI script must be located on a functioning Web server, such as the one noted at *www.FlashTrainingDesign.com/FlashSendMail* in order to work. You use the level parameter to specify which movies to load into the Flash Player. You must assign a level number in the Flash Player even if you will not be using the specific parameter. Recall that level 0 is the base level from which all subsequent levels are loaded. The final parameter is the POST transfer method in combination with the CGI script. The POST method is a more secure method of transferring data because it is contained in the header of the HTTP request from the CGI script.

In the following steps, you use a CGI script named FormMail.pl to deliver a Flash form via e-mail. The CGI script will deliver the e-mail to the administrator of the domain *www.flashtrainingdesign.com*, including all the text fields in the form. CGIEmail.fla is already set up for you with a form, all of the form fields, and the code to validate the input of the data. In this set of steps, you enter the variable name for the person to whom you are sending the e-mail, add and name another text field, and address the CGI script in code. You can also test the working example at the following Web address: *www.FlashTrainingDesign.com/FlashSendMail.*

If you are using a Macintosh, press Ctrl + click instead of right-clicking throughout this chapter.

1. Open **CGIEmail.fla** from the Chapter8 folder in your FlashSamples folder. Save the file as **myCGIEmail.fla** in the same location. The movie uses text boxes to collect user information and send it to a CGI script named FormMail.pl, which takes form data such as the Flash text field variable values, and delivers that data in an e-mail message. You must create the editable text fields to accept the user's input, and then assign actions to a button the user clicks to send the form data to the CGI script. The CGI script then forwards the form data to an e-mail message.

2. Using the **Arrow** tool, double-click the Email text box on the Stage to open the form in Edit mode. Click the **Line type** list arrow, and then click **Single Line**, if necessary. Then click the **Var** text field and assign it a variable name of **Email** in the Property inspector, as shown in Figure 8-9. This field will accept the e-mail address of the person receiving the form.

Figure 8-9 Property inspector and Email text field

3. Right-click the arrow-shaped **Send** button at the bottom of the form, and then click **Actions** to open the Actions panel. Switch to Expert mode, if necessary, by clicking the **View options** button on the Actions panel, and then clicking **Expert Mode** to select it. Then click the **View options** button again and click **View Line Numbers** to show line numbers. You will use the Actions panel to enter the code for the Send button. You need to indicate that when the Send button is clicked, Flash will send the contents of the text fields to the FormMail.pl CGI script. (FormMail.pl is also stored in the Chapter8 folder of your FlashSamples folder.) To do so, you use the POST command, which packages the form data properly in an e-mail format. Type the following code starting on line 8:

```
} else {
loadVariablesNum("http://www.flashtrainingdesign.com/
cgi-bin/FormMail.pl", "0", "POST");
EmailStatus = "Sending Data... One Moment Please... or
Two...Thank you message sent.";
```

This code continues the if-then-else conditional structure to validate the data entered into the form, such as e-mail addresses that contain the "@" and "." symbols. The code then loads the CGI script and its full path as a variable to the Flash file. Finally, the code displays a status message to the user that the e-mail has been sent. The Actions panel should resemble Figure 8-10.

```
on (release) {
    if (!Email.length || Email.indexOf("@") == -1 || Email.indexOf(".") == -1) {
        EmailStatus = "Please enter a valid E-mail address";
    } else if (!FirstName.length) {
        EmailStatus = "Please Enter your name before Sending";
    } else if (!ToComments.length) {
        EmailStatus = "Please enter some text in your message";
    } else {
        loadVariablesNum("http://www.flashtrainingdesign.com/cgi-bin/FormMail.pl", "0", "POST");
        EmailStatus = "Sending Data... One Moment Please... or Two...Thank you message sent.";
    }
}
```

Figure 8-10   Send button's getURL variables

4. You can publish or test the Flash movie to see how the Send button and script work. To publish the movie, save myCGIEmail.fla, click **File** on the menu bar, and then click **Publish**. To test the movie, save the file, click **Control** on the menu bar, and then click **Test Movie**.

5. In the myCGIEmail.swf file, type an e-mail address, and click the **Send** button to test the movie. If the form is not complete, the movie reminds you to enter the data. A message appears, "Sending Data...One Moment Please..."

6. Close **myCGIEmail.swf** and **myCGIEmail.fla**, but leave Flash open for the next set of steps.

Not all Web servers support CGI scripts. Consult your administrator and ask where you should place and address the CGI script. In the future, you may need to use the entire URL, as in *www.mydomain.com/cgi-bin/FormMail.pl*.

You can find CGI scripts and resources at *www.cgi-resources.com* and *www.perl.com*.

In the next section, you learn to work with JavaScript in the Flash environment.

WORKING WITH THE JAVASCRIPT PROGRAMMING LANGUAGE

JavaScript was created in 1995 in a cooperative effort by Netscape Communications and Sun Microsystems. Like ActionScript, JavaScript is based on the ECMA standard. Unlike ActionScript or Java Applets, however, JavaScript is intended as a client-side scripting language and does not require you to process requests to the Web server. It is integrated directly into the HTML documents and provides an easier development model.

Several versions of JavaScript are supported by different browsers and browser versions, which can lead to confusion and incompatibilities. Netscape originally introduced JavaScript, so JavaScript 1.0 was the language specification supported in Netscape Navigator 2.0. Version 3.0 supported JavaScript 1.1, and Navigator 4.0 now supports JavaScript 1.2.

In parallel, Microsoft attempted to support JavaScript 1.0 in its Internet Explorer 3.0 browser. Known as "JScript," Microsoft's initial JavaScript support was unreliable. A push to standardize the language resulted in an "official" version of JavaScript that was sanctioned by the ECMA. Internet Explorer 4.0 includes robust support for the ECMA-standardized JavaScript; although it is similar to Netscape's JavaScript 1.2, it is not equivalent.

You can do a lot with JavaScript, such as swap images when you move a mouse over one, influence form elements as users work with the form, make calculations, and control the browser's appearance and function.

Integrating JavaScript and Macromedia Flash MX

Flash can communicate with JavaScript and vice versa. Flash can send messages to JavaScript functions, and JavaScript can control Flash movies. Because JavaScript is a fully developed object-oriented scripting language, it can make Flash movies highly interactive.

Customizing the browser window means that you can control the different aspects of that window session. For example, suppose you want a new window to appear to display a news headline in a window smaller than the standard browser window. The window for the news headline will have no toolbars, address bar, or scroll bars, but will have a status bar and menu bar. You will also be able to resize the window by dragging an edge or corner. With JavaScript, you can control all of these aspects of the window, as shown in Figure 8-11.

8

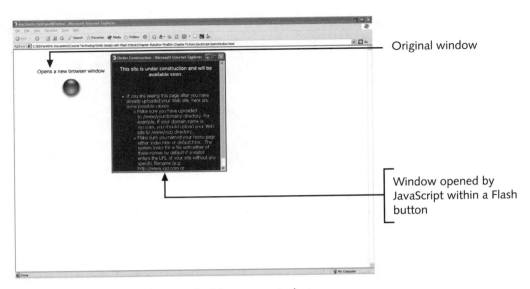

Original window

Window opened by JavaScript within a Flash button

Figure 8-11   JavaScript-controlled browser window

Table 8-2 describes the window options you can set using JavaScript.

Table 8-2   JavaScript Window Options

Option	Parameter	Description
Left	10	Determines the horizontal distance from the upper-left corner of the user's screen to display, measured in pixels
Top	10	Determines the vertical distance from the upper-left corner of the user's screen to display, measured in pixels
Width	500	Determines the window width in pixels
Height	500	Determines the window height in pixels
Toolbar	Yes, No	Determines whether the toolbar will display in the new window
Menu bar	Yes, No	Determines whether the menu will display in the new window
Location	Yes, No	Determines whether the location bar will display in the new window
Scroll bars	Yes, No	Determines whether the horizontal and vertical scroll bars will display in the new window
Status bar	Yes, No	Determines whether the status bar will display in the new window
Resizable	Yes, No	Determines if the new window is resizable by the user

JavaScript does not work on all Web browsers. For a list of compatible browsers, visit *www.macromedia.com/support/flash/ts/documents/java_ script_comm.htm*.

In the following steps, you use JavaScript with your Flash movie to open a new custom browser window. You use an existing Flash movie, edit the button that commands the new browser window, and also edit the HTML file that requires additional JavaScript to be added and coded.

To use JavaScript to open a custom browser window:

1. Open **JavaScriptOpenWindow.fla** from the Chapter8 folder in your FlashSamples folder, and then save the file as **myJavaScriptOpenWindow.fla** in the same location. Notice the button on the Stage to which you will add code.

2. Use the **Arrow** tool to click and select the button, if necessary.

3. Right-click the **button**, and then click the **Actions** command to open the Actions panel. Be sure the Actions panel is in Expert mode.

4. Type the following code into the Actions panel for the button:

```
on (release) {
getURL("javascript:openNewWindow('http://www.flashtrainingdesign.com',
'thewin','height=400,width=400,toolbar=no,scrollbars=yes') ");
}
```

This code displays the new window with the settings you set. The first line is the on release event, which means as soon as the user releases the mouse button, the next lines of code are executed. The next line of code is the ActionScript getURL action, which induces the JavaScript code and opens the new browser window. The parameters of this code are in sequence and are important to the execution of getURL and JavaScript actions. The first parameter is the full URL path to the Web address of the page you want to open. The next is a variable name you need to specify for the window, followed by the specific elements of the browser window itself.

5. Publish the Flash and HTML files by clicking **File** on the menu bar and then clicking **Publish Settings**. The Publish Settings dialog box opens. Make sure the Formats tab is selected. You will learn more about the Publish Settings dialog box in Chapter 9, "Optimizing and Publishing Macromedia Flash MX Movies."

6. If they are not checked, click the **Flash** and **HTML** check boxes. Ensure that only the check boxes are checked, as shown in Figure 8-12.

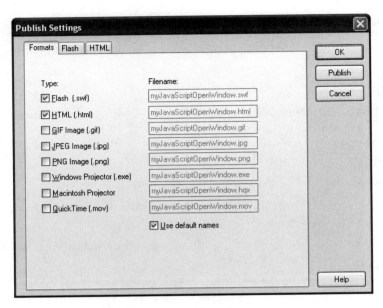

Figure 8-12   Publish Settings dialog box

7. Click the **Publish** button, and then the **OK** button to publish the movie in the SWF format and the HTML format.

8. Use a text editor, such as Notepad or SimpleText, to open your newly published HTML file, myJavaScriptOpenWindow.html, from the Chapter8 folder in your FlashSamples folder.

9. Find the Title tag within the heading of the HTML file. After the Title tag line of code, click to place your cursor and press the **Enter** key to create a new line. (Press **Return** on the Macintosh.)

10. Type the following lines of code:

```
<SCRIPT LANGUAGE=JavaScript>
function openNewWindow(URLtoOpen, windowName, windowFeatures) {
  newWindow=window.open(URLtoOpen, windowName, windowFeatures);
}
</SCRIPT>
```

This code is a necessary JavaScript function that uses the window.open event to open the new browser window. Without this JavaScript function located in the header of the HTML document that opens the new window, you would receive an error message.

11. Save the HTML file and close your text editor.

12. Open the HTML file in a browser.

13. Click the **Flash** button. The new browser window opens with the referenced URL and the JavaScript parameters you set. Figure 8-13 shows the code that Flash uses to open the browser window.

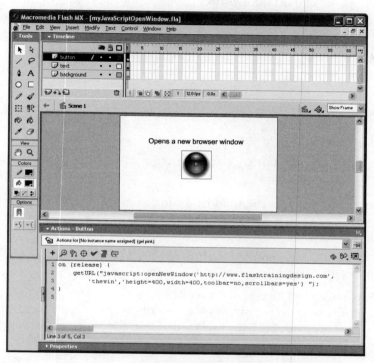

Figure 8-13   Code used to open the HTML file in the new browser window

14. Close all browser windows, and then close Flash.

The getURL and JavaScript actions are required to provide the full path to the Web address as the previous exercise indicates. If you are opening a specific HTML page, then you need to provide that path and file name as well. For example, to open the page called news.html located in the news folder, you would provide a path similar to the following: *http://www.flashtrainingde-sign.com/news/news.html*.

CHAPTER SUMMARY

❏ Extensible Markup Language (XML) is a language for documents containing structured information. Structured information includes not only content, such as words and pictures, but an indication of what role the content plays.

❏ XML lets you separate data from the presentation. XML documents contain data only, not formatting instructions, so the programs that process XML documents can determine how to display its information. XML is a complement to HTML, not a substitution.

❏ CGI is a standard protocol that allows Web users to interact with programs on Web servers. CGI is a protocol, not a programming language, so you create a CGI script to process information.

❏ You use JavaScript to enhance the way Web pages look and work, making them more dynamic and interactive.

❏ Language integration provides the foundation for a new generation of tools for Flash designers, who can now use Flash as a user-interface development tool for Web-based applications.

❏ Using components you have worked with in previous chapters, Flash can communicate with Common Gateway Interface (CGI) technology.

❏ XML is a complement to HTML, not a replacement for it. The two languages were designed with different goals in mind: XML describes data, carries data, and focuses on what the data represents; HTML displays data and focuses on how it looks.

❏ CGI permits interactivity between a client (Web browser) and a host operating system (Web server) through the World Wide Web via the Hypertext Transfer Protocol (HTTP). CGI is a standard for external gateway programs or scripts to interface with HTTP servers or Web servers.

❏ JavaScript was created in 1995 in a cooperative effort by Netscape Communications and Sun Microsystems. Like ActionScript, JavaScript is based on the ECMA standard. Unlike ActionScript or Java Applets, JavaScript is intended as a client-oriented scripting language, and does not require you to process requests to the Web server. It is integrated directly into the HTML documents and provides an easier development model.

REVIEW QUESTIONS

1. Flash cannot work with any other languages or technologies other than ActionScript. True or false?

2. Which of the following is not a standard technology for programming languages used with Flash?

   a. JavaScript

   b. Java

   c. XML

   d. Common Gateway Interface

3. Flash MX components can work directly with the _____ technology.

   a. ActionScript

   b. Common Gateway Interface

   c. XML

   d. all of the above

4. Flash MX technology integration replaces functionality provided by Macromedia Generator. True or false?

5. Flash can be used for which types of Web applications?

   a. online form generation

   b. user interface design

   c. database integration

   d. all of the above

6. The coding syntax for XML is stricter than for HTML. True or false?

7. _____ is a markup language much like HTML, and was designed to describe data.

8. XML is used for displaying information, and HTML is used for describing information. True or false?

9. XML tags are not _____.

   a. structured

   b. organized

   c. predefined

   d. none of the above

10. XML can be used in a _____ and hardware-independent environment.

11. What must you use with CGI to interact with information servers, such as HTTP or Web servers?

    a. hardware devices

    b. middleware

    c. programs or scripts

    d. none of the above

12. CGI can be hosted on a Web server or hosted remotely on a CGI provider's server, which handles information requests and then returns the appropriate information or generates a document in real time. True or false?

13. The most common use of CGI scripts is handling HTML form data requests. True or false?

14. Some of the more popular languages used to program CGI include _____.

    a. C or C++

    b. Perl

    c. Python

    d. all of the above

15. Running a CGI script requires specific _____ on the Web server.

16. JavaScript is based on the ECMA standard. True or false?

17. You can use _____ to control the browser window.

18. JavaScript is useful for tasks such as _____.

    a. image swapping or rollovers

    b. calculations

    c. form handling

    d. all of the above

HANDS-ON PROJECTS

These projects demonstrate how to use XML, CGI, and JavaScript development techniques.

Project 8-1

In this project, you create a JPEG slide show with XML. You design a structured XML document and integrate it into an existing Flash movie. The movie already contains movie elements, ActionScript, and functions to support the slide show. You only need to focus on XML in this exercise.

1. Create an XML document by opening an ASCII text editor such as Notepad or SimpleText.

2. Name the XML file **slides.xml** and save it in the Chapter8\Projects folder in your FlashSamples folder.

3. Add the following lines of XML text and then save **slides.xml**:

```
<slides>
  <slideNode jpegURL="images/image1.jpg">A sea
horse</slideNode>
  <slideNode jpegURL="images/image2.jpg">Sea
anemone</slideNode>
  <slideNode jpegURL="images/image3.jpg">Sardines!
</slideNode>
  <slideNode jpegURL="images/image4.jpg">Another sea
horse</slideNode>
  <slideNode jpegURL="images/image5.jpg">Some kind of
jellyfish</slideNode>
</slides>
```

4. Open the **Slides.fla** file from the FlashSamples\Chapter8\Projects folder in your FlashSamples folder. The scenes and movie elements are already in place. Save the file as **mySlides.fla** in the same location.

5. Right-click frame 1 of the Scripts layer and click the Actions command. The Actions panel opens.

6. Add the following line of syntax directly after the comments in the third line:

```
slides_xml.load("slides.xml");
```

This will integrate the XML document into the Flash environment and use the images associated with the XML syntax structure.

7. Test and then close the FLA and XML files.

Project 8-2

In this project, you create a project estimator using a series of input text fields and a CGI script to send the project data to an e-mail address.

1. Open the **EstimatorEmail.fla** file from the FlashSamples\Chapter8\Projects folder in your FlashSamples folder. Save the file as **myEstimatorEmail.fla** in the same location.

2. Double-click the button to open the form's movie clip in Edit mode.

3. Use the Text tool to add four text boxes to your Stage, one under each heading. Configure each text box as input with the following variable parameters: ProjectName, ProjectDescription, ProjectStage, WebURL.

4. Set the Project Description and Project Stage fields to be Multiline.

5. Add another text field; position it directly to the right of the button.

6. Set this text field as multiline dynamic text, and give it a variable name of EmailStatus. This text field has no static text and will display a confirmation that the form data was sent in an e-mail.

7. Still in the movie clip Edit mode, right-click the button and click the Actions command on the shortcut menu to open the Actions panel.

8. Type the following code in Expert mode. This code will use a preexisting CGI script on a live Web server to transfer the text field data to the Web server administrator.

```
on (release) {
    loadVariablesNum("http://www.flashtrainingdesign.com/cgi-
bin/FormMail.pl", "0", "POST");
    EmailStatus = "Thank you message sent.";
}
```

9. Click Scene1 on your Timeline.

10. Test the functionality of the code and text fields with the Test Movie command on the Control menu.

11. Save and then close the file.

Project 8-3

In this project, you experiment with JavaScript and ActionScript in Flash MX by creating a movie to load another HTML browser window, and providing a close link to ease the use of the new window. The new window will have the getURL parameters for you to experiment and try with different types of HTML pages, such as other Flash movies, QuickTime videos, static HTML pages, or various Web sites of interest.

1. Use a text editor to open the **LoadPage.html** file from the FlashSamples\ Chapter8\Projects folder in your FlashSamples folder. Save the file as **myLoadPage.html** in the same location.

2. Within the HTML header tags (<HEAD> and </HEAD>), place the following code:

```
<script language="javascript">
function closeMe()
{
onClick=window.close()
}
</script>
```

This code stores the function to execute the JavaScript window.close method. This JavaScript method closes the active browser window.

3. Within the HTML body tags just above the closing body tag </body>, place the following code:

```
<A HREF="javascript:closeMe()">Close Window</A>
```

This code references the window.close method located in the heading of the HTML tags and provides a link for you to click on to close the browser window.

4. Save and close the **myLoadPage.html** file.

5. Open the **LoaderPage.html** file from the FlashSamples\Chapter8\Projects folder in your FlashSamples folder. Save the file as **myLoaderPage.html** in the same location.

6. Within the HTML header tags, place the following code:

```
<SCRIPT LANGUAGE="JavaScript">
function openNewWindow(URLtoOpen, windowName, windowFeatures) {
  newWindow=window.open(URLtoOpen, windowName, windowFeatures);
}
</SCRIPT>
```

This code will use the window.open JavaScript function to open the browser window with the parameters set in the Flash file's settings. Save and close **myLoaderPage.html**.

7. Open **LoaderPage.fla** file from the Chapter8\Projects folder in your FlashSamples folder. Save the file as **myLoaderPage.fla** in the same location.

8. Right-click the basketball icon, which is a button, and click the Actions command to open the Actions panel.

9. Add the following lines of code in Expert mode.

```
on (release) {
    getURL("javascript:openNewWindow('LoadPage.html','thewin',
    'height=400,width=400,toolbar=no,scrollbars=yes') ");
}
```

10. Save and publish the Flash file in both SWF and HTML formats.

11. Open the **myLoaderPage.html** file in a browser window, and click the basketball icon to load the new browser window.

12. Click the Close Window link to close the new browser window.

13. Close Flash and all browser windows.

CASE PROJECTS

Case Project

Case Project 8-1

A software manufacturing company has commissioned you to design an Enterprise Information System to track data from its Web site. Your role is to put together a set of user controls that will help management examine and report on various Web trends. Use your XML skills to design a charting series that provides a visual demonstration of the trends you find.

Case Project 8-2

Your associates are asking you to help upgrade their marketing efforts with a design and mailing of CD-ROMS to their prospect base. Your role is to increase the effectiveness of their presentations communications. You will accomplish this by creating the presentations forms that will send an e-mail message to the CD-ROM's administrator. The CD-ROM's presentation is entirely Flash based, and will allow you to integrate a new scene into the existing movie. Capture the viewers name, title, company, address, phone, and e-mail address, and have it sent in an e-mail using the CGI method. For testing and development purposes, you can use the existing CGI script located at the following path: *www.flashtrainingdesign.com/cgi-bin/FormMail.pl*; or you can download the FormMail.pl script from a scripts resource at *nms-cgi.sourceforge.net./scripts.shtml*.

Case Project 8-3

As a personal or fictional business piece for your portfolio, add a Flash presentation that uses the XML schema to create a chart, such as a pie chart or bar chart. Chart any topic of interest, such as sports scores, test ratios, class attendance, or financial figures to be presented to a board of directors. Design a multi-scene Flash presentation with a navigational system to browse through the presentation effectively.

CHAPTER 9

OPTIMIZING AND PUBLISHING MACROMEDIA FLASH MX MOVIES

Techniques for Delivering Macromedia Flash MX Movies

In this chapter, you will:

♦ Optimize Macromedia Flash MX movies for publishing

♦ Optimize your work with Quick Start templates

♦ Publish in different file formats

♦ Publish Macromedia Flash MX movies for the Web

In prior chapters, you learned both basic and advanced techniques for using Macromedia Flash to create movies and presentations. In this chapter, you will learn how to optimize your Flash movies, which involves generating your final output with the highest possible quality and the lowest possible file size for your SWF file. Optimizing requires that you know how to reduce the size of the files for your imported images, audio, and video.

This chapter also explains how to print Flash documents easily, and how to allow your audience to print some or all of the movies they view. For example, if your Flash movie includes a form designed for printing, you can set a Print dialog box to open when users click a Print Form button.

This chapter also discusses publishing your Flash movies to the Web. In addition, you can also publish your movies to many file formats, including animated GIF files, QuickTime movie files, and static images. The following sections provide guidelines for minimizing file sizes, using multiple file formats, and printing and publishing your Flash MX movies.

OPTIMIZING MACROMEDIA FLASH MX MOVIES FOR PRINTING AND PUBLISHING

In this section, you learn guidelines and techniques for printing and optimizing your movies. In versions of Flash prior to Flash MX, printing movies usually meant producing poor-quality images on the printer. In Flash MX, you can now provide online content in a printable format that does not seriously degrade quality. To do so, you use Print actions and the browser's Print dialog box.

Publishing for speed, as you already know, is a challenge in Web and Flash design because you must balance download speed, which is enhanced by small file size, and visual quality, which usually requires large files. Typically, a high-resolution image that looks good when printed takes a long time to download. However, even if you use simple images displayed at a low resolution, the file size can remain high if the movie contains audio or video. For example, the streaming track from web-radio.com (*www.web-radio.com*) shown in Figure 9-1 can require a large amount of space on your computer to stream from the server. However, streaming only a few frames at a time makes it easier for users to download the audio track.

Figure 9-1   Streaming audio

In the following sections, you learn how to design your Flash movies with images, audio, and video.

Printing Macromedia Flash MX Movies

Once you have completed a Flash MX movie, you can use the Flash Player printing feature to allow users to print forms, coupons, information sheets, invoices, confirmation notices, or other documents in your Flash movies. Using the Flash Player, users can print Flash content as vector graphics at the same resolution their printers and other output devices offer. Flash scales vector graphics so that they print clearly at any size without the fuzzy, pixelated effects that often appear when printing low-resolution bitmap images.

You can provide ways to have users print some or all of your Flash movies. Printing Flash content is most useful when the content is designed for printed rather than online output. For example, you can let users print forms or informational resources, such as company descriptions, maps, or personal profiles. As you develop a Flash presentation, you might also want to print scenes or frames as separate pages to analyze your design or examine a preview of the completed project.

With standard HTML Web sites, printing Web information simply involves right-clicking the page and selecting Print on the shortcut menu; clicking File on the browser menu bar and then clicking Print; or clicking the Print icon on the browser toolbar. Some Web sites also include JavaScript code to prompt users to print. Now, with Flash MX, you can let users print information in a SWF file using the File menu on the Flash Player menu bar or the Print button on the browser toolbar, or by right-clicking the movie and then selecting Print on the shortcut menu. Figure 9-2 shows the Flash Player shortcut menu, including the Print command.

Additionally, you can assign a Print action to a button or other object. When users click the button, the browser's Print dialog box opens. Using a Print action gives you more control over how users print content from a Flash movie—you can let users print frames in any Timeline, including the main Timeline, or the Timeline of any movie clip or loaded movie level. You can also include color effects, such as transparency, in the printed output. The Flash Player shortcut menu, on the other hand, can print frames only in the main Timeline and does not let you print transparency or other color effects.

Using a Print action, you can specify which frames users can print in a Flash movie. This lets you design some pages for printing, and prevent users from printing other pages. You can also use a Print action to determine which part of a frame will print. For example, if the material you want users to print appears in part of a frame, you can specify that users can print only that area of the frame. To control the appearance of printed information, you can specify whether frames print as vectors or bitmaps. Print graphics as vectors when you want to take advantage of high resolution and as bitmaps when you want to preserve transparency and color effects. To provide printed material without using space on a Web page, you can print frames from movie clips, even if the movie clips are not visible. For example, if you set the visible property of a movie clip to false, the movie clip does not appear in the movie, but you can still specify the movie clip in the Print action to print the clip.

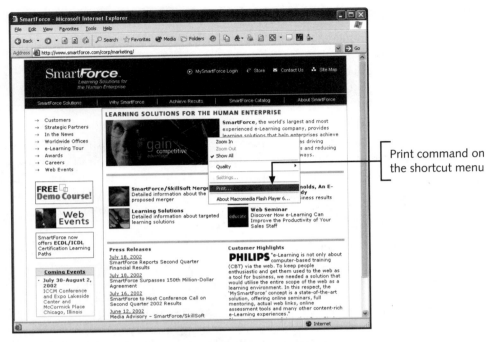

Figure 9-2   Printing from the Flash Player shortcut menu

The Print actions you can use in your Flash movie are described in Table 9-1.

Table 9-1   Print Actions

Action	Description
print (target, "bmovie")	The Print action prints the target movie clip according to the boundaries specified in the parameter. This action is useful for printing entire movies.
printAsBitmap (target, "Bounding box")	The printAsBitmap action prints the target movie clip as a bitmap instead of in vector format. The bitmap format produces higher quality than the vector format.
printAsBitmapNum (level, "Bounding box")	The printAsBitmapNum action prints a level in the Flash Player as a bitmap. This action is useful for printing the scenes as separate bitmaps.
printNum (level, "Bounding box")	The printNum action prints the level in the Flash Player according to the boundaries specified in the Bounding box parameter (bmovie, bmax, bframe). This action is useful for printing scenes as separate vector graphics.

When setting up movies that allow users to print content, consider the Stage size, which should not be larger than the standard 8-1/2 × 11-inch sheet of paper. To print the contents of a movie clip in a SWF file, the Timeline must be on the Stage and the movie clip must have an instance name. Before you can print the content of frames, the frames must first be fully loaded into the SWF file. Use the _framesloaded property to check whether all Stage elements and frames have fully loaded.

The Print action allows you to define a print area, print Timelines, and determine whether to print as vector or bitmap images. You can add a Print action to a frame, movie clip, or button instance. By default, a Print action prints all frames in a Timeline. However, you can limit the number of frames that can print, which is especially helpful in a long movie. In the following steps, you learn how to set up a Print action to establish print settings for your movie. You use the printNum action to open the Print dialog box when viewing a SWF file. You set the printNum action to print only a specified frame's contents, and not the entire movie contents.

 If you are using a Macintosh, press Ctrl+click instead of right-clicking in this chapter.

To use the Print action:

1. Open **FlashPrint.fla** from the Chapter9 folder in your FlashSamples folder. Save the file as **myFlashPrint.fla** in the same location. The Stage and layers are already set up for you. The Stage has text, button, and image elements on separate layers. The last frame on the Image layer has a #p label, indicating that this frame contains the printNum action and is the only frame that prints in this movie. Note also that this frame is slightly longer than the other layers.

2. Right-click **frame 1** on the Actions layer, and then click **Actions**. The Actions panel opens. Make sure you are working in Normal mode. (Click the **View Options** button, and then click **Normal Mode**.) In the Action list, click **Actions**, if necessary, and then **Printing**. Double-click the **print** action to add it to the print statement in the script.

3. In the parameters section, click the **Bounding** (**Bounds** on the Macintosh) list arrow, and then click **Frame**. Keep the Location settings as Levels and zero, and keep the Print setting as vectors. By changing the Bounding setting to Frame, you are giving the Print action instructions to print only the frame that contains the #p label. See Figure 9-3.

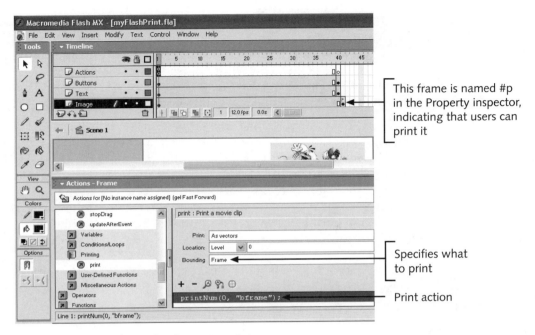

This frame is named #p in the Property inspector, indicating that users can print it

Specifies what to print

Print action

Figure 9-3 Specifying the frame to print

4. Test your movie by clicking **Control** on the menu bar and then clicking **Test Movie**. Immediately, a Print dialog box opens, as shown in Figure 9-4.

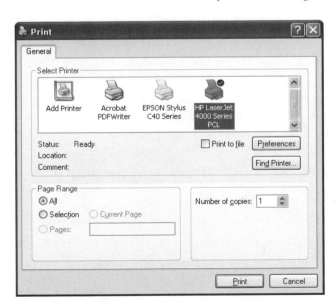

Figure 9-4 Print dialog box opens so users can print the specified frame

You need at least the Macromedia Flash Player 4.0.20 or greater for high-quality Flash printing.

5. Click the icon for the printer connected to your computer, and then click the **Print** button. Flash prints only the frame you specified, in this case the contents of frame 41 on the Image layer. Close **myFlashPrint.swf** and **myFlashPrint.fla**.

Optimizing Images for Macromedia Flash MX Publishing

As you add images and other objects to a movie, its file size increases, as does its download time and playback speed. To ensure that the movie plays back at the best possible speed and quality, you should optimize the images in the movie. When you publish a movie, Flash automatically optimizes some elements. For example, it checks for duplicate shapes and inserts only one copy in the file. You can further optimize the images in movies by cropping and compressing the images, converting images to symbols, and using system rather than embedded fonts.

Recall that Flash movies can use vector images created in other programs, such as Macromedia Freehand, Macromedia Fireworks, Adobe Illustrator, or Corel Draw. In other situations, you might need a raster (bitmapped) image, such as photographs or realistic representations of animate objects. When you import images created in programs other than Flash, be aware of the file size of each element you import into Flash. This way, you can monitor the size of your Flash file, and balance the tradeoffs between download speed and output quality.

To optimize images, you should compress JPG files in the Flash environment only. Working with tools such as Adobe Photoshop, you can manage and compress images before importing them into Flash. However, if you compress a JPG in Photoshop, and then use Flash's default compression settings for the JPG again, you compress the image twice, leaving it distorted. Minimize the size of the file before importing it into Flash by scaling it to reduce the size and pixel definition or by cropping it. For example, you may not need the entire contents of a photograph imported into your Flash movie. In an image-editing program, such as Adobe Photoshop, open the image and crop it to necessary content only, just as you may do with a traditional photograph. Cropping helps to reduce the image's file size.

You can also reduce file size by converting imported images into symbols and then reusing them as necessary. Each image then becomes an instance of an original symbol that you can scale and manipulate. In fact, you can use animated and static symbols for every element that appears more than once in your movie.

Fonts can increase file size. Limit the number of fonts and font styles, and don't embed fonts; instead, use a system font such as "_sans" as your text font. This reduces the file size of your SWF file, and also maintains the integrity of fonts. Especially in a team work-group environment, this will reduce the error messages when some computers do not have all of the fonts used in your Flash file.

In the following steps, you import a JPG file and use the Flash tools to reduce the file size of that image. As a result, you reduce the file size of the entire Flash FLA and SWF files. The JPG is currently 156 KB, which is too large for a conventional HTML Web presentation. Web designers would work to reduce this image's size to a maximum of 30 to 40 KB. After you import the image, you convert it into a graphic symbol. This creates a format that can be copied or reused on your Stage, if necessary, and reduces the file size. You also set bitmap properties and publishing settings to reduce the file size.

You can also examine the published SWF files at every stage of the following steps. For example, myOptimizeImage-1.swf is published with no image reduction, and is 153 KB. The myOptimizeImage-2.swf file is published with the image converted to a symbol and the graphic image's properties reduced, making the file size 26 KB, a dramatic reduction that does not sacrifice output quality.

To import a JPG file, and then reduce the file size of the Flash SWF output:

1. In Windows Explorer or the Finder on a Macintosh, navigate to the Chapter9 folder in your FlashSamples folder. If necessary, switch to Details view in Windows or List view on a Macintosh. Record the sizes of the OptimizeImage.fla, OptimizeImage.swf, and OptimizeImage.jpg files.

2. In Flash, open **OptimizeImage.fla** from the Chapter9 folder in your FlashSamples folder. Save the file as **myOptimizeImage.fla** in the same location.

3. Click **File** on the menu bar, and then click **Import**. Use the Import dialog box to import the JPG file named **OptimizeImage.jpg** from the same folder location.

4. Convert the image into a symbol by pressing **F8**. Name the symbol **Image** and then click **OK**. Both the original image and the symbol are in the current document's library.

5. Use the **Free Transform** tool to reduce the size of the symbol to about half its size.

6. Press **Ctrl+L** to open the Library panel, if necessary. Your Stage, symbol, and library should resemble Figure 9-5.

7. Right-click **OptimizeImage.jpg** in the library (not the symbol on the Stage), and then click **Properties** on the shortcut menu. The Bitmap Properties dialog box opens.

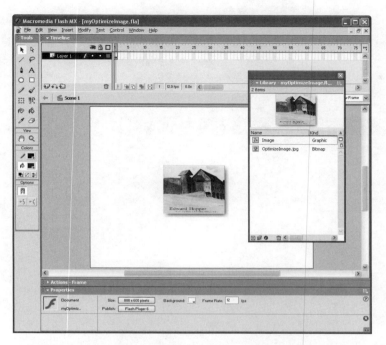

Figure 9-5 JPG converted to a symbol and scaled on the Stage

8. Click the **Use imported JPG data** check box to remove the check mark. Keep 50 as the image Quality setting. See Figure 9-6. Converting the image to a symbol, reducing the image size, and not using JPG data significantly reduces the final SWF file size. Click **OK**.

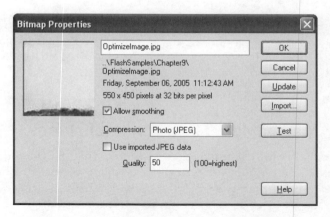

Figure 9-6 Bitmap Properties dialog box settings

9. Click **File** on the menu bar, and then click **Publish Settings**. The Publish Settings dialog box opens. Ensure the Formats tab is active.

10. Make sure the Flash check box is selected, and then click the **Flash** tab.

11. Type **50** in the JPEG Quality text box (or drag the JPEG Quality slider). Setting the quality to 50 usually provides a good baseline to start comparing the quality of output with the size reduction. See Figure 9-7. Your dialog box might contain other tabs.

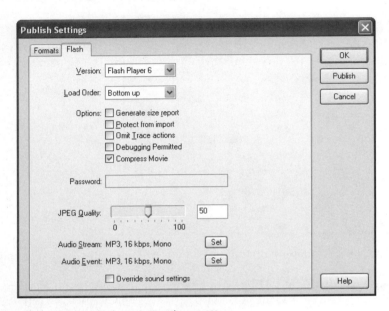

Figure 9-7   Flash JPG Quality settings

12. Click the **Publish** button, and then click the **OK** button.

13. You can now compare the file sizes of the original FLA and SWF files with the myOptimizeImage.fla and myOptimizeImage.swf files in Windows Explorer or the Finder on a Macintosh. The files containing the optimized image should be significantly smaller than the original files.

14. Leave Flash open, but close all other windows.

Optimizing Video for Macromedia Flash MX Publishing

As you learned in Chapter 4, Flash MX supports native video, which is video displayed in the Flash Player, without using QuickTime or another video player as your video delivery tool. Flash MX accomplishes this through the Sorenson Spark codec. The codec is a method that Macromedia licenses from Sorenson to compress and display video.

The Sorenson Spark codec is integrated with Flash MX. Additionally, the Sorenson Spark Pro Edition is part of Sorenson Squeeze and is available separately. The Macromedia Flash Player 6 supports Standard and Spark Pro SWF output. Sorenson Spark Pro is intended for

Flash MX designers who want highest quality video compression available at the smallest possible file size.

Before Flash integrated the Sorenson Spark codec, designers had to deliver video by creating multiple scenes, each containing a different version of the video designed for a specific connection speed. Using the Sorenson Spark codec means that your users do not have to page through a series of scenes to find one suitable for their current connection speed. Using the Flash native video format, you can create a movie within a single SWF file (or multiple files, depending on your movie's size and construction), that users navigate without having to load other HTML pages. Additionally, this methodology does not require the QuickTime plug-in or application to view the video. Table 9-2 lists advantages and disadvantages of streaming video with the Sorenson codec and downloading video with QuickTime.

Table 9-2   Comparing Sorenson Streaming with QuickTime Downloads

Benefit	Sorenson streaming	QuickTime download
Real-time broadcasts	X	
Minimum lag time	X	
Long clips	X	
Broadcasts and multicasts	X	
Immediate random access to different parts of a movie	X	
Downloads entire movie		X
Constant data rate		X
Consistent high-quality playback at any connection speed		X
Can be stopped by firewalls	X	
Content remains on server	X	
Retransmits lost packets		X

9

Table 9-2 compares the two popular video delivery formats by delivery method. The benefits marked as provided by Sorenson streaming require a streaming delivery format or a "play as needed" delivery format. The goal of streaming video is to maintain real-time playback at various connection speeds without sacrificing significant quality.

Movies that download entirely, have a constant data rate, have a consistent high-quality playback at any connection speed; or movies that can retransmit lost packets are better suited for a progressive download. A **progressive download** is a video that must be buffered or preloaded into memory before you can play it. Progressive downloads provide a better quality in delivered movies.

Consider the benefits listed in Table 9-2 when you choose a method for providing videos in your Flash movies. By using streaming video or the Flash native format, a user's machine plays a video segment as it is received and then removes it from memory. Streaming allows broadcasts to run as long as necessary. In progressive movie delivery, such as QuickTime, content plays as soon as it is available; therefore, on fast connections progressive movies can appear to be streaming. However, if you want to play some video, and then skip to another segment, you must download all the video from the point currently in view to the segment you want to play.

 For Flash MX SWF files to play back native video properly, the Flash Player 6 must be installed.

Optimizing Audio for Macromedia Flash MX Publishing

Much like video, audio adds to the quality of a Flash movie, but also adds file size. You can easily reduce the size of audio files; the challenge again is to preserve the quality of the output when doing so. You can use two settings in the Publish Settings dialog box to reduce audio output: Audio Stream and Audio Event. These settings affect all audio files in your current Flash document. In Flash files containing movie audio elements that are used for the same purpose, such as all streaming audio, the Audio Stream and Audio Event sound settings are good ways to compress and publish your movie. However, these settings are not recommended for movies that have different types of audio elements, such as audio for streaming music, audio for button click events, and audio for an online narrative. The best way to manage the audio compression in such a movie is to compress each audio file in the current document's library. Following are guidelines for compressing audio effectively:

- When you set the Sync option for your sound and Timeline in the Property inspector, the stream setting gives priority to the audio over the visual elements in your movie.

- For streaming long audio files such as music or songs, load them behind the scenes after your priority scenes load.

- Use export options that focus on individual audio elements, and not on a whole set of audio elements at once. For example, with a library of multiple audio symbols, edit each export option uniquely, as shown in Figure 9-8. Do not set the export options for a set of audio elements unless they are all in the same format.

- Avoid looping a streaming audio loop.

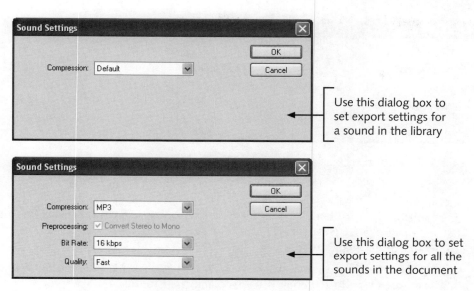

Figure 9-8   Audio export settings

To effectively export audio:

1. Open **AudioCompression.fla** from the Chapter9 folder in your FlashSamples folder. Save the file as **myAudioCompression.fla** in the same location. The Stage and layers are already set up for you with a button and sound effect on the Down frame, and an audio file suitable for streaming.

   Because each sound in this movie has a different purpose and size, you will compress these elements individually.

2. Press **Ctrl+L** to open the Library panel, if necessary. Right-click the **Brick Drops** sound, and then click **Export Settings**. The Sound Settings dialog box opens.

3. The Brick Drops sound is used when the user's mouse rolls off the button. A good compression format for shorter audio formats is the ADPCM, due to its compression method. Click the **Compression** list arrow, and then click **ADPCM**.

4. Ensure the Convert Stereo to Mono check box is selected. This converts any stereo sound effect to a mono, or single-channel, sound, further compressing the sound.

5. Click the **Sample Rate** list arrow, and then click **5kHz**, the lowest rate.

6. Click the **ADPCM Bits** list arrow, and then click **2 bit**, the lowest possible setting required to hear a quality button-clicking sound. See Figure 9-9 for the audio settings. For the button sound, using the lowest settings possible is usually a good practice.

Figure 9-9   Button click audio settings

7. Click **OK** to accept your settings.

8. In the Library panel, right-click the **Ambient – Saunton.wav** file, and then click **Export Settings**. The Sound Settings dialog box opens so you can set the options for this file.

9. Click the **Compression** list arrow, and then click **MP3**. Click the **Bit Rate** list arrow, and then click **8 kbps**. Click the **Quality** list arrow, and then click **Medium**. The Ambient – Saunton.wav sound is a large audio file containing background music. MP3 is an ideal compression method for streaming or for large audio formats due to its delivery size and audible quality. For most music, using 8 kbps and a medium quality is a good practice. See Figure 9-10 for the audio settings. Click **OK** to close the dialog box.

Figure 9-10   Audio streaming compression settings

10. Click **File** on the menu bar, and then click **Publish** to publish the SWF file.

11. In Windows Explorer or the Finder on the Macintosh, review the file size, and open and test the quality of output for the SWF file.

12. Close all folders, and then save and close the Flash files, leaving Flash open for the next set of steps.

OPTIMIZING YOUR WORK WITH QUICK START TEMPLATES

Flash MX, like the popular office suite programs, now comes equipped with movie templates called Quick Start templates. A **template** is a predefined Flash document that gives you a starting point from which to work. These templates allow you to quickly create presentations, photo albums, advertisements, and learning content, as shown in Figure 9-11.

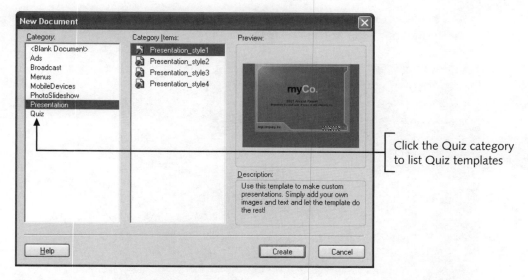

Click the Quiz category to list Quiz templates

9

Figure 9-11   Flash Quick Start templates

The banner or pop-up templates are good for designing a pop-up styles window, displaying recent news, or offering a special service. A broadcast and special device template would be used for streaming broadcast video or movies where the final output is displayed on a smaller device, such as a Web-enabled phone or handheld computer such as a Palm Pilot or Handspring. The XML and quiz templates are ready for you to enter data; they include information and structure so you can start providing data-driven presentations, such as XML navigational menus or an online quiz or survey. The types of templates are included in the following list:

- Banner and pop-up style advertisements
- Broadcast template
- XML menu-driven template
- Template for mobile devices, Pocket PC, and some Nokia devices
- Slideshow for images
- Presentation-style templates
- Online-quiz templates

To use a Quick Start template:

1. Click **File** on the menu bar, and then click **New From Template**. The New Document dialog box opens.

2. Click the **Quiz** category, and then click the **Quiz_style1** category item. Click the **Create** button. A new movie is started for you from the quiz category. Save the movie as **myQuiz.fla**. This quiz is an already working model for you to revise and edit.

3. Immediately test the quiz with the Test Movie command on the Control menu. The quiz runs as shown in Figure 9-12.

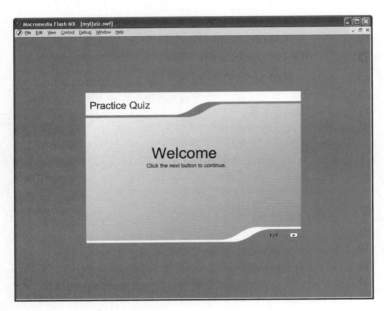

Figure 9-12   Working quiz template

4. Close the Flash Player window, and then return to Edit mode.

5. Click **frame 2** in the Instructions layer to view the content of that frame on the Stage.

6. To edit the parameters of the quiz, click the **Eye** icon above the layers in the Timeline. Click the **Eye** icon again to remove any Xs from the layers. Click the **Quiz Component** instruction box.

7. Click **Window** on the menu bar, and then click **Component Parameters**. The Component Parameters panel appears.

8. Drag the lower-right corner of the panel to enlarge the panel enough to read it, as shown in Figure 9-13.

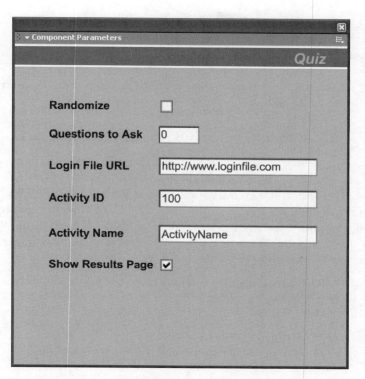

Figure 9-13   Component Parameters panel

9. Click the **Randomize** check box to have the quiz questions appear in random order.

10. Enter **4** as the number of questions to ask.

11. Enter **http://www.FlashTrainingDesign.com** as the Login File URL.

12. Close the panel, and test your movie again.

13. Save the myQuiz file and then close it, leaving Flash open.

PUBLISHING IN DIFFERENT FILE FORMATS

Publishing your movie is in most cases your final task. As you analyze your intended audience, however, you may find that a Web-based SWF file is not appropriate. For example, you might need to deliver a CD-based presentation; therefore, a stand-alone projector would work best without the need of a browser. In this section, you will learn how to save your Flash file as an animated GIF89a and QuickTime file, as a stand-alone SWF Projector file for both the PC and Mac platforms, and as a static image.

Both GIF89a and QuickTime provide alternate animated file formats to the animated SWF file. If you are going to use your movie for CD or download distribution, then a stand-alone projector is well suited for that delivery format. You can present a static set of images from your Flash movie one scene or one Timeline at a time, as in a slideshow instead of a movie. To import your Flash scenes into a PowerPoint presentation, you export the scenes as static images first.

Publishing as an Animated File in GIF89a and QuickTime

An animated GIF89a file format is an easy way to export short animation sequences for Web publishing. Flash optimizes an animated GIF, storing only frame-to-frame changes. By using an animated GIF, you can increase your audience acceptance for small and non-complex movies. Doing so increases your audience by attracting those with older browsers that do not support the Flash Player, such as the older Microsoft Internet Explorer version 3, or Netscape Navigator 2. Movies that play for a short while and are not large in file size are a good choice for this medium.

As you learned in earlier chapters, the GIF file format is a CompuServe proprietary file format and is largely used for Web production. The GIF image format uses a built-in LZW compression algorithm, which is patented technology and is currently owned by Unisys Corporation. GIF89a is an extension of the 87a specification; GIF89a adds the following advantages: lets you specify wait time before displaying the next frame, which gives you more control of the timing of the individual frames; lets you specify transparent color to set the page background color in HTML files; lets you include unprintable comments, which can be useful for future editing or team communication.

To publish an animated GIF file:

1. Open **PublishGIF.fla** from the Chapter9 folder in your FlashSamples folder. Save the file as **myPublishGIF.fla** in the same location. The Stage and a small animation are already set for you.

2. To change the stage dimensions, click **Modify** on the menu bar, and then click **Document**. Change the dimensions to **150 × 100**, and then click **OK**.

3. Click **File** on the menu bar, and then click **Publish Settings**. The Publish Settings dialog box opens.

4. On the Formats tab, select the **GIF Image** and **Flash** check boxes only.

5. Click the **GIF** tab shown in Figure 9-14, and then click the **Animated** option button in the Playback section. Make sure the Match Movie check box is selected. Accept all the other settings.

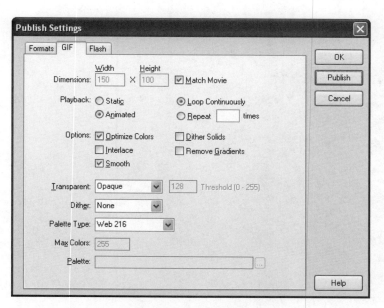

Figure 9-14   GIF Publish Settings dialog box

6. Click the **Publish** button, and then click **OK**.

7. Open the GIF file in a Web browser to test the file. The GIF animation plays the same animation that a Flash SWF would play.

8. Close your browser, and then save and close myPublishGIF.fla. Leave Flash open.

PUBLISHING MACROMEDIA FLASH MX MOVIES FOR THE WEB

Publishing movies on the Web is the most common usage of Flash. In this section, you learn how to configure the settings in Flash and in HTML dialog boxes. These settings appear when the Flash file is ready to publish, and you select the Publish Settings command on the File menu. Macromedia's Flash Player is a widely accepted medium for both Web and stand-alone access. As of March 2002, over 400 million people use the Flash Player on a browser. Most of these users are on a 56k, DSL, or cable modem connection and are home or work users, as stated on the Macromedia Web site.

Figure 9-15 can be used as a guide to selecting HTML settings when publishing Flash files.

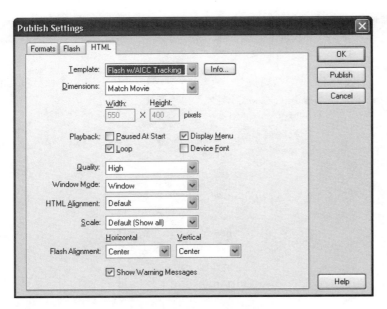

Figure 9-15   HTML settings for publishing Flash files

The Version settings allow you to publish movies for lower Flash Player versions. Thus, if you perform a very detailed audience assessment, and find that most of your viewers are on the Flash Player version 4, then it would make sense to design your movies accordingly, and publish to that version. The load order sets the order in which the frames will load into the Flash Player. Generate size report creates a text file with detailed information on the size of the FLA and SWF files. To adjust the output of the JPG and audio files, these controls override any previous settings. Overriding settings can degrade the quality of your movie, so be sure to optimize movie elements as discussed in the previous sections. The following list provides a description of the various Flash settings you can use:

- Version allows you to choose a final output for the Flash Player. In some cases, you may want to publish for previous versions depending on your intended audience. Doing so could cause incompatibilities and inconsistencies within your output.

- Load Order sets the order in which the Flash Player loads a movie's layers for displaying the first frame of your movie: Bottom Up or Top Down. Use this option to control which parts of the movie Flash draws first over a slow network or modem connection.

- Generate Size Report provides you with a report on the size of your Flash file.

- Protect from Import prevents others from importing the Flash movie and converting it back into a Flash (FLA) document.

- Omit Trace Actions and Debugging Permitted are advanced debugging options.

- Use the Compress Movie setting to create a compressed file, which can only play in the Flash 6 Player, and is most beneficial where there is a lot of ActionScript to compress.

- If you selected the Debugging Permitted option, you can also specify a password to prevent unauthorized users from debugging your Flash movie.

- Adjust the JPEG Quality slider or enter a value to control the quality of bitmapped images within your movie.

- Audio Stream and Audio Event allows you to set the sampling and compression rates for all audio collectively. If you are using different types of audio for different purposes, do not change this setting; instead, adjust the different audio elements independently.

- To override the settings for individual sounds selected in the Sound section of the Property inspector, select the Override Sound Settings option.

In the following steps, you use the Publish Settings dialog box to configure your move for HTML output over the Web.

To publish a Flash movie to the Web:

1. Open **PublishHTML.fla** from the Chapter9 folder in your FlashSamples folder. Save the file as **myPublishHTML.fla** in the same location. The Stage and a small animation is already set for you.

2. Click **File** on the menu bar, and then click **Publish Settings**. The Publish Settings dialog box opens.

3. On the Formats tab, select the **Flash**, and **HTML** check boxes only, if necessary.

4. Click the **HTML** tab. The HTML property sheet opens, shown earlier in Figure 9-15.

5. The most important settings here are the quality and alignment settings. Click the **Quality** list arrow, and then click **High**, if necessary.

6. Click the **HTML Alignment** list arrow, and then click **Top**.

7. Click each **Flash Alignment** list arrow, and then click **Center** for both settings, if necessary.

8. Click the **Publish** button to publish both the Flash SWF file and the associated HTML file. Click **OK**.

9. Use Windows Explorer or the Finder to open the HTML file. As long as the SWF is in the same folder as the HTML file, the SWF file will open and play within your browser.

10. Close your browser and Flash, saving any changes.

9

CHAPTER SUMMARY

❏ In versions of Flash prior to Flash MX, printing movies usually meant producing poor-quality images on the printer. In Flash MX, you can now provide online content in a printable format that does not seriously degrade quality. To do so, you use Print actions and the browser's Print dialog box.

❏ Printing Flash MX movies can be achieved in two ways: Your user can print from the shortcut menu by right-clicking, or you can implement a Print action associated with a button, for example.

❏ Once you have completed a Flash MX movie, you can use the Flash Player printing feature to allow users to print forms, coupons, information sheets, invoices, confirmation notices, or other documents in your Flash movies. Using the Flash Player, users can print Flash content as vector graphics at the same resolution their printers and other output devices offer. Flash scales vector graphics so that they print clearly at any size without the fuzzy, pixelated effects that often appear when printing low-resolution bitmap images.

❏ Be aware of the file size of each element you import into Flash and the overall file size in the SWF.

❏ The specific ways to optimize images are to compress JPG files in the Flash environment only. Working with tools such as Adobe Photoshop, you can manage and compress images before importing them into Flash.

❏ Much like video, audio adds to the quality of a Flash movie, but also adds file size. You can easily reduce the size of audio files; the challenge again is to preserve the quality of the output when doing so. You can use two settings in the Publish Settings dialog box to reduce audio output: Audio Stream and Audio Event.

❏ Once dominated by the popular MPEG codec, Flash and the Sorenson Spark codec now offers a progressive workflow to increase the usability of your movies.

❏ Flash MX comes equipped with movie templates called Quick Start templates. These templates allow you to quickly create presentations, photo albums, advertisements, and learning content.

❏ You can save your Flash file as an animated GIF89a and QuickTime file, a stand-alone SWF Projector file for both the PC and MAC platforms, or as a static image.

REVIEW QUESTIONS

1. Flash can be published for non-Web mediums. True or false?

2. Which of the following is used for printing single frames in Flash movies?

    a. ##print label

    b. #p label

c. #b

d. none of the above

3. To optimize images for Web access, the ideal image format is _____.

4. When using raster images such as JPG, it is best to compress JPG files with the Flash environment only. True or false?

5. The best type of fonts to use in a Flash movie are:

   a. Postscript fonts

   b. True type fonts

   c. System fonts

   d. Printer fonts

6. Flash MX accomplishes native video support through the Sorenson Spark codec. True or false?

7. The Flash Player _____ must be installed to play back video support.

8. The stream audio is best compressed with the MP3 method. True or false?

9. Flash MX Quick Start templates allow you to create:

   a. banner-style adds

   b. XML menus

   c. slide shows

   d. all of the above

10. The predesigned quiz _____ is used to tally the selected results.

11. Publishing in different file formats allows you to publish as:

    a. GIF89a

    b. Stand–alone Projector

    c. Static images

    d. all of the above

12. A stand-alone project can be published for both PC and Mac platforms. True or false?

13. The GIF file format uses a proprietary compression algorithm called LZW. True or false?

14. Some advantages of the GIF89a format are:

    a. specifying the accuracy per frame

    b. transparent colors

    c. unprintable comments

    d. all of the above

15. Publishing to a stand-alone file does not require a(n) _____.

16. Less than 4 million users have Flash Player access. True or false?

17. You can publish to lower Flash Player versions with the _____ option.

18. To publish a static image, which of the following formats should you use?

   a. PNG

   b. JPG

   c. GIF

   d. all of the above

19. Button-click sounds require a high quality compression to sound proper. True or false?

20. You can publish audio formats with the _____ command in the movie's library.

HANDS-ON PROJECTS

This series of projects enforces the topics you covered in the sections of this chapter. You work with a Flash presentation that requires optimization, publish in multiple file formats, and then publish your presentation for Web usage.

Project 9-1

In this project, you optimize your Flash movie by compressing both audio and imported images. After compressing and saving your Flash file in the SWF file format, you will review your individual files and compare the file sizes. With this information, you will determine the viability of the compression settings you used. There is a JPG and a large WAV file in your Chapter9 Projects folder. By using large files, you will be able to measure the efficiency of the compression.

1. Open the file **OptimizeMedia.fla** from the Chapter9\Projects folder in your FlashSamples folder. Save the file as **myOptimizeMedia.fla** in the same location. There are two layers created for you, one for the image and one for the audio file.

2. Click to select the Image layer to import the image on that layer.

3. Click File on the menu bar, and then click Import to import **Project 09-01.JPG** from the Chapter9\Projects folder in your FlashSamples folder.

4. Use the Property inspector to scale the image to 685 width and 450 height.

5. Press F8 to convert the image into a graphic symbol and reduce the Flash file size if the symbol is reused. Name the symbol Image.

6. Click to select the Audio layer.

7. Click File on the menu bar, and then click Import to Library.

8. Import the WAV file named **Project 09-01.wav** into the library from the Chapter9\Projects folder in your FlashSamples folder.

9. Select frame 100 of both layers, and press F6 to insert keyframes.

10. Click to select frame 1 on the Audio layer.

11. With the Audio layer still selected, drag the audio file from the library onto the Stage. The WAV file should appear in all frames in the Audio layer.

12. Right-click the bitmap in the library, and then click Properties.

13. Uncheck the Use imported JPEG data check box, and keep 50 as the value in the Quality setting. This will greatly reduce the Flash file size.

14. Click OK to accept your changes.

15. Right-click the WAV file in the library, and then click Properties.

16. Choose MP3 as the Compression method.

17. Choose 8 kbps as the Bit Rate.

18. Ensure the Quality setting is set to Fast.

19. Click OK to save your settings.

20. Test your movie by clicking the Test Movie command on the Control menu. The audio file should play for 100 frames with the image in view.

21. Next, use the Windows Explorer or the Finder to analyze the file sizes of all the audio, JPG, and SWF files. The file sizes should be close to the following: original JPG size is 2,389 KB (over 2 MB), the original audio WAV file size is 5,229 (over 5 MB), and the total file size for the published SWF file is 1,108 (just over 1 MB).

22. Close Flash and all folders and files, saving any changes within your Flash FLA file.

Project 9-2

In this project, you save a Flash presentation in three separate file formats. You save the presentation in static image formats (JPG) for use in documentation, marketing, or design delivery purposes. Then you save the presentation in a Windows AVI and a Flash Projector format based on your audience's needs.

1. Open the file **PublishFormats.fla** from the Chapter9\Projects folder in your FlashSamples folder. Save the file as **myPublishFormats.fla** in the same location. There is already a brief animation set on the Stage for you.

2. First, you practice saving each keyframe in a static JPG image. Select the first keyframe, click File on the menu bar, and then click Export Image.

3. Export the image as a JPEG sequence file type. Use the name **myPublishFormats-1.jpg** and the Chapter9\Projects folder in your FlashSamples folder as the location. Click the Save button, and then click OK.

4. Export each keyframe in the Flash document. The purpose of exporting is to reuse the Flash keyframes in a non-Flash environment, such as PowerPoint.

5. Next, you convert your Flash movie into a Windows AVI file format. Click File on the menu bar, and then click Export Movie.

6. Choose **myPublishFormats.avi** in the Chapter9\Projects folder in your FlashSamples folder as the AVI file name, and select the Windows AVI file type.

7. Select a Video format of 24-bit color. This option provides color without saving the file with an enormous file size.

8. Ensure the Compress video check box is selected to compress the video on export, reducing the file size. Then click the OK button.

9. In the Video Compression dialog box, choose the Microsoft Video 1 as the Compressor, a common video compression method for the PC format.

10. Use 50 as the Compression Quality, again a good practice to balance quality with file size. Click OK.

11. Save the file, and then use the Windows Explorer or the Finder to open and play the file.

To create a Windows or Macintosh stand-alone Projector file to run and play your movie:

1. Click File on the menu bar, and then click Publish Settings.

2. Select only the Flash and Windows Projector format options. Use the Macintosh Projector if you are using a Macintosh.

3. Click the Publish button, and then click the OK button.

4. Save and close your Flash file.

5. Open the Projector file, and play the movie. The .exe format is very portable, meaning you can use it for downloads or copy it to a disk.

6. Close all files and folders.

Project 9-3

In this project, you prepare and save your presentation in a Web-ready format. You set your HTML options accordingly, and use only the most necessary files and movie elements; then you will generate the SWF and HTML files to view your Web site. Afterwards, you will review the contents of the HTML code and identify where the Flash SWF file is referenced.

1. Open the file **PublishWeb.fla** from the Chapter9\Projects folder in your FlashSamples folder. Save the file as **myPublishWeb.fla** in the same location.

2. Click File on the menu bar, and then click Publish Settings.

3. Select only the Flash and HTML formats.

4. Click the HTML tab.

5. Set the Quality to High, if necessary.

6. Set the HTML Alignment to Top.

7. Set the Horizontal and Vertical alignment to Center, if necessary.

8. Click the Publish button, and then click the OK button.

9. Close and save your Flash file.

10. From your Chapter9\Projects folder, open the HTML file and watch the animation play in your browser.

11. Close your browser, and open the HTML file in a text editor such as Notepad or SimpleText.

12. Examine the code, and notice the lines of code that represent the options you chose, and the SWF file name.

```
WIDTH="200" HEIGHT="200" id="myPublishWeb" ALIGN="top">
 <PARAM NAME=movie VALUE="myPublishWeb.swf"> <PARAM NAME=quality
VALUE=high>
```

This entire block of code is important, especially when you are using this to integrate the SWF file into other HTML files.

13. Close all files and windows.

CASE PROJECTS

Case Project 9-1

In this case project, you import a video file using the Embed method. This method uses Flash native resources to display and render the video, the Sorenson Spark licensed method. Next, you import the video using the "Link to external video file" method. This creates a link to a QuickTime format, and will use the Apple QuickTime Player to render and play back the video. Your deliverables are both the Flash presentation and a research report with your findings on the advantages and disadvantages of both uses. A video file named **Sample.mov** is in the Chapter9\Projects folder in your FlashSamples folder.

Case Project 9-2

In this case project, you design a multi-scene presentation. The scenes are based on a series of portfolios for an artist or photographer. Once you build the scenes, practice using the Print action and its parameters. Create a small button or menu system that will allow a user to navigate to the various scenes and prompt users to print on every occasion except the main scene. You can find artwork or photos for educational use at a variety of Web sites, including *www.artville.com* or *www.photography.com*.

Case Project 9-3

Design a small Flash presentation that reflects personal interest. Use five to seven scenes, each reflecting a different topic or interest. For example, use one scene to show vacations you have taken. Use another scene for sporting activities you perform. Save the Flash presentation as a Flash Projector file, instead of in a Web-based format. This way, you can e-mail or copy the file to a disk and share it among friends.

CHAPTER

10

EXPLORING THE MACROMEDIA FLASH RESOURCES

Using Third-Party Tools, Technologies, and Resources

> **In this chapter, you will:**
> ♦ Use Macromedia Flash resources
> ♦ Explore 3-D Tools for Macromedia Flash Designers
> ♦ Explore video applications
> ♦ Explore audio applications

In this chapter, you will explore a variety of tools and technologies available for enhancing your Macromedia Flash movies. You will examine software programs that may or may not work directly with Macromedia Flash MX, but can be part of the toolkit you use as a Macromedia Flash designer. Some products produce a SWF file, some use a proprietary format, and some can be integrated with Macromedia Flash. In addition, you will review the many resources available online.

In addition to third-party software and resources, Macromedia provides you with a set of resources that can help you design professional-quality Flash movies. These resources contain tips, tutorials, how-to videos, reference materials, and product extensions, all available on the Macromedia Designer Developer Resources Web page. These resources focus on accessibility, eLearning solutions, and topics for templates, tutorials, and content for Macromedia Flash and Dreamweaver. Other resources that Macromedia provides include the Application Developer Toolkit (ADT) and the Macromedia Flash MX Deployment Kit. The ADT contains components, white papers, tutorials, trial software, and sample Flash applications for you to download. You will learn how to use the contents of these Macromedia kits in this chapter.

USING MACROMEDIA FLASH RESOURCES

Macromedia provides tools for making your Web content accessible to those with physical disabilities; and software resources and guidelines for engaging online learners, measuring performance, and tracking results in computer-based training (CBT). You can download many of these resources from the Macromedia Web site.

The accessibility resources include information on adding text equivalents for graphics and captions for sound in Flash, videos that show you how to develop content for users with disabilities, and a template you can use to create accessible Flash documents. You can also download a free accessibility test that checks Web sites against Section 508 and W3C accessibility guidelines. Recall that Section 508 of the Rehabilitation Act requires public Web sites to be accessible to all users. The Flash Web site also provides links to Flash movies that demonstrate accessible design.

In addition to guides and tutorials, the eLearning resources include software extensions, tutorials, product guides, white papers, and other resources. Using the Flash eLearning resources and templates can help you create instructional content and interfaces that load quickly and look the same on different platforms such as Windows, Macintosh, and hand-held devices. The Flash eLearning resources also help you design presentations that comply with the Aviation Industry CBT Committee (AICC) protocol. The AICC is an international association of technology-based training professionals that develops guidelines for the aviation industry to develop, deliver, and evaluate CBT and related training technologies. The AICC is setting the standard for all CBT courseware.

The accessibility and eLearning resources are available online at the following Web sites. The Macromedia Dreamweaver resources are valuable if you are using Flash to design Web content and Dreamweaver to build the Web site on a Web server.

- Accessibility topics and resources:
  www.macromedia.com/macromedia/accessibility

- eLearning topics and resources:
  www.macromedia.com/resources/elearning

- Flash topics and resources:
  www.macromedia.com/software/flash

- Dreamweaver topics and resources:
  www.macromedia.com/software/dreamweaver

- Designer and developer topics and resources:
  www.macromedia.com/desdev

On the Macromedia Web site, you can also access the Application Developer Toolkit (ADT) and the Macromedia Flash MX Deployment Kit. Use the ADT to assist you in distributing your Flash presentations to a variety of formats and platforms, such as Web-ready for the Windows and Macintosh platforms. You use the deployment kit to post Macromedia Flash SWF files to your Web site and control the experience of visitors who do not have the Macromedia Flash Player installed in their browsers. This kit allows the user to download the Flash Player, and then view your movie as it was designed to be viewed. The deployment kit contains a detection tool called the Macromedia Flash Dispatcher, which consists of several integrated files that detect whether a suitable version of Macromedia Flash Player is installed in a visitor's browser. When users visit your Web site, the Macromedia Flash Dispatcher determines whether their browsers can play the movies on your Web site. If an appropriate version of the Flash Player is installed on the browser, the movie plays. If an incompatible version of the Flash Player is installed, or if the Flash Player is not installed at all, the user is redirected to the Flash Player download page. You can find these resources at the Flash MX Application Development Center: *www.macromedia.com/desdev/mx/flash*.

EXPLORING 3-D TOOLS FOR MACROMEDIA FLASH DESIGNERS

A current trend in Web development is to include three-dimensional images to enhance Web sites. To explore 3-D digital design, you need to be familiar with terms such as NURBS, rendering, and 3-D animation. **NURBS** is an acronym for Non-Uniform Rational B-Spline, a computer method for constructing smooth, freeform curves and surfaces. Most of today's 3-D modeling programs rely on NURBS for constructing surface models, and sometimes solid models. **3-D rendering** is the process of producing an image based on three-dimensional data. 3-D rendering is a creative process that is similar to photography or cinematography, because it involves lighting and staging scenes and then producing images. Unlike regular photography, however, the scenes being photographed are imaginary, and everything appearing in a 3-D rendering needs to be created before it can be rendered.

3-D has matured and is used in a wide assortment of industry applications, such as industrial and toy design; automotive, marine, and aviation design; gaming; mechanical and computer-aided design (CAD); and traditional film and broadcast video. Figure 10-1 shows what you can accomplish with 3-D rendering tools.

10

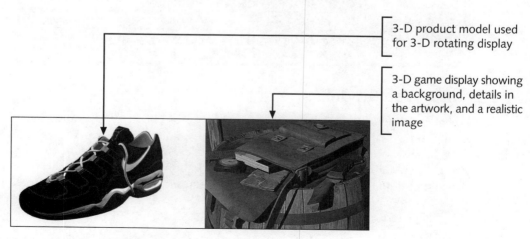

3-D product model used
for 3-D rotating display

3-D game display showing
a background, details in
the artwork, and a realistic
image

Figure 10-1   Diversity in 3-D rendering

In the next sections, you will explore 3-D software and how industries use 3-D images. As a Flash designer or developer, look for 3-D software that works with Flash FLA and SWF files. Because most Web users have browsers that can play SWF files, being able to deliver 3-D interfaces and animations in the SWF format offers a significant advantage over 3-D tools that do not support SWF. This means that you can design and use 3-D artwork with your Flash movies and HTML files without requiring your visitors to download special plug-ins or interface viewers. Table 10-1 lists the tools and the Web sites where you can learn more about each tool.

Table 10-1   3-D Companies and Products

Company	Product name	Product Web site
Discreet	3ds max Web Studio	www.discreet.com/products/3dsmax
Discreet	Plasma 1.0	www.discreet.com/products/plasma
Alias I Wavefront	Maya	www.aliaswavefront.com/en/products/maya/index.shtml
NewTek, Inc.	LightWave 3D	www.lightwave3d.com
Corastar, Inc.	Strata 3D Pro	www.strata.com/products/strata3d.html
Corel Corporation	Bryce	www.corel.com
Softimage Co.	Softimage I XSI	www.softimage.com/products/xsi/v2/default.asp
Curious Labs	Poser and Poser Pro Pack	www.curiouslabs.com/products/poser4/index.html
Eovia	Carrara Studio	www.eovia.com/carrara/product_intro_car.jsp
Mind Avenue	Axel Edge	www.mindavenue.com/en/products/index.html
Caligari	True Space, I Space, and the I Space Flash Plug-in	www.caligari.com/Products/trueSpace/ts6
Electric Rain, Inc.	Swift 3D	www.erain.com/
Robert McNeel & Associates	Rhinoceros	www.rhino3d.com/
Ulead Systems	Cool 3D	www.ulead.com/cool3d/runme.htm
Right Hemisphere	Deep Paint 3D, Deep Exploration, and Deep UV	www.righthemisphere.com/products

3ds max Web Studio

3ds max is one of the leading professional tools for character animation, game development, and visual effects production. Designers and developers primarily use 3Ds max Web Studio to create 3-D content for game development platforms such as Microsoft Xbox and Sony Playstation 2. As Figure 10-2 shows, the 3Ds max interface appeals to the digital designer and includes a toolbar set, multiple viewpoints, and floating panels.

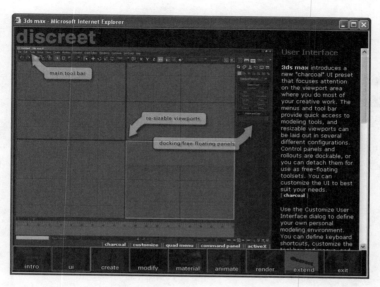

Figure 10-2   3ds max interface

Use 3ds for professional design projects that involve 2-D and 3-D modeling, animation, rendering, lighting, and multiple points of view.

Plasma 1.0

Plasma, Discreet's newest 3-D tool, can produce files in Macromedia Shockwave and Flash output formats. With Plasma, you can design 3-D models, animate them, and then publish them in a SWF format ready for Web viewing. Plasma offers a familiar 3-D user interface, shown in Figure 10-3, equipped with a collection of tools to create and modify Plasma graphics. You can also use these tools to convert Plasma graphics to Flash SWF output.

Besides supporting Flash rendering and exporting Shockwave files, Plasma also integrates with 3ds max and supports **Havok dynamics**, a physics-based technology that adds interactivity and realistic dynamics to virtual worlds produced by Havok. These virtual worlds appear in products such as Discreet's 3ds max Web Studio and Reactor; Adobe's Atmosphere; and Cyan, the makers of the popular games Mist and Riven. Havok dynamics work with other software vendors such as Discreet to integrate 3-D elements, including rigid and soft body effects to represent the form of both human and robotic figures, cloth and rope to provide a realistic material, and lifelike movements for all hardware platforms to include PS2, GameCube, Xbox, PC, Mac, and Linux.

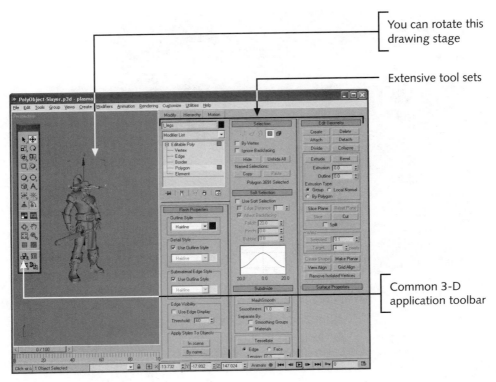

You can rotate this drawing stage

Extensive tool sets

Common 3-D application toolbar

Figure 10-3   Plasma user interface

Use Plasma for projects that involve 2-D and 3-D modeling, character and path animation, 3-D Web user interface design, and Havok dynamics.

Maya

Alias | Wavefront Maya is one of the most complete production solutions for 3-D artists in animation and visual effects. Maya specializes in NURBS modeling, animation, dynamic rendering, and paint effects. It provides its own scripting language called MEL, and is equipped with a wide range of Web 3-D plug-ins, including a Shockwave 3D exporter.

Maya's user interface, as Figure 10-4 shows, makes the software easy to use. Maya provides many tools on the main window, including the menu bar, status bar, shelf, scene menu bar and toolbox, time and range slider, command line, channel box, and layer editor. The interface is also customized, allowing you to assign hotkeys, navigate using the hotbox instead of menus, mark menus in a pop-up for quick access, and hide interface components.

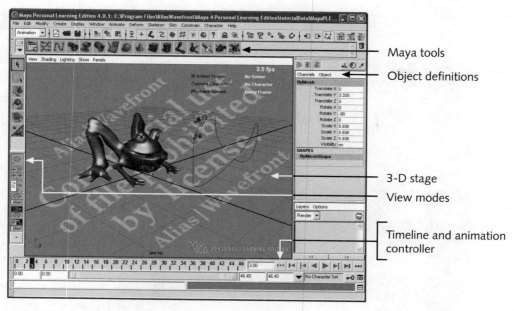

Maya tools

Object definitions

3-D stage

View modes

Timeline and animation controller

Figure 10-4   Maya user interface

Use Maya for projects that involve polygonal modeling, NURBS modeling, character setup and animation, dynamic animation, 3-D rendering, and 2-D and 3-D painting and sculpture. A polygon is a multi-sided shape defined by a group of vertices; the edges are defined by pairs of those vertices. A polygonal object is a collection of polygons called polygonal faces. Polygonal objects can be either simple shapes, such as 3-D cubes or cones, or custom shapes. You can use the various polygonal tools and operations to build complex models such as figures and backdrops.

LightWave 3D

LightWave 3D from NewTek is used primarily to create computer games and special effects in film. LightWave 3D is also being used to create graphics for print, Web, industrial design, architecture, and medical imaging. Because it provides a Shockwave 3D exporter, you can use LightWave 3D to create 3-D Web sites that can export scenes, complete with images, objects, surfaces, and animations as Macromedia Shockwave files. You can then use these files in Macromedia Director to create and distribute multimedia content.

LightWave 3D provides excellent handling of digital 3-D effects, including caustic light reflection, depth–of–field filters, high dynamic range images, Hypervoxel, and a spreadsheet scene manager. **Caustics** in LightWave 3D provide light reflection and refraction, which appear in the real world when light reflects off a curved surface or refracts through a transparent surface. **Depth–of–field filters** offer traditional depth–of–field control, a technique used in film photography to change the perspective of rendered

10

objects. The depth-of-field filter also blurs backgrounds accurately and provides optional iris shapes to match various camera styles, a benefit when you want to match the optical characteristics of a camera perspective. **High dynamic range images** are used to create a single image containing more color information than traditional photographic equipment can offer. A **Hypervoxel** is a 3-D pixel used with volume-based effects to create images such as liquids, fire, smoke, dust, ash, gelatin, rusted materials, and clouds. The spreadsheet scene manager shown in Figure 10-5 organizes and allows you to access and edit the properties of scene objects. The scene manager includes expandable and collapsible sections so you can view sections of the scene and edit elements as needed.

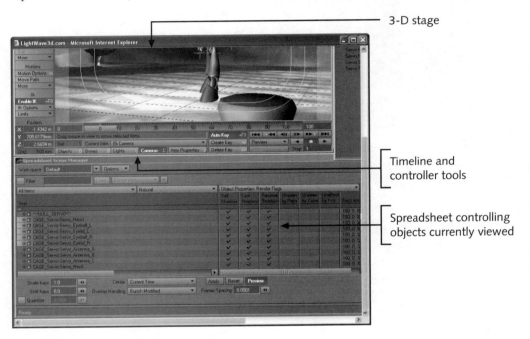

3-D stage

Timeline and controller tools

Spreadsheet controlling objects currently viewed

Figure 10-5   Spreadsheet scene manager

Use LightWave 3D for developing computer games and graphic design projects that require interactive guides, animation, game development, rendering, special FX, surface and texturing, UV mapping, and 3-D modeling.

Strata 3D Pro

Strata 3D Pro from Corastar, Inc., is an ideal 3-D graphics program for Flash designers who are new to working with three-dimensional graphics. You can create a variety of content for the Web or for Flash SWF output, as shown in Figure 10-6. Strata is known for its superior image quality and ease of use. Strata has been used to create advanced 3-D Web site content, print illustrations, adventure games, and video on CD and DVD media.

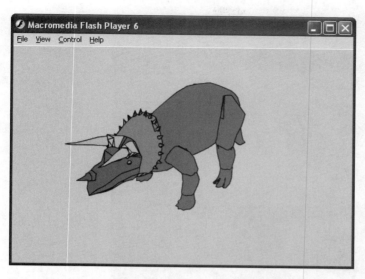

Figure 10-6   Strata 3D Pro output in the Flash SWF format

Flash SWF format compatibility means that you can save your rendered movie as an SWF file, complete with 3-D content, to play on a Web site. By default, Strata 3D Pro saves SWF files in a pixel-based format, not a vector-based format. However, Strata 3D Pro licenses the Ravix Swift 3D feature to convert your pixel images to a vector-based SWF format. Strata 3D Pro also can export sequential EPS and Adobe Illustrator file formats.

The Strata 3D Pro interface, shown in Figure 10-7, is designed to fit into your existing suite of design applications. It includes a tool palette to create and edit objects; view management tools to control how your model appears in the modeling window; object manipulation tools to move, rotate, and scale objects; modeling tools to create 3-D elements; predefined 3-D objects; 2-D drawing tools; imaging tools to capture stills and create animations; and resource palettes for textures and backgrounds.

Use Strata 3D Pro for Web design projects that require modeling, texturing, lighting, rendering, and animating.

Bryce 5

Bryce, from Corel Corporation, is a 3-D graphics application that lets you design, render, and animate natural 3-D worlds and abstract 3-D sculptures, landscape planes, procedural objects, primitive objects, and various lighting. You build landscape planes by creating graphic terrains, mountains, trees, stones, and other objects. Procedural objects or multi-dimensional objects, such as terrains, trees, or rocks require special constructions to create. Primitive ojects are basic geometric shapes such as the sphere, torus, cylinder, cube, pyramid, cone, plane, and disks, which are used to create more complex shapes. Figure 10-8 shows a typical 3-D landscape designed in Bryce.

10

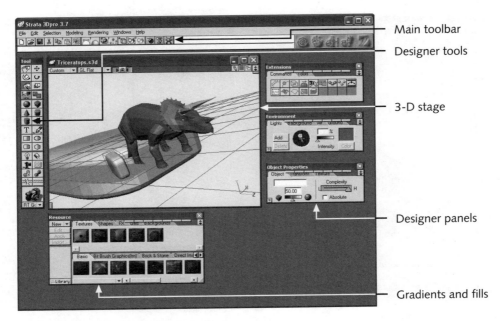

Figure 10-7   Strata 3D Pro interface

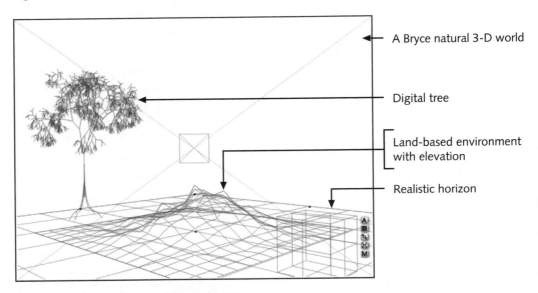

Figure 10-8   Landscape designed in Bryce

Bryce provides you with a metaphoric and intuitive user interface shown in Figure 10-9. New features include a terrain editor and a real-time preview mode that lets you preview changes to landscapes and objects.

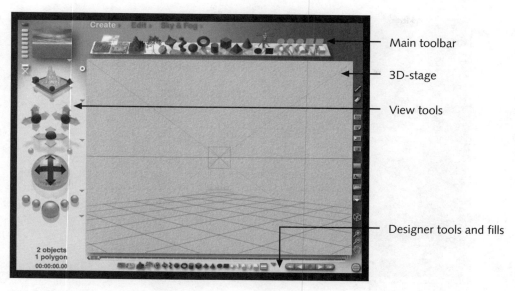

— Main toolbar

— 3D-stage

— View tools

— Designer tools and fills

Figure 10-9   Bryce user interface

Bryce also provides a rich set of predesigned effects, such as the sky lab, which lets you use a single panel to control the appearance and attributes of sky effects, including clouds, smoke, fog, sun, moon, comet, star field, and halo effects. You can edit volume sky effects, such as haze, fog, and rainbow, to create a more realistic atmosphere. You can also use a shading mode to enhance light interaction with sky effects. The star field controls allow you to create landscapes with star patterns as they appear from earth, and specify the intensity and number of stars. You can view animation effects frame by frame in a story-board preview format, shown in Figure 10-10. Using the storyboard, you can select and render specific frames of animated effects and change individual frames within the animation sequence, and then publish your animations in the Apple QuickTime format.

Poser and Poser Pro Pack

Poser and the Poser Pro Pack from Curious Labs together offer a complete package for you to begin 3-D design. The Pro Pack provides a Flash SWF sequence exporter so you can use Flash SWF output for your Web and CD presentations. The presentation shown in Figure 10-11 was designed in Poser and exported into the SWF format. The Pro Pack allows you to export your Poser file in Flash, Viewpoint, 3ds max, LightWave, and other formats as well.

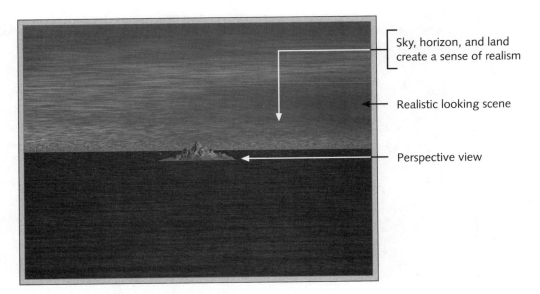

Sky, horizon, and land
create a sense of realism

Realistic looking scene

Perspective view

Figure 10-10   Bryce storyboard preview

Figure 10-11   Flash SWF format designed in Poser

The Poser interface shown in Figure 10-12 is unique, using human parts as the camera controls; 2-D and 3-D buttons for the editing tools, display styles, lighting control; animation sequencing; and playback.

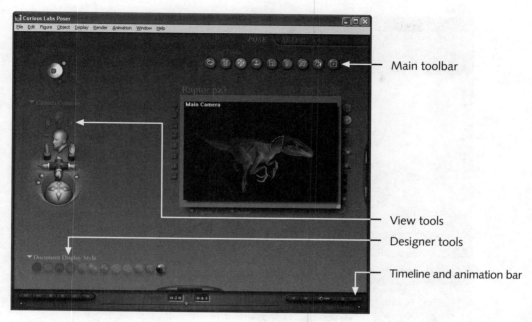

Main toolbar

View tools

Designer tools

Timeline and animation bar

Figure 10-12 Poser interface

Use Poser for Web design projects that require 3-D character design and animation, advanced texture controls, lighting controls, figure creation, 3-D character animation, and brush-stroked renderings.

Axel Edge

Axel Edge from Mind Avenue is a high-end 3-D design tool used to create 3-D models, animations, texture, and light. Axel Edge can also preview and publish 3-D interactive content directly to the Web. The interactivity allows your user to control and view your 3-D design, as shown in Figure 10-13.

Axel Edge includes functions such as Inverse Kinematics scripting, the option of using a scripting language based on the ECMA JavaScript, as well as ability to import 3-D models from other high-end software such as LightWave. You can produce presentations for interactive marketing, games and entertainment, 3-D navigational interfaces and content, and educational content.

10

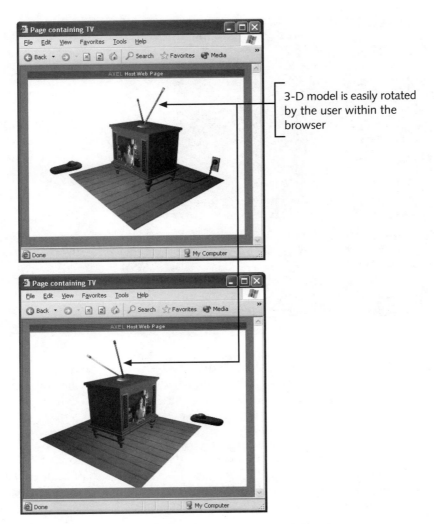

3-D model is easily rotated by the user within the browser

Figure 10-13   3-D model allows user to control the view

The Axel Edge interface combines many familiar animation and Internet techniques, such as object views and editing; a top, front, right, and rendered production view; a timeline; and toolbars, as shown in Figure 10-14.

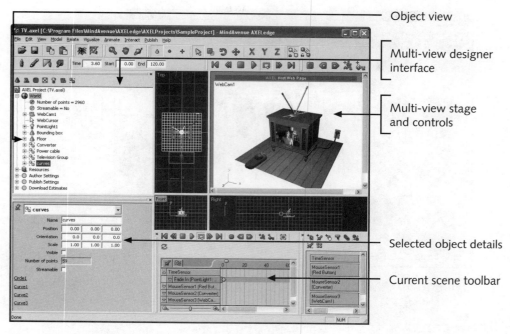

Object view

Multi-view designer interface

Multi-view stage and controls

Selected object details

Current scene toolbar

Figure 10-14   Axel Edge multi-view interface

Use Axel Edge for Web design projects that involve geometrical and character modeling; object relations; image and movie textures; shaded, cartoon, and custom wireframe; geometrical, shape, character, and particle animation; and publishing.

Swift 3D

Swift 3D from Electric Rain, Inc., is a three-dimensional vector graphics tool that you use to create high-quality, low-bandwidth, scaleable 3-D vector animations. Like other 3-D tools, Swift 3D can produce output in the Flash SWF format. Swift 3D provides multiple views, panels, and editors, such as the scene editor for creating and editing objects shown in Figure 10-15, an extrusion editor for creating 2-D paths that can be automatically turned into 3-D extrusions, a lathe editor to create the point of the 3-D model, and a preview and export editor to render and preview your artwork.

Swift 3D can create objects with effects such as diffuse or ambient lighting, bevels and edges, and animation sequences.

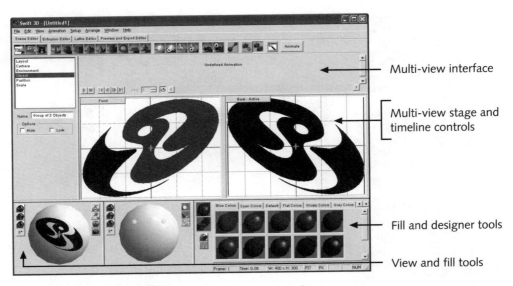

Figure 10-15   Swift 3D interface and the scene editor

Rhinoceros

Rhinoceros from Robert McNeel & Associates is a 3-D NURBS modeling application that you can use to design objects such as NURBS geometry, NURBS surfaces, polygon meshes, lighting effects, and shading and rendering. Rhinoceros can also create photorealistic images from 3-D models using the raytracing and radiosity effects with the Flamingo add-in. Raytracing is a feature in Flamingo that calculates the brightness, transparence, and reflectivity of each object. Radiosity, another Flamingo feature, creates an effect of indirect light in a scene. It does not produce a rendered image; it is only the lighting calculations for effects such as shadows, reflection, and lighted materials.

The Rhinoceros interface shown in Figure 10-16 provides a series of toolbars, a command line, and a multi-view scene to help you visualize three-dimensional objects on a two-dimensional screen. The viewpoints you can view are the top, front, right, and a perspective view where you can create, edit, and render objects. You can view objects in a Wireframe, shaded preview, and a fully rendered view.

Rhinoceros can create objects with 3-D effects such as two-dimensional modeling; precision modeling; 3-D modeling; deformable shapes such as curve editing, rendering, dimensions, advanced surfacing techniques, and sculpting.

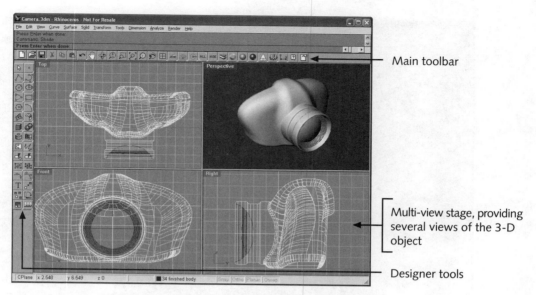

Figure 10-16   Rhinoceros interface with multiple viewpoints

Cool 3D

Cool 3D from Ulead Systems is a beginner's platform for stepping into the 3-D world, yet it still allows you to design sophisticated 3-D objects. Cool 3D allows you to create high-impact animated 3-D titles and graphics for output as still images, GIF animation, broadcast-quality video, or even 3-D in the Flash SWF file format.

With Cool 3D, you can create effects such as 3-D shapes and text; add effects such as shadow, lightning, and fire; animate the objects with keyframes; and then output your design in a raster or vector Flash SWF, animated GIF, or video sequence file. Cool 3D also provides a familiar intuitive user interface, shown in Figure 10-17.

Deep Paint 3D, Deep UV, and Deep Exploration

Deep Paint 3D from Right Hemisphere provides you with an intuitive tool, shown in Figure 10-18, to paint and texture 3-D models. It uses textures or natural media that can be brushed directly onto 3-D models and scenes. Natural media are artistic tools such as airbrush, oils, watercolors, colored and charcoal pencils, felt-tipped pens, chalks, pastels, gouache, acrylics, impasto, and various textures. Deep Paint integrates with 3ds max, Maya, and other 3-D applications; and comes complete with a bidirectional interface to Adobe Photoshop and special support for the Wacom Intuos pressure-sensitive tablet. This is a hardware device that lets you use a pen and mouse, combined with a pressure-sensitive tablet to control various effects such as pressing harder or softer to affect brush size, opacity, or color. Deep Paint 3D is used by film studios, broadcast companies, and game developers.

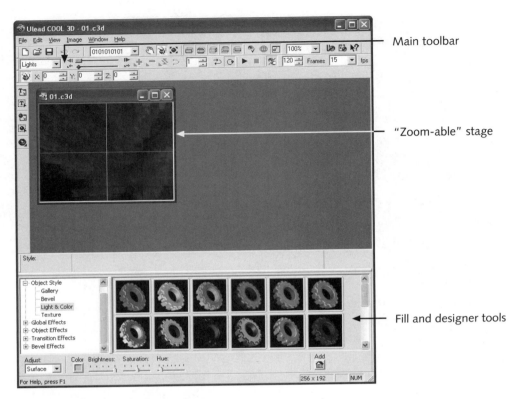

Main toolbar

"Zoom-able" stage

Fill and designer tools

Figure 10-17   Cool 3D interface

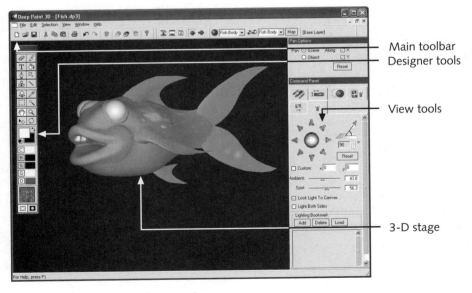

Main toolbar
Designer tools

View tools

3-D stage

Figure 10-18   Deep Paint interface

Deep Paint includes some unique features, such as an image and clone brush that can capture any image instantly and use it as an image stamp or texture paint in 2-D or 3-D. Deep Paint also lets you perform real-time 3-D painting and texturing on 3-D models; paint across multiple materials; view objects using dynamic 3-D zoom, pan, and rotate; use 3-D masking and selection tools; paint with artistic tools such as a true airbrush, oils, watercolors, colored and charcoal pencils, felt pens, chalks, pastels, gouache, acrylics, impasto, and various textures.

Deep Paint 3D can operate in three modes:

- 3D mode is active whenever a 3-D model is loaded into Deep Paint 3D, and allows you to paint your model in three dimensional space with real-time rendering of color, bump, shine, glow, and opacity.

- 2D mode allows you to view and paint bitmaps while painting a 3-D model.

- 2½D mode lets you paint two-dimensional images with color, bump, and shine rendered in real time.

Deep UV from Right Hemisphere is a UV-mapping technology using unique mathematical techniques that let you create and modify UV mapping for n-polygonal models within an interactive 2-D and 3-D mapping environment. Two-dimensional surface points allow a texture to fill an area, while you are working on a 3-D object. UV mapping describes the relationship between a three-dimensional surface point as described by X, Y, and Z values, and a two-dimensional surface point. It also describes the relationship between 2-D texture maps and their position on a 3-D model. A common example of UV-mapping projection involves the problem of representing the earth, which is spherical, with a flat 2-D world map. On a two-dimensional map, the geography closer to the north and south poles is distorted.

Figure 10-19 shows the Deep UV interface.

Following are some of the Deep UV features:

- Unfold is a revolutionary new automated UV unwrapping tool, used to automatically unwrap folded or twisted surfaces.

- Preserve Bitmap lets you change the UV mapping after the object has been textured and preserves the texturing regardless of UV changes.

- Real-time preview of UV lets you edit simultaneously in 2-D and 3-D.

- Advanced relax tools automatically minimize local or global distortions by selection.

10

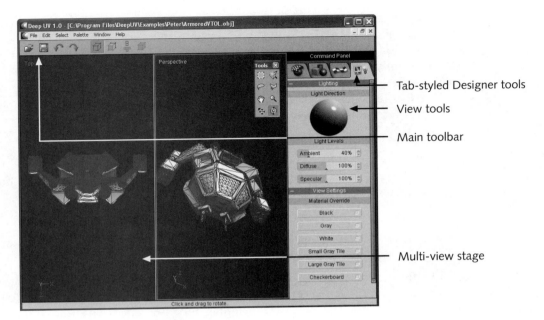

Tab-styled Designer tools

View tools

Main toolbar

Multi-view stage

Figure 10-19   Deep UV interface

Deep Exploration from Right Hemisphere provides navigation tools that let you manage your digital content, including 2-D files and 3-D models. Deep Exploration also lets you translate and convert graphics within an easy-to-use viewer and a Windows Explorer-like interface (shown in Figure 10-20) and Open GL hardware accelerator support. Deep Exploration allows you to browse many popular 3-D file formats such as 3-D Studio, LightWave, Caligari, Direct X, AutoCAD, and many others, as well as the common 2-D file types. Deep Exploration solves the problem of finding and managing the many files you use in 3-D design.

Following are some of Deep Exploration's features:

- A familiar Windows Explorer and IE-style interface
- Fast import process
- Easy zoom, rotate, and pan
- 3-D objects and materials browser
- Search
- Turbo Squid Search
- 3-D model and texture Web search
- Browsed file history
- Easy 3-D file organization

- Ability to show or hide separate objects
- Slide show
- Thumbnail generation
- Built-in export features
- Ability to copy to Clipboard as BMP
- Batch processing

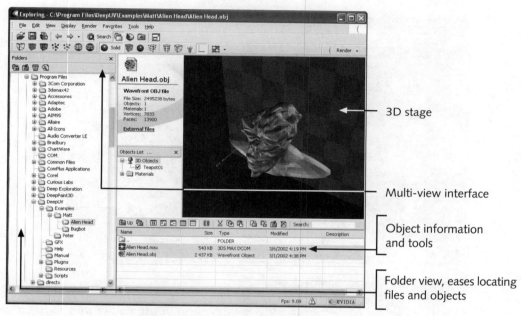

Figure 10-20   Deep Exploration interface

In the next sections, you will explore audio and video applications, and how they work with Flash movies.

EXPLORING VIDEO APPLICATIONS

Web users increasingly demand video elements on Web sites. Video creates dynamic entertainment, enhances the experience of visiting a Web site, and helps users retain information. Because people now use a variety of hardware devices, including handheld computers, cell phones, notebook computers, and desktop computers to access the Web, the programs you use to create multimedia have become less dependent on hardware. This section discusses the programs you can use to create video elements in your Flash movies.

Cauldron 1.0

The Cauldron Media authoring tool from Sorceron, Inc., shown in Figure 10-21, integrates virtually any media type into a streaming show. It lets you combine and stream video, audio, 2-D objects, 3-D objects, HTML, text, PowerPoint files, and Flash files. Cauldron provides a high-quality, object-based video stream, which creates large, high-quality pictures over low-bandwidth connections. Each element is transmitted separately, so shapes and text are always sharp over a wide range of displays. Over broadband, Cauldron technology provides an experience similar to digital TV.

Figure 10-21   Cauldron interface

Cauldron enables content creators to assemble and distribute dynamic video, audio, graphics, text, HTML, and even application files, such as a Microsoft PowerPoint, which provides a timeline and a common media designer's interface. Each media file becomes an object that the author manipulates. The author encodes each object to optimize the bandwidth required to stream the release to a user. The Cauldron Player, shown in Figure 10-22, receives these individually streamed objects and renders the presentation.

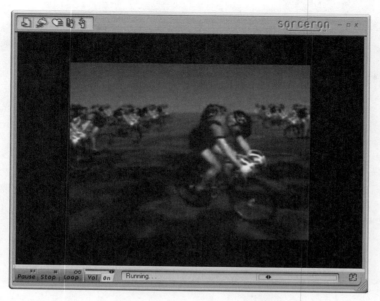

Figure 10-22   Cauldron Player

Vegas Video 3.0

Vegas Video from Sonic Foundry is a multi-track media-editing system. Vegas Video lets you edit audio and video tracks, video effects and transitions, and audio effects. You can also use multiple audio busses, print from timeline to tape, encode files with MPEG 1 and 2, and burn CDs. MPEG is a set of standards for video and audio compression and for multimedia delivery developed by the Moving Picture Experts Group. MPEG 1 was designed for coding progressive video at a transmission rate of about 1.5 million bits per second. It was designed specifically for Video-CD media. MPEG 2 was designed for coding interlaced images at transmission rates above 4 million bits per second, and is used for digital TV broadcast and DVD playback. Figure 10-23 shows the track view, where you arrange and edit multiple tracks and your project events. The window docking area is where you use windows such as the effects window, the Explorer window, the trimmer window for editing media files, and the mixer window.

10

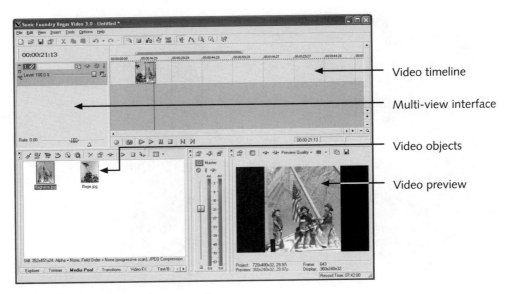

Video timeline

Multi-view interface

Video objects

Video preview

Figure 10-23 Vegas Video interface

EXPLORING AUDIO APPLICATIONS

Today's users increasingly demand audio effects on Web sites such as streaming music loops, event sounds effects, and voice over narration. The applications used to create audio can be used to create royalty-free music and produce effects like drumbeats and DJ-style effects. They also import and save audio files in a variety of formats such as WAV, Windows Media audio, MPEG 1 and 2, RealAudio, and MP3. This section discusses the programs you can use to create audio elements in your Flash movies using digital audio editors.

Sound Forge 6.0

Sound Forge from Sonic Foundry, Inc., shown in Figure 10-24, is a two-track digital audio editor that includes audio processes, tools, and effects for manipulating audio you use to create, record, and edit audio files. You can import, create, or copy an audio track from a CD, and then burn your own CDs.

Sound Forge provides an assortment of features to open, play, edit, and create audio files. The Playbar and the Transport bar are the main toolbars to record, play, and use the audio files.

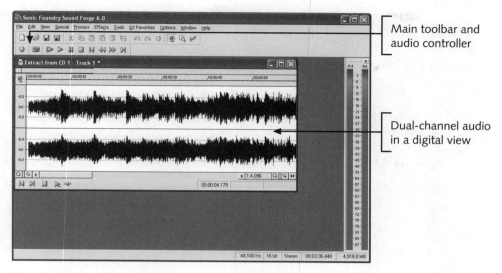

Figure 10-24   Sound Forge

ACID Pro 3.0

ACID Pro from Sonic Foundry is a loop-based music creation program that provides a multi-featured and multi-view interface, shown in Figure 10-25. The interface is divided between a track list, a track view, a Windows Explorer view for searching files, and a multi-purpose docking area for features such as a mixer.

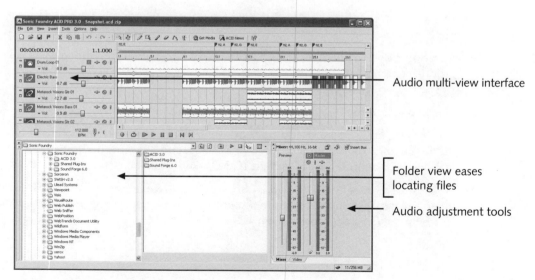

Figure 10-25   ACID Pro interface

ACID allows you to create music loop projects and audio such as streaming music loops or event sounds that you add to Flash projects. Once you create or import audio tracks, you can edit them. ACID creates a track for each media file you add to a project. Track types are loops, one-shots, beatmapped, or MIDI. Loops are small audio files meant to repeat a continuous beat when played. One-shots are similar—they repeat without looping. Beatmapped files are larger and longer than loops, and can respond to tempo changes if they play longer than thirty seconds. MIDI files are edited through external editors, and are imported through a .mid, .smf, or .rmi file.

Other Audio and Video Resources

The following list includes some of the audio resources available to you when you add sound and music to your Flash movies.

- Sound Rangers, *www.soundrangers.com*
- Sonic Foundry, *www.sonicfoundry.com*
- Flash Sound, *www.flashsound.com*
- Killer Sound, *www.killersound.com*
- Garn Creative, *pulse.garncreative.com*
- Getty Images/Photo disk, *www.photodisk.com*

CHAPTER SUMMARY

- ❏ Macromedia provides you with a set of resources that can help you design Flash movies.

- ❏ The Solutions Kit contains tips, tutorials, how-to videos, reference materials, and product extensions for your use.

- ❏ The Application Developer Toolkit is full of components, white papers, sample Flash applications for you to download, tutorials, and trial software.

- ❏ 3-D has matured to be used in a wide assortment of industry applications, such as industrial and toy design; automotive, marine, and aviation design; gaming; mechanical design; computer aided design (CAD); and traditional film or broadcast.

- ❏ Web users increasingly demand audio and video elements on Web sites. Audio and video create dynamic entertainment, enhance the experience of visiting a Web site, and help users retain information.

REVIEW QUESTIONS

1. 3-D rendering is a useful technology in professional industries. True or false?

2. The Macromedia Application Developer Toolkit includes:

   a. trial software

   b. tutorials

   c. white papers

   d. all of the above

3. A computer method for constructing smooth, freeform curves and surfaces is called _____.

4. 3-D rendering is the process of producing an image based on three-dimensional data. True or false?

5. Discreet 3ds max is used on which of the following platforms?

   a. Microsoft Xbox

   b. Sony Playstation 2

   c. PC

   d. all of the above

6. Plasma can produce 3-D files in Macromedia Shockwave and Flash output formats. True or false?

7. _____ is a physics-based technology that adds interactivity and realistic dynamics into virtual worlds.

8. Maya specializes in NURBS modeling. True or false?

9. Maya can produce which of the following?

   a. 2-D illustration

   b. line and airbrush design

   c. drag and drop delivery

   d. none of the above

10. LightWave 3D provides excellent handling for _____ as a series of effects.

11. Light reflection means:

    a. light reflects off a curved surface

    b. light refracts through a transparent surface

    c. light reflects off a beveled surface

    d. all of the above

12. Strata is known for its superior image quality and ease of use. True or false?

10

13. Strata 3-D Pro saves your pixel renderings to the SWF format in a pixel-based format as well as a vector-based format. True or false?

14. Bryce is a 3-D graphics application that lets you design:

    a. natural 3-D worlds

    b. abstract 3-D sculptures

    c. landscape planes

    d. all of the above

15. The Poser Pro Pack comes equipped with a _____ for Flash.

16. Axel Edge includes a scripting language based on the ECMA JavaScript standard. True or false?

17. Rhinoceros is a NURBS application that can be used to design a variety of objects such as _____.

18. The Cauldron Media authoring tool can import and stream:

    a. PowerPoint files

    b. Flash files

    c. video files

    d. all of the above

HANDS-ON PROJECTS

In these projects, you research and practice 3-D and audio development techniques.

Project 10-1

Research and document which 3-D-based software programs can produce output in the Flash SWF file format. List the companies and products included in Table 10-1, and indicate whether they support the SWF format. As you create 3-D Web projects, you can refer to this research to determine whether you should create files in the Flash SWF format or use another media type. Using your browser, visit the Web sites listed in Table 10-1.

Project 10-2

In this project, you download a trial version of Strata 3D Pro, and create a series of 3-D designs. The designs are listed below for you to create. For ideas and inspiration, go to Strata's online gallery at *www.strata.com/gallery*. The Web URL for the software is *shop.strata.com/?Product=83*. Because you are working with demo software, you cannot save files, though you can view them in the Flash Player.

To download and start the Strata 3-D Pro demo:

1. Open your Web browser, and go to the Strata Shopping Web address: *shop.strata.com*.

2. Click the Related Products button next to the Strata 3D Pro edition.

3. Click the Strata 3Dpro v 3.7 Demo link.

4. Click the Add To Cart link. This adds the free download to your shopping cart. The left side of the screen displays the cart contents.

5. Click the Checkout button.

6. Click Windows or Macintosh as your delivery method, and then click Continue.

7. Click US Academic Customer, and then click Check Out.

8. Check out and download the demo version to your computer.

9. Unzip the file, and then double-click the downloaded icon to install the demo version. Follow the instructions that appear on the screen.

10. Double-click the Strata 3-D icon to start the application, located in the Strata/Strata 3-Dpro 3.7 folder.

11. Once Strata starts, click the Continue button, if necessary.

12. If necessary, enter the serial number the download provided, your name, and a fictitious or class name in the Company field. When Strata starts, close any Information dialog boxes or panels that appear.

To create a 3-D scene with Strata 3-D Pro:

1. Click File on the menu bar, and then click New. A new scene appears on your Stage.

2. Click the Sphere tool located on the Designer tool panel, hold down the Shift key, and drag a sphere on your Stage.

3. Click the Object Move tool to center the sphere on your Stage. (The Object Move tool looks like a four-headed arrow.)

4. In the Resource panel, click the Textures tab, and then scroll and click a texture to fill the sphere.

5. Click the Apply button on the Resource panel. The sphere fills with a gradient color, and not the texture you selected.

6. Click the Render command on the Rendering menu. The Render dialog box opens.

7. Click the Render button to view the sphere in the texture you selected.

8. Close the render preview window, and then close the file, leaving Strata 3D open.

10

Project 10-3

In this project, you use Strata 3D to create a three-dimensional key. You use predefined shapes, apply texture and fill to those shapes, and then add a background to the scene.

1. To start a new file, click File on the menu bar, and then click New.
2. Drag the scene edge to enlarge the scene.
3. In the Resource panel, click the Shapes tab.
4. In the Shapes tab, use the navigation arrows on the lower-right of the Resource panel to scroll to the Basic tab. Click the Basic tab, if necessary.
5. Scroll to find the **Key.ssh** object, select it, and then click the Insert button.
6. Click the Object Scale tool, located on the right of the Tool panel, third from the top. The object now has eight points that you can use to drag and scale the object.
7. Drag a corner of the object to enlarge it. Then use the Object Move tool to center it on the stage.
8. With the key object still selected, click the Textures tab.
9. In the Textures tab, click the navigation arrows to find and then click the Basic tab.
10. Scroll until you find the **Stucco.ssh** (or **Stucco.sft**) texture, select it, and then click the Apply button.
11. For the background, you will apply a white fill. Click the Background tab in the Environment panel.
12. Click the Vis. list arrow, and then click the **White.sbg** background.
13. Click Rendering on the menu bar, and then click Render. Click the Render button in the dialog box. The background is now white instead of black, and the key you added and applied texture to is rendered in the appropriate colors and textures.
14. Close the new file, and leave Strata 3D open.

Project 10-4

Use Strata 3D to create a realistic world and background scene, and then apply a lighting effect.

1. To create a Strata document, click File on the menu bar, and then click New.
2. Drag the scene edge to enlarge the scene.
3. In the Resource panel, click the Shapes tab.
4. On the Shapes tab, scroll to and then click the Basic tab.
5. Select the Earth.ssh object, and click the Insert button.
6. Click the Object Scale tool to enlarge the shape slightly. Hold the Shift key as you drag to scale the shape proportionately. Note that the shape already includes a texture.

7. Click Rendering on the menu bar, and then click Render to see the effect. Click the Render button. Close the Render Preview window.

8. Click the Background tab in the Environment panel.

9. Click the Vis. list arrow, and then click Metaloid.sbg. This creates a metallic background behind the earth shape.

10. Click Rendering on the menu bar, and then click Render to see the effect. Click the Render button. Close the Render Preview window.

11. Click the Lights tab on the Environment window.

12. Click the upper-right corner of the circle to the left of the Intensity text box and then drag the handle clockwise to define the direction from which the light source comes.

13. Add a second smaller sphere in the upper-right corner of the Stage. This will act as a moon. Use the Object Move tool to click the sphere.

14. Click Rendering on the menu bar, and then click Render to see the effect. Click the Render button. Then close the Render Preview window.

15. Close Strata 3D.

10

CASE PROJECTS

Case Project 10-1

A new musician has requested that you design a Web site and record his music digitally. Research the audio programs introduced in this chapter, and write an e-mail message to the musician explaining the most economical way to record music and make the music available to stream or download.

Case Project 10-2

Visit several game Web sites, and try to determine if the 3-D technology or application used was published in a Flash SWF file. For example, you can visit these popular Web sites for research:

- ❐ *www.myst.com*
- ❐ *www.cyanworlds.com*
- ❐ *www.gamers.com*
- ❐ *www.animationmagazine.net*
- ❐ *www.computerandvideogames.com*

Case Project 10-3

For your personal or fictional business Web site, create a Flash scene that lists your favorite 3-D and audio and video applications, or those applications you might use for your business. List the application name and the software manufacturer, and assign the application to a general audio or video software category. Use the getURL action to link to the software manufacturer's Web site. Add a text box and scroll bar component to add comments and what you liked about the applications. Publish this as a SWF file, and print it as a report to hand in to your instructor.

Index

optimizing images for publishing, 363–366

optimizing video for publishing, 366–368

for printing, 359–363

Quick Start templates, 371–373

option buttons, 307–310

organizing movie objects, 236–237

Orient to path check box, Property inspector, 97

Oval tool, 25, 39

P

Paint Bucket tool, 25, 42–44

panels, 9–11, 22, 23. *See also specific panels*

panning movie clips, 315

parameters, 118

Parameters pane, Actions panel, 118

parentheses (()), ActionScript, 275

parent movie, 187

parsers, 335

paths, 30

  absolute, 188

  objects on, motion guide layers, 103–106

  relative, 188–189

.pct filename extension, 141

Pencil tool, 25, 40

Pen tool, 9, 25, 34–36

.pic filename extension, 141

PICT file format, 141

pinning, Actions panel, 257

Plasma 1.0, 388, 389–390

playhead, Timeline, 49, 51

plug-ins, 2

  for movies, 5

PNG (Portable Network Graphic), 141

.png filename extension, 141

Polygon Mode, Lasso tool, 33

Portable Network Graphic (PNG), 141

Poser/Poser Pro Pack, 388, 395–397

preferences, customizing ActionScript, 259–260

preloaders, 182, 192–200

  Bandwidth Profiler, 193–194, 197–200

  creating, 194–197

primary colors, 217

Print actions, 359–363

Print dialog box, 362

printing movies, 359–363

programming languages, 333–350

  integration in Flash MX, 334–336

progressive downloads, 367–368

Properties tab, Debugger, 281

Property inspector, 9, 22, 23, 56

  motion-tween properties, 92–93, 96–97

publishing, file formats, 373–375

publishing movies

  optimizing files. *See* optimizing movies

  QuickTime movies, 166–167

  for Web, 375–377

publishing options, 8

Publish Preview command, 167

Publish Settings dialog box, 160, 166–167, 347–348

quaternary colors, 217

Q

Quick Start templates, 371–373

QuickTime movies, 163–167

  downloads, 367

  importing into Flash, 164–166

  publishing, 166–167

R

radio buttons, 307–310

raw compression method, 163

Rectangle tool, 25, 39–40

Reddick VBA (RVBA) Naming Convention, 236–237

Reference panel, ActionScript, 264–265

registration point, 187

  dragging symbols by, 106

relative paths, 188–189

Remove all breakpoints button, Debugger, 281

Replace command, 257–259

Replace dialog box, 259

reusing elements. *See* symbol(s)

reusing movie elements, 51

RGB model, 217, 218

Rhinoceros, 388, 400–401

rolling text boxes, 208–211

rollovers, 200

  movie clip. *See* movie clip rollovers

Rotate list box, Property inspector, 97

Rotate option, Arrow tool, 29

Ruler Units property, documents, 54

RVBA (Reddick VBA) Naming Convention, 236–237

S

Salomon Nordic Web site, 221, 222

Salomon Sports Web site, 229, 230

samples per inch (SPI), 217

sampling, 217

Scale check box, Property inspector, 96

ScaleMode property, Stage, 256

Scale option, Arrow tool, 29

scenes, movies, multiple, 181, 182–186

W

WAI (Web Accessibility Initiative), 233–234
Watch tab, Debugger, 281
wave files, 154
Waveform (WAV) files, 5, 154
Web
  copyrighted sound files, 155
  history of multimedia on Web, 2
  publishing movies for, 375–377
Web Accessibility Initiative (WAI), 233–234

Web-safe color palette, 58
Web sites. *See also specific sites*
  creating, 14–15
  designing, 12–14
while loops, ActionScript, 278
Width property, Stage, 256
wipe effects, 213–214
work environment, features, 22, 23
World Wide Web, 2

X

XML (Extensible Markup Language), 5, 333, 334, 335, 337–341
  HTML compared, 338
  integrating with Flash MX, 339–341
  rules and syntax, 338–339

Z

Zoom tool, 25, 46
z-order, grouping images, 56